Effective
Group Discussion

Effective Group Discussion

Sixth Edition

John K. Brilhart
University of Nebraska, Omaha (Emeritus)

Gloria J. Galanes
Southwest Missouri State University

wcb
Wm. C. Brown Publishers
Dubuque, Iowa

Book Team

Editor *Stan Stoga*
Developmental Editor *Michael Lange*
Production Editor *Michelle M. Kiefer*
Designer *Tara L. Bazata*
Photo Research Editor *Carol M. Smith*
Visuals Processor *Vickie Werner*

wcb group

Chairman of the Board *Wm. C. Brown*
President and Chief Executive Officer *Mark C. Falb*

wcb

Wm. C. Brown Publishers, College Division

President *G. Franklin Lewis*
Vice President, Editor-in-Chief *George Wm. Bergquist*
Vice President, Director of Production *Beverly Kolz*
Vice President, National Sales Manager *Bob McLaughlin*
Director of Marketing *Thomas E. Doran*
Marketing Communications Manager *Edward Bartell*
Marketing Information Systems Manager *Craig S. Marty*
Marketing Manager *Kathy Law Laube*
Production Editorial Manager *Colleen A. Yonda*
Production Editorial Manager *Julie A. Kennedy*
Publishing Services Manager *Karen J. Slaght*
Manager of Visuals and Design *Faye M. Schilling*

Cover and part openers: © George Elich

Photo Credits: James L. Shaffer: **13, 72, 313**, Fig. 14.1; Courtesy of Archbishop Bergan Mercy Hospital, Omaha, Nebraska: **15**; Paul Conklin: **45, 141**; © Jean-Claude Lejeune: **49**; © C&W Shields, Inc.: Fig. 6.1; Courtesy of the authors: **143, 153**; James Ballard: **344**.

Library of Congress Catalog Card Number: 88–070018

ISBN 0–697–03046–6

Printed in the United States of America by Wm. C. Brown Publishers
2460 Kerper Boulevard, Dubuque, IA 52001

10   9   8   7   6   5

Contents

9 Leadership in Small Groups 188

10 Conflict in the Small Group 226

Part 5 Small Group Outputs 257

11 Which Shall It Be? Decision Making in Small Groups 258

12 Group Problem Solving 274

Part 6 Group Discussion and Observation Techniques 299

13 Special Discussion Techniques and Methods for Learning and Organizational Settings 300

Preface

This sixth edition of *Effective Group Discussion* continues the dual emphases of the previous three editions: a comprehensive survey and interpretation of research literature concerning communication in small problem-solving groups accompanied by practical, prescriptive guidance to help the reader/student become a more productive member and leader of the ubiquitous small working groups which are a part of all organized human society. The quality of our lives and the joy we feel are in large part determined by the interpersonal and small group relationships we experience. We both believe that humans have a need to contribute, to participate actively in all areas of endeavor. The small group can provide a vehicle for this participation. We believe strongly that persons who understand how small groups function and have a variety of techniques for making communication in them effective will be happier and more satisfied than persons to whom small groups remain largely a mystery. We believe that one must *understand* what is going on before a small group technique can be introduced that will help the group.

A major portion of our lives is spent in various kinds of task and activity groups: work groups, committees, task forces, quality circles, and other small groups which have as their objectives the production of goods, creation of policies, and solutions to specific problems. *Effective Group Discussion* is about secondary groups of all types. Written for the beginning student of small group communication, group discussion, and group dynamics courses, this book should also serve well as a reference source for persons appointed to posts of leadership, for consultants, and for anyone active in small groups. Instructors in such academic fields as communication, social psychology, business communication, and education will find it an appropriate and teachable textbook for their small group-oriented courses.

New Features

Several changes have been made from the fifth edition. First, you have noticed that this edition is the product of collaboration between two authors. Gloria Galanes is actively involved in small group research, with specialization in the effect of conflict in small groups and conflict management in organizational contexts. One immediate output of the new collaboration is chapter 10, "Conflict in the Small Group," which greatly expands the coverage of this vital topic over that provided in the fifth edition. Some streamlining and stylistic efficiency have been accomplished in the revision. Readers familiar with the fifth edition will find some sections of the book shortened considerably without loss of important ideas or information. Chapters have been rearranged so that general interpersonal communication theory and group communication processes have been introduced before the study of group development. We have replaced Tuckman's global theory of phases in the development of small groups with two major development phases that are more typical of problem-solving groups (not necessarily appropriate to therapy, encounter, or primary groups). We combined this two-stage development model with Fisher's description of four phases in decision making to produce a two-dimensional paradigm that is typical of problem-solving groups.

This book continues to be written primarily for *students,* many of whom lack extensive experience with committees, task forces, work teams, quality circles, and other small groups which are so large a part of the modern productive or service organization. Numerous specific examples from both campus and industry are included for this reason. Visual illustrations were composed or selected to teach rather than to entertain or capture attention. A freshman prepared for college should find the text understandable; upperclass students will find their needs for research summaries and theoretical explanations well met.

Approach

As before, the general model of open systems was used to unify the book. We believe this is the most appropriate paradigm available for understanding small groups. Much of the complexity and jargon of general systems theory was intentionally avoided. Early chapters will help the reader view small groups as open systems of input, throughput, and output variables.

Both authors advocate sharing of responsibility, work, and the rewards of small group life. To both of us, *leader* means *servant* more than controller. We believe that Theory Z is the most humane, productive, and democratic approach to management in both political and economic senses. This is what we advocate for small groups. The Theory Z philosophy of management implies much small group problem solving with all members of a corporate family involved. Small groups are a major part of the "renewal factor" seen in such corporate entities as IBM, Ford, and Morgan Guaranty Trust. Much of this information underscores the belief that our ability to compete in world markets by being both effective and efficient in the workplace depends on our ability to function creatively and cooperatively in groups. Every young American who would like to contribute to our success as a nation in the world economy needs to understand both the philosophy and practical techniques (quality circles, autonomous work groups, job security, employee ownership and profit sharing, etc.) that have spelled the difference between renewal and stagnation of organizations in the political, production, service, and voluntary association phases of life as we experience it. We cannot afford the waste of destructive internal strife. We must learn means of collaborating and using individual disagreements to forge superior solutions. This is first and most basically learned in the study of small group dynamics and communication.

As before, the book was written so that the chapters may be used selectively. Each chapter is self-contained in terms of content, but in this edition an attempt has been made to integrate information from throughout the book. Part 1 presents an overview of small group theory. Chapter 1 introduces the importance and types of small groups in our lives and chapter 2 explains the small, human group as an open system. Part 2, "Small Group Inputs," deals with the human and informational resources and other factors that exist at the beginning of the group's life. Chapter 3 focuses on the members of the group and chapter 4 on the group's purpose, setting, and available information. Part 3 lays the foundation, drawn from basic communication theory, which will enable you to understand the complex interaction that occurs within a group. Chapter 5 discusses the communication process in general. Chapter 6 concentrates on verbal interaction and language and chapter 7 on nonverbal communication. Part 4 elaborates on the groundwork established in part 3 and continues the discussion of group interaction as a throughput process. Chapter 8 explores the development of a group. Chapter 9 develops the concepts of leader and leadership, and chapter 10 examines the role of conflict in a group and its effective management. The next section, part 5, focuses on the outcomes produced by the group, with chapter 11 examining how decisions are made and chapter 12 looking at problem-solving procedures. The final section, part 6, contains specific techniques and tools for evaluating and improving small groups. Chapter 13 presents special discussion techniques designed to facilitate learning and to improve the operation of production and service organizations. Specific techniques and tools for observing, analyzing, and evaluating small group communication are presented in chapter 14.

The chapters were written to explain small group input, throughput, and output in a logical way, but instructors need not assign them in the sequence presented in the book. Some teachers may want to address problem solving or leadership very early in the course. Others may want their students to know how to observe and evaluate interaction in groups so that the theoretical explanations can be applied to specific real-life examples. In addition, some instructors may want or need to omit some chapters or sections. This should present no problems. More is said about this in the Instructor's Manual.

To understand any field of study, one must acquire the special vocabulary of that field. To this end, we have included a list of key terms for each chapter. Study objectives are also provided to guide the reader. A summary, list of supplementary readings, and some exercises are provided at the end of each chapter. The Instructor's Manual provides additional exercises and teaching supplements for the faculty member.

We gratefully appreciate your use of *Effective Group Discussion.* We welcome your written reactions to its content and composition. You can send such comments to us via Wm. C. Brown Publishers or at the Department of Communications, Southwest Missouri State University, Springfield, MO.

May all your groups be enjoyable and satisfying!

Acknowledgments   We appreciate the contributions made to this book by numerous persons; we can name only a few. First, we acknowledge our debt to such instructors and writers as Freed Bales, Ernest Bormann, Elton S. Carter, B. Aubrey Fisher, Kenneth Hance, Randy Hirokawa, Alex Osborn, Sidney J. Parnes, J. Donald Phillips, Marvin Shaw, and Victor Wall. Many colleagues in the study of small group dynamics and communication have expanded our vision through their papers and research reports. We thank our department head, Donal J. Stanton, for both his moral and tangible support.

The reviewers provided through Wm. C. Brown Publishers were exceptionally helpful in supplying thoughtful, carefully considered suggestions: Kathy Adams, California State University-Fresno; Ferald J. Bryan, Mount Union College; Angela M. Campbell, The Ohio State University; William Dresser, Denison University; Thomas Droessler, Owens Technical College; Randy Y. Hirokawa, University of Iowa, Iowa City; Albert Katz, University of Wisconsin, Superior; Bruce Kinghorn, American River College; Dorotha O. Norton, The University of Tennessee at Martin; Lisa Ray, University of California-Davis; Anita Taylor, George Mason University; Victor Wall, The Ohio State University; Doris Werkman, Portland State University; Sally Widenmann Harrison, University of California-Davis. We have chosen to incorporate many of their suggestions and thereby improved the book appreciably. Fellow members of many small groups provided numerous examples, many of which we have included in the book. Students in our classes continue to teach us, and their insights have been incorporated as well. Finally, our friends and families have supplied support in countless ways. To all these people, and many left unmentioned, our sincere thanks!

J.K.B.
G.J.G.

Effective
Group Discussion

Part 1

Introduction to the Study of Small Groups

Chapter 1

The Small Groups in Everyone's Life

As a result of studying chapter 1 you should be able to:

1. Explain why it is important for you to understand the dynamics of small groups and be able to participate productively in small group discussions of many types.

2. Use correctly the terms presented in this chapter, particularly *group, small group, discussion, small group discussion, group dynamics, and small group communication.*

3. Classify any small group on the basis of its major purpose and source.

Key Terms

Activity group a group formed for members to participate in some collaborative activity.

Committee a small group of people given an assigned task or responsibility by a larger group (parent organization) or person with authority.

    Ad hoc or *special* a group given a specific task to perform that goes out of existence when this job is completed.

    Standing a group given an area of responsibility that includes many tasks and continues indefinitely.

Conference discussion by representatives from two or more groups to find ways to coordinate efforts, reduce conflict, etc.

Discussion (small group discussion) a small group of people talking with each other face-to-face in order to achieve some interdependent goal, such as increased understanding, coordination of activity, or solution to a shared problem.

Forum discussion large audience interacting verbally, usually following some presentation.

Group three or more persons united for some purpose(s) and interacting in such a way that they influence each other.

Group dynamics a field of inquiry concerned with the nature of small groups, including how they develop and interact and their relationships with individuals, other groups, and institutions.

Grouphate the feeling of antipathy and hostility many people have against working in a group, fostered by the many ineffective, time-wasting groups that exist.

Interaction mutual influence by two or more persons via the communication process.

Learning group (growth group) a group that discusses in order to enhance the knowledge, perceptions, and interactions of the members.

Panel discussion a small group whose members interact informally and impromptu for the benefit of a listening audience.

Primary group a group whose major purpose is to meet members' needs for affiliation and affection.

Problem-solving group a group that discusses to devise a course of action to solve a problem.

Promotively interdependent goal an objective shared by members of a small group in such a way that achievement of the goal by any member is dependent on achievement by all members.

Public discussion group a small group that plans and presents before an audience a discussion-type program, such as a panel or interview.

Public interview one or more interviewers asking questions of one or more respondents for the benefit of a listening audience.

Secondary group a group whose major purpose is to complete a task, such as making a decision, solving a problem, writing a report, or providing recommendations to a parent organization.

Small group a group of few enough members for each to perceive all others as individuals, who meet face-to-face, share some identity or common purpose, and share standards for governing their activities as members.

Small group communication the scholarly study of communication among members of a small group, among two or more groups, and between groups and larger organizations; the body of communication theory produced by such study.

Small groups constitute the basic fabric of social and work life in the last part of this century. Humans do not exist in isolation from one another, but as members of families, work groups, clubs, and circles of friends. While we may admire Henry David Thoreau for retreating to Walden Pond in relative isolation, that decision fascinates us in part because it is so unusual for a human being to choose prolonged solitude. The desire for social **interaction** is part of our genetic inheritance. Most of us spend a major portion of each day involved as members of various small groups. Even examination of our large corporations reveals a structure of interdependent small work groups, task forces, committees, and boards.

Four important ideas are introduced in this chapter. First, groups exist because they meet distinctly human needs. Schutz summarized these as needs for inclusion, affection, and control: the need to belong or be included in groups with others, a need for love, and a need for power in relation to both other persons and our environment.[1] These are needs that humans cannot meet by themselves—the presence of other people is mandatory. However, groups do not just permit individuals to satisfy several of their basic needs. They are also better problem solvers in the long run than individuals. Group members can see the blind spots and biases in each other's thinking, thus helping protect against faulty solutions. For many of the decisions we must make there is no "correct answer at the back of the book;" only the judgment of our peers arrived at through consensus can guide us in choosing among alternatives. Moreover, if people participate in planning the work or solving the problem it is more likely that they will work harder and better at carrying out the plans. No plan of action is good if the people who must implement it don't like it and work halfheartedly. A long line of investigations has shown that groups are powerful persuaders of their members, leading to more personal change than individual study, lectures, or a one-on-one pitch. Thus, participation in decision making and problem solving helps guarantee continued commitment to those decisions and solutions.

A second important point is that because the formation of groups is natural to humans, groups are found everywhere. List all the small groups in which you participated during the past week, regardless of how brief the time spent with the group. Students in college classes have listed from two to twenty-four groups, with a typical response being about eight to ten. If your list does not include at least eight groups, probably you are unaware of much of the fabric of communication in your life. Does your list resemble one of the following examples? A factory worker: quality control circle, union bargaining committee, family (current nuclear, parental, in-law family), fishing trio, church building committee, bowling team. A student: family, Bible study group, sorority, executive committee of sorority, discussion group in psychology class, intramural volleyball team, car pool, work group of clerks in clothing department. A faculty member: family, collective bargaining team, arrangements committee for professional convention, research team, executive committee of state historical association, steering committee of AAUP, two committees of academic department, gourmet club, two graduate student committees, and numerous informal discussion groups among faculty and student acquaintances.

The amount of time spent in formal groups alone can be overwhelming. Kriesberg found that executives spend an average of ten hours per week in formal committee meetings.[2] Goldhaber found that at the University of New Mexico the average tenured faculty member served on six committees simultaneously and spent eleven hours per week in meetings of various kinds.[3] Add to these figures the amounts of time spent in informal groups, and you can see the pervasiveness of groups in modern society. Moreover, the higher a person goes in any organizational hierarchy, the more time he or she will spend in group situations.

Reliance on groups in our society is expected to increase, perhaps dramatically. American managers are recognizing the value of participative decision making, with the small group as one important vehicle through which employee participation can be encouraged. A hallmark of Japanese management, which American companies are using with growing frequency, is the quality circle, a small group of employees who meet regularly on company time to solve job-related problems. Volvo, the Swedish car manufacturer, has used the concept of the autonomous work group or team with great success. American industry, faced with the need to compete and to make the best possible use of its resources, including its human resources, is looking to the small group as a means to these ends. William Ouchi, creator of the concept of Theory Z management, went so far as to say that how well American business uses groups will determine how effectively it counters Japanese competition.[4] Robert Waterman, examining the characteristics of companies that have kept their competitive edge, identified teamwork as a key element.[5] Teamwork, which enables individuals to work together toward common ends and shared values, is a distinguishing quality of the best American companies. For example, at Morgan Guaranty, one of the companies Waterman described, employees are chastized for attempting to solve problems entirely on their own. Instead, they are encouraged to put together a team of employees and work on the problem as a group.

It should be apparent to you that understanding something about how groups operate and knowing how to communicate productively in groups is essential for anyone who hopes to operate effectively today. Robert Theobald, communication theorist, argued that as group participation increases, especially in the workplace and as part of the political process, individuals need to develop "a far more conscious understanding of the basic communication styles that are required" for decision-making groups to be successful.[6]

The third key point is this: communicating in small groups is so much a part of our lives that most of us take it for granted, failing to perceive and understand what is happening in these groups or how to make them more effective. We need to understand how to communicate effectively in them or we are doomed to unsatisfying and ineffectual discussions ad nauseam. It would be delightful if we could say that most of the talk in these ubiquitous small groups to which we belong produces personal satisfaction for the participants, achieves its purposes, and unifies group members, but it is hardly so. Why else would we chuckle at the truth we recognize in such sayings as: "A camel is a horse designed by a committee," or "Committees are groups that keep minutes and waste hours." We as teachers have experienced on many occasions the groans from students when we tell them that a major portion of their grade will be based upon a group project. Sorensen has coined the term **grouphate** to describe the antipathy many people feel about working in a group.[7] Interestingly, she found that *lack of training in effective group communication skills is associated with grouphate. Knowledge of the process of group communication and education in effective discussion techniques is crucial.* According to Patton and Giffin:

> Since the individual today is experiencing a growing dependency on groups of all descriptions, it is important that people be familiar with the dynamics of group interaction. Once a person has acquired an understanding of the nature of groups, the bases of their development, and their interrelationships with individuals and other groups he [*sic*] has the basis for prediction and control.[8]

The fourth and final point is this: groups help provide the vehicle by which the individual can make a contribution to the organization and the society as a whole. Larkin postulated:

> The basic ingredient cementing social cohesion is not the satisfaction of basic needs, but rather the availability for contribution. What best binds individuals to groups may not be so much the pressure to obtain necessities as the opportunities to give of oneself to something beyond merely self-interested acquisition.[9]

The dignity of individuals, he states, comes not from these basic needs but from people's contributions to something greater than themselves. Groups facilitate these contributions, enabling individuals to participate directly in that something greater than self. We agree with the humanistic principles outlined by Larkin. There is a motivation to *give,* which we believe transcends the usual motivations attributed to humans by most motivational theorists. The success of work-related committees, we believe, stems from this need to create and to share one's creation with others. And, what better way to do this than through the group?

The focus of this book is the communicative behavior of group members. While we will draw upon findings from other fields, we will concentrate on the process of communication among members, especially on how you as a member can influence this process. In sociology classes, you may have studied the role of groups in establishing and maintaining social organization as the link between the individual and society. In psychology you may have examined how the small group modifies the individual's personality and how groups can be therapeutic. In communication, you will study what is happening as members talk and work together and what you can do to make your own communication behavior as productive as possible.

Small group discussion, the talk among group members, cannot be reduced to a set of formulae; it is far too complex for simplistic prescriptions or rules. In *Effective Group Discussion* we have used the concept *system* as a framework to help you understand how groups develop and function, with numerous guidelines but no absolute prescriptions for success. We define the systems concept in depth in chapter 2. System implies interdependence among components in an ongoing process. In a small group this means everything that happens in any part of the system makes a difference in every other component of the group. Because the only person you can directly influence and control is yourself, this book is designed to promote your awareness of your own behavior in small groups and its implications for other members. Therefore, we are aiming at developing the art of communicating effectively in a variety of problem-solving and learning groups. As Spich and Keleman noted, ". . . learning to work as an effective member of a group will be an asset, if not a necessity in future work."[10]

Definitions of key terms we will be using throughout the book are needed in order to reduce the possibility of misunderstandings among you, your classmates, and your instructor. Throughout this book, lists of key terms are included at the beginning of each chapter. To begin, we will introduce several important terms that are fundamental to your understanding of the rest of the book.

Discussion and Related Concepts

Group is the first term we must consider. Although groups have been categorized by others using a variety of classification schemes, we chose the following definition by Marvin Shaw as most suitable to a study of small group communication:

> A group is defined as [three] or more persons who are interacting with one another in such a manner that each person influences and is influenced by each other.[11]

This definition emphasizes interaction and mutual influence. Interaction implies *communication,* the exchange of signals between or among persons who belong to the group, and that at least some of these signals are perceived and responded to in such a way that each group member makes some difference in how each other member acts in the future. By this definition, a collection of people in one place would not necessarily constitute a group unless there were reciprocal awareness and influence. On the other hand, one could argue that group members who are widely scattered geographically but who interact and mutually influence each other via newsletters, telephone conversations, computer networks, closed circuit TV, or radio *do* constitute a group.

This brings us to a basic concept in this book: **small group.** Attempts to define the term on the basis of number of members have never worked. *Small* is at best imprecise, but we are stuck with it when we talk about the basic social unit of a few persons who perceive themselves as an entity. The essence of small is not the number but the *perceptual awareness,* with the upward limit being the numbers of persons one is able to include in awareness and recall. There are limits to how much information humans can perceive and retain.[12] At one glance, most of us can take in from one to at most eleven similar units, although with training, such as learning to use behavioral classification schemes, we may learn to handle twelve or fourteen units.[13] In this sense, a small group is one in which the members can perceive, at least peripherally, all the other members at once, with some awareness of who is and who is not in the group, and the role each is taking. We arbitrarily eliminate the dyad (two persons), since it functions differently from entities of three or more. We include within the definition groups that meet only once, provided that the sense of shared purpose, interaction, and mutual influence exist.

One key feature of a group is its **promotively interdependent goal,** meaning that all members succeed or fail together in the accomplishment of that purpose. With a softball team, for example, one player cannot win while the others on the same team lose. The players are interdependent, and what one does affects the others. Their fates are linked together—they all succeed or fail as a group. Thus, calling several people a group just because they happen to have been thrown together by time and circumstance does not make them such if they lack promotive interdependence.

Discussion is another key term essential to the concept of group. In this book, **small group discussion** refers to *a small group of persons talking with each other face-to-face in order to achieve some interdependent goal, such as increased understanding, coordination of activity, or a solution to a shared problem.* This definition implies certain characteristics of small group discussion, several of which have been presented earlier:

1. A small enough number of persons for each to be aware of and have some reaction to each other (typically three to seven; rarely more than fifteen).
2. A mutually interdependent purpose where the success of one is contingent upon the success of all.
3. Each person has a sense of belonging, of being part of the group.
4. Oral interaction involving communication via verbal and nonverbal channels. This interaction is continuous during a discussion so that the members are constantly reacting, adapting, and modifying their actions in response to each other. Impromptu speaking rather than prepared speeches is the essence of small group discussion, which entails give and take.
5. A sense of cooperation exists among members. While there may be disagreement and conflict, all members perceive themselves as searching for a group outcome that will be as satisfactory as possible to all. Argument is viewed as a means for testing ideas so the best ones can be selected rather than as a way of winning.

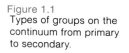
Figure 1.1
Types of groups on the
continuum from primary
to secondary.

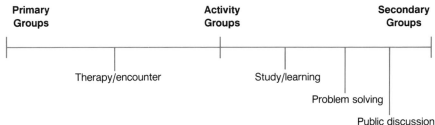

The term **small group communication** will be used in this book to refer to the study of interaction among small group members as well as to the body of communication theory yielded by such study that will be used to produce more effective discussion among members. Later, we will examine in detail this body of theory and principles.

Group dynamics is used in this book to refer to a field of study much broader than that of small group communication:

> . . . a field of inquiry dedicated to advancing knowledge about the nature of groups, the laws of their development, and their interrelations with individuals, other groups, and larger institutions.[14]

We must examine the knowledge gained by scholars of group dynamics if we are to understand the communication going on in small groups and thus make our discussions as effective as possible. Being an effective discussant in a variety of small groups calls for an understanding of the dynamics or forces at work in the group. You must be able both to understand the processes and to be skilled in the way communication is effected in the group. You also must experience a personal involvement or commitment to the group and use your knowledge of group dynamics to the betterment of the group. You can be an effective public speaker and a poor group member, and vice versa.

Types of Small Groups That Discuss

Discussions among members of small groups are held for many purposes. The student of small group communication and discussion needs a simplified scheme for classifying both small groups and the discussions in which they engage. This will promote clarity as you observe, analyze, or talk about a variety of discussions. The classification scheme presented in this section is based on the purpose or major objective of the group. Since groups form for a variety of reasons ranging from having fun to solving major problems, classifying them will help you communicate efficiently with your instructor and fellow students. The two major types of groups we will discuss are primary and secondary. A number of subtypes fall between these two main groupings, as shown in figure 1.1.

Primary Groups

Primary groups exist chiefly for the purpose of satisfying human needs for inclusion (affiliation) and affection rather than for accomplishing some specific task. All primary groups are long-term. Examples include a nuclear family, roommates, several friends who meet daily around a table in the student center, four women who eat lunch and attend movies together, co-workers who regularly share their coffee breaks, and white-collar workers who periodically drop into each other's offices for a chat. Such groups may take on specific tasks and often make decisions, but more often they provide personal attention and support, chat about a variety of topics, let off steam, and generally enjoy each other. The decisions they make are secondary to their primary purpose of providing affection. Their talk is often disorganized and informal because it is not the means to an end so much as it is the end itself, a part of human companionship. Universal human needs to symbolize and share experiences and to listen and be listened to are met through informal discussion in primary groups. More than any other force in our lives, primary groups socialize and mold us into the people we become; their importance is *tremendous*. However, primary groups are not the major focus of this book, though most of the information and advice regarding effective communication in groups applies to them. *Effective Group Discussion* focuses on such secondary groups as problem-solving or decision-making committees and task forces, work groups, and learning groups. The reader who wants to focus on primary groups is encouraged to direct attention to books and courses labeled "interpersonal" communication.

Secondary Groups

Secondary groups are formed for the specific purpose of completing a task, such as making a decision or solving a problem. Primary and secondary groups are not totally distinct; rather, they represent endpoints on a continuum. A "pure" secondary group might be one organized to produce a change in the environment without having any impact on members' needs for belonging or affecting them as persons, whereas a "pure" primary group might exist solely for the socializing of its members. Activity groups fall in between. All groups initiated to accomplish some task are more secondary than primary, although many task groups do help members achieve primary human needs for socialization and affiliation. A variety of secondary groups exists, and you will note that there are not necessarily clear distinctions among the categories; in some cases the differences are a matter of degree or *principal* purpose.

Activity Groups

Activity groups are secondary groups that enable members to engage cooperatively in an activity, often both for the sake of doing the activity and for the affiliation provided by doing the activity with others. Thus, the activity group combines elements of the primary group and the secondary, or task, group to be discussed later. For example, the following represent activity groups: a dinner group of people who meet at intervals to eat together at a new restaurant; game-playing groups such as bridge, poker, chess, and pinochle clubs; a road rally club; hunting groups; and bird-watching or other interest groups. Members of such groups do solve problems and make choices,

Sharing information and ideas in a small group is usually more enjoyable and enlightening than being silent in a large group.

such as when and where to meet, how to pay for their activities, and all the other decisions that must occur in coordinating the efforts of several people. In addition, they often enjoy the fellowship and camaraderie of the other members. Thus, they fall between pure primary and pure secondary groups. The main purpose, however, is participation in the activity that brings the members together.

Therapy and Encounter Groups

All therapy and encounter groups are called collectively *personal growth groups*. They are composed of persons who have come together to develop personal insights, overcome personality problems, and grow as individuals from the feedback and support of others—to engage in personal learning and growth. Examples include local chapters of self-help groups like Alcoholics Anonymous, mutual support groups like gay or women's rights groups, and outpatient groups for clients with personal adjustment problems. Members of such groups do not choose each other, nor are they appointed; they join to help themselves with problems that are both highly personal and social. No group goal is sought; rather, members meet their individual needs for learning, awareness, and help in the context of the group. Many such groups have a professional facilitator to guide the interaction. Most such groups have a relatively limited term of existence; in some, membership changes gradually while the group itself continues.

Study or Learning Groups

Learning groups are similar to encounter and therapy groups in that they are formed as a medium for learning and growth of the participants. If you are reading this book for a course concerned with small group discussion, your class may be organized into several learning groups. Rather than seeking growth in the personality as the primary end, members of such groups have as their major purpose meeting to understand a subject more thoroughly by pooling their knowledge, perceptions, and beliefs. While they are exchanging information, the participants also gain practice in speaking, listening, critical thinking, and other communication skills.

Both of us are strong believers in the value of such groups and have received enormous pleasure from such participation. One of us is a breeder and trainer of hounds and had learned an immense amount from discussions with friends while driving to field trials for dogs, for example. Both of us participated regularly in study groups as graduate students. Opportunities for participation abound on most college campuses, as posters announce Bible study groups, meditation groups, philosophy discussion groups, issue discussion groups, and many others. In addition, many churches, libraries, schools, hospitals, and volunteer organizations produce opportunities for such informal learning.

Problem-Solving Groups

Problem-solving groups vary widely in their composition and functioning, but all of them are formed to help alleviate some unsatisfactory condition (problem). Problem-solving groups may be asked to give advice to someone in authority who will make the actual decision, may be asked to choose one alternative from among several, or may go through a complex procedure that begins with exploration of a problem to be solved and ends with implementation of the solution created by the group. While primary and learning groups periodically tackle problems and engage in occasional problem-solving discussions, that is not their originating purpose. A problem-solving group, on the other hand, is so classified because it was created expressly to solve a problem or problems. There are many subtypes of problem-solving groups. Much of this book deals with four major categories of problem-solving groups: committees, conference groups, quality control circles, and autonomous work groups. The latter two are relatively new to the American scene but can be expected to grow in importance.

Committees   **Committees** are groups that have been assigned a task by a parent organization or person of authority in an organization. Committees may be formed to investigate and report findings, recommend a course of action for the parent group, formulate policies, or plan and carry out some action. All these tasks require discussion among members. Boards, councils, and staffs are special types of committees. For example, the board of directors is often called an executive committee and represents the larger organization, often with extensive power to make and execute policy.

Committees are usually classified as either *ad hoc* or standing. The **ad hoc** or **special committee** is established to perform a specific task and normally ceases to exist when that task has been completed. A special committee is often referred to as a *task force,* with members appointed from various departments of an organization or political body. Examples of what special committees might be asked to do include evaluating credentials of job applicants,

A committee of nurses preparing a recommendation.

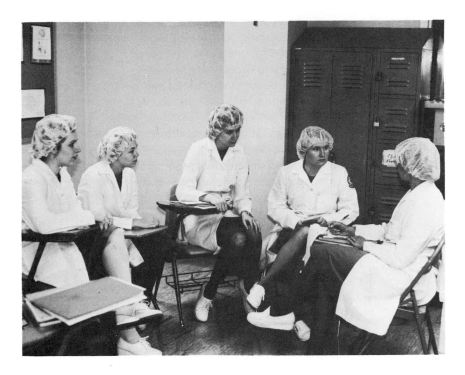

drafting bylaws, hearing grievances, planning social events, conducting investigations, devising plans to solve work-related problems, advising legislators on what to do about statewide problems, and evaluating programs and institutions. Once the task force has reported its action or recommendations, it goes out of existence.

Standing committees are on-going committees established through the constitution or bylaws of an organization to deal with particular types of problems or perform specific organizational functions. The most important standing committee of most organizations is given a name, such as "executive committee," "board," or "steering committee." Usually this group is charged with overall management of the organization and can function for the entire organization when general membership meetings are not possible. Other commonly encountered standing committees go under such names as "membership committee," "personnel committee," "parking and traffic committee," and "program committee." These groups continue indefinitely even though the membership may change. Frequently, some portion of the members of a standing committee is replaced annually so that the group includes both experienced members and those with a fresh perspective. Standing committees often meet regularly, typically resolving a number of problems at a single meeting.

Conference Groups   By general usage, *conference* refers to almost any type of face-to-face communication, whether between two persons or among many participants at large gatherings. However, we use **conference** in this book to refer to a meeting of representatives from two or more other groups. Since every large organization contains within it many functioning small groups, conferences are critical for coordination within and among organizations. Conferees communicate information from one group to another, perhaps coordinating their efforts. Intergroup conflicts and competition must be mediated to find a solution acceptable to all groups represented. For example, representatives of various arts organizations meet to plan a yearly schedule of events and coordinate their marketing and publicity efforts so that individual events do not compete with one another. Conferences between delegates of the Senate and House of Representatives attempt to resolve differences in legislation bearing on the same issue. In the workplace, representatives of business and labor meet to negotiate contractual matters. Often, conferees must submit their tentative decisions to their respective constituent groups for final approval.

Quality Control Circles   The quality control circle is a relatively recent development in American organizations and represents an attempt to capitalize on the fact that groups usually make better and more readily accepted decisions on complex problems than do individuals. Workers in a production or service company volunteer or are selected for membership in a quality control circle. The circle meets periodically (often weekly) on company time to develop recommendations for improving the quality of finished products, efficiency, worker safety, and other work-related problems. A few conditions are essential if the quality control circle procedure is to work. The people who lead the groups must be trained as problem-solving discussion leaders. Upper management must be committed to the concept, must respond to all recommended solutions, and must either act upon these recommendations or explain why they are being delayed or rejected. Workers must share in the benefits of their cost-saving ideas, job security must be guaranteed when efficiency is increased, and discussion leaders must be open-minded toward all ideas suggested. The typical quality control circle has from five to seven members.

Autonomous Work Groups   Groups of workers are given a defined area of freedom to manage their productive work ("autonomous" does not imply unlimited scope, as there are clearly defined restrictions on the group's freedom to decide and act). Autonomous work groups elect their own leaders rather than having first-line supervisors appointed. The group may decide such managerial issues as who will do what task and in what order assigned jobs will be completed. The claim in support of autonomous work groups is that an immediate group can allocate resources more effectively than can a somewhat distant manager, that employees with some say in their work are more committed and productive than workers given less choice, and involvement in decision making meets the psychological needs of the employees without reducing the technical quality of their work. After workers have been given such authority it is very hard for management to take it back from them. Workers need to be trained for autonomous work groups to work optimally.[15] In the future, it is likely that more employees will be involved in quality control circles and autonomous work groups, which makes sensitivity to group phenomena and skills in discussion leadership increasingly important.

Public Discussion Groups

Public discussion groups are created for the stimulation and enlightenment of a listening audience whose members may become participants in a large group discussion or forum. Small group public discussions permit a number of perspectives or beliefs about a problem to be expressed and allow listeners to make direct comparisons of the merits of differing beliefs, values, and policies.

Panel Discussion   A **panel discussion** is a public presentation in which a small group of persons representing varying perspectives discusses informally, in front of a listening audience, a few issues relevant to an important question. For example, a panel might discuss abortion laws, solutions to congested parking on campus, pros and cons of quality circles, or the responsibility of society to victims of crimes. A panel format is sometimes used with a group of aspirants for nomination by a political party to the presidency or some other high office. A *moderator* coordinates the discussion so it does not ramble and so all points of view are given representation. Participants need to be both knowledgeable about the question under discussion and articulate in expressing their opinions. Panelists generally have an outline of questions to follow, but their speaking is relatively impromptu. Panelists need not agree on anything except which issues to discuss; the lively argument which often ensues can make for an intellectually stimulating program. The panel format is excellent for presenting an overview of different points of view on an issue of public concern.

Public Interviews   A **public interview** may be conducted by one or more interviewers of one or more interviewees at a time. "Meet the Press" and "The Oprah Winfrey Show" are examples of this format as are press conferences and presidential debates. Interviewers and interviewees may agree in advance on a list of major questions or topics to be discussed, on the range of topics for discussion, or the program may be entirely spontaneous. The interviewees are selected for their expertise or special roles. The interviewer's responsibility is to represent the audience by asking questions he or she believes the audience most wants or needs to have answered and to help the interviewees clarify responses.

Forum Discussion   **Forum discussion** refers to a period of verbal interaction during which audience members are invited to ask questions or express opinions. Frequently a forum follows a panel or interview program; it may also follow a film, speech, or other presentation. Audience members should be told in advance that a forum will follow the public presentation so they can think of (and possibly write down) questions or comments. The term *forum* also refers to a discussion held by a large gathering of people, such as a hearing on a proposed zoning change or a town meeting scheduled by a mayor, legislator, commissioner, or other governmental official.

Summary

In this opening chapter, we have considered the vital and ubiquitous roles small groups play in our lives. They provide a source for our identity, a vehicle to satisfy many basic human needs, and a means for decision making and problem solving in a complex society. Yet grouphate is pervasive, because small groups are often ineffectual and frustrating to their members. Even so, the use of groups in the workplace and in society is steadily increasing. Operating effectively in groups is ". . . a learned skill requiring increased understanding of interpersonal dynamics and personal sensitivities to the subtleties of group work."[16]

Key terms have been defined to facilitate communication, and a scheme for classifying small groups according to purpose and source was presented: primary groups, secondary groups (therapy and encounter groups; study or learning groups; and problem-solving groups like committees, conference groups, quality control circles, and autonomous work groups), activity groups, and public discussion groups (panel discussions, public interviews, and forums).

With your understanding of these basic terms and concepts, we can now turn to a more detailed consideration of the dynamics of the small group.

Exercises

1. This icebreaker exercise is designed to help you get acquainted with classmates and to reduce tensions and formality that exist within a collection of strangers. The entire class should sit in a circle so that members can see each other face-to-face. Use a name tag or card large enough to be read across the circle.
   a. First, draw a picture (stick figures are fine!) to illustrate each of the following statements about yourself. Each person respond to the first statement before proceeding to the next. Begin each set of answers with a different person and proceed around the circle until all have answered.

   I am taking this course because
   Being in a small group makes me feel
   The thing I like best about myself is
   The thing I like least about myself is
   It would surprise most people if they knew that I
   No matter what anyone says, I will not change my mind about
   I really dislike
   My favorite activity is
   Ten years from now I see myself as
   The thing I am most proud of about myself is

    b. Briefly discuss the following:

       Who is most like you?
       Did anybody's answers particularly surprise you?
       Who impressed you most? Why?
       How do you feel now about your class?
       What have we learned from this exercise?

2. For the next week, keep a list of all the small groups in which you actively participate. See if you can classify these groups according to the scheme presented in this chapter. Next, rate your personal satisfaction with each group, from 1 (very dissatisfied) to 7 (very satisfied). Compare your lists in class. What do you conclude? Do your classmates like and dislike the same things in a group that you do?

Bibliography

Barker, Larry A., Kathy J. Wahlers, Kittie W. Watson, and Robert J. Kibler. *Groups in Process: An Introduction to Small Group Communication.* 3d ed. Englewood Cliffs, N.J.: Prentice-Hall, 1987, chapter 1.

Randy Y. Hirokawa and Marshall Scott Poole, eds. *Communication in Group Decision-Making.* Beverly Hills: Sage Publications, 1986.

Notes

1. William C. Schutz, *FIRO: A Three-Dimensional Theory of Interpersonal Behavior* (New York: Rinehart, 1958).
2. M. Kriesberg, "Executives Evaluate Administrative Conferences," *Advanced Management* 15 (1950): 15–17.
3. Gerald Goldhaber, "Communication and Student Unrest," (Unpublished report to the president of the University of New Mexico, undated).
4. William Ouchi, *Theory Z: How American Business Can Meet the Japanese Challenge* (Reading, Mass.: Addison-Wesley, 1981).
5. Robert H. Waterman, Jr., *The Renewal Factor: How the Best Get and Keep the Competitive Edge* (New York: Bantam Books, Inc., 1987).
6. Robert Theobald, "The Communications Era from the Year 2000," *National Forum* 60 (Summer 1980): 20.
7. S. Sorensen, "Grouphate," (Paper presented at International Communication Association, Minneapolis, May 1981).
8. Bobby R. Patton and Kim Giffin, *Problem-Solving Group Interaction* (New York: Harper & Row, Publishers, 1973), 6.
9. T. J. Larkin, "Humanistic Principles for Organization Management," *Central States Speech Journal* 37 (1986): 37.
10. Robert S. Spich and Kenneth Keleman, "Explicit Norm Structuring Process: A Strategy for Increasing Task Group Effectiveness," *Group and Organization Studies* 10 (1985): 55.

11. Marvin E. Shaw, *Group Dynamics: The Psychology of Small Group Behavior,* 2d ed. (New York: McGraw-Hill, 1976), 11.

12. Robert S. Woodworth and H. Schlosberg, *Experimental Psychology,* rev. ed. (New York: Henry Holt and Company, 1954), 90–94.

13. Robert F. Bales, *Interaction Process Analysis* (Cambridge, Mass.: Addison-Wesley, 1950), viii, 35–39.

14. Dorwin Cartwright and Alvin Zander, *Group Dynamics: Research and Theory,* 3d ed. (New York: Harper & Row, Publishers, 1968), 7.

15. Charles C. Manz and Henry P. Sims, Jr., "The Potential for 'Groupthink' in Autonomous Work Groups," *Human Relations* 35 (1982): 773–84.

16. Spich and Keleman, "Explicit Norm Structuring Process," 56.

Chapter 2

The Small Group as a System

Study Objectives

As a result of studying chapter 2 you should be able to:

1. Consciously and intentionally adopt a participant-observer perspective when engaged in discussions.

2. List and explain the major input, throughput, and output variables in a small group as an open system.

3. Describe the characteristics of an ideal discussion group.

Key Terms

Environment the context or setting in which a small group (system) exists.

Feedback some part of the output of a system that is returned to the system and that influences or controls future operations of the system; also refers to the control process.

Individual-level variables features or characteristics of the individual members of a group, such as traits, attitudes, values, beliefs, and skills that affect the group's interaction.

Input variable an observable source of energy and raw material used by an open system; resources from which a system is formed and on which it operates to produce outputs.

Interdependence the property of a system that all parts are interrelated and affect each other as well as the whole system.

Non-summativity the property of a system that the whole is greater than the sum of the system's parts.

Norm a rule, usually informal and unstated, that governs the behavior of members of a small group.

Open system a system whose boundaries to the environment are highly permeable, permitting a relatively free flow of material and energy back and forth; within limits, a balance must be maintained between an open system and its environment.

Output variable anything produced by the system; an observable consequence or product resulting from the functioning of the system, including changes in the inputs, the components, outcomes, and environment.

Participant-observer active participant in a small group who is at the same time observing and evaluating its processes and procedures.

Process variable see *throughput variable.*

System an entity made up of components patterned in interdependent relationship to each other, requiring constant adaptation among its parts to maintain organic wholeness.

System-level variables features or characteristics of the group as a whole, such as cohesiveness, interaction patterns, norms, roles, and so forth, that affect the group's interaction.

Throughput variable also called *process* variable; what the system does to transform the inputs into outputs and to adapt to its environment; a characteristic of the *functioning* of a system.

Variable an observable characteristic that can change in magnitude or quality from time to time.

We have already discussed how pervasive small groups are in our daily lives and why it is important to study them. What we present in this chapter is a general framework, from systems theory, that will enable you to see how a small group operates; how the group's parts relate to each other; and how the input, throughput, and output variables function together. Once you understand the basic principles of systems theory, you will be able to apply what you know to any type of small group. You can then understand what is happening and why, and adjust your behavior to achieve desired outcomes for yourself and your group.

The Participant-Observer Perspective

A major purpose of this book is to help you develop a **participant-observer** perspective. The participant-observer is a regular member of the group, engaging actively in its deliberations while at the same time observing, evaluating, and adapting to its processes and procedures. Participant-observers direct part of their attention to participating in the group and part to studying how the group is functioning, trying always to be aware of what the group needs at the moment. Because such members make conscious efforts to monitor the group's processes to help ensure that the group is functioning as smoothly as possible, they supply essential information, ideas, procedural suggestions, and interpersonal communication skills *when needed*. They also seek such input from other members of the group who may not realize what is needed at the moment. Lacking such an orientation, which considers the good of the group to be paramount, the member may become a drag on the system, hindering its effectiveness.

Many group members do not contribute to the group's task as completely as they might. For example, some members are valuable because of their expertise or skill but have little understanding of the process variables in small groups. As long as the group is operating well, these members can make contributions, but they are of no help in resolving conflicts, reducing misunderstandings, offering procedural suggestions, or helping to solve other process problems.

Other members are participants in name only. They add almost nothing to the inputs of the group, even though they may detract little from its energy and resources. They are observers who watch and listen but do little or nothing. We all have experienced groups with observerlike members: the committee member who makes no suggestions, the classmate in a discussion group who has not read the assignment to be discussed. This may be the result of lack of knowledge relevant to the group's purpose, lack of small group communication skills, or lack of sophistication regarding small group processes and procedures.

In contrast, members with extensive knowledge of small group dynamics as well as skills in communication techniques can contribute both to the process and the product of the group. They can articulate relevant information and ideas, promote harmonious relationships among members, call attention to deficiencies in the group's process, and suggest procedures and discussion techniques. To be an all-around valuable member of the group, one must have **both** a participant-observer focus and information and expertise needed by the group to achieve its objectives.

Throughout the rest of this book, we will be examining the major variables in the small group as a system so that you can become a more knowledgeable participant-observer member, gaining the knowledge and skills needed to accomplish the task of your group. As a beginning student of small group discussion, you need an overall image of interaction in an ideal small group, one that you can use as a standard against which to compare the groups to which you belong. For this reason, we present an actual example of an exceptionally productive small group, then develop a model of the small group as an open system, and finally establish a standard of excellence for each major small group variable.

An Example of an Ideal Problem-Solving Group

From the hundreds of small groups in which we have participated or observed as researchers, we have selected one as an example to illustrate the ideal model. This committee of five faculty members of a college of Arts and Sciences had been elected by their colleagues and charged with the task of creating a constitution for the college, which was a component of a large university. A new bylaw of the board of regents of the university authorized colleges to develop constitutions for their internal governance. The committee members each came from different academic disciplines. The dean of the college acted as chair *pro tem* at the first meeting to explain his understanding of the charge of the committee, then asked the committee to elect a chair. The group then discussed the chair's duties: calling meetings, seeing that detailed records were kept, providing tentative agendas for meetings, seeing that multiple copies of all the writing the committee had done were prepared, and providing equal opportunity for each member to speak. Following that discussion, Professor Orin Miller was elected by secret vote. The dean asked that, if possible, a completed constitution be presented to the college faculty at a meeting in six months, then left the meeting.

Fortunately, all members of the new committee were acquainted with each other from participation in previous committees. They had chosen wisely; Orin was accepted completely as chair. He suggested efficient procedures; clarified and summarized progress; and encouraged, organized, and coordinated, but he never dominated or manipulated.

After the dean had left, Orin asked the group how they viewed their assignment and how they might go about producing a constitution. The following discussion ensued:

Paul: This is a tremendous opportunity to create a model of democratic academic governance. We've never had anything like this at our university, so the constitution we write will be a groundbreaking thing. We have a great challenge and a great responsibility.

Joan: Amen! I really feel that this is important, and that we must and can do a great job. If we do our job well, the faculty will adopt the constitution we propose, and it will serve them well.

Tom: Yeah, that's how I see it, too. I'm not much of a lover of committees, but this one matters. I can't think of a finer group of people to work with on drawing up our first constitution.

Ray: And how—this is the cream of our faculty. I'm sure we can work well together and do a fine job. But I think we ought to plan out how we will go about this.

Orin: I'm pleased that we all feel that our task is so important, and that we have such a fine group. Okay, Ray, why don't we discuss the problems we face in writing a constitution, then how we might go about it, and come up with a general plan for our meetings.

Group: Fine. Yes. Good. Let's do it.

Orin: Well, then what do we need in a constitution? I suggest we make a list of all the things we think need to be addressed in it.

Ray: Definitely it must state the purpose of the faculty as a group, such as setting standards, approving degree programs, examining courses and evaluating them, advising the dean on recommendations for promotion and tenure of faculty, and similar academic matters.

Joan: It will need a committee structure, with the purposes, selection, and organizing of standing committees to do all these things.

Paul: And a section on how the constitution is both adopted and amended as needed at a later date.

This listing of possible components of a constitution for the college went on for about twenty minutes, with the chair asking a few questions to clarify ("Do you mean have the departments represented on a rotating basis?"), asking if there was anything else anyone could think of, and recording everything. He summarized the growing list of components:

Orin: Well, that's quite a list! Let me read it all over to you, and see if I've left anything out. Then, we might discuss whether this is all we need and if we need it all. Before we end this discussion, I think we should decide how to proceed from here.

Following nods of approval, Orin read the list, thus summarizing the group output to that time. This summary provoked further discussion:

Joan: We don't have anything about membership. We need to define how one qualifies for voting in the faculty.

Paul: Right.

Orin: Okay, it's added to the list. I think we've made a good beginning on setting our goals. I'll have this typed, run off, and send each of you a copy so you can think it over and maybe suggest additions or deletions at our next meeting. Also, I guess we should put these in some order. Would anyone be willing to try that?

Joan: Well, I've done a lot of work on constitutions in the past, so I guess I could do that. But now I'm anxious to get to talking about what we need to do and how to go about it in the months ahead.

Group: Yes. Me, too. Let's.

Orin: Okay, I think one of the first things we ought to do is draw up a list of similar institutions, then divide up the list among us and everyone write to several of them for copies of their constitutions, and note sections that impress you and things we have overlooked as possible topics in our constitution.

Tom: Good idea. We sure ought to write to Iowa State and Penn State.

Ray: And Michigan State and Western Michigan. I heard they have a fine setup there.

Orin: Those all sound like good places to get examples, but before we get further into that, I think we should plan out our long-range agenda, the general procedure to follow through our meetings. Is that all right with all of you? [Nods of agreement from all.] First, when should we meet and how often?

Ray: This is as good a time as any for me. How about the rest of you?

Paul: Well, I can make it, but because of having no classes on this day I'd rather keep it free for research and writing. How about another time? Could we all compare schedules?

The group members did so, and chose unanimously to meet every Wednesday from 2:00 P.M. until as late as necessary.

Orin: We have an awful lot of work to do, so I think we ought to meet every week, at least at first, until we are sure we will have a draft ready for the faculty meeting in April. What do the rest of you think?

Paul: I agree wholeheartedly, but I think we should skip a week or two until we get back the copies of constitutions we request and have time to analyze them.

Joan: I guess I agree, Paul, but I think we should meet next week to finish up our list of possible topics and maybe write a sort of preamble to help us get our sights set and our values in order as to what we want to achieve from or through a constitution.

Paul: Yeah, I hadn't thought of that, but you're right.

Orin: Is that agreeable to you fellows [to Tom and Ray]?

Both replied that it was.

Orin: Why don't we each write down what we think is the purpose of our constitution and what we think the preamble ought to say about those things?

Group: Fine. Okay. I'll do what I can. That's a good place to start.

Orin: Now let's get on with our long-range plan. We get a list of schools, divide it up and write to them for copies, and revise our outline of a constitution. We could then take it up a section at at time, one or two sections per meeting, being sure we have time to go over it as a whole and get it prepared before the faculty meeting. How does that strike you as a procedure?

Paul: That sounds good to me, but I've noticed how easy it is if we begin in a group with something to shoot at. So why don't we form one- or two-person subcommittees to write tentative drafts of the various articles and sections?

Joan: I think that's a good way to proceed, if we can choose what sections we begin work on and agree that each of us is to do about the same amount of work.

Tom: That's fine by me, if we can write other tentative sections than those we are assigned when we don't agree with what has been presented to us.

Ray: Yes. I think it is vital that we be very open with each other on what we think and believe and that we don't have to agree with what someone wrote. It's too important not to bring out all the pros and cons on each issue.

Orin: I certainly would hope we examine everything we propose from all angles. How do the rest of you see that?

There was a consensus that this was necessary and that they could disagree openly, yet remain friends working in cooperation. The committee then set up a list of schools from which to request copies of constitutions.

Throughout their entire eighteen meetings, this group followed the general procedure and agenda laid out at the first meeting. Sometimes a proposed article would be accepted with minor revision; sometimes it would be argued in depth and with strong feelings, but never in the approximately fifty hours of discussion did any name-calling occur. Orin sent out an outline agenda for each meeting, along with a copy of articles to be considered at the meeting so members could look them over in advance. At the next to last meeting, the following discussion occurred:

Orin: I think we now need to talk about how we introduce this constitution to the faculty and get them to vote for it. I'm really proud of us and the constitution we have drafted, and I don't want it to get chopped up or beaten down by people who don't understand it so well as we do.

Joan: Right, Orin. As chair, you will make the motion for adoption, and explain what we designed it to accomplish, and why.

Paul: Yes, and now I think we should consider all the things people might raise as objections, what they might want to change, and how we can argue against those changes.

Orin: Do you all agree? [Everyone did, so they proceeded, dividing up the main responsibility for thinking up rebuttals on each section.]

At the final meeting of the group:

Orin: I'm really sort of sad to see our "Ben Franklin" committee come to an end, though I can sure use the time to get back to some research I had to put aside. This has been the finest group I've ever been in. As chairman, I can't thank you enough.

Tom: I feel the same—we've been a great group. But, Orin, you've been a model chair, by far the best I've ever seen.

To this there were strong expressions of agreement, a tribute to Orin, and to themselves for how proud they were of their work. The college was given the constitution, discussed it in great detail section by section, made two relatively minor amendments to it, and then adopted it by unanimous vote, something exceptional for a group of 160 people with strongly held beliefs from a wide divergence of backgrounds. This constitution is still in effect, with some amendments over the years, and is regarded as the best college constitution in that university.

This group, from both of our standpoints, represents an ideal example of how a problem-solving group should operate. Especially important were the sense of commitment each member brought to the task and the availability of needed resources. These resources included information in the form of constitutions from elsewhere and many informal polls of fellow faculty members, ideas, writing skills, members' skills in cooperation and communication, an ideal setting in which to work—a quiet, comfortable conference room with chairs in a circle around a table—and a systematic procedure that all had helped to develop. All decisions were made by consensus, which helped build the sense of teamwork throughout. Orin never acted bossy or dogmatic in his role. He worked very hard to keep the group following agreed-upon procedures, to see that all points of view were heard and respected, and to ensure that consensus was reached. Tom was especially skilled at bringing a sense of good humor and calm to the group when anyone seemed upset over a conflict of ideas. As the group succeeded on each part of the document, that success added to their enthusiasm and ability to work well, including being open about any doubts or disagreements they held. The final products included not only a fine constitution and ready adoption by the faculty, but a sense of unity and satisfaction among the members. Orin made a statement of tribute to the whole group, saying they deserved the credit for what was accomplished for the faculty, not he. This committee manifested to an exceptional degree the characteristics of an ideal small group as an open system with optimal inputs, throughput procedures, and outputs. With the example of this real group as a foundation, we are now ready to consider the meaning of the phrase "a small group as a system."

The Small Group as an Open System

You have probably noticed that when a new person joins a group the group changes in some ways. This illustrates the idea of a **system**—a set of relationships among interdependent components and forces. General systems theory is built on an analysis of living things that attempt to remain in dynamic balance with the **environment** in which they live by constant adjustments throughout the system. A system is living, dynamic, and everchanging. Several principles of systems theory are important to your understanding of the small group as a system.

One important principle, discussed earlier, is the idea of **interdependence.** The parts of a system do not operate in isolation; each part affects the other parts as well as the system as a whole. If a new person comes into the group, that member's arrival will affect every other member of the group in some manner. Similarly, if the normally cheerful chair of a committee comes to a group meeting in a grouchy mood, the other members will feel uneasy and the group's normally effective decision-making processes may be impaired. Notice in the constitution committee transcript provided earlier how the members were interdependent. The chair, Orin, set a climate that fostered full participation. Everything from selecting a meeting time to determining the overall philosophy and direction of the constitution was accomplished through open discussion that emphasized member interdependence. Members engaged in a mutual influence process; no individual's views, including Orin's, were more important than another's. Notice also that this group recognized its interdependence with the rest of the college. Members strove to create something that would be fully acceptable to the other faculty they represented.

Another key principle is the system property of **non-summativity** (non-additivity). In other words, the whole is greater than the sum of its parts. For example, a collection of individuals in one place who happen to know how to play basketball does not constitute a group. If these individuals form a basketball team, begin to interact, and coordinate their efforts in playing against another team, we see that the team (or group) involves more than the simple addition of the abilities of each player. The group will take on a life of its own and will become an entity, something more than a mere addition (summing) of the abilities of the members.

Sports enthusiasts know that they will lose money on a basketball or football game if they add up the statistics for each player, arrive at team totals, and bet on the team with the higher total. On any given day, a team with superior statistics can be beaten by a so-called "lesser" team. How can this happen? This can happen because a team or group is a living system with a life of its own that cannot be predicted by summing the individual capabilities (or statistics) of the players. In other arenas of endeavor, groups can design technologies beyond the collective capacities of members as individuals or collectivities. For example, most recent Nobel prizes in science have been given for breakthroughs that required teams of scientists. Both these examples illustrate non-summativity.

One benefit of thinking of the small group as a system is the emphasis this gives to the notion of multiple causation, which says that whatever happens is not the result of a single, simple cause but the result of complex interrelationships among several forces. Another benefit of the systems perspective is that it leads us to look for multiple outcomes of any change in the group. With a systems perspective, we are less likely to oversimplify our understanding of how a group functions and perhaps miss something important.

The **variables** (characteristics or dimensions) of a system, including a small group, are classified in three broad categories: **input, throughput (process),** and **output** variables. Input variables are the components taken from the environment from which a small group is formed and which it uses to do its work: the members of the group; the reason for the group's formation; resources, such as information, expertise, and tools; and environmental conditions and forces that influence the group. In our illustrative example, the members with diverse interests can be considered inputs. Recall that Ray had heard that Michigan State and Western Michigan had model constitutions. That information, possessed by one member, served as a resource input variable, which ultimately affected both the group's deliberations as well as its final proposal.

Throughput variables include the structure of relationships among members: the roles, rules, and norms that emerge; the procedures followed; the communication and interaction among members; and all the other things that are part of the process in which the group engages as it works toward completing its task. In our ideal committee, observe how certain rules and procedures evolved. First, the members complimented each other, indicating their pleasure at working together. This began to constitute a pattern of expressing cohesiveness and mutual respect, which made it easier during the group's subsequent interaction for members to contribute freely. Orin established his role as a democratic chair ("Is that all right with all of you?"). Other members felt comfortable in jumping in with suggestions and comments, which established norms of participation and equality.

Output variables are the results or products of the group's throughput processes, including the tangible work accomplished (such as items built, policies developed, reports written), changes in the members themselves (such as increases in positive feelings toward each other), the group's effects on its environment, and changes in the group's procedures themselves. Many outputs affect the group's environment. As you can see, these categories of variables are not separable; everything influences and is influenced by everything else in the small group system. Our ideal group's most obvious output to the environment was a constitution that was not only adopted by the college but was widely praised. Internal outputs included the increase in mutual respect and cohesiveness ("I'm really sort of sad to see our 'Ben Franklin' committee come to an end."). Can you start to see how each of these variables—inputs, throughputs, outputs—is related to the others? For example, attitudes affect interaction which in turn influences the outcome. Moreover, the interaction and outcome can produce changes in members' attitudes. In addition, this reciprocal relationship among a system's parts and processes illustrates the interdependence discussed earlier.

In addition, these variables may be classified as either **individual-level** or **system-level** features of a group.[1] The characteristics the members bring with them, such as traits, skills, abilities, values, and attitudes, clearly affect the way the group functions. These individual-level variables are interdependent with each other as well as the system-level variables that influence the group, such as pre-existing social and cultural norms, degree of cohesiveness, and decision rules which are characteristics of the group itself. For example, a new group member may be very well informed about a topic the group is discussing, but if the group has established a norm that new members should be seen and not heard until they have received some tangible form of acceptance from long-standing members, then the group will not benefit from the new member's information. Thus, individual characteristics and group, or system, characteristics mutually influence each other as well as the group's final outputs.

Figure 2.1 is a diagrammatic model of some of the many variables in each of the three categories: input, throughput, and output. The hopper at the top of the figure represents inputs into the throughput machinery of the system, where they are processed and changed. The exit channel at the bottom of the diagram represents the outputs of the system. The tube on the left side looping from output to input represents the **feedback** channels through which a portion of the outputs are cycled back to the system to modify future operations and processes of the system. For example, if the basketball team we mentioned earlier is successful, the output of repeated winning will produce more enthusiasm and commitment to the team by the players, who will continue to polish their performance together and to feel positive about each other and the coach. Their success may produce greater attendance at the games, more funds to buy better equipment, and perhaps will lead to even greater success.

This model of a small group is an **open system,** meaning that the group interacts with its environment rather than existing in social isolation. There is a relatively free exchange between the group and its environment, which includes all the forces surrounding the group and which impinge upon it. A classroom discussion group, for example, may receive relevant information from the instructor, from other classmates, or from news media sources. In contrast, a closed group receives relatively little input or feedback from the environment. A cloistered monastery, where the members interact with each other but not as a group with outsiders, illustrates such a closed system. We can think of no completely closed group system.

Now that you have seen an example of the interaction of an outstanding committee and have an understanding of the small group as a system, we can proceed to identify standards against which you can evaluate the major input, throughput, and output variables of any small group in which you might participate.

Standards for an Ideal Discussion Group

The quality of any discussion group can be determined only from its outputs, its effectiveness. The very title of this book emphasizes the importance of achieving desired outputs (see figure 2.1). Of course, outputs can be evaluated by comparing them with what the group set out to accomplish and in relation to environmental restraints on goal accomplishment. For example, no matter how skilled a team of physicians may be, if they are trying to treat a disease of unknown origin for which there is no therapeutic procedure (such as AIDS), they cannot be expected to cure the victim. A more realistic goal would be to

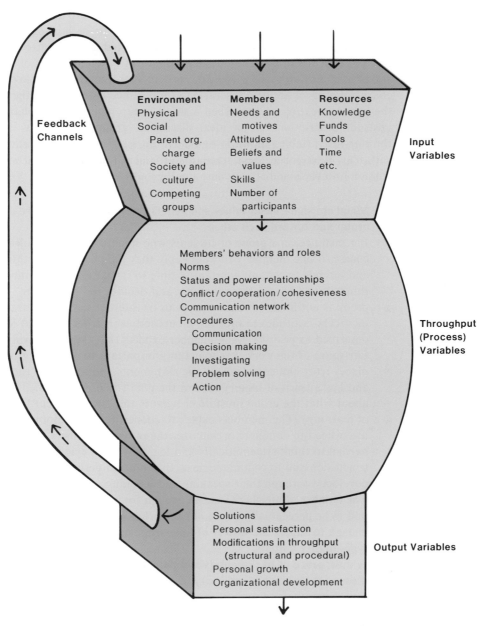

Feedback Channels

Environment
Physical
Social
  Parent org.
    charge
  Society and
    culture
  Competing
    groups

Members
Needs and
  motives
Attitudes
Beliefs and
  values
Skills
Number of
  participants

Resources
Knowledge
Funds
Tools
Time
etc.

Input Variables

Members' behaviors and roles
Norms
Status and power relationships
Conflict / cooperation / cohesiveness
Communication network
Procedures
  Communication
  Decision making
  Investigating
  Problem solving
  Action

Throughput (Process) Variables

Solutions
Personal satisfaction
Modifications in throughput
  (structural and procedural)
Personal growth
Organizational development

Output Variables

Figure 2.1
A model of the small group as an open system.

eliminate as much suffering as possible for the patient. No matter how skilled and informed the members of a committee may be or how excellent their throughput processes, the organization that created the committee may have limited what it can do. The interdependence of all components of a system, and of a system with its environment, is demonstrated as we seek to define the characteristics of an ideal discussion group. Since *discussion* is the name of the communication process when a small group meets, the emphasis in the abstract descriptions of an ideal discussion group that follow is on the throughput variables shown in figure 2.1 rather than on the input or output variables. Remember, these standards represent the ideal toward which discussion groups should strive; most small groups will fall short.

Input Variables

1. **Members share basic values and beliefs relevant to the purpose of the group and toward each other.**
   For instance, in a group of students who must complete a project for a course, if one member believes deeply that the project is worthwhile and intends to commit substantial time to it, but another member thinks it is a busywork assignment and decides to "blow it off," the group is not likely to reach consensus or interact smoothly. Ideally, members' attitudes toward the group and each other would at least be described as positive. Each member expects that the others will do a fair share of the work, has something important to offer the group, places trust and confidence in the statements and actions of the others, and has a spirit of inquiry toward the goal (no predetermined belief about what the group must do or what is the "truth" about the subject of learning). The members expect to cooperate and compromise. None has a need to dominate or win over the others. Members have the skills needed to think systematically and logically from evidence to a conclusion and to communicate so that mutual perceptions are developed through their speaking and listening.

2. **The number of members is small enough for all to be active participants and to be perceptually aware of each other as individuals, yet large enough to supply the variety of knowledge and skills needed to achieve high-quality outputs.**
   A divergence of backgrounds and perspectives will characterize an ideal discussion group, yet similarity in goals and values will make it possible for all members to support group decisions. For example, five people with similar values might agree on a goal, yet bring five largely different sets of information about the problem and possible solutions to it. Thus, they could consider many different interpretations of what is causing the problem and solve it better than a group of ten people with very similar knowledge and ideas. The five can communicate more informally and efficiently than the ten. A group of three persons who can't agree on basic values and goals (for example, what should be achieved by a policy on public prayer) can accomplish little even though the group is small.

3. **Resources to achieve the goals of the group are available.**
   Reliable facts are known or accessible to members and they have or can generate reasoned opinions and ideas about the topic or problem. They have the physical resources of tools, communication media, funds, and any other needed objects. For instance, one group could not do its work until a highly detailed set of data on computer tapes was made available from a government agency and a member with computer programming skills was added to the group. This group also needed access to computer time and money to pay for the time.

4. **Relationships to other groups and organizations in the group's environment provide a clearly defined mission and necessary resources to accomplish it.**
   Group members understand their environment, especially how they relate to any organization that created the group, any competing groups, and sources of needed resources. Both the area of freedom and limitations on the group are understood by the group and concerned persons in its environment. The group makes constant adaptations to changes in conditions facing it. The group can obtain needed resources from other groups, and cooperate with them when necessary. If there are competing discussion groups, such a group is more likely than others to have its suggestions accepted and implemented.

5. **The group's purpose is understood and accepted by all members.**
   All members give the group goal priority over personal goals or needs not in harmony with the group objectives. Members whose personal values are at odds with a group's task will interfere greatly with efficiency in the group process (i.e., one juror opposed to capital punishment on a jury considering the penalty for a convicted murderer). For example, if one or two members of a religious study group attempt to convert others, whereas other members agree that the purpose is to understand each other's beliefs, the group will have problems.

6. **The group has a place to meet that provides for members' needs and allows discussions without distractions.**
   A committee that has no adequate room in which to meet regularly will expend much energy just finding and changing meeting places and trying to get members to those places. A quality circle cannot discuss well in an assembly room, nor can a personnel committee evaluate job candidates in a room where privacy is compromised by strangers entering the room.

7. **The group has sufficient time in which to do its work.**
   If research is needed to understand the problem, group members should have enough time to do it thoroughly. Enough meetings can be held to work through all phases of the problem-solving procedure or to digest and process information and ideas. In short, members both have and commit enough time to do their work as a group and do it well. They do not try to find a solution to congested parking on an urban campus in a forty-minute meeting!

Throughput
Variables

1. **Behaviors of members are predictable to each other.**
   A member who undertakes an assignment can be counted on to carry it
   out, such as gathering certain needed information, typing up and
   distributing a report, or doing something as part of solving a problem.
   Members can be counted on to attend scheduled meetings or notify the
   group if this is not possible.

2. **Roles of members are relatively stable, mutually understood, and
   accepted by all members.**
   There is both sufficient role definition to permit members to predict
   each other's behavior as well as sufficient flexibility to permit anyone to
   make needed contributions to the task or group maintenance. There is a
   division of labor such that each member has some worthwhile
   contributions to make to the group's task. The leadership position has
   been settled in the minds of the members. The leader has a group-
   centered orientation, but leadership functions are optimally shared by
   everyone. In the example provided earlier, Orin was the elected leader
   of the group, but in his coordinating role, he typically sought the
   opinions and ideas of the group (e.g., "How do the rest of you see
   that?").

3. **Members have relatively equal status, so all can exert influence based on
   their own knowledge, skill, and ideas rather than on status differences
   internal or external to the group.**
   In the example, note that each member contributed at least one
   suggestion regarding what the group should do or how it should
   proceed. Equal status promotes teamwork in the sharing of rewards,
   mutual support, and decision making by consensus. Members expend
   their energy to achieve the goals of the group, not in competing for
   power and position over each other. Thus, cooperation is maximized and
   disagreement is limited to the evaluation of ideas in searching for the
   best solutions.

4. **Norms (rules) and the values underlying them are understood and
   adhered to, or else discussed openly and changed when found to be
   unproductive.**
   The group has a culture of beliefs, values, and standards that
   encourages thorough searching for and testing of facts and ideas and
   open conflict over the merits of ideas. Recall Ray's statement that he
   hoped members would be open with each other and Orin's agreement
   that the group should examine everything "from all angles." The group
   demonstrates affection, support, and solidarity. In the example, Tom
   says, "I can't think of a finer group of people to work with . . . ," and
   later Orin says, "I'm really sort of sad to see our 'Ben Franklin'
   committee come to an end. . . ."

5. **The flow of communication reveals an all-channel network.**
   A high proportion of remarks are directed to all members. Remarks are
   rarely directed to one person. There are no dialogues within subgroups.
   Members are free to approach any and all other group members when
   the group is not meeting as a group.

6. **Members are skilled in expressing themselves interpersonally and are considerate of other members.**
They express their knowledge and ideas in ways that evoke similarity of understanding of facts and ideas without causing defensiveness in each other. For instance, in our extended example, Tom wants the opportunity to have input into all sections of the report. When Paul suggests that the writing task be split up into smaller chunks with subcommittees working on them, Tom doesn't say, "That's a lousy idea—what if I don't like what someone else has written!" Instead, he demonstrates his basic *agreement* with the idea of distributing the work ". . . if we can write other tentative sections than those we are assigned if we don't agree with what has been presented to us." His statement is formulated to preserve the feelings of the others while making an important point.

7. **In an ideal group, all members understand and share procedures that are efficient, prevent overlooking important issues and facts, and lead to goal achievement.**
In a problem-solving group, this means all members understand and follow a procedure that is based on scientific methods of problem solving. They share in exercising control over this procedure; procedures are decided by the group, not imposed on it. This is apparent in our example. Specific discussion techniques appropriate to the purpose of the group are known and accepted by all members. In learning groups, the sequence of issues is decided by the group with changes made only by consent of all members.

Output Variables

1. **Members of the group perceive that its purpose has been achieved.**
Decisions and solutions to problems are supported by members as the best ones possible (note in the example that the members were so proud of their work that they didn't want it "to get chopped up or beaten down by people who don't understand it so well as we do"). Solutions decided upon will achieve the desired results and will be accepted by most or all of the people affected.

2. **Members experience personal satisfaction with their respective roles in the group, the discussion and group-work process, and their relationships with group members.**
For example, Orin says, "This has been the finest group to work with I've ever been in . . . ," and Tom replies, "We've been a great group. . . . But, Orin, you've been a model chairman. . . ."

3. **Cohesiveness is high.**
Members have a strong sense of identification with the group and give it high priority among competing demands for their time and energy. Affectively, members will have a sense of "we-ness" and so express their attitudes toward the group both in action and work. A high degree of interpersonal trust exists among members.

4. **There is consensus on the role and leadership structure of the group.**
   If asked independently, each would name the same person(s) as leader of the group and as choice for leader in the future. Roles and procedures have been developed that worked to the satisfaction of all members and will be used in the future if the group must deal with similar problems.
5. **The parent organization (if any) is strengthened as a result of the small group's work.**
   The organization is more productive and viable in its environment. Note that the constitution developed by our model committee was accepted unanimously and is still in effect today—the ultimate compliment!

   Probably, few groups you experience will measure up to these standards so well as did the constitution committee described early in the chapter. However, you should now be able to determine at least some of the sources of difficulty in any group not producing satisfactory outputs, and you have a model of a small group as a perspective for studying specific details of small group communication.

Summary

In this chapter the small group was described as an open system with input, throughput (process), and output variables and as demonstrating the properties of interdependence and non-summativity. Furthermore, these variables may be classified as individual- or system-level features of the group. Input variables include such items as members' skills, knowledge, and other resources. The group as a system processes these resources via interaction among members. This interaction involves speech communication as the primary medium and produces outputs of physical products, solutions to problems, recommendations, perceptions, and changes in the group members and in the group's procedures and cohesiveness. A model of an ideal group was presented as a standard by which to evaluate any secondary small group and as perspective for further study. In the next section, we will examine input variables in more detail, beginning in chapter 3 with the group members themselves.

Exercises

1. Discuss the following issues with a small group of classmates or with the entire class sitting in a circle.
   a. How important is it to develop a participant-observer focus?
   b. How could you tell whether a group member had such a focus?
   c. How can we develop such a focus while working in this class?
2. Compare a small group as a living system to other living systems: an individual plant cell, the human body, a country (for example, the United States or the Soviet Union). Discuss the following terms in relation to these other systems.
   a. Open versus closed systems
   b. Interdependence of the parts of the system on each other
   c. Non-summativity

3. In this chapter several input, throughput, and output variables of small discussion groups were identified. What others do you think should be included? Why? Your answer should include a modification of figure 2.1.

4. Think of the best and the worst small groups in which you have participated. Why were they the best and worst? What characteristics of the components and the process seem to have made the most difference? Compare your ideas with your classmates.

5. Study carefully the excerpts from the discussion of the constitution committee presented in this chapter. What are the characteristics of the variables that made this a highly productive, satisfying, and cohesive group? Compare your answers with those of classmates.

Bibliography

Andersen, Martin P. "A Model of Group Discussion." In *Small Group Communication: A Reader*. 3d ed., eds. Robert S. Cathcart and Larry A. Samovar. Dubuque, Iowa: Wm. C. Brown Publishers, 1979, 43–54. A detailed model of the process of small group discussion.

Barker, Larry L., Kathy J. Wahlers, Kittie W. Watson, and Robert J. Kibler. *Groups in Process: An Introduction to Small Group Communication*. 3d ed. Englewood Cliffs, N.J.: Prentice-Hall, 1987. See chapter 2, "A Systems Approach to Small Group Communication."

Johnson, R. A., F. E. Kast, and J. E. Rosenzweig. *The Theory and Management of Systems*. 3d ed. New York: McGraw-Hill, 1973.

Katz, Daniel, and Robert L. Kahn. *The Social Psychology of Organizations*. 2d ed. New York: John Wiley, 1978. See chapter 2, "Organizations and the Systems Concept."

Tubbs, Stewart L. *A Systems Approach to Small Group Interaction*. Reading, Mass.: Addison-Wesley, 1978.

Von Bertalanffy, Ludwig. *General System Theory*. New York: George Braziller, 1968.

Notes

1. Randy Y. Hirokawa and Dierdre D. Johnston, "Toward a General Theory of Group Decision-making: Development of an Integrated Model," *Small Group Behavior* (in press).

Part 2

Small Group Inputs

Chapter 3

The Members of the Group

Study Objectives

As a result of studying chapter 3 you should be able to:

1. Describe behaviors that characterize an attitude of responsibility for a small group and the importance of such an attitude.

2. Explain how a positive self-concept contributes to being a productive small group member, assess your own self-concept, and name three techniques for enhancing it.

3. Explain why the most desirable group member is one who is assertive with a strong desire to communicate.

4. Describe an authoritarian attitude and why it is harmful to most groups.

5. Explain why it is important for members to trust each other.

6. List five components of rhetorical sensitivity and explain how such an attitude facilitates small group communication.

7. Contrast the attitudes of skeptical inquiry and dogmatism and explain how members with these attitudes behave during discussions.

8. Describe nine communicator styles and the effects each may have on a group.

Key Terms

Aggressiveness behavior designed to win or dominate that fails to respect the rights and beliefs of others.

Argumentativeness behavior that indicates desire to defend one's own position and attack another's position regarding an issue or idea.

Assertiveness behavior that manifests respect both for one's own and others' rights as opposed to aggressiveness and nonassertiveness.

Attitude a complex of beliefs and values, not directly measurable, that a person holds toward some concept or class of objects; produces a tendency to react in specific ways toward the concept or member of the class.

Authoritarianism tendency to accept uncritically the information, ideas, and proposals of high status persons and to prefer strong, dominating leaders.

Communication apprehension anxiety or fear of speaking in any type of social situation; reticence; shyness.

Communicator style an individual's consistent pattern of verbal and nonverbal interaction.

Dogmatism a tendency to hold rigidly to personal beliefs; closed-mindedness to evidence and reasoning contrary to one's beliefs.

Dialectic discussion in which arguments are compared and contrasted in order to arrive at the best possible answer to a question or solution to a problem.

Hidden agenda item a private goal that an individual member or subgroup hopes to achieve through participation in a small group; differs from the group's public, or announced, agenda.

Homophily a high degree of similarity among group members in such attributes as attitudes, values, and beliefs.

Passiveness (nonassertiveness) behavior that allows one's own rights and beliefs to be ignored or dominated, including avoiding conflict, even at the expense of a good group decision.

Prejudice an attitude, accompanied by a tendency to reject contrary evidence, toward a class of objects based on experience with one or few members of the class; a belief based on partial information about the object.

Principle of least-sized groups maxim stating that a group should be no larger than necessary to include members who collectively possess the information, skills, and other resources needed to achieve the goal.

Rhetorical sensitivity an attitude that encourages thinking before one speaks to phrase statements taking into account the feelings and beliefs of the receiver.

Skeptical inquiry open-minded inquiry characterized by cautious search for new information and ideas. It is demonstrated by discussants who are willing to change their points of view when acceptable new evidence or reasoning is presented.

Among the most important input variables in the small group communication process are the members themselves: how many of them belong to the group, what their attitudes and behaviors are, how well they perform together. These individual-level features, which members bring with them to the group, substantially affect the group's interaction and ultimately its outcome. We all know from painful experience that it often is easier to make a decision alone than to work with a group whose members are incompetent, unwilling to contribute, or selfishly interested in their own needs more than those of the group. On the other hand, those of us who have been fortunate to be part of an outstanding athletic team, productive committee, or supportive family know just how rewarding a group of the right people can be. For complex decisions or problems, groups are valuable because members provide more information and resources than one person working alone. However, that advantage is realized only if everyone has the opportunity to participate, willingly cooperates, and remains open-minded toward other members, and there is enough similarity of values that members are able to work together. This chapter examines factors that contribute to that winning combination of people.

Group Size

The number of persons in a group has a major impact on the group's resources and discussion process. Recall that the variety of knowledge, abilities, and skills supplied by members is an advantage for a group. However, this apparent gain is offset at some point by the increasing difficulty of coordinating the work and likelihood of internal conflicts. The group, therefore, must have enough people to provide needed diversity, but not so many that members feel anonymous and reluctant to take part or that the group's energies are depleted with organizational matters. Following the principle of the **least-sized groups,** a group should be as small as possible so long as it has the necessary variety of information and skills to accomplish its task.

As group size increases, the complexity of interpersonal relationships increases geometrically. For example, in a dyad (two-person group) there is only one two-person relationship possible. In a three-person group, three such relationships are possible. In a group of five members, there can be ten dyadic relationships, and in a group of ten there can be forty-five.

The opportunity for each member to participate in discussion decreases as size increases. Not only is talking time for each member reduced, but evidence suggests that the total amount of talking decreases as well.[1] More importantly, the distribution of participation becomes more uneven as the number of members increases, with a few members tending to dominate the discussion. Bales found that while the amount of participation in groups of three or four members was relatively equal, as groups increased to eight members, the discrepancy in percentage of remarks between the most and least active members increased as well.[2] There is a tendency for one central person to do relatively more of the talking.[3] In addition, as size increases, more centralized control of the procedures is expected and needed. Leadership roles become more specialized and formal with demands made on leaders to keep order, organize the

Groups as large as this
seminar tend to have
directive leaders.

discussion, and regulate the flow of ideas. Reliance on formal rules of parliamentary procedure makes it easier, then, for an autocrat to dominate a large
group.

Increased size has other outcomes as well. Members' satisfaction and cohesiveness are negatively affected. Lower individual rates of participation in
relatively larger student learning groups result in reduced satisfaction with
the discussions.[4] The increased frustration is associated with decreased cohesiveness; therefore, the group loses power to attract its members and maintain their loyalty. Groups larger than six seem to encourage personal
aggressiveness, inconsiderateness, competitiveness, centralization, and fragmentation.[5] In larger groups, fewer cooperative choices are made and people
are more likely to withdraw.[6] On the other hand, a group that is too small also
has problems, with groups of fewer than four seen as tension-producing and
constraining.[7] The optimum group size from the standpoint of satisfaction
seems to be about five or six for student discussion groups.*

Problems with size increases also include greater difficulty in establishing
criteria or values, more time reaching a decision, lessened cohesiveness, and
a tendency for cliques or subgroups to develop.[8] No wonder students proficient
with discussions in groups of five to seven often flounder in confusion when
they try to maintain the same informality for a discussion involving the entire
class. The loose structure simply doesn't work.

How large should a discussion group be to have enough members to accomplish the work yet maximize personal involvement and promote member
satisfaction through opportunity for frequent participation? Thelen's principle of least-sized groups seems to apply here: we should strive for "the smallest
groups in which it is possible to have represented at a functional level all the
social and achievement skills required for the particular required activity."[9]

---

*Informal surveys of Dr. Brilhart's students over the years consistently have shown that
    discussion groups of five or six members are more satisfying than either groups of
    fifteen to eighteen or groups of two to three members.

Other factors being equal, the ideal task-oriented discussion group seems to be five. This is small enough to promote face-to-face interaction between and among all members and informality and ease in reaching decisions, yet is large enough to have the variety of information and diverse points of view needed for wise decisions. However, remember that all parts of a system are interdependent, and optimum size greatly depends on the group's objectives. If the purpose is to encourage individual thinking and questioning, choose a small group. If the purpose is to expose the participants to as many points of view as possible, a larger group is better.

Attitudes toward Self and Others

The most important resource a small group has is its members: their knowledge, attitudes, and skills. How well they work together toward a common goal depends partly on the attitudes they have toward themselves, each other, the group, and the information and ideas presented in the discussions. Thus, the attitudes of the members are crucial determinants of the group's success.

An **attitude** is defined as a cluster of values and beliefs held by one person toward some concept, object, or person that influences that person's behavior regarding the concept, object, or person. Attitudes cannot be observed directly but are inferred from someone's behavior. We attempt to measure attitudes with opinion scales (often called attitude scales) on which respondents indicate how much they agree or disagree with some statement. We listen to what people say during a discussion and watch how they behave as members of the group, and we form impressions about the kinds of attitudes they hold. Thus, although the term "attitude" remains somewhat vague in concept, certain attitudes are particularly relevant to the dynamics and processes of a small group. Especially helpful are attitudes which promote a group orientation as opposed to an individual orientation. In addition, although one of the chief advantages of asking a group to solve a problem is the diversity of information and ideas, similarity of the attitudes and values of group members (often called **homophily**) will help a group agree upon and eventually achieve its goals.

Attitude toward the Group

The ideal set of constructive attitudes, which promote effective group work, is summarized in the phrase *a sense of responsibility for the success of the group.* Constructive discussants feel a personal responsibility to see that the group achieves its goals and do what they can to help insure this. They also encourage others to manifest responsible behavior. This attitude of responsibility is shown in several ways.

First, group members demonstrate a sense of commitment to the group by indicating that they belong to the group and have put accomplishment of the group's goals ahead of individual, perhaps selfish, needs. For instance, the kinds of pronouns used by group members reveal a sense of belonging. Groups that reach consensus use a higher ratio of other- or group-referent pronouns (you, your, we, us, our) than nonconsensus groups that use more self-referent pronouns (I, me, mine, myself). The pronouns indicate the degree to which the discussant feels a part of the group and responsible to it. Be wary of group members who consistently refer to the group as "you" instead of "we." They may be revealing a lack of commitment.

Group members must be willing to give up their **hidden agendas** when these interfere with the group's process. The term "hidden agenda" refers to any objectives of individual members or subgroups that are unannounced, covert, or different from the group's public agenda or stated purpose. For example, one may join a committee in order to enhance one's application to graduate school. Another may join a group out of loneliness. These are not inappropriate reasons for joining a group. The problems occur, however, when the hidden agenda clashes with the public agenda. For example, one member of a student group kept trying to take charge of the direction of the group, even when the other student members resisted his attempt to do so and confronted his controlling behavior. He admitted that his hidden agenda was to become the eventual chair of the group for the purpose of listing this position on his résumé. This kind of selfishness and self-centeredness interferes with the group's needs, resulting in unnecessary conflict. Techniques for handling members whom you suspect have hidden agendas are described in chapter 13.

A second way members indicate their responsibility to the group is by participating actively. Responsible members speak up and follow through on assignments. Burgoon, Heston, and McCroskey describe the good group member as

> willing to commit himself to the group process and product. . . . He is willing to devote time and energy to the group's activities. He gives as well as takes. . . .The individual who has no initial commitment to a group, whose entering attitude is one of "wait and see," is not likely to be an asset. In times of stress, he is more likely to "abandon ship" than to address problems seriously.[10]

Occasionally project groups formed in a small group communication class have a member who wants credit for the work of the group but is not willing to do a fair share of the work. Such irresponsible behavior is the biggest source of friction among members of student groups and of poor quality projects. This behavior will not "take care of itself," as many students believe. It is best to address this lack of dependability as soon as you observe it, for if you ignore it, you allow a norm of "members need do little work in this group" to become entrenched.

A third way members demonstrate responsibility to the group is by continuing to support and show loyalty to the group after the discussion. This means they support the group's decisions. They say, "We decided . . ." not "They decided. . . ." They also respect the trust of the other members by not revealing what has transpired in confidence during meetings.

In short, the valuable group member has an attitude of personal responsibility for the success of the group as shown by commitments of time and energy, dependability in carrying out assignments, putting aside self-centered concerns for the sake of the group, and loyalty in times of stress. If you lack such an attitude, it will be better for the group if you are not a member.

Attitudes toward Self

There is a consensus among human relations writers that only people who hold positive and objective self-concepts can relate openly, honestly, and objectively toward others. While an in-depth study of self-esteem and its development is more appropriate subject matter for a psychology or interpersonal communication class than a small group communication class, one's self-esteem has an important bearing on one's behavior in a group. In order to be a productive group member, the ideal self-attitude is, "I'm okay."[11] One must like and trust oneself before it is possible to like and trust others. Although none of us can have a perfect and complete image of self, the more fully we can understand our own motives and needs and accept them, the more openly we can communicate and work with others in a group. Members who are constantly worried about how their remarks will be judged by others will not be as likely to challenge information and ideas advanced by others, no matter how poor those ideas may be. Thus, they will withhold information and thinking the group needs to do a good job. Also, they will be more stinting in giving positive support and compliments to others, the kinds of statements and acts that make discussion rewarding and pleasant to participants.

People who have low self-esteem are more easily influenced by other people. They feel their ideas have less worth than the ideas of others, so they are more likely to go along with the group than provide critical thinking. They tend to be reticent, participating as little as possible and allowing others to dominate. These people may have good ideas to contribute, but the group may never know this because they are often unwilling to speak.

The single most beneficial attitude you can have about yourself if you want to be a valuable group member is to value yourself—to have high self-esteem. If you believe your own self-esteem is impaired, you should investigate the support services provided by your college or university. Many such centers provide individual or group growth opportunities such as assertiveness training or cognitive restructuring, which can lead you to a new level of self-acceptance.

Attitudes toward Others

Attitudes you have about yourself and about others are inextricably interrelated; we separate them only for analysis. There are hundreds of attitudes that can be examined. We have selected for discussion those that seem to have a significant bearing on small group discussion processes.

Desire to Communicate

A number of attitude scales exist that measure attitudes toward speaking which we call collectively "the degree of desire to communicate." Individuals who do not want to or are afraid to talk can severely hinder a group. Reticence in speaking (Philips), communication apprehension (McCroskey), shyness (Zimbardo), and willingness to communicate (J. Burgoon) are major concepts applicable to group discussions. In potential interaction situations, **communication apprehension,** or fear of expressing oneself, manifests itself in varying degrees, by self-concern, self-doubt, anxiety, fear, and defensiveness toward

The desire to communicate is evident during group interaction.

others.[12] People lacking a desire to communicate usually avoid group inter-action. Their remarks are often irrelevant or ill-timed. They are unlikely to disagree because that calls for an explanation; instead they keep silent, often depriving the group of useful information.

If you have a high degree of apprehension about speaking in general or about participating in small groups, there are several things that may help. A group norm of accepting without ridicule each other's different beliefs and opinions may furnish enough security for you to speak. A group whose members express support for others' ideas may provide apprehensive members the courage to be open. A designated leader who monitors the group's discussion process, encourages shy members to contribute, and ensures that all members are treated kindly and with respect, can be invaluable in helping the appre-hensive member. The more you can overcome apprehension by speaking up, the more comfortable you will be. If that doesn't help, try contributing by preparing written materials and distributing them to members, or writing out your suggestions so someone else can present them.

Specific training techniques usually available at college counseling cen-ters also can help. For example, systematic desensitization teaches you to relax gradually and control your tension level while you imagine yourself speaking,

Aggressive	Assertive	Nonassertive (passive)

then practice speaking. The technique of cognitive modification teaches you to replace the negative messages you give yourself ("Nobody wants to hear what I have to say;" "That's a dumb idea, so I won't say it.") with positive messages ("The group needs to hear what I have to say;" "My idea is as good as anyone else's."). Both techniques can be very effective.

Assertiveness

An **assertive** attitude reflects respect for both oneself and for other members in a group. Productive discussants are generally assertive when they communicate in a small group.

Assertive communication lies on a continuum between **passive (nonassertive)** and **aggressive** communication behavior. Figure 3.1 illustrates this continuum. An aggressive person attempts to force ideas and practices on others. An assertive person demonstrates equal respect for both personal rights as a group member and the rights of all other members. Passive members allow their rights to be trampled and themselves to be dominated rather than confront or conflict with others. Most people fall somewhere between pure passivity and pure aggression. We vary our degrees of assertiveness in groups depending on the situation. For example, we may be assertive at times, but become passive in the face of aggression.

The aggressive person acts autocratically, dominates, demands, and pushes others around. Aggressive members try to force ideas and practices down the throats of others by name calling, innuendos, insults, threats, or commands. Sarcasm and ridicule are other common aggressive tactics. By talking loudly, pounding the table, and making exaggerated gestures, aggressors prevent others from talking. They are emotional bullies, interrupting without apology, changing the subject, or hogging attention. "Do it my way or fight" is the aggressive member's motto. This person falls into the "I'm okay, you're not" quadrant of figure 3.2.

Verbally aggressive people, as described by Infante and Wigley, attack not just the ideas but the self-concepts of other people (e.g., "Boy, are you stupid for suggesting that!"). Several reasons have been proposed for this behavior: it could have been learned socially by observing others, it may result from the frustration of having a goal blocked, it may show the person's lack of verbal skills for dealing constructively with conflict, and it may involve psychopathology.[13] No matter what the cause, this clearly is unacceptable behavior in a group. It indicates a lack of respect for other members, and it is a detriment to the cohesiveness of the group. This irresponsible behavior tends to dampen discussion, resulting in an output that is less than ideal.

The passive discussant presents the group with other problems. Like those who are apprehensive about communicating, passive members go along with the group rather than argue, even if they don't agree. The group does not receive a full contribution from nonassertive people. They make little eye con-

Figure 3.2
Attitudes about self and
attitudes about others
contribute to group
members' behavior.

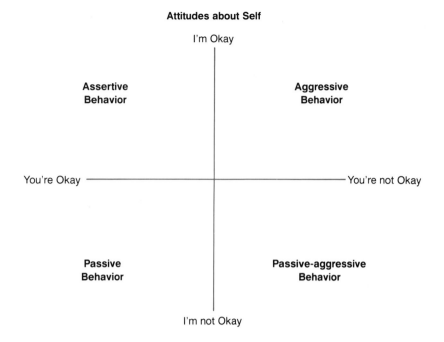

Attitudes about Self

I'm Okay

**Assertive
Behavior**

**Aggressive
Behavior**

You're Okay ———————————————— You're not Okay

**Passive
Behavior**

**Passive-aggressive
Behavior**

I'm not Okay

tact with other members, speak so softly they often cannot be heard and won't stand up when their rights are violated by an aggressor. The stereotyped yes-man illustrated in figure 3.3 epitomizes passive behavior. The motto is "I'll do it your way. Nothing is worth fighting over." This person can be located in the "I'm not okay, you're okay" quadrant.

A special type of nonassertive member engages in passive-aggressive behavior. These members attempt to manipulate subtly, to control without expressing clearly and directly what they believe or want. They sabotage rather than confront. A passive-aggressive member expresses disagreement or displeasure indirectly by being late with an assigned report, "forgetting" to carry out an assigned task, failing to appear for a meeting, or neglecting to complete his or her share of the group's work. Such behavior violates everyone's rights and is counterproductive to effective group functioning. The passive-aggressive motto is "I'm not okay, and you're not okay."

In contrast to these types, the assertive discussant has a positive attitude both toward self and others—"I'm okay and so are you." A model depicting all four types is shown in figure 3.2. Assertive members respect others' rights and their own as well. If interrupted such a member might say, "I had the floor; please let me finish my statement," whereas an aggressive member would shout "Damn it, don't interrupt me!" and a passive member would say nothing at all. Assertive discussants do not try to dictate to others and will not allow dictation from peers. They express ideas as directly and clearly as possible and look for new alternatives or compromises when other members have competing interests. They listen carefully when others have the floor and insist

Figure 3.3
Passive "yessers" do
not express
disagreement.

"All those is favor say 'Aye.' "

"Aye."   *"Aye."*   *"Aye."*

"Aye."   *"Aye."*

that others give them the same courtesy. In problem-solving groups, they do not require that their own pet solutions be adopted but strive for consensus through careful exploration of all relevant information and points of view. Shaw summarized research about ascendant (assertive) persons this way:

> They attempt leadership, participate in group activities, are assertive and are creative. They tend to emerge as leaders, promote group cohesiveness, influence group decisions, conform to group norms and are popular.[14]

Argumentativeness   If a small group is to achieve the best possible solution or decision, it must allow all members the freedom to express their ideas but at the same time must engage in critical thinking to test these ideas for soundness. A balance must be found between uncritical acceptance and automatic attacks on members' ideas. **Argumentative** persons tend to argue strongly for their own positions and attack the positions of others on the same issue. Infante and Rancer conceive of argumentativeness as both a personality predisposition and a set of behaviors that manifest themselves in certain situations.[15] Argumentative people are intellectually stimulated by the process of arguing and feel invigorated and challenged. They are competitive and feel satisfied when they score points in a verbal argument. They want to WIN!

In certain areas of the group's deliberations, argumentative people can provide a valuable service. Because they do not shy away from argument (in fact, they seek it), they can be counted on to express an opinion. They can be expected to participate in a group and to find the weaknesses in the information and alternatives being considered by the group. Argumentative people help stimulate the group's collective critical thinking skills because they will not hesitate to point out what they consider wrong with a proposal. So, having argumentative people in a group should help keep the group on its toes. Infante and Rancer found, for instance, that highly argumentative people have higher grade point averages than those low on argumentativeness. On the other hand, constant argument can be draining, and in the extreme case, argumentative people have the tendency to argue for the pleasure they find in verbal combat. This will ultimately be detrimental to the group.

It seems then that the best stance for a group member to adopt is one between avoiding argumentation and debate completely on the one hand and arguing every point vociferously on the other hand, no matter how stimulating this may be personally. The group is best served by an intermediate position.

Authoritarianism   **Authoritarianism** partially overlaps the concept of aggressiveness in that the authoritarian person is likely to make a dominating leader. However, high authoritarians have other distinguishing characteristics and may be very passive in certain instances. Authoritarianism is characterized by an uncritical acceptance of ideas or information from a source identified as an authority, resulting in doing what the authority figure orders without examining the implications of the action. A group of high authoritarians will seek a strong leader who will tell them what to do and are uncritical in supporting the decisions of an authority. Milgram found, for instance, that they were willing to give dangerous electric shocks to other persons when instructed to do so by an experimenter (an authority figure).[16] Thus, as group members, they usually act subservient, waiting for the designated leader to give instructions or opinions about the best source of action. Appoint or elect such people to leadership positions, however, and they will begin to give orders and act like the rest of the group members are subordinates serving at the pleasure of the boss.

The implications for a group are obvious. Authoritarians are preoccupied with power relationships and either take charge or follow a dominant leader. Janis describes how acquiescing to the beliefs of high-status leaders can be disastrous.[17] Thus, authoritarians in a group can lead to poor decision making in the group. Moreover, Haythorn and associates found that groups of authoritarians show less positive affect toward each other, ask for fewer opinions from others, and make more directive remarks than groups of egalitarians.[18] Authoritarians may be bossy as leaders, servile as followers, and may rebel against a democratic leader for not being dominant enough. Such an attitude spoils teamwork among peers.

Interpersonal Trust

Rotter defines trust as a general expectancy that ". . . the word, the promise, the verbal or written statement of another individual or group can be relied on."[19] High-trust people are not more gullible than low-trust people, but they will opt to trust a stranger until that person provides evidence that he or she cannot be trusted. Rotter believes that trust results from one's past experiences and that persons display a stable attitude of generally trusting or distrusting others. People who are not trustworthy see others as untrustworthy and so cannot work well in group discussions. People who are trusting of others tend to be regarded as more trustworthy and dependable themselves. People who score low in trustworthiness on Rotter's Interpersonal Trust scale are not only seen as less trustworthy by others, they are actually more likely to lie, cheat, and steal. High-trust college students have fewer personality conflicts and are better liked by both high- and low-trust students.

In a group, cooperation depends on trust. For discussions to be satisfying, promote cohesiveness, and produce quality decisions, group members should make positive assumptions about each other (at least until proven wrong) and operate from the belief that the other participants want to arrive at a reasonable outcome in a reasonable way. Otherwise, the group's climate will be suspicious; there will be little sharing of information and ideas; and competition will be unrestrained.

Rhetorical Sensitivity

Rhetorically sensitive individuals monitor what they say, considering what the consequence will be with respect to other group members. The rhetorically sensitive individual occupies a communicative position midway between saying everything that comes to mind and trying to second guess the position of the majority or the high-status group members to reflect only those positions (the yes-man type).

Each of the following five components of rhetorical sensitivity is relevant to small group communication:

1. **Acceptance of personal complexity.**
   The speaker views persons as having many selves, only some of which will be involved in the role(s) taken by the discussant in a particular group.
2. **Avoidance of communicative rigidity.**
   The person is free from fixed patterns of speaking and interacting and so is free to speak and act flexibly depending on the needs of the given situation.
3. **Interaction consciousness.**
   A high degree of awareness of the process of interaction. The person neither sacrifices ideas and feelings in order to placate others, nor disregards the needs and feelings of other members. Thus, rhetorically sensitive people communicate neither aggressively nor passively; they are neither habitually argumentative nor acquiescent.

4. **Appreciation of the communicability of ideas.**
   Not *all* of our ideas and feelings ought to be uttered in a given discussion even if expressing some of them might make us feel better temporarily. The criterion used by rhetorically sensitive persons is "will communication of this feeling or idea facilitate achievement of my own and the group's goals at this moment?"

5. **Tolerance for inventional searching.**
   The speaker realizes that there may be many ways to express an idea and, therefore, searches consciously for the most effective way to evoke a desired response from fellow discussants before speaking.[20]

Developing an attitude of rhetorical sensitivity, especially of interaction consciousness, will help you speak in ways that are both true to yourself yet clear and acceptable to fellow group members. This, in turn, will enhance mutual understanding, reduce defensiveness, and contribute both to group cohesiveness and consensus decisions.

Attitudes toward Information and Ideas

In addition to attitudes that people have toward themselves and each other, people have attitudes toward information and ideas. Some attitudes promote group effectiveness but others interfere. It is appropriate for group members both to be open-minded toward information, and also to examine information carefully and critically. The following attitudes bear upon effective discussion.

Skeptical Inquiry

Ideally, group members achieve perceptual congruity through the give and take of the group interaction process. This means that they have a similar awareness of events and compatible beliefs about these events and their implications. Without this convergence of attitudes, perceptions, and values, meaningful problem solving or decision making will be difficult at best. Achieving congruity requires that members have an attitude of **skeptical inquiry** toward information and ideas as they engage in **dialectic,** the search for the truth in the form of the best possible answer to a question, solution to a problem, or decision. Attitudes of certainty or authoritarianism hamper the group's search. Attitudes of skeptical inquiry, on the other hand, sharpen the group's critical thinking abilities and enable it to evaluate information, ideas, and opinions thoroughly and accurately.

People who have made up their minds cannot honestly engage in a problem-solving discussion; they can only practice persuasion, not dialectic, as they try to persuade others to their point of view. While persuasion is an important process during group discussions, it must be reciprocated by a willingness to be persuaded. Persuasion and debate block learning discussions where the intent is to share, explore differing conceptions, and foster mutual understandings out of which common values, images, and action emerge among equals. People who are not interested in understanding dissimilar opinions, values, and ways of doing things cannot genuinely engage in decision-making discussions—only pseudodiscussions. Thus, all forms of discussion are obstructed if members demand of others what they are not willing to do themselves—change positions.

This does not mean that argumentation has no place in discussions or that group members should give in rather than take a strong stand. Critical examination of ideas helps the group discover its best options. Discussants should weigh evidence, evaluate all reasoning, detect and test assumptions, and constructively debate differing points of view to help insure the quality of group decisions. The best forge for testing ideas is to bring in contrary evidence and arguments. Moreover, open and honest conflict is a sign of a cohesive, involved group, whereas concealing differences of opinion merely indicates lack of unity or lack of concern and interest. Avoiding conflict doesn't eliminate it; it just sends conflict underground. Thus, for effective discussion, conformity for its own sake and dogmatic rejection of information or reasoning should be avoided.

Dogmatism

The attitude opposite skeptical inquiry is **dogmatism** or closed-mindedness. The more dogmatic people are, the less willing they are to try to understand new ideas, to listen to or accept evidence that contradicts presently held beliefs, and to base conclusions on the total pool of information available to the group.[21] Arguments based on evidence and sound reasoning will not influence dogmatic people because their decisions are based on internal needs and emotions rather than a desire to be logically consistent.

The degree of dogmatism in members of a group affects the group's discussions. Unless members rely on evidence and reasoning to solve a problem when they hold different beliefs about it, much time and effort will be expended but no consensus will emerge from the discussion. Instead, the group will suffer from tension and unresolved conflict. This produces either a split or other members finally yielding to the dogmatists, with a poor decision or solution resulting.

As one famous cartoon character put it, "It ain't what people don't know hurts 'em so much as what they know that ain't so." Lee calls this attitude the "mood of allness" in which a person indicates "he wishes to go no farther, to talk no more about something which is to him impossible, unthinkable, wrong, unnecessary or just plain out of the question. He has spoken and there is little use in trying to make him see otherwise."[22] A dogmatic person may declare, "We've never done it that way and we just aren't going to try something new and dangerous. I refuse to listen to such nonsense." Such comments illustrate the game Philips calls "It Can't Be Done," in which a speaker gives what may be a tightly reasoned argument to show how impossible it is to solve a problem or implement a proposal.[23]

Dogmatic people see things in black and white terms. One of us recently discussed the relative merits of collective bargaining with several highly educated individuals and heard such closed-minded statements as "I'm just against unions in principle. They're wrong. I wouldn't even consider joining one." Others said, "Unionism is good. Management just doesn't care about us who do the real work." Neither statement demonstrates use of evidence or reasoning and no allowance is made for exceptions, just an extreme, unqualified position. You can see how this kind of thinking can block group consensus.

A special kind of closed-mindedness is called **prejudice,** which indicates a judgment that is unreasonable, an opinion formed without full and sufficient inquiry. Actually, we can never know everything about anything, so we need to be open to new ideas and different evidence. As Allport said, "Attitudes become prejudices only if they are not reversible when exposed to new knowledge."[24] It would be ideal if we were always open to new information and reasoning, but that is not the case. We all hold on to prejudices. While we like to think that we are open-minded, careful analysis of many statements from discussions indicates that we are more dogmatic than we think. Your mind is closed to the degree that you consistently reject ideas that you disbelieve, cannot distinguish nuances among beliefs different from your own, and see no similarities between your own beliefs and disbeliefs.[25]

If your group has this problem, you can take steps to replace closed-mindedness with an attitude of inquiry. First, accept your own tendency to act dogmatically and prejudicially as normal, then be on guard whenever you are tempted to reject information that contradicts personal belief. Try to give such information special attention, no matter how hard that is. State it aloud until the person who uttered it is satisfied. This insures that at least you understand it. Second, try to ask for points of view other than your own and train yourself to listen. Finally, in a continuing group it may be wise to tackle the problem head-on by bringing it out into the open. An effective way to do this is to discuss specific instances of members automatically dismissing information without giving it a fair hearing. Few people will persist in making "allness" statements if they know that others see them as closed-minded. It may help to keep reminding the group that mutual respect is essential for group cooperation.

Communication Behaviors in the Group

We have presented a variety of attitudes that have a bearing on a group's interaction. The assumption we make is that one's attitudes and beliefs are related to behavior and influence a group member's **communicator style.** However, it is possible to describe someone's style and assess its effectiveness without understanding that person's attitudes. Robert Norton, who has studied communicator style extensively, defines communicator style as consistently occurring, observable verbal and nonverbal behavior with important consequences.[26] A communicator with a good image is one who interacts easily with others and seems to know just the right thing to do or say. Norton describes nine communicator styles that contribute in varying degrees to the perception that an individual is an effective communicator. These styles are listed and described briefly in figure 3.4. Most individuals do not operate in only one style but incorporate elements of several styles in their repertoire of communication behaviors.

Figure 3.4
Communicator styles.

Communicator Style	Description
Dominant	Confident, forceful, active, and self-assured. Talks more than others and more loudly, is less compliant.
Dramatic	Tells stories, exaggerates, uses metaphor, rhythm, voice, and other devices to emphasize content.
Contentious	Argumentative and quick to challenge others. Demands that others back up their assertions with evidence.
Animated	Lively and expressive. Uses facial expressions and gestures. Emotional state is easy for others to read.
Impression-leaving	Memorable. Others remember what this person says and how he or she says it.
Relaxed	Calm and collected, confident. Relaxed even under pressure, not tense.
Attentive	Considered a good listener, empathic, pays attention to the speaker. Listens carefully and reacts deliberately.
Open	Frank and outspoken, gregarious, extroverted, easy to read. Readily reveals personal information about self.
Friendly	Affectionate, sociable, and tactful. Encourages others, consistently acknowledging other's contributions.

Style is related to effectiveness in a variety of situations. For example, Norton notes that effective teachers are perceived as more active, sender-oriented, and precise, whereas ineffective teachers are seen as not being attentive, friendly, relaxed, precise, or dramatic. The most effective group members are those who readily participate, are sensitive to the needs of other group members and the needs of the group as a whole, and can perform those functions that help a group complete its charge. In terms of style, we can speculate that the most valuable group members incorporate elements of the dominant and friendly styles, since these behaviors will help the group move toward completion of its task. Submissive individuals, the low participators, rob the group of their ideas and input.

Summary

In this chapter, we have considered group members as inputs, the number of members in a group, and their attitudes toward self, other members, and information.

To function well, a group should have enough members to supply the skills and knowledge needed to accomplish group objectives, yet be small enough to keep the level of interpersonal and organizational formality low. We have suggested the principle of "least-sized groups." An ideal number seems to be five. With more than that, members have fewer opportunities to participate and satisfaction, cohesiveness, and sharing of leadership decrease.

Positive member attitudes toward the group, self, other members, and information and ideas are major resources for the group. It is especially important for members to relinquish their hidden agendas so that individual needs will not interfere unduly with the group's goal accomplishment. A high degree of responsibility and dependability toward the group, self-acceptance, willingness to communicate openly and honestly, assertiveness, low authoritarianism, trust, and rhetorical sensitivity contribute to making a learning or problem-solving group productive. Attitudes of skeptical inquiry and open-mindedness toward information and ideas are equally important if the group is to reach sound, logical conclusions. A communicator style that is friendly and dominant is appropriate for group discussions and will help the group achieve its objectives.

Members with the positive attitudes described in this chapter are essential. However, a group must also have a clear purpose, a setting conducive to thoughtful deliberation, and a fund of information and ideas relevant to the group's task. In the next chapter we will consider these additional inputs in detail.

Exercises

1. Discuss the following question with your classmates, first in small groups, then as an entire class: How much can we trust each other to be truthful and to carry a fair share of the work in the small groups we form in this class?

2. Think of the various groups in which you have belonged and recall members who had high self-esteem and those who had low self-esteem. What specific behaviors did they manifest? Do you see any relationship between one's self-esteem and behavior in a group? On a scale of 0 to 100, where would you place your own level of own self-esteem? How does it affect your behavior?

3. Are there any kinds of groups in which an authoritarian person might be beneficial to goal achievement? Under what conditions are such persons likely to be detrimental to the group's purpose?

4. In a small group of fellow students, discuss each of the following questions in turn. One person should report your conclusions to the class.

   a. What kinds of behaviors indicate that a discussant is dogmatic? Open-minded?

   b. What effects have dogmatic persons had in groups to which you have belonged?

   c. What differences are there in how you feel when a fellow group member speaks dogmatically and when the member speaks with an attitude of inquiry?

5. Assume that a fellow group member has been dominating the group's discussion for a period of time. Write what you think three different types of people might say to try to stop such dominating behavior: an assertive member, an aggressive member, a passive member. With which of these three types of communicative attitudes are you most comfortable? Why?

6. Observe a small discussion group. When you finish observing, rate each member on the following scale.

10	0
very responsible and committed	totally irresponsible and uncommitted

List the specific behaviors and utterances, for each member, which contributed to your judgment. Compare your ratings and observations with two or three classmates who observed the same group independently. How closely do you agree? What general conclusions can you reach regarding the behaviors indicating to you that a group member is responsible and committed?

7. Read your paper's letters to the editor for a few days and clip out the three or four letters that have the clearest examples of dogmatic or closed-minded statements. Revise each dogmatic statement so it reflects an attitude of inquiry while still expressing an opinion.

8. List three or four prejudices you once held but have since abandoned. Describe how you changed each. Then, see if you can identify two or three prejudices you still hold and describe how you will have to behave differently to manifest an attitude of inquiry in each case.

9. The concepts of assertiveness, authoritarianism, argumentativeness, and verbal aggressiveness and dogmatism overlap to some extent. What factors do you feel link them together? What are the major differences between them? Discuss this in a small group, then report your conclusions to the class.

Bibliography

Adler, Ronald B. *Confidence in Communication: A Guide to Assertive and Social Skills*. New York: Holt, Rinehart, and Winston, 1977. An excellent book to help you develop effective attitudes and skills.

Lee, Irving J. *How to Talk with People*. New York: Harper & Row, Publishers,1952.

Norton, Robert. *Communicator Style: Theory, Applications, and Measures*. Beverly Hills: Sage Publications, 1983.

Rokeach, Milton. *The Open and Closed Mind*. New York: Basic Books, 1960.

Shaw, Marvin E. *Group Dynamics: The Psychology of Small Group Behavior*. 3d ed. New York: McGraw Hill, 1981, chapter 6.

Notes

1. R. M. Williams and M. L. Mattson, "The Effects of Social Groupings upon the Language of Pre-School Children," *Child Development* 13 (1942): 233–45; B. P. Indik, "Organization Size and Member Participation: Some Empirical Tests of Alternatives," *Human Relations* 18 (1965): 339–50.

2. Robert F. Bales et al., "Channels of Communication in Small Groups," *American Sociological Review* 16 (1952): 461–68.

3. E. F. Stephan and E. G. Mishler, "The Distribution of Participation in Small Groups," *American Sociological Review* 17 (1952): 598–608.

4. James A. Schellenberg, "Group Size as a Factor in Success of Academic Discussion Groups," *Journal of Educational Psychology* 33 (1959): 73–79.

5. E. B. Smith, "Some Psychological Aspects of Committee Work," *Journal of Abnormal and Social Psychology* 11 (1927): 348–68.

6. Richard B. Powers and William Boyle, "Common Dilemma Choices in Small vs. Large Groups," (Paper presented at American Psychological Association, Anaheim, Cal., 23–30 August, 1983).

7. Philip E. Slater, "Contrasting Correlates of Group Size," *Sociometry* 21 (1958): 129–39.

8. Marvin E. Shaw, *Group Dynamics: The Psychology of Small Group Behavior,* 3d ed. (New York: McGraw-Hill, 1981).

9. Herbert A. Thelen, *Dynamics of Groups at Work* (Chicago: University of Chicago Press, 1954), 187.

10. Michael Burgoon, Judie K. Heston, and James C. McCroskey, *Small Group Communication: A Functional Approach* (New York: Holt, Rinehart and Winston, 1974), 159.

11. Thomas A. Harris, *I'm OK—You're OK* (New York: Harper & Row, Publishers, 1969).

12. James C. McCroskey, "Oral Communication Apprehension," *Human Communication Research* 4 (1977): 78–96.

13. Dominic A. Infante and Charles J. Wigley III, "Verbal Aggressiveness: An Interpersonal Model and Measure," *Communication Monographs* 53 (1986): 61–67.

14. Marvin Shaw, *Group Dynamics,* 2d ed. (New York: McGraw-Hill, 1976), 180.

15. Dominic A. Infante and Andrew S. Rancer, "A Conceptualization and Measure of Argumentativeness," *Journal of Personality Assessment* 46 (1982): 72–80.

16. Stanley Milgram, "Some Conditions of Obedience and Disobedience to Authority," *Human Relations* 18 (1965): 57–76.

17. Irving L. Janis, *Groupthink: Psychological Studies of Policy Decisions and Fiascoes,* 2d ed. (Boston: Houghton-Mifflin Company, 1983).

18. William W. Haythorn, Arthur Couch, D. Haefner, P. Langham, and L. F. Carter, "The Behavior of Authoritarian and Equalitive Personalities in Groups," *Human Relations* 9 (1956): 54–74.

19. Julian B. Rotter, "Trust and Gullibility," *Psychology Today* 14 (October 1980): 35–52, 102.
20. Roderick P. Hart, Robert E. Carlson, and William F. Eadie, "Attitudes toward Communication and the Assessment of Rhetorical Sensitivity," *Communication Monographs* 47 (1980): 2–22.
21. Milton Rokeach, *The Open and Closed Mind* (New York: Basic Books, 1960).
22. Irving J. Lee, *How to Talk with People* (New York: Harper & Row, Publishers, 1952), 46.
23. Gerald M. Philips, *Communicating and the Small Group,* 2d ed. (Indianapolis: The Bobbs-Merrill Company, 1973), 145.
24. Gordon Allport, *The Nature of Prejudice* (Garden City, N.Y.: Doubleday, 1958), 9.
25. Dale G. Leathers, "Belief-disbelief Systems: The Communicative Vacuum of the Radical Right," in *Explorations in Rhetorical Criticism,* eds. C. J. Stewart, D. J. Ochs, and G. P. Mohrman (University Park, Pa.: The Pennsylvania State University Press, 1973), 127–31.
26. Robert Norton, *Communicator Style: Theory, Applications, and Measures* (Beverly Hills: Sage Publications, 1983).

Chapter 4

Purpose, Setting, and Information as Input Variables

As a result of studying chapter 4 you should be able to:

1. Explain why having an interdependent goal is vital to effective group discussion.

2. Give examples of parent organizations and their committees and explain the relationship between them.

3. Detect the absence of a clear group objective or charge and help any group lacking such to establish one.

4. Explain the impact of such environmental features as room size, decoration, and seating arrangements on small group members and communication among them.

5. Make physical arrangements that facilitate effective group discussion.

6. Explain and follow a systematic procedure for locating, gathering, evaluating, and organizing information needed for productive small group discussions.

Key Terms

Area of freedom the scope of authority and responsibility of a small group, including limits on that freedom.

Bibliography a list of sources of information bearing on a given topic, problem, or issue; a bibliography includes books, journal and magazine articles, newspaper stories, interviews, etc.

Charge a statement of the purpose or goal for which a parent organization has created a small group (committee or task force), usually given to the group by an officer or administrator of the parent organization.

Fact, question of asking for a description of some specific observation; a question of fact is not discussable because the answer is a report of whatever was observed.

Fact, statement of a description of a specific event observed by some person; the statement includes or implies a method of observing by which the statement could be tested for accuracy.

Group goal question the goal of a group expressed as a question to be answered through the collective efforts of the members.

  Question of interpretation question asking for judgments or opinions about the meaning of a fact or body of related facts.

  Question of policy a question asking for a general solution or plan of action.

  Question of value question seeking a judgment about the goodness, merit, or worth of something; special type of question of interpretation.

Implication a statement that is a logical derivative, extension, or conclusion drawn from a belief or opinion.

Inference, statement of any statement that includes more than a description of some event; involves some degree of uncertainty or probability and cannot be checked for accuracy by direct observation.

Interdependent purpose an objective shared by members of a small group in such a way that achievement of the goal by any member is dependent on achievement by all members.

We will now consider three additional input variables which affect a group. Its purpose, its physical setting, and the information and ideas available to it are vital to both the group's process and ultimately its outcomes.

Purpose of the Group

By the definition given earlier, a group must have some purpose shared by all members. Members have individual needs and purposes that can be met by belonging to a group, such as the need for affiliation, the need to share thoughts with others, the need for affection and social esteem, and the need for self-development and actualization. While these needs can be met without interfering with the group's purpose, members must also have an **interdependent purpose,** one which cannot be achieved by one group member unless it is achieved by all. A balanced tug-of-war illustrates this. For any one person to win, all on the team will win, and if they want to win badly enough, the members will exert a maximum effort. If members of conflicting teams during labor negotiations really want to avoid a breakdown, that common purpose may be enough for them to overcome their disagreements and continue negotiating until a mutually acceptable solution is reached. This type of interdependence is the basis of the kind of decision we call consensus. In a strong group, there is an understanding that all members are needed to succeed. They share a common fate of success or failure as a group. Conflicts among individuals are subordinated to the interdependent goal, which may require the best collaborative and cooperative behavior to produce necessary consensus decisions.

The type of task the group is working on has a significant effect on several aspects of the group's interaction and determines, in part, appropriate communication patterns and other features of group discussion. Hirokawa, synthesizing information regarding the group task, has identified three task dimensions that should be considered in combination by a group searching for the best way to proceed.[1] These are task difficulty, cooperation requirements (the degree to which group members must coordinate their efforts in arriving at a solution), and solution multiplicity (whether there is only one correct solution that will work, or whether many possible alternatives will succeed). For example, if a group is faced with an easy task that requires minimal coordination and interaction and for which there is one correct solution, then the quality of the group's solution will depend on the expertise available to the group. In this instance, it is possible that one competent member of the group with expertise on the topic can decide on behalf of the rest of the group. On the other hand, if the task is difficult and complicated, requiring the collective expertise of members and having several possible acceptable solutions, then the quality of the group's ultimate solution will depend upon the quality of the group members' information, their communication skills, and their ability to attend to the process of discussion. You can see that consideration of the type of task is important!

Any newly formed small group should first determine, clarify, and achieve agreement from all members on the purpose of the group. Members must ask and get answers to the following types of questions:

Why have we formed or been appointed as a group? What are we to accomplish?

What exactly is our goal?

What will be the nature of the output we are to produce? Will this output take the form of some personal growth, such as new understandings or solving personal problems, a report to a parent organization such as a summary of findings or a recommendation, or some concrete product such as a barn, dinner-dance, or set of bylaws?

How will we know when we have met our goal and finished our work?

Only after the group purpose has been understood and accepted by all members can the group design procedures for doing its work. The individual members' purposes for belonging to the group must contribute to (or at least not detract from) the group's primary objective if the group is to be truly productive. Members who value the group and its purpose will willingly subordinate private goals to group goals.

The importance of having a clear purpose understood by all hit home with one of us some time ago. Jack was appointed to a special committee to evaluate and make recommendations about an academic program to the chief administrator of the university. Members didn't know what they were to accomplish or why they had been chosen. For months, committee meetings were apathetic, accomplishing nothing. Finally, the group determined what it was supposed to do, that it was a very important charge, and each member had been selected for good reasons. Meetings then came to life and in a relatively short time a well-documented report and set of recommendations was produced, for which members received much praise. If members had insisted on receiving a clear charge at the onset, how much time would have been saved!

Sometimes a group will ostensibly be working for one purpose but actually be working toward another. Many discussion groups lose sight of their original reason for being. This can result in inefficiency, dissatisfaction, member loss, and decay. Just as with living organisms, decay leads eventually to death. How many friendship groups have you known, for instance, that went stumbling along even after most of the positive feelings for each other were gone? How many functionless committees and councils are you aware of that exhaust members' energies? We need to help small groups who have met their original purpose either adopt new objectives or end rapidly before they become a drain.

Even when there is something specific to be accomplished by the group, the goal may not be understood alike by all members. In classes, we have asked each member of a discussion group to write down the purpose(s) of the discussion, only to find that each person had a decidedly different idea about the group's purpose. This lack of goal clarity makes progress impossible.

The group's purpose may arise from the needs of the members themselves, as in a friendship or activity group, or may be given to the group by a parent organization or individual in authority. For instance, the curriculum committee which one of us chairs was created by the Department of Communications and instructed by the chair to submit a redesign of the undergraduate curriculum to the full faculty for consideration. However the group receives its purpose, it *must have one,* and the members must have a common understanding of that purpose.

The Charge

A **charge** is the assignment given to a subordinate group by a parent organization or administrator of an organization. A major component of the charge is the group's **area of freedom.** The charge specifies what the group is to do, whereas the area of freedom defines both the authority of the group and the limits on what the group may do to complete its charge. As an example, the following charge, created originally by a special task force and published in booklet form, details what the Committee on Improvement of Instruction is supposed to do:

> This committee shall be responsible for the granting of monies to full-time . . . faculty for the improvement of their instructional capabilities. Such grants shall be awarded, but not necessarily limited to, worthy projects in innovative instructional methods, instructional research, pedagogical applications of new technologies, development of instructional materials, and professional development in accordance with established criteria.

> The University committee on Improvement of Instruction shall make its funding recommendations to the Director of the Center for Improvement of Instruction and shall report its activities to the Chancellor.

This charge makes it clear that the committee does not have the freedom to recommend that a faculty member be dismissed for poor teaching, that monies be spent to improve a research laboratory, or that new instructional programs be created. A committee that one of us observed exceeded its charge and created serious problems for its parent organization. A special task force was created to make recommendations regarding the types of student-related activities offered on the campus. This committee took it upon itself to recommend the complete redesign of the student services office, in some cases suggesting that certain people be replaced. Naturally, the chief administrative officer who charged the committee rejected the recommendations. The resulting furor caused hurt feelings, mistrust, suspicion, and dissatisfaction, not just on the part of the committee members but among other campus personnel as well—all because the area of freedom was not observed.

No subordinate group should be created if there is not a real and demonstrable need for it that can be stated as a charge. Otherwise, confusion, frustration, and waste are the inevitable results. One of our graduate students in a small group communication seminar wrote an unusual paper on "non-group meetings."[2] She had observed meetings of committees created by statute as part of the organization of a large, public medical complex. These standing committees were required by charter and had to meet at designated times. They were given very general responsibility for dealing with problems that might arise in the management of the hospital complex, including such matters as violations of laws and unethical practices. Most of the time, however, when they met there was no business to attend to. People had not found anything wrong in their scope of responsibility. The result was considerable discussion in general and abstract terms, expressions of boredom, and complaints that members were wasting valuable time. Yet they met, and said they must, because the charter required them to do so.

A few years ago, one of us was involved in a major conflict while serving on a committee that heard faculty appeals to decisions made by a dean. The committee members thought the bylaws of the board of regents granted them the power to overturn the administrator's decisions, but the dean believed members had only the power to *recommend* that he change decisions. A great deal of professorial time was spent trying to resolve this conflict over the area of freedom. For a time, members refused to consider any appeals. Finally, the dean agreed to abide by the committee's decision, and once again, the committee began to function. In short, it is vital that a group be constantly aware of its charge and the limits on its authority.

Classroom Project Groups

Instructors frequently assign projects to be done by groups in small group communication courses. When you have an assignment to produce some output as a group for a grade, you have been given a charge. Make sure that all group members understand the charge as given by the instructor. What form is your output to take? A panel discussion presented to the class? A dramatization of some principle or theory? A written recommendation, resulting from an investigation, designed to solve a campus or local problem? How will you be graded, as a group, as individuals, or some combination of both? Will you as an individual be required to write a paper analyzing your group from some perspective? If so, what form will the paper take? What records will you need to keep?

Sometimes student groups tackle issues that are beyond their area of freedom or competence, such as "What should be our position in arms negotiations with the Soviet Union?" or "How might we get America to place less emphasis on material things and more on spiritual matters?" These questions are limitless in scope. Experts might work for years and still arrive at nothing precise or specific. Also, the materials needed to answer these questions are likely to be classified or unavailable. Students will be able to do little more than express opinions, and no one is likely to consider their ideas seriously.

As a classroom group, you need to decide early what you can realistically do as a group that would interest all members. Trying to impress your instructor with what sounds like an intellectual topic will backfire. Coming up with a new and defensible solution to a campus problem or conducting a panel discussion that airs thoroughly the issues on a bill being considered by your city council is more than enough challenge and will be worthwhile to the people who receive it. Only when your goal fits your charge and members' interests are you ready to create a procedure to follow, or an agenda of steps toward completion of your assignment.

Frequently, some members of such classroom groups begin with hidden agendas detrimental to group accomplishment. They may want credit for the project but not be willing to attend meetings or turn in assigned work. Some need a social or play group. Ignoring these problems will not resolve them. You need to be serious about the public agenda of the group by asserting yourself in suggesting that the group get on with its task. Suggestions made in this book, such as the ones included in chapter 13 on how to deal with hidden agendas, will work only if you use them. Otherwise, your group and most of all you will be the losers.

Group Goal Questions

Discussion is always a form of inquiry and dialectical search on the part of group members for solutions to personal problems, the meaning or the value of something, what to recommend, or what course of action to pursue. A group's charge can always be stated in the form of a question or questions. For example, "What should XYZ Corporation do to reduce the effects of employee drug usage on its productivity?" or "How shall funds appropriated for improving instruction at ABC College be expended?"

Such **group goal questions** have traditionally been classified into three broad categories: questions of interpretation (often called **questions of fact**), questions of value, and questions of policy.

Questions of Interpretation

Questions of interpretation (judgment or opinion) are those concerned with the meaning of a fact or group of facts. Such questions ask not what happened, but what the facts mean to the discussants. Since the answers are matters of opinion, many different answers are possible. Many groups have this as their goal. Grand juries, for example, collect information, then decide whether or not to file charges against suspects. The Iran-Contra hearings first ascertained what happened, then interpreted the meanings of the facts and have contributed to policy actions as a result. The following are some examples of questions of interpretation:

Has auto theft increased in our city since 1983?

What conditions have contributed to the decline in the number of family-owned farms?

What is the effect of capital punishment on the murder rate?

How does legalized gambling affect the crime rate?

Questions of Value

These are subtypes of questions of interpretation. **Questions of value** ask a group to make a judgment about the effectiveness, merit, or goodness of something. A comparison is always implied: to an absolute standard of judgment;

to a basic value shared by group members; to other items of the same class; or to other proposed solutions to a problem. The following are examples of questions of value:

Which American political party has done more to improve the living conditions of people living in poverty?

Is it more beneficial to humanity to give food to starving people in overpopulated countries or to teach them birth control techniques?

How well has court-ordered integration by busing achieved its educational aims?

How effective is Bob Blank as governor of this state?

When individual and personal valuations are called for, remember that there is no need for agreement. There is no sense arguing about answers to such questions as "Is this a good painting?" or "Does pork or chicken taste better?" Rather than agreeing, a learning group should strive to understand what the questions imply and the basis for differing answers to them. On the other hand, if a group is trying to arrive at a solution to a problem, it must agree on values or criteria in order to arrive at specific recommendations or courses of action. For such a problem-solving group, arriving at agreement on values may be essential for it to agree on a solution. Rubenstein gave an example that highlighted how differences in the values of different people contributed to disagreement over an appropriate course of action. Imagine that a man is in a small boat with his mother, wife, and child when it capsizes. Only the man can swim, and he can save only one of the other three people. Whom should he save? Rubenstein found that all the Arabs he asked would save the mother because a man can always get another wife and child but not another mother. Of the 100 American college freshmen, 60 said they would save the wife and 40 would have saved the child. These Americans laughed at the idea of saving the mother.[3] The solutions are based upon quite different values. Thus, lack of agreement on basic values makes group problem solving difficult or even impossible.

Questions of Policy   **Questions of policy** ask "What should be done in order to. . . ?" The key word in this question is *should*. The group is searching for a solution to a specific problem or a general procedure to follow. The following are examples of questions of policy:

What laboratory science courses should be required of liberal arts graduates? as opposed to What laboratory science courses are required? (a question of fact) or What is the value of lab science to a liberal arts graduate? (a question of value).

What should be done by the public schools to combat the spread of AIDS?

What should be the federal law governing abortions?

What should we do to recruit more members for our organization?

Meeting room ready for
the committee.

Answers to such questions, if they are to be acceptable to all members, will be found only after answers to questions of interpretation and value have been agreed upon. When communication breaks down in a group trying to agree on a solution, it is wise to raise questions of value, asking what criteria are actually being applied. It may also be necessary to collect more facts and interpret them. Sometimes a group needs to backtrack to answer questions of fact, interpretation, or value previously overlooked. When a group begins to search for solutions to a problem, it may be better to phrase the question as "What *might* be done to. . . ?" (rather than *should*) in order to encourage a variety of ideas before discussion of pros and cons ensues.

Members may agree that the purpose of their group is important and may have a clearly worded and agreed-upon charge, yet still be unproductive unless the physical setting allows uninterrupted dialectical exchange. We can now consider the effects of the physical setting on the group.

Physical Facilities and Arrangements

Researchers have found that the characteristics of a room or space influence individual behavior and group interaction. An ugly room with stark gray walls, a bare light bulb, junk lying around, and hard floors evoked such responses as fatigue, headaches, irritability, and hostility. A room with warm beige walls, draperies, windows, comfortable furniture, and adequate lighting evoked feelings of pleasure, importance, comfort, and a desire to remain in the room.[4]

Not only the atmosphere of a room but its size affects the group as well. Sommer found that the larger the room, the closer to each other discussants chose to sit.[5] It seems that a group can meet just as well in a large room as a small one so long as the room is attractive, comfortable, and free of distractions.

It is especially important that the room be free from distractions and provide privacy. Listening to fellow members is taxing enough without the competing stimuli of a television set in the background, nonmembers moving about, pets, and similar distractions. Most student groups report that meeting in a quiet room on campus or a simple apartment works best. Always be sure you have a setting conducive to group discussion *before* you meet.

Seating arrangements are particularly crucial to productive discussions. Hare and Bales found that the way chairs are placed in a room influences the pattern of interaction.[6] In a circle, members tend to talk most often to those opposite them rather than to those sitting on either side. If the group has a dominating leader, members will conduct side-bar conversations with their neighbors. At rectangular tables, such as those typically found in meeting rooms, members at either end and in central positions on the sides contribute more than members at the corners. It seems a widely accepted norm that the leader should sit at the end of a rectangular table. A chairperson of a small group tried sitting in a corner spot, only to discover signs of discomfort. When asked whether they wanted the chair to sit at the end, all said "yes." This produced an obvious improvement in the discussion. One company president asked what could be done to facilitate more responses from store managers' regular meetings to discuss corporate policies and problems. One of us suggested removing all corner chairs and changing the T arrangement of tables to form a large square. The president reported that this made a big improvement in subsequent meetings.

What guidelines can we derive from such research and observations? The optimum for private discussion is a circular seating arrangement with members seated close together. Most discussions also call for a writing surface for members. If the group meets in a classroom with flexible seating, participants should push their chairs in a circle (or semicircle for a clear view of the blackboard). With fixed seating, use portable chairs or have some members sit sideways. With a long, rectangular table, have the members in the middle push their chairs away from the table to allow eye contact between all members. If possible, do not seat anyone at the corners. A few small tables can be arranged to approximate a circle. See figure 4.1 for examples.

If group members are not well acquainted, each should have a name tag or tent large enough to be seen across the circle. Adhesive-backed name tags or three by five inch file cards work well. Large file cards can be used to make name tents.

Adequate lighting, comfortable temperature, and adequate ventilation should be provided. The issue of smoking should be discussed initially and not permitted if any member is adversely affected. If allowed, each member should have an ashtray.

Also helpful is access to a blackboard or large pad of plain paper for recording information, ideas, and questions. Other necessary supplies (projector and slides, tape recorder, charts, pencils, note pads) depend on the group's purpose and should be assembled and distributed before the meeting begins to avoid disrupting the interaction.

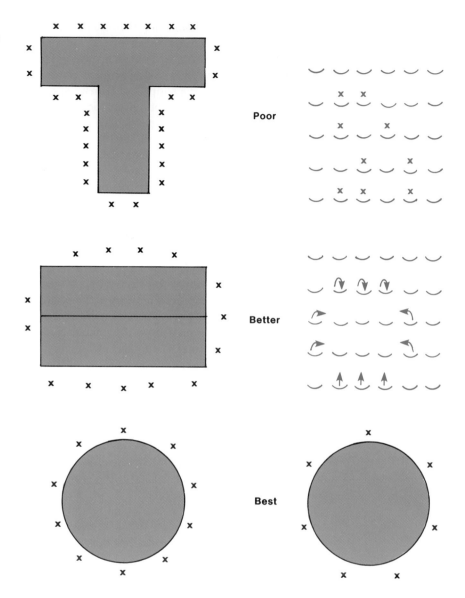

Figure 4.1
Seating arrangements
for small discussion
groups.

Poor

Better

Best

Informational Resources

Because many of our interactions occur in spontaneous primary group meetings, we don't usually look upon an upcoming discussion as something for which
to prepare. This is a counterproductive attitude. "Garbage in, garbage out"
is as applicable to small groups as to computer programs. No matter how skilled
discussants are at the process of communicating, the outputs of their discussions will be no better than the informational resources they bring to and use
in the group.

Effective group discussion grows out of dependable knowledge and clear thinking; it is never a pooling of ignorance. Every appropriate conclusion, solution, interpretation, or belief rests on dependable evidence and valid reasoning from that evidence. Half-informed participants reach only half-informed decisions. Think for a moment of a group of college students trying to discuss intelligently such topics as capital punishment or the control of atomic arms without having first done extensive reading on the subject. Would you give credence to the conclusions of such a group?

Prepared, informed participants are valued by other members, according to research on emergent leadership in leaderless discussion groups. Geier found that being perceived as uninformed was the greatest reason why members of leaderless discussion groups were quickly eliminated from consideration as major influences in the group.[7] You can't bluff for long if others are the least bit informed and critical of information and ideas. Your best response is to be well-informed.

Groups, especially student groups, are frequently plagued by members who keep telling irrelevant jokes or pulling the group off the topic. Such nuisances are almost always poorly informed. Study-discussion leaders report that when participants are unprepared, the ensuing discussion is listless, disorganized, shallow, and frustrating. Many students in our small group communication classes have noted that their project groups made little progress until everyone did the research needed. Then, a lot was accomplished in a relatively short time. To combat problems like this, one promotor of study-discussion programs advocated this policy: "If anyone has not read the materials, he is not permitted to speak unless to ask a question."

Discussants not only need information, they need accurate, relevant, valid, and complete information to perform effectively. Can you imagine an academic committee basing its creation of a new communication degree program on an outdated list of course offerings? This means that the information must be tested for quality before as well as during the discussions. The evidence may include nonverbal materials like maps, photos, or objects and verbal materials like statements of fact, opinion, and policy. The group members as a whole are responsible for ensuring that the information on which conclusions are based is current and accurate.

The contrast between being uninformed and informed was discovered by a group of students at a large university. The students began attacking the food service with a host of complaints and suggestions for improvement. Realizing, fortunately, that they had few facts other than secondhand opinions of others, they conducted a careful investigation. The labor was divided so that some members studied menu planning, others food preparation, others looked into costs, and still others investigated food service at other schools. Information was gathered from a variety of credible sources: home economists, dietitians, journals, and books. At their next meeting, after pooling their knowledge, the students concluded that they had the finest food service of any university in their section of the country, that menus were reasonably priced, better planned than most family diets, and most of the complaints resulted from ignorance or misuse of the service by students. The question now became, "How can we get the students at our university to appreciate the excellence of our food service and to take better advantage of it?" The group made a few recommendations, all based on the facts, for minor improvements to the food service. These suggestions were well received by the food service manager, who expressed his appreciation and implemented several of the group's suggestions.

Since valid information is so important, the question now becomes, "What can we do to gather the information we need as a group?" The answer depends in part on the purpose of the group and the knowledge members already possess. A general procedure for locating information and evaluating and organizing it is presented next. The steps, presented in order, are (1) review and organize your present stock of information and ideas, (2) gather needed additional information, (3) evaluate the information and ideas you now have collected, and (4) organize the information and ideas into a tentative outline. While the procedure may be modified somewhat if you are well versed in the problem area, you can't omit any steps without losing group effectiveness.

1. Review and Organize Your Present Stock of Information and Ideas

You probably already have some information and experience on the subject or you would not be discussing it. Taking a systematic inventory of the knowledge you have will both save you time and make it easier for you to recall what you have when you need it.

1. **Place the problem or subject in perspective.**
   To what is it related? What will it affect, and what affects it? For example, in trying to plan a scholarship program for a company, a task force would consider the corporation's financial condition, long-range plans, obligations to the community, public relations, types of employees, and the like.
2. **Make an inventory of what you know about the subject.**
   For instance, list relevant courses taken, jobs held, reports, firsthand experiences, articles read, books, ideas, and so forth. Additional headings will suggest themselves. Jot down everything that occurs to you as you let your mind freewheel.
3. **Organize your information into a rough draft of a problem-solving outline.**
   Look over your notes for main issues, topics, or questions about the problems. A guideline is suggested in chapter 12.
4. **Look for deficiencies.**
   Your outline will reveal what you don't know, where specific information is needed and which opinions or ideas are unsupported.

2. Gather Needed Information

You are now ready to plan research to correct deficiencies in your knowledge and thinking. Don't assume, as some students do, that you can begin looking for evidence anywhere and get what you need for effective group work. Students often take whatever they happen to find in recent magazines, newspapers, and encyclopedias as valid and sufficient. The result of haphazard preparation is "garbage in" information resulting in "garbage out" conclusions. A systematic procedure prevents such an undesirable outcome.

Groups cannot expect to deal with all this information in a single meeting, even if members know about the topic in advance. They need time to think about the information and to spot gaps. This usually takes at least two meetings, often more. Recall the example in chapter 2 of the committee of professors drafting a college constitution. This group spent part of its first meeting making a list of areas to be covered and planned to spend additional meetings reviewing the list, adding to it information from the members as well as from the other colleges and universities to whom they wrote. The following three-step procedure will help assure that the group overlooks nothing of importance:

1. **The group should identify and list as many as possible of the issues and topics it will need to explore.**
2. **The group should assess the adequacy of its collective knowledge on the topic or problem.**
   Then it should determine what information is needed, thus preparing a list of headings for members' research. As Harnack, Fest, and Jones say, "Groups more often err on the side of too little evidence; but it is important to remember that it is never possible to gather all the evidence there is."[8]
3. **The group should assign research responsibilities to individual members.** This increases individual responsibility and involvement although it is frequently overlooked as a way of preventing gaps in knowledge and wasted time. Ideally, members are allowed to choose voluntarily from a list of topics and sources, with a group secretary or chair keeping a written list of who has undertaken what task. Deadlines should be established for each person or subgroup to report to the group as a whole.

As a general rule, all members should do some common background study with two or more persons examining every major article, book, or other source on the subject. This helps offset individual perceptual biases and helps prevent errors creeping in because each member has become a specialist and other members don't know enough to test the information supplied. Group "experts" also tend to dampen interaction when they are the only ones with detailed knowledge.

Once you have a list of topics or sources, you are ready to begin detailed personal preparation. How to gather and record information has been covered previously in your communication and composition classes, so we review it only briefly.

LEADER RATINGS   Affected by Subordinates' Beliefs about Leadership

Martin M. Chemers, "Leadership Theory and Research: A Systems-Process Integration," in Paul B. Paulus, Basic Group Processes. New York: Springer-Verlag, 1983, p. 26.

". . . subordinates ratings of leader behavior may reflect what the subordinate thinks good or bad leaders do, rather than any objective measure of what their leader really does. A number of recent studies . . . strongly indicate that implicit theories of leadership held by individuals affect their ratings of leader behavior."

Figure 4.2
A note card listing a topic heading, a specific subject, and exact details of the source.

Note Taking

Information and ideas slip from memory or become distorted unless we make accurate and complete notes. It is virtually useless to say that some key piece of information appeared "in a book by some psychologist." This makes it impossible for fellow members to evaluate the credibility of the information. The best system of note taking is to record each bit of information or idea on a separate three by five inch note card. Put a topic heading followed by the specific subject on the card. Then, list exact details of the source, just as you would for a bibliography. Finally, record the information, idea, or quotation. Figure 4.2 shows how to do this.

Note cards provide both accuracy and flexibility. They can be arranged in various groups to help synthesize and interpret the evidence collected. They can be consulted with ease during a discussion without having to leaf through a disorganized notebook. For those of you with a computer and a data-base management program, the information supplied on your note cards can be entered into your computer and sorted in a variety of ways with ease.

Three important sources for information helpful in preparing for group discussions are direct observation, reading, and interviews.

Direct Observation

Many times, needed information can come only from firsthand observation by group members, and often only direct observation can breathe life into a table of statistics or survey results. For example, in Omaha a commission charged with recommending potential sites for government subsidized housing found it necessary to visit proposed building sites even though they had available maps and reports of what was available. A group of students wanting to improve conditions in a self-service coffee shop of a student union spent some time observing what happened there at various times of the day. They recorded how many customers did and did not bus their waste materials, the kinds of litter on the floor and tables, placement and condition of waste containers and signs encouraging users to keep the room clean. Your small group can decide whether direct observation is required, then assign the task to those members most interested in doing this type of information gathering.

Reading

For many topics and problems, the major source for information will be books, journals, newspapers, government documents, and other printed pages. First, it is important to narrow down the print resources likely to yield relevant information: the number, type, and quality of the sources. To do that, you need to compile a **bibliography,** which is a list of published sources on a particular topic or issue. Although ideally you would like to locate and evaluate all recent printed information on your topic before making any final decision, it is not always possible. Be sure, however, that you do not limit yourself to only one or two sources, or to sources that support only one point of view. This will produce a bias in your information with no way to cross-check the validity.

To compile your bibliography as efficiently as possible, first prepare a list of key terms—descriptors—on the topic to guide your search for print items. For instance, a group investigating "What type of lottery, if any, should our state conduct?" might include the following descriptors: lottery, sweepstakes, gambling, crime, revenue, tax, and betting. A reference librarian can often be of invaluable help, along with printed sources of all kinds, such as *Sociological Abstracts, Psychological Abstracts, Facts on File,* and others. The abstract sources are significant time savers since they provide brief summaries of articles or books that can help you decide whether you should read the entire publication for details.

In addition, most major bibliographies, indexes, and compilations of abstracts are now in computer files, each of which has a thesaurus of key descriptor terms. Although some of these services may entail a fee, they make it extremely easy for you to locate relevant items and are usually worth the money. Whether or not you have access to such services, the list of descriptor terms your group generated will provide a starting point. As you proceed on your search, other key terms will be discovered. For instance, in your search for information about lotteries, you might encounter the additional terms "victimless" and "wagering."

A good library manual, available at virtually every college or university library, is a great help in building a bibliography and locating materials. Also helpful are bibliographies of bibliographies, such as *A World Bibliography of Bibliographies and Bibliographic Sources* and *Bibliographic Sources.* Bibliographies are also found at the end of most books, doctoral dissertations, and research articles. Do not overlook special indexes, such as *The Readers Guide to Periodical Literature, New York Times Index,* and *Education Index.* Federal and state government publications, in special sections of many libraries, also contain vast amounts of information. The *Monthly Catalog of U.S. Government Publications* and the *Monthly Checklist of State Publications* will help you locate relevant information in these publications. Other useful sources include the *Congressional Quarterly Weekly Report* and the *Congressional Digest*.

Even while you are compiling a bibliography you can begin reading. A good strategy is for all members of the group to read some of the same things to provide a common background. As we shall see later, learning discussions depend on all members having read or shared the same sources. When you are trying to evaluate a book for relevance, read the index and table of contents for clues. Skim rapidly until you find something pertinent to your group, then read carefully. Take notes of the most important ideas and facts and make copies of particularly valuable information for the rest of the group.

When reading in preparation for a learning discussion of a controversial issue, you should read as many contrasting interpretations and points of view as possible. For example, before discussing the relative merits of capital punishment, study the writings of those who favor and those who oppose it. *To learn, we must consider that which does not conform to our present beliefs.* It is easier to be accepting of sources who agree with us and critical of those who don't. It has been shown that we tend to forget evidence or beliefs inconsistent with our own.[9] However, if we are to be open-minded and well-informed group members, it is imperative that we make the effort.

Interviews

When you can observe only a small part of an entire operation (a nuclear reactor or the operation of a farm for example) or when you are not sufficiently knowledgeable to observe meaningfully, you may need to interview persons who are trained observers and have firsthand contact with your subject. Members of the group that observed the operation of the campus coffee shop also interviewed a number of users to determine how they felt about its condition and to ask their reasons for not busing their wastepaper and leftovers. They also interviewed the manager to determine why materials that contributed to litter were being used. Members of the faculty constitution committee asked friends at other universities how their constitutions worked in practice. Remember that your interviewees are busy and would prefer that you prepare by reading first, then interviewing them for clarification.

Interview questions may be open-ended or closed-ended. If only a few persons need to be consulted, your group may want to conduct in-depth interviews with open-ended questions, which often elicit unexpected information and provide richer data. However, answers to open-ended questions are more difficult and time-consuming to tabulate. If a larger number of people are to be interviewed, your group may want to use closed-ended questions instead, which can be quickly tabulated if they are formulated properly. Sometimes you may want to use both. One group of discussion students decided to compare first dates of today with thirty years ago. They selected respondents from each age group and asked each person the same set of open and closed questions:

1. Do you remember your first date? Yes _____ No _____
2. How old were you at the time of your first date? _____
3. How did you become acquainted with the person you dated?
4. Was this a solo or a double date?
5. If you remember, what did you do on this date?
6. Did you get a kiss on this date? Yes _____ No _____
   It is invalid to generalize the findings from a casual or haphazard

It is invalid to generalize the findings from a casual or haphazard sample to a larger population. For example, interviews on some public issue with fifty people who walk past a particular street corner will not yield an accurate picture of the beliefs of all residents of that city, or even of people who go downtown. Interviewing members of a class about some campus issue may produce a distorted picture. A scientifically designed sample (a representative sample) must be taken if results of interviews are to be generalized to members of the larger population. *Student groups generally should not undertake a sample survey unless some member of the group has been trained as a survey researcher, perhaps in a research methods course. If you have such a member, that person should design the sampling and interview procedures for the rest of the group.*

Other Sources of Information

Useful information may crop up anywhere, anytime. You may hear something important to your forthcoming discussion while listening to the radio or watching television. Lectures or public speeches are another source. An idea may occur to you when you are not consciously thinking about the problem—for example, while riding to school, jogging, or talking with friends. Most of us find it helpful to keep a small notepad with us so we can jot down ideas when they occur, lest we forget or distort them. The important thing is to be alert for unexpected information and record it promptly.

3. Evaluate the Information and Ideas You Have Collected

You will need to evaluate the information and ideas you have gathered for accuracy and credibility. Many of your ideas may collapse in the presence of contradictory evidence. Some of your information may be spurious, from suspect sources, in direct contradiction to other evidence or irrelevant. Now is the time for your group to cull the misleading, unsubstantiated, or false information so you will not misinform or confuse others.

Distinguishing between Statements of Fact and Inference

It is especially important to distinguish between statements of fact and statements of inference, opinion, advice, preference, or taste. Failure to do so may lead your group to adopt faulty solutions or arrive at inappropriate conclusions.

The major difference between statements of fact and all other types of statements is that factual statements can be verified as *true* or *false*. Facts either exist or do not exist; they are not discussable as such. A **statement of fact** is a declarative sentence that refers to an observation of some event in the world. "It is raining outside " is a statement of fact. The event is described and the statement includes or implies a method of observing by which the statement could be tested for truth or accuracy. It is a true statement if it accurately describes the observed events (it really *is* raining). If the statement refers to a presently ongoing situation accessible to the group, it can be verified. If referring to a *past* event, that past event must have actually been observed by somebody. However, past events themselves are not presently accessible to the group; therefore, only statements about them can be verified. For example, we could not verify that George III occupied the throne of England in 1773, but we could verify that records indicate that he was king. However, if several independent sources report the same information as fact, you can be more confident than if it comes from only one unverified source. As benchmarks to help you recognize them, statements of fact

are limited to description;

can be made only *after* observation;

are limited in the number that can be made;

are as close to certain as humans can get.

On the other hand, **statements of inference** (or opinion):

go beyond what was directly observed;

can be made at any time without regard to observation;

are unlimited in the number that can be made about anything;

can be made by anyone, observer or not;

entail some degree of probability, or inferential risk or uncertainty.

Statements of advice, taste, or preference do not refer to direct observation but report a personal liking, choice, value, or taste. The following examples may help clarify these differences:

Statements of Fact	Statements of Opinion and Inference
The population of Omaha recorded in the 1970 census was 363,421.	Omaha is growing rapidly.
On June 3, 1976, Jack Egart owned two cats.	Jack Egart likes cats.
The University library contained 2,437,532 volumes in its catalog on May 18, 1984.	The heart of a good university is its library.
After instituting lotteries, three states reduced their tax rates.	We should legalize gambling to reduce the state tax.
I–80 runs near both Cleveland and New York City.	You will get to New York from Cleveland by following I–80 (not if you have a wreck!).

Evaluating Survey and Statistical Data

Factual-type statements including statistics or the results of surveys need to be evaluated carefully for dependability. Surveying is a sophisticated operation and must be done correctly or the results can be misleading, especially if they are based on other than random or scientific sampling. What the questions are and who asks them can make a big difference in the results.

Ask the following questions when evaluating statistics. Who commissioned the study? How were the data gathered and analyzed? How were questions phrased? You may need the help of an expert to evaluate statistical data and interpret it properly, especially if you are basing an important conclusion on those data.

Evaluating the Sources and Implications of Opinions

Occasionally a student, when first introduced to the differences between statements of fact and of opinion, acts as if statements of opinion are less valuable in a discussion. Hardly so! Facts themselves are not discussable but provide the basis for discussion. Groups must deal not only with what has been verified but also determine priorities of value, ethics, goals, and procedures acceptable to all. Members make inferences about what will probably happen *if* we adopt each possible alternative. For example, facts regarding AIDS and how it is spread must be examined, but what a particular board of education should do about it depends on values, opinions, and judgments for the development of rational policies acceptable to all.

Not all opinions are equal, although persons have an equal right to express their opinions. Unexamined opinions are poor guides to belief or action, and while opinions cannot be verified for truth, they can be evaluated for their validity and appropriate use of fact. First, consider the source of the opinion.

1. Is this person (or other source) a recognized expert on the subject? How do other experts in the field regard the person? If their opinions are different, how might this be explained?
2. Does the source have a vested interest that might have influenced the opinion? For example, a corporate executive, union member, and politician will have different opinions about whether the government should supply special funds to help a large corporation avoid bankruptcy.
3. How well does the source support the opinion with documented evidence? Is the evidence well organized, with supporting statistics and tables and clear reasoning?
4. How consistent is this opinion with others expressed by the source? If not consistent, is there an acceptable explanation for the person's change?

Second, consider the **implications** of the opinion. To what further inferences or conclusions does it lead, and are these acceptable to the group? For example, a writer may argue that outlawing private ownership of handguns would protect us from accidents and murderers. What are the implications of this statement? That dangerous devices should not be allowed in the hands of the citizens at large? That only nonessential dangerous tools that could be used as murder weapons should be restricted? That eventually all potential weapons of murder should be removed from citizens? Another writer may argue that anyone should be allowed to own a handgun after demonstrating competence in handling it safely and correctly and if the person has no felony record. What are the implications of that opinion? That only convicted felons use handguns to kill another person? That most accidents would be prevented if persons knew how to handle guns safely? That handguns are useful to many people? The point is that when a group decision depends on opinions, it is most important to test these opinions, especially for what they assume and imply. To do so is the essence of discussion. Not to do so assures poor decisions and policies.

4. Organize Your Information and Ideas

The most efficient way to organize your knowledge is to write a tentative outline based on either a sequence for problem solving (see chapter 12) or one of the patterns for organizing a learning discussion (see chapter 13). Ask yourself "What are the questions that must be answered by our group to arrive at a full understanding of the problem or subject?" Your answers will serve as tentative main points in your preparation outline.

With some tentative major issues you can now arrange your notes into piles, one per issue or outline item. Some of the piles can be further subdivided into subheadings. For example, information concerning the nature of the problem might be arranged under such subheadings as "who is affected," "seriousness of the problem," "where the problem exists," "contributing causes," and so on. Organizing your information like this helps you decide what is important and what is not, makes it easier for you to locate pertinent information when a topic arises in discussion, helps you prepare questions the group needs to consider, and generally helps you and the group maintain an orderly and comprehensive discussion of a complex topic.

When you are preparing for a problem-solving discussion your outline likely contains some possible solutions you have found or thought of. You may have evidence or reasoning that shows how similar solutions were tried on similar problems and even some suggestions on how to implement a plan, check to see whether it works, and adjust it as needed. However, such thinking and planning should be tentative. It is easy to become dogmatic about an issue after you have spent hours preparing and discussing it, but it is absolutely essential that your mind be open. It is inappropriate and harmful to the group if members come to a discussion prepared to defend their solutions against all comers or if they feel their personal understanding of the problem is complete. Remember that experts at the cutting edge of their fields are the least dogmatic and sure of themselves. Instead, the ideal group member has the attitude of being prepared to contribute some reliable information and perhaps some ideas for testing by the other members, to listen with more understanding, and to ask perceptive questions, thereby shaping but not forcing the solution.

When preparing for a learning discussion you may or may not need to prepare an outline. Sometimes one will be supplied by the instructor or moderator. For most academic discussions, outlines help participants presort and organize their information. Regardless, you will get much more from the discussion as well as be prepared to give more to your fellow discussants if you write down the following kinds of items as you prepare:

Significant issues for the group to discuss

Controversial points of view or policies the group should examine

Passages that are unclear and any questions you want to raise

How a writer's proposition relates to his or her personal life and experience

Any other related information or experience that comes to mind

Summary

In this chapter we have examined three input variables important to effective discussions: the reason for forming a group, the physical setting, and informational resources.

Only if group members share an interdependent purpose to which they are committed can small group discussions be productive. The purpose may be assigned by some parent organization as a charge. The charge and the group's area of freedom must be clear to and accepted by all members, or frustration and time-wasting will result. The group's purpose can be formulated as a group goal question of interpretation, value, or policy. Classroom groups especially need to be clear and realistic when wording their group goal questions.

A meeting place conducive to discussion is free from distractions, comfortable, provides group members with a face-to-face view of each other, reflects egalitarian relationships among participants, and includes facilities for group recording and note taking. A circular seating pattern is ideal.

Clear objectives and ideal physical facilities merely set the stage for effective discussions. Adequate informational resources are the grist on which the mill of discussion grinds; outputs are no better than the information and ideas put into discussion. Such resources come from discussants who are well armed with information, ideas, and questions. Groups dealing with extensive problems need to plan initially how they will obtain such materials and assign responsibility for their acquisition. Members can begin by reviewing and organizing what they already know. Then they should compile a bibliography of sources and do the observing, reading, interviewing, note taking, and outlining required to obtain, evaluate, and organize their information. A preparation outline will make it possible to gain perspective on a mass of information, raise needed questions, and help locate notes relevant to the issues being discussed. To fail to prepare thoroughly for discussions is to prepare the group to fail in its stated goal.

We have discussed key input variables that affect the group. Next, we turn our attention to the throughput, or process, variables. The next section presents basic communication theory, which serves as the groundwork for understanding the group's interaction processes.

Exercises

1. Think of a committee with which you are familiar that had trouble because members ignored their area of freedom or otherwise violated their charge. How did the parent organization react? Share your example with classmates. What guidelines can you establish from your examples?

2. List examples of the kinds of interdependent purposes a group can have. How important is this for a group? Explain the reasons for your answer.

3. How would you arrange your classroom for a problem-solving discussion by the entire class? For a series of simultaneous small group meetings? Make a pictorial diagram of these plans.

4. Select an article which contains commentary (both *Time* and *Newsweek* regularly have such columns or perhaps your instructor will supply you with an example). Locate examples of statements of fact, inference, and taste or value. If you classify a statement as one of fact, indicate whether or not it could be verified and how that could be accomplished. If you classify a statement as inference, what evidence does the writer supply to support that inference?

5. In class, select a topic or problem of interest to all. Then do all the following:

   a. Prepare a bibliography of references on the topic, keeping a record of all the bibliographic sources you used.

   b. Prepare yourself to discuss the subject, including a detailed outline and the note cards from all sources you consulted which you may submit to your instructor after the discussion. Be sure your outline contains all the questions you can think of that the class must answer to understand the problem fully, arrive at common goals and values, and reach a decision.

Bibliography

Babbie, Earl R. *The Practice of Social Research*. 4th ed. Belmont, Cal.: Wadsworth Publishing Company, 1983, chapters 7 and 9. These chapters present a clear and complete explanation of survey research.

Burgoon, Judee K. "Spatial Relationships in Small Groups," In *Small Group Communication: A Reader*. 4th ed., eds. Robert S. Cathcart and Larry A. Samovar. Dubuque, Iowa: Wm. C. Brown Publishers, 1984, 276–292.

Stewart, Charles J., and William B. Cash. *Interviewing: Principles and Practices*. Dubuque, Iowa: Wm. C. Brown Publishers, 1978.

Notes

1. Randy Y. Hirokawa, "The Role of Communication in Group Decision-Making Efficacy: A Task-Contingency Perspective," (Unpublished manuscript, University of Iowa, 1987).

2. Mary Ann Strider, "The Non-Group Meeting,"(Unpublished paper, 1974).

3. Moshe F. Rubenstein, *Patterns of Problem Solving* (Englewood Cliffs, N.J.: Prentice-Hall, 1975), 1–2.

4. J. Bilodeau and H. Schlosberg, "Similarity in Stimulating Conditions as a Variable in Retroactive Inhibition," *Journal of Experimental Psychology* 41 (1959): 199–204; A. Maslow and N. L. Mintz, "Effects upon Perceived 'Energy' and 'Well-being' in Faces," *Journal of Psychology* 41 (1956): 247–54; N. L. Mintz, "Effects of Esthetic Surroundings: II. Prolonged and Repeated Experience in a 'Beautiful' and an 'Ugly' Room," *Journal of Psychology* 41 (1956): 459–66.

5. Robert Sommer, "The Distance for Comfortable Conversation: A Further Study," *Sociometry* 25 (1962): 111–16.

6. A. Paul Hare and R. F. Bales, "Seating Position and Small Group Interaction," *Sociometry* 25 (1963): 480–86.

7. John G. Geier, "A Trait Approach to the Study of Leadership in Small Groups," in *Small Group Communication: A Reader,* eds. Robert S. Cathcart and Larry A. Samovar (Dubuque, Iowa: Wm. C. Brown Publishers, 1970), 414.

8. R. Victor Harnack, T. B. Fest, and B. S. Jones, *Group Discussion: Theory and Technique,* 2d ed. (Englewood Cliffs, N.J.: Prentice-Hall, 1977), 119.

9. Sir Frederic Bartlett, *Thinking: An Experiment and Social Study* (New York: Basic Books, 1958).

Part 3

Communication Theory
Foundation for Understanding Small Group Processes

Chapter 5

The Communication Process in Small Groups

Study Objectives

As a result of studying chapter 5 you should be able to:

1. Explain communication as a complex, symbolic, transactional process requiring participation of a receiver.

2. Describe how signals are encoded, transmitted, received, transformed, interpreted, and responded to in both intrapersonal and small group communication systems.

3. Differentiate between the content, affective, and relational components of interpersonal messages.

4. Name and describe the fallacy in each of five myths of communication.

5. Demonstrate active listening.

6. Explain and identify each of seven pitfalls to effective listening.

7. Explain how selective note taking and focused listening can improve recall and continuity in discussion.

Key Terms

Active listening listening to understand what a speaker means, then paraphrasing one's understanding so the speaker can correct or confirm the paraphrase.

Communication process in which symbols and other signals produced by people are received, interpreted, and responded to by other people.

Complete communication transaction open interchange system in which both persons send and receive signals, so that a signal from one is responded to by the other and the response is acknowledged.

Defensive listening thinking of how to defend some aspect of one's image while apparently attending to the message of another.

Feedback information regarding one's own messages or someone else's response to one's own messages that leads to change in subsequent message output.

Focused listening focusing attention on major ideas and issues rather than details of another's message. This includes attempting to review and recall those issues with mental and written summaries.

Forcing meaning listener insisting that speaker meant by some statement what the listener would have meant by the same words even though the speaker insists he or she meant something different.

Interpersonal communication transactional process in which one person's verbal and nonverbal behavior evokes meaning in another.

Intrapersonal communication process of signal generation, transmission, interpretation, and response within the nervous system of one individual.

Listening receiving and interpreting oral and other signals from another person or source.

Message either a set of signals from one person to other(s) or interpretation and response of listener to a set of signals.

Nonverbal cues signals other than words to which listeners react.

Paraphrase restatement by listener in his or her own language of what he or she understood the previous speaker to mean.

Pseudolistening responding overtly as if listening attentively while thinking about something other than the speaker and his or her message.

Sign a trace or vestige of something, having an *inherent* relationship with the thing which it represents to a perceiver; e.g., a footprint, scar, or blush.

Signal any stimulus a person can receive and interpret, including both signs and symbols.

Symbol arbitrary, human-created signal used to represent something with which it has no inherent relationship; all words are symbols.

Communication is what we call the process by which group members put their thoughts into words, share information, develop interdependence, coordinate their efforts, reach agreement on ends and means, and forge a collection of individuals into a group. The purpose of chapter 5 is to provide the foundation for your understanding of the term *communication,* which is essential to your grasp of the throughput processes of a small group.

Much of this section may be a review for you, especially if you have taken other communication courses. Nevertheless, because communication scholars use the key terms to mean many different things, we recommend that you at least survey the next three chapters to see how we are using them.

What Is Communication?

Many definitions of the term *communication* exist. We are using Stephen King's: "Communication is the process whereby symbols generated by people are received and are responded to by other people."[1] This definition implies that a person, the sender, has a thought, feeling, or idea that he or she puts into words and/or gestures. By this definition, there is no requirement that our sender consciously attempts to communicate the thought or feeling. Another person, a receiver, may or may not pick up the message being sent, respond to it, or attach significant meaning to it, but if he or she *does,* then communication has occurred. Communication, then, is a process. It is a complex, symbolic, and receiver-oriented phenomenon. Because the definition is so important to understanding concepts in this book, elaboration is warranted. Much of the following explanation is derived from King's article about the nature of communication:

1. **Communication is a process.**
   Communication is everchanging, without clear beginning or ending points. It involves at least two people whose interaction proceeds, never returning exactly to the same place. For instance, if you have an argument with a fellow group member, even if you resolve that argument chances are neither of you will be able to forget it. Consequently, the memory of that argument will be carried with you into your subsequent interaction with one another. Communication is not static but constantly shifts and moves.

2. **Communication is a complex process.**
   Many variables are involved, making communication intricate rather than simple. Messages are sent along verbal and nonverbal pathways simultaneously by senders and receivers. The communicative environment includes variables, such as the topic, the goal of the participants, the setting, the individual needs and characteristics of the interactants, and a host of other factors, some of which we have already discussed. A complete understanding of the communication process must comprise each of these factors plus many more.

   Many changes in the form a message takes occur during the process, and at each of these changes there is a chance that the intended message will be altered somewhat. Beginning as electrochemical patterns in the brain, the message is in sequence converted to nerve signals, muscle movements, light and sound waves (vibrations), mechanical movements of sensor-endings, nerve messages, receiver electrochemical patterns in the nervous system, and finally perceptions or ideas. With so many transformations in form, a *lot* can go wrong.

3. **Communication is symbolic.**

Meaning is not transferred from one person to another; rather, people send **messages** to each other. In the movie "Brainstorm," the main character invented a headphone device which could transfer experiences directly from the brain of one person to the brain of another, without having to translate the experiences first into words. Of course, humans cannot do this, at least not yet. We must resort to using the media of language and nonverbal communication to attempt to convey our beliefs and emotions. One person converts his or her thoughts into signals (e.g., words, gestures) and sends the signals to another person who converts the signals perceived back into thoughts. Note that **signals** embrace both symbols (words and symbolic gestures) and nonverbal **signs** (tone of voice, face and body characteristics, clothing, etc.). Communication is the study of this signaling behavior, which in humans is largely symbolic.

An important characteristic of human communicating is the heavy reliance on symbols. **Symbols** are arbitrary signals, created by people and used to represent experiences, things, concepts, or other components of thought *with which they have no inherent relationship or connection.* They are convenient, but they can also be sources of great confusion. There is no inherent or natural connection between any symbol and what it represents to speaker or listener, so each can easily have different meanings for a single symbol (such as a word) or a set of signals (phrase, sentence, statement). Think of a symbolic gesture, such as the one you likely use to indicate "okay" or approval, in which thumb and index finger are circled. Okay is an arbitrary use or meaning of this gesture, based in cultural usage and experience. Don't try to use it in much of South America, though—there it indicates something obscene!

4. **Communication is a receiver phenomenon.**

The presence of a receiver is a necessary component in our definition of communication. If you, alone in your room, shake your fist and swear at the rainclouds outside, you have not communicated. Likewise, if a fellow group member makes a suggestion but none of the other group members hears that suggestion, that person has not communicated because our definition of communication requires a receiver who invests the message with some meaning. The group member, on the other hand, may pick up a set of messages that the rest of the group did not intend to send, such as "We don't agree with your suggestion" or "Who cares what you have to say?" This implies that the intent of the sender may be relatively immaterial to how a receiver responds. The important thing is what meaning the *receiver* attaches to the communicative message. It may transpire that your "ignored" member feels slighted enough to fail to complete key assignments for the group. This demonstrates that the meaning the receiver derives from the message will affect both his or her perceptions and behavior, in this case to the detriment of the group. Even though the rest of you did not mean to hurt this member's feelings, what counts is what meaning the member (the receiver) got from the message.

Many people, especially those who have not systematically studied communication, perpetuate a number of communication myths. The following are five of the most pervasive myths about the communication process presented by King:

1. **I understand communication. I've been communicating all my life.**
   Doing something frequently does not mean that one does it well or with understanding. Look at how some people walk, drive, or stand! The group member with this attitude believes he or she has nothing to learn and will likely continue to repeat past mistakes.

2. **Communication can be improved simply by improving communication skills.**
   The problems with this myth are twofold. First, communication is reduced to a list of techniques. Use the techniques, and presto, you are a good communicator. Instead, communication almost always is improved most by enhancing the communicator's understanding of the process and attitudes toward that process and other people. Second, this myth implies that the *speaker* is the important element in the process. As we have discussed, it is what happens to the *receiver* that is the more appropriate focus.

3. **I didn't misunderstand him, he misunderstood me.**
   If a message is misunderstood, the effective communicator accepts a share of the responsibility for that misunderstanding, recognizing that both sender and receiver must cooperate to create clear communication. Both share the credit or blame for the outcome of a communicative episode.

4. **Most problems in human relationships are caused by communication breakdowns. Breakdowns are unusual and can easily be corrected.**
   This myth, propagated by the popular media, ignores the social, economic, and political realities contributing to conflicts and disagreements. I may want to use a public waterway for fishing and swimming, while you may want to use it for motorboating and waterskiing. We understand each other very well; we simply have competing values. To call this a communication breakdown cheapens the real disagreement we have. In addition, ineffective communication is the rule, not the exception. It is complex and incompletely understood, particularly by the layperson.

5. **Good communication achieves perfect understanding among participants.**
Perfect understanding is impossible. Moreover, some communication is
designed to mislead rather than enlighten. Did you know that "revenue
enhancement" (uttered by a politician) means "taxation," for instance?
Have you ever answered vaguely to the question, "How do you like my
new hair style?" In these cases, the lack of clear, unambiguous
communication is purposeful. Even when we refer to the same object or
image with a symbolic statement, we have differences in our
experiences with it and somewhat different feelings about it. Therefore,
the symbolic message has slightly different meanings for every speaker
and receiver.

Some signals of group members are not communicative. Any behavior,
including words uttered and intentional gestures, must be perceived for communication to occur. Thus, an unheard remark or an unseen gesture is not a
part of the group's communication. Neither is the behavior that was seen or
heard but to which no meaning was attached by the receiver. For instance, at
the conclusion of a group meeting, often people are not attentive to one another, jostle one another to leave the room, all talk at once, and interrupt.
Members perceive this, but do not attach any particular significance to it. They
typically do not leave one another thinking, "How inconsiderate;" they simply
go about their business. Thus, ". . . behavior that is not perceived by another
or to which no significant meaning is attached is not communication. Behavior
that is both perceived and meaningful is communication."[2]

Communication Systems

Human communication systems can be examined from the individual to the
societal level. A system was defined as an entity composed of interdependent
components patterned in interdependent relationships to each other and requiring constant adaptation among the parts. **Intrapersonal communication**
refers to communication occurring within an individual, involving the flow of
electrochemical energy throughout the nervous system. It includes the study
of cognitive processes we call perception and thinking as well as sensation,
muscle control, and coordination of the entire organism.

Social systems of communication involve two or more persons exchanging
and responding to each other's signals; they are generally categorized into one
of five levels. At the *interpersonal level,* the communication process involves
two or a few persons interacting. *Small group communication* refers to interpersonal communication that occurs in the context of a *small group as defined in chapter 1,* with three or more group members simultaneously sending,
receiving, internally processing, and responding to signals from each other.
The upper level of small group communication occurs at some point when
members lose awareness of other members as distinct individuals. At that point
a large group may or may not exist, but *public communication* occurs. Public
communication involves a primary source of verbal signals (public speaker)
communicating to others not generally perceived by the source as persons with
unique characteristics. The listeners in the public communication system are

Figure 5.1
An intrapersonal
communication system.

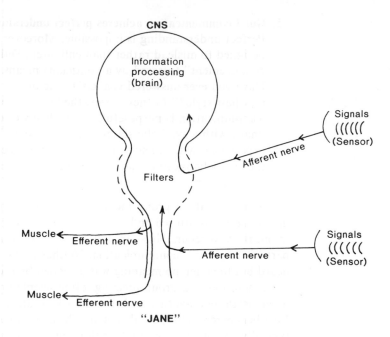

referred to as an audience. The most common forms involve live public speeches or written, visual, or oral messages carried across a closed-circuit electrical system to a limited audience. Public communication becomes *mass communication* when the messages are carried by some medium available to an indeterminately large number of people—television and radio, newspaper, magazine, book, film, etc.

Of these five categories, the most important to understanding the small group are the intrapersonal, interpersonal, and small group system levels. Communication is the process by which these systems influence each other.

Intrapersonal Communication Systems

Entire books are written about the functioning of the brain, central nervous system, signals, and how humans interpret them. These are the components of intrapersonal communication. We include here general information about intrapersonal communicating needed to understanding the behavior of individuals in the group and to appreciate what may go wrong when group members interact.

Remember that a necessary element for communication to occur is a receiver who is aware of the signals being sent. This awareness first happens at the physiological level. As illustrated in figure 5.1, a given intrapersonal communication episode begins the moment a signal from some source reaches one of the sensors, such as the visual or auditory sensors, causing the sensor to react to the signal. The person, in this case "Jane," may receive the signal from inside or outside the body: a hunger pang, a rise in heart rate, pressure on a toe, a sudden noise, a flashing light, a voice. The responding sensor emits signals to an afferent nerve that carries them to the central nervous system of spinal cord and brain. Here various switching operations occur to send the signals to one or more divisions of the great central information processor, the brain. Based on Jane's physical and psychosocial needs, the condition of Jane's systems, past experiences and knowledge, values, expectations, and many other variables, the central nervous system (CNS) will respond in some way—a decision is made and action taken. For instance, the sensation of sudden pain in a finger will proceed to the brain, register there as pain, and send a subsequent signal to the efferent nerve, causing the muscles of the finger to retreat from the pain source. Sometimes the sensory filters of the CNS may decide that no action is needed and "kill" the signal. Thus, the response is not overt. In deep sleep, for example, you may not awaken to your alarm, although the noise has registered on the ears and caused the auditory nerve to send the signal to the brain. In this case, the response may be to weave the signal into a dream. However, if your brain interprets the signal as being especially important or if the signal is of sufficient power, you will waken, try to interpret the sound, and respond in some overt way. If the clanging alarm is supposed to wake you for an important job interview, for instance, it is unlikely that you will sleep through it. In a small group, when a member who has had little to say finally does speak up, the more active members may not even be aware of the verbal contribution unless the speaking is particularly forceful.

Only one signal at a time can be the focus of attention. The other signals that constantly bombard Jane's CNS are dealt with by the autonomic nervous system below the level of conscious awareness. To reach the awareness threshold, the signal must be of some minimum strength or duration. Thresholds vary depending on the sensor, time, and person. Thus, one group member may not be aware of what another member says, while a third participant listens quite well. On the other hand, when members are energetic and alert they may be attuned to most of the contributions made by the group, but when they are tired they may miss important suggestions.

Interpersonal Communication Systems

Interpersonal communication has been defined in a variety of ways. We use it here to mean those transactions involving a minimum of two people who are exchanging verbal and nonverbal signals and responding to each other's signals simultaneously. All small group communication involves interpersonal communication since to become a group the members send and respond to one another's signals at the personal level. Awareness of each other as unique individuals is part of the definition of small group. Communication at the interpersonal level is only part of the small group process; therefore, we have incorporated interpersonal information along with the explanation of small group communication systems. We do not treat in-depth factors which impinge primarily on communication at the interpersonal level, such as self-concept development, self-disclosure, expression of feelings, and perception.

Figure 5.2
A small group
communication system.

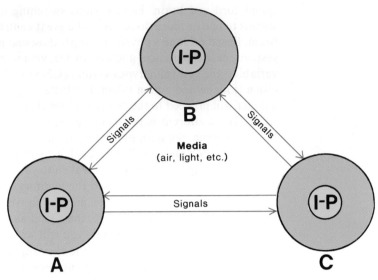

I-P = Information Processors

Small Group Communication Systems

Small group communication occurs when three or more members, with promotively interdependent goals, simultaneously emit and respond to signals from each other. Figure 5.2 represents communication in a small group with three members, *A, B,* and *C.* They interact in a transactional process. Each is both sender and receiver, influencer and influenced, and each creates a personal meaning for the signals to which he or she responds. As with the model depicting intrapersonal communication, members are responding to the visual and vocal signals they are sending. If member *A* wishes to make a suggestion to the other participants, he or she encodes the suggestion (thinks about what he or she means and decides what to say) and delivers it by speaking the words in a particular tone of voice, perhaps with accompanying gestures. Thus, both verbal and nonverbal signals are sent, to be decoded by *A*'s fellow group members in a process that reverses the one used by *A* to send the suggestion. What originated as meaning in one person has been transformed into electrochemical signals in efferent nerves, converted to muscle actions, sent as sound and visual cues, picked up by the sensors belonging to the receivers, transformed again into electrochemical nerve signals in the receivers' afferent nerves, processed in the CNS, and given meaning as perception, thought or mental image. Again we emphasize that it is not *meaning itself* that is transmitted; the meaning is first encoded and later decoded by another individual.

Communication is complex; it is easy to see how many things can go awry at any number of junctures in the process. If a group is to keep misunderstandings to a minimum, attention and effort must be given to this complicated process. Otherwise, the result will be low cohesiveness, dissatisfaction, members perceiving things in dissimilar ways, and poor solutions to problems. A group is more efficient if members see things in similar ways and act correspondingly, but achieving compatible understanding requires deliberate concentration and cannot be taken for granted.

The Complete Communicative Transaction

A **complete communication transaction** occurs when the receiver verifies the sender's meaning during discussion. For a valid interpersonal transaction to occur, the receiver must respond to the initial message and the sender in turn must acknowledge that response. This way, both parties to the interchange know whether they have communicated as desired. For example, if member A says, "What happened in the student center that everyone is talking about?" (initiation), B might say, "A big fight broke out between members of two fraternities" (response) to which A might nod or say, "Oh, I see" (acknowledgment). In the case of a small group, each speaker addressing the group as a whole needs an overt, perceivable response of some kind (maybe only a nod or a frown) and needs, in turn, to acknowledge those responses. The speaker may find it necessary to revise or correct the original message if the responses indicate lack of understanding. For instance, if puzzled looks follow a statement, the speaker will sense confusion and may rephrase the remark. The members may make no response, in which case the speaker has three choices: to give up, to restate in a more forceful or different way, or to ask for an overt response.

Nothing dampens solidarity, interest, and enthusiasm more than lack of a perceivable response—**feedback**—denying the speaker's existence by indicating "You are not worth responding to." This kind of destructive response disconfirms the speaker's very existence, in contrast to confirming statements and actions that say "You are a valued member of this group." Sieburg defines confirming actions as those that reinforce an individual's sense of self-worth, while disconfirming actions are those which cheapen it.[3] In addition to ignoring a speaker, specific disconfirming behaviors include interrupting the speaker, making a response which is irrelevant to what preceded it, and responding tangentially by acknowledging minimally what the speaker said but taking the conversation in another direction. Confirming responses, on the other hand, include direct acknowledgement of the speaker, indicating agreement, expressing support, clarifying to understand the speaker's meaning, and expressing positive feelings toward the speaker. Many of the groups studied by Sieburg exhibited impervious and tangential remarks. Members of effective groups had fewer impervious, tangential, and ambiguous remarks and responded more to the content. Clearly, confirming behaviors contribute positively to understanding, helping to complete the communicative transaction, while disconfirming behaviors short-circuit it. Chopra observed, for instance, that when group members did not respond to and reinforce one another, retaliation, withdrawal, and defensive behaviors increased.[4] We all want to be responded to, and responded to positively, in a group.

In the groups to which you belong, notice whether there is a difference in how much the members respond to each other. In what kind of group are you most comfortable, one where members react openly and clearly (even to disagree) or one where reaction is minimal? Do you agree with Jablin, who found that subordinates would rather have a boss disagree openly than disconfirm, which is perceived as highly insulting?[5] We suggest that you monitor your own response behavior and change it if you find you routinely fail to respond to speakers. In short, don't break the communication circuit. Many student journals have contained observations of disconfirming behavior: "Even though Jean didn't say much, I was able to tell where she stood. You could tell from her face and movements that she was involved. Ed was another story. It was hard to tell how he felt, and I never could trust him."

The Message Sent

Message can refer either to a set of signals from some person to others, or to the interpretation and response of a discussant to a message received from another. A *sent* message consists of both verbal and nonverbal signals. A short speech by a group member, including all the words and the **nonverbal cues** accompanying the words, such as gestures, vocal tones, pitch changes, and eye movements, is a sent message. So is a nonverbal message like a facial expression or a shift in posture. In this case, a person who received the message of those nonverbal cues might interpret them as "Charles is not interested in what I have to say." Notice that the response in this transaction is verbal at the intrapersonal level. An entirely nonverbal or verbal human communicative transaction is rare in small group discussion. Every verbal statement has its nonverbal elements, and responses to entirely nonverbal signals always include words in the mind (intrapersonal level) of the receiver. To illustrate this point, try to look at another person with whom you have some involvement but who is saying nothing, then see if you can avoid thinking with words while you interpret what you see. It can't be done! Although we divide them for the purposes of analysis, in practice they are inseparable.

In addition to its verbal and nonverbal signals, every verbal message contains three elements: content, affective, and relational. The content level, also called the denotative aspect, is what the speaker is actually talking about. A group member might say, "Mary, you take the minutes for the meeting." At the content level, Mary is instructed to pay attention to the content of the interaction to be able to reproduce it in written form. The affective level concerns how the speaker feels about what has been denoted. For instance, the speaker may be angry with Mary for some perceived slight and may be speaking in a hostile tone of voice or, the remark may be spoken in a questioning manner. The relational implication of the statement, usually conveyed nonverbally, concerns how the speaker sees his or her relationship to the listeners. In the previous example, a hostile, commanding tone of voice indicates that the speaker is attempting to establish dominance over Mary. A pleading, questioning tone connotes subservience, whereas a straightforward request suggests equality. Attitudes of arrogance, dominance, submissiveness, distrust, superiority, neutrality, or concern are not often stated as directly as this; rather, listeners interpret them from nonverbal cues.

Listening and Responding during Discussions

Mutual understanding among group members depends more on how they listen and respond than on how they speak. **Listening** has been defined as a "selective process of attending to, hearing, understanding and remembering aural (and at times visual) symbols."[6] Hearing, the reception by the ear of sound waves and transformation of them into auditory nerve signals, is only a part of listening, which also includes the interpretation of signals heard. During a discussion participants must first hear, then assign meaning to the aural signals in order for us to say they have listened. A person with acute hearing may be a poor listener who does not interpret and respond appropriately to others' statements, whereas someone with considerable hearing loss may be an excellent listener who is motivated to understand the other group members. Such individuals attend closely to the interaction, ask others to speak up, and interpret accurately despite the loss.

It is easier to detect poor listening in a dyad than in a small group where one person can avoid speaking for long periods of time. Because people can fake listening, only when someone speaks do other participants have a basis for judging how well he or she has listened. Irrelevant comments and obvious misunderstandings give the poor listener away.

Few of us consider ourselves poor listeners, but evidence suggests that most of us are pretty poor at getting information from listening, interpreting others' meanings accurately, and retaining in long-term memory what we have heard. At times, group members are not even aware of the current topic of discussion. Berg found, for instance, that topics were switched about one time per minute in discussions he observed. It seemed as if hardly anyone was listening to and responding to what previous speakers had said.[7] This finding has been confirmed by other investigators in a variety of cultures and situations.[8] Nichols and Stevens reported that students listening to lectures on which they knew they would be tested retained even for a short time only about half of the new information presented.[9] One of us has found that when members of small groups (whether college students or corporate personnel in training groups) are required to paraphrase what a previous discussant said to that person's satisfaction, they can do so only about half the time. This is true even when they know that they will be assessed for accuracy in listening. How much, then, must group discussants misunderstand when they are *not* on guard, trying their utmost to listen well?

The cost of poor listening is high. In the work scene many jobs are done incorrectly, shipments go awry, time and material are wasted, and people are hurt or killed because they did not understand what was intended. In small groups, much time is lost repeating ideas for people who weren't listening or who could have understood readily had they been listening well. We pay a price; we cannot afford to indulge poor listening habits.

Pitfalls to
Listening
Effectively

Our listening is impaired when we are tired, preoccupied, or overloaded with information and noise. But even when we are not bothered by such concerns, we still may listen poorly as a result of bad habits we have acquired and probably are not aware of. Some of the patterns of behavior that interfere with good listening follow:

1. **Pseudolistening.**
   Pseudolistening refers to faking the real thing by appearing to listen and understand. Pseudolisteners nod, smile, murmur polite responses, look the speaker in the eye, and may even give verbal support like "Right" or "Good idea." Behind the mask the pseudolistener is off on a personal train of thought: a daydream, a personal problem, sizing up the speaker as a target, mentally preparing a verbal response. When their behavior is challenged, most pseudolisteners say something like "That stuff he was saying is boring," when in truth they had dismissed the topic in a stereotyped way without giving the speaker a chance.

2. **Silent arguing.**
   Many people listen selectively to information that confirms the views they already hold. Instead of listening well to contrary evidence and arguments, necessary if one plans to help a group find the best possible course of action, the selective listener ignores these or carries on a silent argument. Without fully understanding the opposing positions, he or she argues that the other is wrong.

   You cannot listen both to self and to a fellow discussant. You cannot mentally rehearse a reply (listening to yourself) at the same time you are supposedly listening to another. If you listen primarily to find flaws and argue them in your mind, you are unlikely to perceive and understand an idea or the evidence and reasoning supporting it. Silent arguing is closed-mindedness in action. It is the dogmatism we have already discussed in chapter 3. Such behavior is counterproductive to helping the group search for and evaluate the best alternatives at its disposal. You can stop this habit if you are aware of your biases and realize when you start your internal argument. Try to overcome it by making extra efforts to understand what others are saying well enough to paraphrase it from their point of view. If you have understood *to the other's satisfaction* what he or she means, then (and only then) you are in a position to disagree and construct valid arguments against the position.

3. **Premature replying.**
   This can take two forms. Most commonly, a person prepares mentally to make a remark before fully understanding a question or statement by another member of the group. Similar to silent arguing, the premature reply need not involve disagreement. It is also common for group members who know each other well to think they know what other members will say before they say it. Before the other has finished,

the listener jumps to a conclusion and readies a reply without allowing time to listen to the full statement. The result is misunderstanding and disjointed discussions where the subject seems to be changing constantly. Sometimes the premature replier *stagehogs* by switching the conversation to a favorite topic or to a more familiar aspect of the problem.

4. **Focusing on irrelevancies and distractions.**

   Instead of keeping attention focused on what other members are saying or doing nonverbally, some members allow themselves to be distracted by background noises, furnishings, statements made by nonmembers, or less than ideal environmental conditions. Some will pay undue attention to a speaker's dialect, appearance, or personal mannerisms and miss his or her meaning. As one woman from Georgia said to group members, "Damn it, listen to what I have to say, not to how I speak. I can't change that now. It makes me really mad when someone says 'Oh, how you talk is so cute I just can't pay attention to what you are saying.' "

5. **Sidetracking.**

   A fellow group member mentions some experience or idea, and you begin a reverie as you recall a past experience triggered by the statement. Meanwhile, you have missed several points in the discussion. Watch out for the tendency to sidetrack into your personal storehouse of memories while others are still speaking.

6. **Listening defensively.**

   When we feel psychologically threatened, we are likely to become defensive. In that state, we do not listen well. Instead, if we feel defensive about an idea or self-concept, we generally quit listening in order to invent ways to defend ourselves and attack the perceived threat. This is called **defensive listening.** Unfortunately, this is the very time when we need most to understand the perception and values of the other person that we find irritating. There may be a genuine clash of values, the speaker may be trying to assume a position of dominance, or merely has a different way of verbalizing a belief or value that we as listeners actually share.

   It is especially important to watch for emotive or trigger words so we do not miss the other's point in a burst of negative reaction to a word. For instance, you may be sensitive to perceived attempts of others to control your behavior, so when a group member suggests you take notes for the group, you fly off the handle. That suggestion may not evoke a defensive reaction in another person who is not sensitive to dominance attempts, but it produced one in you because it touched one of your "hot buttons." Other examples include people who have strong negative reactions to such terms as *nuclear energy, abortion,* or *right to life;* they fail to listen to what the speaker means and why. When you get too emotionally involved, take a deep breath, back off, and try to understand the meaning of the speaker to whom you are reacting with such vigor. Take another look—check your understanding.

7. **Forcing meaning.**

This behavior is not common in small group discussions, but when it happens the cost is high. **Forcing meaning** refers to the listener who insists that what the speaker meant by a statement was what the listener would have meant if he or she had uttered those words. "I heard what you said, and I know exactly what you meant by that," says the meaning forcer, insisting that his or her interpretation is correct despite the protests of the speaker. Underlying this behavior is the faulty assumption that words have only one meaning. Meaning forcers are unwilling to accept the fact that meanings are in people, and they are too rigid to admit to a variety of possible meanings for the same utterance.

You may have noticed that the common thread binding these nonlistening behaviors together is the element of evaluation or judgment. Poor listeners are so busy judging the speaker and the speaker's ideas that they do not take the time to respond empathically and supportively. The sequence is entirely reversed from what it should be. Only after we understand each other's ideas are we able to judge appropriately. As Kelley put it, we need to be empathic listeners who try to understand what the other means from his or her point of view, with the motivation to receive information being greater that the motivation to evaluate and criticize.[10]

Early in a new group's formative stage, when the normal jockeying for leadership and role positions prevails, not much effective listening is evident. If this continues the group will accomplish nothing and may disintegrate. We will now explain what you as a committed group member can do to assume responsibility for improving your listening habits.

Active Listening

Effective listening is an active process requiring as much effort as speaking. The person trying hard to understand and recall is an active listener because in that situation such a person shows signs of physical activity, such as an accelerated heartbeat. In contrast, heart rates of poor listeners frequently slow to the level of sleep! Active listening takes an act of will, a decision to apply oneself to understanding before judging and to select what will need to be recalled in the future.

A good test of how well you have been listening is a technique called **active listening.** This technique virtually forces the listener to understand a speaker before replying or adding to a discussion. The main rule is that you must re-state *in your own words,* or **paraphrase,** what you understood the previous speaker to mean, then ask for confirmation or correction of your paraphrase. It is very important that the listener paraphrase, not repeat word for word. A tape recorder can repeat, but that does not demonstrate understanding. A paraphrase in the listener's own words forces the listener to process the information cognitively and gives the speaker a good basis for determining whether the message was understood accurately, whether the listener comprehended only a portion of the intended message, or whether it was misunderstood in its entirety. The original speaker can then reply to the paraphrase (feedback) by indicating acceptance, adding what was omitted, or revising the statement and asking the active listener to try again. Only when the original speaker is fully satisfied that the listener has understood what was intended does the discussion proceed with agreement, disagreement, elaboration, change of topic, or whatever the active listener wants to say. The following dialogue will clarify the technique:

Ed: Requiring landowners to farm in such a way that topsoil is not lost is absolutely necessary if we are to protect the earth as a habitation for our descendants. (opinion)

Gail: If I understand you, you think we should require that farming practices prevent possible erosion of the topsoil, for such erosion destroys the earth for growing things. (paraphrase of Ed's opinion)

Ed: Right, Gail. (confirmation and acceptance of the paraphrase)

Another example:

Ann: If every college graduate were required to demonstrate some competence in using a computer, that might help right at graduation, but computers are changing so rapidly that grads would be no better off than if they had no such training in a few years unless they kept up-to-date or had to use a computer all along. (opinion)

Charles: Do I understand you correctly? Are you saying that a computer science course should *not* be required to get a degree? (attempted paraphrase of Ann's opinion)

Ann: No, just that it should be more than just how to use a computer. You ought to understand computers, and what they do and don't do. (rejects the paraphrase and attempts to clarify)

Charles: So you think there should be a requirement for a graduate to be able to explain what computers can and can't do as well as to be comfortable with a computer. (second attempt at paraphrasing Ann's opinion)

Ann: Yes, more than a course as such. (confirms paraphrase)

Charles: I agree with that idea, and think we should also have a requirement for ability to investigate, organize, and write a term paper. (his paraphrase confirmed, Charles now is free to add his opinion, on a new topic, to the discussion)

Every idea proposed in a discussion should be evaluated but only when you are sure you understand it to the satisfaction of the speaker. Active listeners confirm their understanding *before* they express their positive or negative evaluation. Only at that point is critical listening in order, where the listener may comment on whether the statement is pertinent to the previous theme of the discussion, whether there is sufficient evidence to support it, whether it reflects a prejudice or stereotype, etc. Productive listening during discussion enables accurate and fair evaluation of ideas and information.

Sometimes active listeners cannot hear adequately or are not confident of their understandings. If so, they will say so quickly, asking the speaker to repeat or clarify. Once understanding is established, active listeners openly agree, ask for more information, indicate skepticism, or express whatever is their honest reaction.

A side effect of active listening is a slowdown in the pace of interaction. If you are not used to listening actively, you may at first find yourself with nothing to say for a moment after the other finishes speaking. Keep practicing; soon you will find yourself making spontaneous responses instead of pre-planned remarks or irrelevant statements that sidetrack the discussion. Note the compatibility between the communicative model presented in figure 5.2 and the concept of active listening. Only overt feedback can provide the speaker with the responses needed, and confirming feedback is the best response of all. Positive feedback indicating that a message has been received can take the vocal form of an "um-hum," "gotcha," or "yeah," or such nonverbal gestures as head nodding, smiling, frowning, changing body angle, or hand gesturing. More expansive nonverbal cues usually indicate agreement, so loosen up when you listen and allow yourself to be spontaneous. Above all, do not pseudolisten by sending responsive signals when you are not really paying attention but are just trying to be polite and accepted. Pseudolistening is often more damaging to trust and cooperation than is argumentative listening, for the speaker at first thinks the responder understands and agrees, but later realizes the re-sponder's nonverbal and verbal responses cannot be trusted.

Becoming an active listener in group discussions takes practice, but the confirming climate you help create when you listen actively should increase cohesiveness and cooperation in your group.

Focused Listening

A common problem for many groups is the lack of functional memory for important ideas or issues that have been raised during discussion and agreed upon. During the excitement of exploring a new idea or argument, it is easy to forget vital information or reasoning accepted earlier. The skilled leader or group secretary probably has a written record of these, but only occasionally might the other participants be reminded of them. Remembering what the issue of the moment is, what has previously been discussed, and what has been decided earlier is the responsibility of each group member. **Focused listening** for such recall is an important skill for all participants.

Human memory is limited; we have a finite number of things we can re-member. We have a terrible time memorizing unrelated lists of single items, but we can more easily recall information grouped into sets of related items. Try to remember the following list of numbers: 4178365218. Now try again: (417) 836–5218. Grouping a string of digits into area code, exchange, and number simplifies the process. This is the key to focused listening.

Members of highly productive groups are able to maintain their perspec-tive on the discussion as a whole by focusing their listening on the *main points* of the discussion. They keep a notepad to record important information. They listen primarily for issues rather than specific facts and opinions. They organize the details—the specific facts and opinions—by issue. Thus, they are able to retain considerably more of the conversation. You will recall far more information if you keep a mental summary of the main issues and how each is settled than if you try to memorize specific but isolated facts. You can keep written track of the facts as you need them, organizing them by issue. Such listening will keep you on track and allow you to reorient a group when someone switches the topic before the group has reached a decision regarding the original issue. All too often, groups flit from topic to topic without achieving closure on any of them. The focused listener helps prevent this by being a process observer who points out the problem and teaches members how to listen well. The focused listener may also provide an internal summary, a brief review of what has transpired up to that point in the discussion. With members who are focused listeners, the group will benefit by being able to maintain a focus on its purpose as well as the content and progress of its discussion.

Summary

Human communication is a complex transactional process that involves the generation of symbolic signals and transformation of those signals as they are transmitted, received, and interpreted. The communicative transaction can break down at numerous places. To be an optimal discussant, you need to understand the communication process as it occurs at the intrapersonal and interpersonal levels during small group communication. Intense attention both to encoding and decoding is required if members of a small group are to achieve the similar perceptions they need to function smoothly. Productive discussants send positive, confirming messages to one another; they are active listeners who frequently check their understandings with paraphrases. They avoid the pitfalls of pseudolistening, silent arguing, premature replying, focusing on irrelevancies, sidetracking, listening defensively, and forcing meaning. They maintain their focus on issues and ideas of the discussion with mental reviews and notes.

Exercises

1. Discuss in small groups, then share your ideas with the class as a whole: "How and where in the small group system can interferences occur in the process of communication?"
2. Select a topic, preferably a controversial one, and practice active listening in a small group discussion. Remember, a discussant may not have the floor or add anything to the conversation until he or she paraphrases what the previous speaker means (ideas and feelings) to that speaker's complete satisfaction. If the paraphrase is not accepted, the discussant may try again until the speaker accepts the paraphrase. One member of the group should not participate but should keep an accurate count of the number of times paraphrases are accepted and rejected. Be sure to count every attempt to rephrase. Afterward, discuss the implications of listening, how to improve communication, and how you felt during this project.

3. Think of times when you have felt especially confirmed, and especially disconfirmed, in a conversation. Try to recall exactly what was said to you and why you felt as you did. What are the implications of your findings for small groups?

4. Prepare a chart for recording observations of listening behaviors and responses of members of a discussion group. This chart should have four columns headed as follows: active listening, premature replying, sidetracking, and forcing meaning. With several classmates, observe either a live discussion or a recording of one. As you observe, note each instance of these types of behaviors.

Now compare your observations with those of your fellow observers. What do you conclude about the listening-responding behavior of discussants? Were there apparent instances of pseudolistening, silent arguing, defensive listening, focusing on irrelevancies, or disconfirmation? What was the effect of the members' listening behaviors on the group outcomes?

Bibliography

Cathcart, Robert S., and Larry A. Samovar, eds. *Small Group Communication: A Reader,* 4th ed. Dubuque, Iowa: Wm. C. Brown Publishers, 1984, section 5.

Steil, Lyman K. and Larry Barker. *Effective Listening: Key to Your Success.* Reading, Mass.: Addison-Wesley, 1983.

Notes

1. Stephen W. King, "The Nature of Communication," in *Small Group Communication: A Reader,* 4th ed., eds. Robert S. Cathcart and Larry Samovar. (Dubuque, Iowa: Wm. C. Brown Publishers, 1984), 214–23.

2. Ibid., 222.

3. Evelyn R. Sieburg, "Dysfunctional Communication and Interpersonal Responsiveness in Small Groups," (Doctoral dissertation, University of Denver, 1969).

4. Amarjit Chopra, "Motivation in Task-Oriented Groups," *Journal of Nursing Administration* (1973): 55–60.

5. Fred Jablin, "Message-Response and 'Openness' in Superior-Subordinate Communication," in *Communication Yearbook II,* ed. Brent Ruben. (New Brunswick, N.J.: Transaction-International Communication Association, 1978), 293–309.

6. Larry L. Barker, *Listening Behavior* (Englewood Cliffs, N.J.: Prentice-Hall, 1971), 17.

7. David M. Berg, "A Descriptive Analysis of the Distribution and Duration of Themes Discussed by Task-Oriented Small Groups," *Speech Monographs* 34 (1967): 172–75.

8. Ernest G. and Nancy C. Bormann, *Effective Small Group Communication,* 3d ed. (Minneapolis: Burgess, 1980), 97.

9. Ralph G. Nichols and Leonard Stevens, "Listening to People," *Harvard Business Review* 35 (1957): 85–92.

10. Charles M. Kelley, "Empathic Listening," in *Small Group Communication: A Reader,* 4th ed., eds. Robert S. Cathcart and Larry A. Samovar. (Dubuque, Iowa: Wm. C. Brown Publishers, 1984), 296–303.

Chapter 6

The Language of Discussion

As a result of studying chapter 6 you should be able to:

1. Describe the nature and function of each of the three major components of a language.

2. Explain the concept *symbol* and why it is so important to understanding the process of small group communication.

3. Describe the nature and disruptive effects on discussions of bypassing, abstract and ambiguous language, and emotive words, and explain at least one way to prevent or correct each of these types of disruptions.

4. Express your ideas during a discussion so that your statements are organized, unambiguous, and relevant to preceding remarks.

5. Distinguish among the purposes of the six major types of questions raised during discussions.

6. Write minutes or summary reports of small group meetings that are accurate and easy to read.

7. Explain what "meanings are in people, not in words" means.

Key Terms

Abstract general, nonspecific; a word lacking a specific referent is said to be abstract.

Ambiguous any word that can reasonably be understood in two or more senses is ambiguous.

Bypassing misunderstanding that results from two persons not realizing they are referring to different things by the same words or have the same referent for different words.

Cliché a trite, stereotyped phrase or saying used to explain some event.

Code a set of specific symbols used in a language, such as sounds, syllables, and words of a spoken language used by some definable society or population.

Concrete words low-level abstractions referring to specific objects, experiences, relationships, etc.

Emotive words words that refer to specific emotions, connote more than they denote, and serve as triggers for recalling highly pleasant or unpleasant experiences.

High-level abstraction word, phrase, or statement commonly used to refer to a broad category of objects, relationships, concepts, etc.

Minutes written sequential report of every relevant item dealt with during a group meeting, including a record of all motions and decisions.

Question verbal request for a response; interrogational statement.

    Answerable one which can be answered by observation or interpretation of observation.

    Information-seeking request for a specific statement of fact.

    Limited request a specific brief answer; the potential answers are predetermined by the questioner.

    Open-ended imply a variety of possible answers and leave room for the respondent to elaborate and interpret the answer.

    Opinion-seeking request for judgment or opinion; may be for interpretation of a body of facts, value judgment, relative merits of proposed solution, or personal appraisal of any issue.

    Orientation-seeking solicits answer to help define context, direction, or goal during a discussion.

    Policy-seeking request for general position or plan of action.

    Procedure-seeking request for suggestion of procedure that the group can follow; appeal for structure or coordination.

    Relational seeks answer describing how members relate to each other, relative statuses, rights, and responsibilities, or a description of any socio-emotional dimension of the group.

Referent that to which a symbol refers; the object denoted by a word, sentence or statement.

Syntactic rules rules governing the appropriate usage and arrangements among code units of a language, such as the rules for constructing phrases and sentences.

People communicate ideas primarily through the use of language, the verbal rather than nonverbal component of communication. Although it is artificial to separate the verbal signals from the nonverbal signals, we do so for the sake of analyzing the contribution each makes to meaning. In reality, they operate together indivisibly. In this chapter we examine verbalization as a key component in small group communication; in the next chapter, we will focus on nonverbal signals.

When you observe a small group you are first likely to be aware of the spoken messages that flow from member to member. *Discussion* implies verbal messages—lots of words being exchanged. In this chapter, we present an overview of the nature of language, some things that can go wrong when we speak to each other, how sensitive and informed word choices and arrangements can facilitate group progress, how verbalization relates to group formation, and how written verbal messages can be used to enhance group output.

Language

Any language—Spanish, Russian, English—consists of a **code** or codes of symbols, rules about how and when to use the words in the code, and some assumptions about the nature of the world. We will look at how each of these components of language enters into the quality of a discussion.

The code, the set or sets of signals used in a language, is the basic building material of language. In spoken language the codes are the sets of sounds (phonemes) and words along with the patterns in which they are uttered. In the written version of the spoken language, we have the alphabet code and the code of all written words in the language. There are also the codes of punctuation marks. Each language has some code units unique to it (for instance, the English word for *woman* is different from the Spanish word) and may have many sub-languages or dialects. Each community of language users develops its own unique sub-code. For example, every corporation develops some unique words and usages that are signs of membership in the corporation, every family has some idiosyncratic uses of certain words, each craft or professional group has its own jargon, and so on. One of us had a group of young women in a speech class who referred to all men they didn't like as "Ernies." This special use of that name came about because once at a party they encountered a particularly obnoxious man named Ernie. Thereafter, that name took on a special meaning for them. One's membership in a continuing group is contingent upon learning and using the special language accepted by and used among members of the group. For example, use of the term *waiting room* instead of *green room* will mark you as an outsider or novice in any theatre group.

Each literate person has somewhat different codes or vocabularies for reading, writing, listening, and speaking. Most of us have a much larger reading code than we have for writing. Most of us also have a much more extensive vocabulary for writing than we do for speaking. Speaking allows little time to select and seek just the right word. We can interpret many words others may speak to us, even though we may rarely or never utter these words.

In addition to the codes themselves, languages have both formal and informal rules governing the use of these codes, many of which vary depending on the situation. We all have learned different codes for different functions, contexts, and relationships. For instance, none of us would write a love letter in the same code we would write a letter of application. We use a different code (language) when we meet in a church or synagogue from the one we use at a tailgate party in the parking lot at a football game. Physicians use a different code to explain a medical procedure to a patient from the code they use to discuss the procedure with their colleagues. We must learn the code shared by other group members if we are to be understood by them. We must use a code appropriate to the context and group, including the topic, or others may be annoyed and distracted from the purpose of the discussion.

The formal rules governing language use include syntactic and grammatical rules. **Syntactic rules** govern the arrangement of code units. In English one would not say "Out the lights put," but that arrangement of words would conform to the rules of some languages. Another rule of syntax indicates that modifying words should be adjacent to the words modified ("the red dress in the closet" rather than "the dress in the closet red"). We have extensive rules governing where to place verbs in sentences, uses of connectives, sentence length, and so on. If others understand us as intended, violation of syntax rules has little effect on group accomplishment, but such violations may lower one's credibility and status in a group of well-educated persons.

Finally, every language builds into its code and structure some assumptions about the nature of the world and human perception. For example, in English we speak as if the characteristics we perceive in some object are inherent in the object, are relatively unchangeable, and exist apart from our perception. Thus we might say, "The lizard is green," implying that the greenness is part of the lizard, rather than a function of how we perceive it through a unique pair of eyes and nervous system. However, to a person with blue-green colorblindness, *green* is a meaningless term just as it is to an animal lacking retinal cells that respond to different wave frequencies. If the lizard belongs to the chameleon family, the greenness may disappear when the background color changes. A more appropriate statement would be "Greenness is occurring as I perceive the lizard," or "To me the lizard looks green at this moment." Such statements are not only in accord with what we know about perception and the physical world, but also leave room for others to perceive and interpret differently.

Of all the characteristics of language, none is more important to understand and keep in mind than this: *all language is symbolic.* Words have no inherent meanings, but are used in conventional ways by a community of users to represent specific items and classes of experience. Signs, unlike symbols, are directly connected with whatever they represent. For example, a blush is a sign of stress, a track in the snow is a sign that a rabbit hopped past, and profuse sweating is a sign of an increase in temperature. However, with symbols (and words are symbols) this is not the case. *There is no meaning to a word apart from the person using and responding to it.* Different languages

Figure 6.1
Symbolically, he is a
*chien, hund, cane,
perro, hunt,* and *dog* or
Butch to his best
human friend.

use different words to refer to the same objects, further demonstrating the principle that meanings are not in words but in the users of the words. The object or experience is indicated by a symbol called the **referent** (the thing to which the word refers). In figure 6.1, the referent *dog* is symbolized in other languages by the words *chien, hund, cane, perro,* and *hunt.* Same referent, different symbol. The important thing here is that human communication is symbolic. For mutual understanding, two or more persons must refer to the same or similar objects, events, values, or ideas by the symbolic signals they use. Only if speakers and listeners have approximately the same referent for a word will they have perceptual similarity. Such a happy concurrence when using symbols to communicate cannot be taken for granted.

It is clear that speakers in a productive discussion must have the same or similar codes in order to be understood. However, even if discussants speak the same language, they may use the same word to refer to different things. This can be seen readily if we consider a word less concrete than *dog—love,* for example. When Mary says, "I love you" to John, she may mean that she wants to spend all her free time with him, thinks about him all the time, is willing to stop seeing other men, and wants to marry him. When John says,

Figure 6.2
One statement,
different referents.

"I love you" to Mary, he means he enjoys her company, thinks about her when he has free time, will call her first if he wants to do something, and fantasizes about all the other women he will have the chance to love before he finally settles down in the far distant future.

To illustrate further, in figure 6.2 Joe says, "Let's go get some food." Joe's reference is to a cream-filled cupcake and a soft drink from the nearest vending machine. Mary envisions alfalfa sprouts on whole wheat bread and assumes Joe is as health-food conscious as she. To Herbie, *food* means a five-course meal at a fine restaurant, and he wonders how Joe can stay so slim on such a substantial diet. Obviously, Joe's words had very different meanings to these three people.

By social agreement we communicate with symbols effectively only when we have similar referents for them. Imagine if the designated leader of your group asks you to keep a "detailed" list of what the group discussed. The leader means "a word for word account of the entire discussion" and you assume that a "broad description of major decisions" will suffice. Ineffective communication like this results in time wasted, hurt feelings, and mediocre output. It is important to remember that *neither of you is wrong*. Each of you has used the same symbol (word) to refer to something different, emphasizing the personal nature of communication—meanings are in people, not in words. Never forget that symbols have no inherent and certain meaning.

Disruptions from Language Choices

You have seen how easy it is for people, even those speaking the same language, to misunderstand each other. Fortunately, your understanding that symbols (including all words) have no absolute or certain referents can help you prevent a variety of misunderstandings and disruptions common in discussions. Be on guard for bypassing due to different word uses of speakers and listeners, misunderstandings and disruptions resulting from use of highly abstract or ambiguous language, and the potential impact of emotive words.

Bypassing

Two discussants **bypass** each other when they have different referents for the same word or phrase but think they have the same meanings, or when they think they disagree but really do not, because they use different words to indicate the same reference. Each hears the same words, but the images each creates are so different as to represent a serious misunderstanding. They are "talking past each other," as in the previous example of the designated leader; each means something different by *detailed*. For example, one of us once listened to a study group argue for half an hour (wasted time!) about whether or not humans have free will. Two factions formed, one lead by an atheist and the other by an avowed Methodist. After listening to a tape recording of their discussion and getting to specific cases, they realized they were actually in agreement! Each side had been using the term *free will* to refer to a different phenomenon. In fact, they all agreed that people have free will in the sense that they can make conscious choices among alternatives, but do not have free will in that much of what happens in life is beyond human control but is instead determined by the convergence of internal and external forces. In another example, a young nurse reported this: "I left a pan of water, soap, washcloth, and towel with a new patient, telling him it was time for his bed bath. When I returned in half an hour, I found him scrubbing his bed with the cloth, but personally unwashed." As a final example, a man whose car battery was too low to turn over the engine told a helpful motorist who had stopped that she would have to push him about thirty-five miles per hour for the engine to catch. You guessed it—she backed up and rammed into his rear bumper at thirty-five miles per hour, doing $300 worth of damage.[1] We both have watched members of many groups go on talking blithely as if they understood each other when any careful observer could tell that members had very different meanings for some key term. This usually results in conflict at some later date, especially if the misunderstanding is over some course of action to be taken by the group. Tempers flare, individuals go on the defensive, and time is wasted because of bypassing.

Bypassing results from two myths about language: Words have meanings, or right meanings, in and of themselves, and a message coded in words can have only one meaning. Even though we know these are false in light of how communication occurs, *we often act as if they were true.* We sometimes behave as if we thought anyone who doesn't understand what we mean when we utter words is somehow foolish, stubborn, or wrongheaded. In the example mentioned earlier depicting the use of the word *detailed,* if both you and the designated leader act as if the other's use of the word *detailed* is wrong, then the potential for hurt feelings is high, interpersonal conflict is likely to be the result, and the group will be hurt. Instead, remember that it is normal for people to use words differently and that effective communication occurs only if discussants use the same code and definitions; they must be in agreement on the referents for their words at any given time. Just as in poker we agree on the value of the various chip colors, so in small group communication we must have a shared understanding of the referents for the words we use. For optimal verbal communication, we must remember that a key term can be used differently by different group members and that people can refer to the same experience using different words. With these principles in mind, we can often determine what a speaker means from the context of the remark, what we know about the speaker's background, and nonverbal cues that accompany the remark. In addition, we can ask for clarification to make sure we understand key terms similarly. In the "detailed" example, you can prevent friction later by asking, "What do you mean by *detailed?* How much detail do you want me to go into?" Taking a bit of extra time earlier in the discussion will save you time in the long run.

Abstractness and Ambiguity

In discussions of ideas, many statements are necessarily **high-level abstractions,** lacking specific referents. Think of such terms as *justice, fairness, democratic, civil rights,* and so on. As we move away from terms referring to specific and unique items, the degree of abstractness and ambiguity increases as does the potential for misunderstanding. Consider the following set of terms, each of which is higher in level of abstraction and thus more vague than the ones preceding it:

Jantha Whitman, freshman at Booker College

Freshman students at Booker College

College students

Students

Women

Humans

Mammals

Living things

When the first term is used between persons who know Jantha, the picture in the speaker's head is likely to be similar to the picture in the listener's head. However, when we talk of *college students, women, or living things,* the pictures and feelings speakers and listeners experience will vary dramatically. Only terms that name specific and unique objects are likely to be free of any vagueness. For example, one discussant said: "Lecturing is a poor method of teaching." Another responded: "Oh, no it isn't." An argument ensued until a third discussant asked for some **concrete** examples (lower level abstractions). The speakers then were able to agree on specific instances of effective and ineffective lecturing, especially when some quantitative research data were introduced. The vagueness reduced, the group reached agreement on a less abstract statement: "Lecturing, if well organized, filled with concrete instances and done by a skilled speaker, can be an effective means of presenting factual information and theoretical concepts. It is usually less effective than discussion for changing attitudes or developing thinking skills."

Leathers found that high-level abstraction statements consistently disrupted subsequent discussion with the degree of disruption increasing as the statements became more highly abstract. His groups contained "plant" discussants who were trained to say abstract statements like "Don't you think this is a matter of historical dialectism?" After such a statement, most of the other discussants became confused and tense and some just withdrew from further participation.[2]

Several factors can cause **ambiguity.** It can result from phrases that could plausibly have two or more meanings to listeners. For example, one of our colleagues once wrote in a letter of recommendation: "You will indeed be fortunate if you can get him to work for you." The writer meant that the person being "recommended" was a lazy employee and "you'll be lucky if you can get him to do any work." However, the recipient of the letter likely took it to mean that the future employer of this job candidate would be fortunate indeed to have such a promising employee. In this case, the potential employer would be wise to call the writer for clarification.

Ambiguity can also result from a mixed message, one in which the words seem to imply one meaning but the vocal cues indicate something different. For example, the speaker might say, "Take as long as you like to think this through" while glancing at his watch. Such ambiguous messages are highly disruptive to a discussion.

Group members can prevent or at least mitigate the confusion, tension, and serious misunderstandings produced by ambiguous and highly abstract language. As a listener, when you realize that the speaker could have meant more than one thing, ask the speaker to clarify. Ask for specific examples or descriptions. A description or detailed explanation usually reduces or eliminates misunderstandings or uncertainty. Use active listening: paraphrase and ask the speaker to confirm or correct your understanding as reflected in the paraphrase. As a speaker, use concrete examples to illustrate what you mean and limit the possible interpretations of your own abstract statements. Choose terms you think others in the group would probably use to refer to what you have in mind. Use synonyms for key words, such as "detailed list, that is, a word for word summary of the proceedings" or "making the punishment fit the crime, like not demanding a jail sentence for a parking ticket." Whenever possible, use specific descriptions or measurements instead of comparative terms: "six feet, four inches" instead of "tall."

Another form of ambiguity and vagueness occurs when opinions are uttered in sentence fragments or in an evasive manner. It is quite common for spontaneous participants to utter sentence fragments; they mention a subject, but never finish making a point about it, at least not in words. Sometimes a nonverbal signal—a shrug, a face, a gesture—completes the utterance, but anyone not watching will miss the point; moreover, nonverbal signals are notoriously ambiguous. Incomplete sentences occur in any spontaneous group interaction. Fragments like the following can confuse listeners:

Uh, I'm thinking that we might—well, what is going on here anyway?

Maybe we should divide . . . there seem to be a lot of issues . . . a lot of confusing bits and pieces . . . will make for a poor solution.

You know what members of that sorority are like (followed by a roll of the eyes, smirking twist of the mouth and toss of the head).

All these statements could easily enough have been uttered directly and unambiguously, leaving little doubt in attentive listeners' minds what was intended:

I think we might improve our understanding of what made it possible for a mechanic to steal so many auto parts if we ask the head of the motor pool how inventories are kept and revised.

Maybe we should divide our discussion of what to do to improve the registration procedure into component topics of advising, enrolling in a course, departmental assignments of faculty to courses, sources of cheating on enrollment, and the drop-add procedure. Otherwise, we may get all these mixed up, overlook some problems, and have a long discussion characterized by unrelated bits and pieces of dialogue.

I think members of Lumba Dumba Sorority are vain and snobbish. They rarely speak to women in Gamma Raya Sorority, who may not come from such wealthy homes, but seem friendlier to me and have far better grade point averages.

Still another type of unnecessary abstractness that disrupts discussion comes from expressing opinions disguised as loaded or rhetorical questions. While the form of the utterance is a question, it functions to express a judgment. Such verbal constructions often leave the responder in a double-bind where any plausible reply can be attacked. The classic example is "When did you stop beating your wife?" instead of saying unambiguously "I think you were a wife beater." Even the common "Isn't this a nice day?" is an indirect way of saying "I think this is a nice day." "Who made you the boss?" is probably an evasive way of saying "You're not going to tell me what to do. We all have equal authority in this group." Rhetorical questions are not questions in intent; they are leading questions that suggest a particular answer. For example: "Wouldn't it be a good idea to brainstorm this question?" "Why don't we recommend that the school buy a bus to transport debate teams?" or "Don't you think prostitution should be legalized?" If you feel as if you have been backed into a corner with a question, chances are you have been the target of a loaded or rhetorical question. When you hear a question that does not appear to be honest, you can clarify or prevent confusion, and encourage the speaker to take responsibility for his or her opinions, by restating it as a declarative sentence: "You seem to think we should brainstorm this issue. I agree." "You are recommending that the school buy a bus for the debate team." "You seem to favor legalizing prostitution."

People use ambiguous language for a number of reasons. Occasionally a discussant will try to enhance personal status or conceal ignorance by using technical jargon not part of the code of the other members. The resulting "snow job" may intimidate other group members into accepting the jargon-user's opinions without challenging them for supporting evidence and reasoning. Thus, the intimidator does not have to answer probing questions about personal study of the issue, research findings, and assumptions on which the conclusion depends. By using technical jargon, the speaker has assumed a priestlike status, one that is hard to challenge. For instance, few people dare to question the testimony of physicians, psychiatrists, or college professors when they speak in technical codes during discussions. When someone uses such language in a small group discussion of laypeople, you can bet the speaker is trying to evade or cover up a lack of supporting evidence. Ask the person to explain in terms you are familiar with and insist that the *group* understand. Don't allow the "expert" to cow the group members into accepting his or her choice by using a smokescreen of ambiguous language.

Sometimes ambiguous language is used to stop objective evaluation of a proposal. If this is the intent, the speaker is likely to use a **cliché.** All clichés are highly abstract. Although they may be true in a general way, they never fit any two specific situations in exactly the same way, since each event or object is unique. If the intent is to stop a proposal to spend money for a cost accounting program that could control waste and inefficiency, a speaker might say, "Let's not throw more money at the problem. After all, a penny saved is a penny earned." All the steam goes out of the people proposing the idea of spending money now to save it in the long run, or they may be tempted to counter with the cliché "A stitch in time saves nine." Neither cliché is helpful because neither addresses the *specific* merits, or lack of them, of the particular proposal under review. Conventional wisdom is not always wise, and common sense may be based on superstition instead of evidence. Here are a few common "idea killers":

Nothing ventured, nothing gained.

Let's act now. Don't put off 'til tomorrow what you can do today.

No one does it that way anymore.

He won't change. You can't teach an old dog new tricks.

A watched pot never boils.

It can't be done. There's no way to get there from here.

That's a tail wagging the dog. We're too small for that idea.

What can you do when someone uses the trite high-level abstractions we call clichés? First, be on guard for such easy answers as proverbs. When you spot one, point it out as such and suggest that the group examine the specifics of the situation to see whether the cliché fits. Ask how the present problem might be different from others like it. Sometimes you can stop the negative impact by giving a contradictory cliché: "You can't teach an old dog new tricks" can be offset with "But you're never too old to learn. Now let's really evaluate. . . ."

Effective discussions occur when participants have common referents for words and are as clear as possible in expressing themselves. The kinds of abstract, ambiguous, and vague conversational habits reviewed here hurt rather than help group discussions and decision making. The more clearly you speak, and the more you can help fellow members say exactly what they intend, the better off your group will be.

Emotive Words

Emotive words are used mostly to evoke strong feelings; these connotative words have been associated with highly pleasant or unpleasant images and experiences in our culture. Their denotative impact on listeners is minimal compared to their blockbuster connotative impact. Such are the "fighting" or "trigger" words that evoke strong reactions—unthinking, instantaneous responses where the person reacts to the word as if it were the actual thing. For instance, among some people the word *feminist* conjures up an image of a man-hating, bra-burning female with no sense of humor. Powerful physiological reactions to words with highly negative connotations are normal, but they involve non-thinking responses. Some of the more common trigger words are racial and ethnic slurs, sexist terms, and other epithets. In all cases there are alternative denotative terms that are neutral or positive to most people. For example:

Negative Connotation	**Neutral or Positive Connotation**
Egghead	Intellectual
Broad	Woman
Manipulative	Persuasive
Jock	Athlete

When a discussant, or something he or she values, is called one of these negative terms, the response is usually defensive. Constructive, inquiring discussion ends. The group problem-solving process is disrupted as counter-attacks fly back and forth.

Discussants must be sensitive to current usage and to the feelings of other group members. For example, a white group member with no prejudicial intention may say "colored" and a black member may respond defensively. One discussant might say, "Nebraska has socialistic power generation and distribution," meaning that such facilities are owned by the public and managed by a voter-elected board. While technically *socialistic* is used appropriately to define a company owned by the social body (the citizens of Nebraska), some Nebraskans wouldn't take kindly to that adjective. *Publicly-owned* would have been equally descriptive and less loaded with negative connotations. The group may get sidetracked discussing the legitimacy of the description rather than its original topic. The goal is forgotten, harmony is lost, feelings are hurt, and members lose face. Even if the group gets reoriented, residual antagonism will hamper cooperation.

The use of sexist terms is a major problem for many groups. Terms that once were used interchangeably to refer to all people as well as to males specifically are now rejected as biased against women. For instance, the word *man* has been used in the past when the person referred to could be either male or female (patrolman, chairman, businessman, postman). Language is dynamic; it changes constantly to fit changing circumstances. What once was acceptable language is now considered inappropriate. Many people resent any word that implies a sex criterion for filling a role or performing a task that itself has no sex criterion attached. Probably the only jobs intrinsically sex typed are those of wet nurse and sperm donor. Using sexist language will disrupt many discussions. If you view women (or any other identifiable group) as inferior beings who should be "kept in their place," you are in for some serious reeducation. Consciously eliminating all sexually stereotyped terms from your speaking vocabulary is necessary if you are to avoid being disruptive in many discussions.

The worst form of stigmatizing is out-and-out namecalling. Adrenalin rises as we physiologically and psychologically prepare to fight when called by such names as *pig, chauvinist,* or *nigger.* Such behavior deflects attention from the issues before a group, reduces trust, elicits defensive reactions, and generally does *nothing* to promote effective group discussion.

What can you do to prevent, reduce, and alleviate stigmatizing? First, recognize that people have feelings about everything and these feelings are not to be rejected. When people or their beliefs are challenged, their concept of self is also challenged and must be defended. Next, monitor your own behavior; be aware that your feelings and evaluations are just that—YOUR feelings and opinions, not characteristics of some objective reality outside of yourself. Remember, the lizard looks green to me at this moment. Some labeling and stigmatizing occurs normally when people express how they feel about things. We can reduce it in ourselves by taking responsibility for our opinions, reminding ourselves and others that our judgments are our judgments: "*I* don't like . . ." or "It seems to *me* that. . . ," for example.

Finally, when you hear someone else express a trigger term, your leader can reduce the danger of direct and wasteful conflict or defensiveness by restating the stigmatic statement in unloaded form and inviting contrasting feelings or points of view. For example: "Joe has called the ACTION program phony and fascistic. That's one point of view. What are some others?" A statement like "Scientists who use defenseless animals for research are brutes" might be rephrased: "Helen believes that it is brutal to use animals in laboratory research. What do others believe on this issue?" Replacing the stigma term with a denotative one and obtaining expressions of different evaluations and feelings toward the denoted object allows the group to examine the idea objectively, in a mood of skeptical inquiry, basing conclusions on more adequate information than was previously available.

If members are reluctant to express a point of view contrary to the stigmatizer, the leader can remove the block to objectivity by playing the devil's advocate. The leader expresses a differing point of view, indicating that the group should consider it in order to weigh the proposal objectively from all points of view and on its own merits. For instance: "Joan has called public power socialistic. Let's consider another judgment of it that I've heard expressed by. . . ." or "Two political scientists say it helps citizens participate in the democratic process."

All of the foregoing points to the importance of trying to develop group norms against using stigma terms so that the group can make an objective examination of all evidence and points of view. A periodic, explicit examination of the values and norms implicit in the language we choose and the ways we express our feelings and beliefs can help a group plagued by such language barriers to effective communication.

Improving Communication by Organizing Remarks

In addition to choosing words with care, how you put them together makes a lot of difference in how others respond to what you say. Although fluency, the ability to speak smoothly and with ease, is not essential to being a valuable group member, clarity is. How you organize your remarks determines how easy it is for others to interpret your remarks as you intended. The following are some guidelines for organizing remarks:

The syntax (word arrangement) of your remarks should be conventional and clear.

For example, to say "Year last of all automobiles percent seventeen recalled from the past five years were" calls attention to the unusual syntax and away from the content. "Ate the rabbit" and "the rabbit ate" have the same words but the syntactic structure gives them different implications. Conventional sentences that are simple, direct, and clear facilitate mutual understandings. Clarity demands not only that we use symbols our listeners are likely to use, but it also demands that we arrange words by the syntactical rules of English. Thus we say, "Last year seventeen percent of all autos made in the past five years were recalled."

Speak concisely.

If listeners appear bored or restive, you may have talked too long. State your ideas as simply and briefly as possible. We all know participants who restate every point several times or who take two hundred words to say what could be said in twenty. This reduces the opportunity for others to speak and causes members to tune out the speaker. If others seem to restate your ideas more briefly than you uttered them, work toward a more concise style. For instance, the following statement is long and confusing: "Although I have no doubt about the possible efficacy of the operations of this proposal, there remain unresolved complications about it that might eventuate at some indeterminate point if untoward circumstances tending toward time slippages were to arise and signal-exchange operations were conducted." Restated, it becomes clear: "This plan would fail if someone received a late signal or was not prepared to act when he got the signal."

State one point at a time.

This is not an inviolable rule, but generally speaking you should not contribute more than one idea in a single speech. A several-point speech is definitely out—a group can discuss only one idea at a time. If you attempt to give all the data on an issue or present a series of points, the group won't be able to follow you and respond meaningfully. How would you respond to this? "Many persons are injured when bumpers fail. Furthermore, I think brakes need to be designed to prevent fading, and then there is the problem of ignition systems that stop the car when powerful radio signals hit them." One person might begin to reply about brakes, another about how ignition systems could be perfected, and another about a wreck that cost $500 because the bumper failed. The result is confusion! Unless you are setting up an initial agenda that will be discussed one point at a time, and you say so at the outset, then address one issue or idea at a time.

Relate your statements to preceding remarks.

A useful comment does not come at random, nor is it randomly expressed. Follow this general pattern: relate your contribution to what has already been said, state your idea, develop and support it with evidence, and connect it to the topic or phase of the problem being discussed. This format provides an answer to the three basic questions to be asked when evaluating any extended contribution: What is the point? How do you know? How does it matter at this time? For example: "Helen, you said many magazine articles have been cut out. I also found that every encyclopedia had articles removed from it. The librarian told me it costs about $1,000 per year to replace damaged encyclopedias. So we can see that a serious part of the problem is the loss of widely used reference materials."

Improving Communication by Asking Appropriate Questions

Every affirmative statement is an answer to some question, implicit or explicit. It has often been said that "Being educated means that you know how to ask the right questions, not that you have all the answers." The process of dialectic, a search for truth through discussion, is a search for the best possible answers to questions. Phrasing the questions themselves is an important part of this process. If you are to be a valuable group member, you need to know how to ask a variety of types of questions, where and when each is appropriate, and how to ask them so that they are answerable and suitable to the complexity of issues a group faces. We present now information about questions in general as well as specific kinds of questions.

Characteristics of Questions

There are two key characteristics of the way **questions** are formulated that are of special importance. Questions may be answerable or unanswerable and limited or open-ended. Weinberg noted that just because we put a question mark after a string of words does not mean we have asked an answerable question. If "answers" are given to an unanswerable question and we cannot choose among them on any objective basis, there is no way to tell which is the correct or best answer.[3] To illustrate, consider the following four questions:

1. What was the population of Omaha according to the 1986 census?
2. What is the population of China today?
3. How fast can a greyhound run?
4. Why did God punish the Martins by burning their house?

The first question is readily **answerable;** records will give a specific incontrovertible answer to what the report says. The second question is potentially answerable; a factual answer based on specific methods of census taking could provide an objective answer even though that answer may not be available now without extensive research. The third question is **ambiguous** because it contains variable terms. It can be answered only when specific conditions are stated naming the dog, the time, and the place. Thus, we make it answerable by asking, "How fast did Diamond Jack run in the third race at the Atokad Greyhound Race Track on July 3, 1973?" The fourth question, an unanswerable one, is meaningless because it refers to nonobjective concepts, unobservables. That question assumes some personal force called God took some direct, causative action. To answer it, what could we observe? Under what conditions? How? Such a "question" cannot be answered by any known means, so there is nothing to be gained by discussing it except confusion and conflict. You can help a group by pointing this out and suggesting that the question either be dropped as meaningless or rephrased in a meaningful way that provides for an observation-based answer: "What beliefs do each of us have about why the Martins' house may have burned?" Our beliefs at least can be stated and observed *as our beliefs.*

Questions can also be classified as limited or open-ended. **Limited questions** ask for a specific, brief answer. These questions are designed to gather information or to discover whether another agrees or disagrees with us. They do not encourage elaboration or different points of view. They imply that there can be only one or a very few possible responses. Once an answer has been given, there is no room for further response. For example: "How old are you?" "Did you like that movie?" "When must we submit our report?" or "Which side do you think is right, management or the union?" Be especially wary of questions that suggest a one- or two-valued orientation, like that last one. Although there are useful two-valued ways of classifying things, in most cases such thinking leads us to overlook matters of degree. Few things are either all good or all bad. To ask "Is this a beautiful painting?" implies that it either is all beautiful or all ugly. In group discussions it is more appropriate to phrase questions in terms of degree than in *either-or* terms.

Open-ended questions imply a wide variety of possible answers, encouraging elaboration and numerous points of view. They do not direct the respondents to any particular answer or prescribed set of answers. For example: "What did you like about that movie?" or "What are the relative merits of both the students' and the administration's points of view?"

Types of Questions

Questions can be categorized according to the function they attempt to serve. They may be concerned with orienting the group, procedure, relations among members, information, opinion, or policy. The first three types pertain to matters of group process; the latter three to the group's task.

Orientation-Seeking Questions

Early in the discussion of a problem or subject, a group must determine the purpose of the discussion, the area of freedom of the group, and what type of output it is to produce (e.g., understanding, findings, advice, a plan, some recommendation or thing). **Orientation-seeking questions,** asking for information and opinions about group goals, help provide direction if asked early, but may be useful at any time the group seems to have lost direction and purpose in its discussions. Consider the following examples:

What are the purposes of this meeting?

How many nominees are we to report for each position to be filled?

Should we be trying to reach an agreement on what is the best policy regarding capital punishment, or just understanding the arguments for various proposed policies?

Often a discussion can be improved by asking the second-order question "What question are we now discussing?" Getting someone to clarify the issue under discussion by stating it as a question often reveals that the group has gotten off the track or is wandering aimlessly among several issues. Most task group discussions are not supposed to be bull or rap sessions; the discussion has a purpose beyond conversation for its own sake. Whenever groups change topics, participants may lose sight of the goal. Many discussions ramble so badly that they look like a series of disorganized answers looking for questions. However, discussants bothered by aimless talk often do not point it out for fear of being labeled as heavy, all-work types. One way of avoiding this label when you sense that an initially purposeful discussion has degenerated into a bull session is to ask, "Where are we and what are we trying to accomplish by this discussion?" This may be all the group needs to jolt it into purposeful discussion again.

Procedure-Seeking Questions	Questions asking how to proceed as a group are vital for teamwork, though infrequently needed. The **procedure-seeking question** asks such things as how to coordinate activity of members, what techniques to use for organizing interaction, in what sequence to take up items for consideration, how to make a decision, how to outline a problem-solving procedure, or simply what to do next. Unless all members of a small group are following the same general procedure, chaos will result. Here are examples of procedure-seeking questions:

What is our agenda for this meeting?

How shall we organize this discussion?

Do you think we should use brainstorming to come up with alternatives?

How can we get our recommendations written up and reported to Vice
President Garfinkle?

Hirokawa found that effective problem-solving groups spent more time discussing and agreeing upon procedural matters than did ineffective groups.[4] When no procedure has been agreed upon or announced or if you do not understand what to do next or who is supposed to do what for the group, a question of procedure is appropriate to facilitate group productivity.

Relational Questions	**Relational questions** seek clarification regarding the interpersonal relationships among members, especially how well members are relating to each other as persons. They seek information about how members feel toward each other and toward the group, and what members want in their relationships with each other. Sometimes they may ask who is responsible for a particular task or type of task, such as keeping records. If a group member's behavior indicates annoyance, anger, boredom, frustration, or alienation from the rest of the group, a question about what the person is feeling might help to bring the tension out into the open. This permits the group to deal with it before a serious interpersonal clash occurs or the group loses a potentially valuable member. When you feel some negative affect toward the group, asking if others feel likewise may help the group correct a problem with its goal, procedures, or way of interacting. In a continuing group, it is almost always more productive to deal with budding tensions and interpersonal conflicts early, before they become serious, rather than to hope they will disappear. On the other hand, expressing a question that encourages members to voice positive feelings heightens the group's cohesiveness. The following examples of relational questions illustrate this concept:

Are we all acquainted with each other?

Is everyone comfortable with this seating arrangement?

How do we feel about working together on this task force?

Did anyone feel left out during our discussion this evening?

Joan, something seems to be bothering you. Mind sharing it with us?

Do you think we're showing enough respect for each other's ideas and opinions?

Is anyone else angry about anything that has been going on in this meeting?

Such questions about member relationships help reveal hidden agendas, resolve tensions, and help prevent struggles over status, power, and control from weakening or destroying a group.

Information-Seeking Questions

As was stated in chapter 4, these ask for specific statements of fact. They may refer to observations of something that has occurred, factual statements reported elsewhere, what some group member said earlier, or to the need for clarification of a statement. The **information-seeking question** implies an answer limited to a report, without interpretation or inference about that report. The accuracy of a factual statement is discussable, but the fact itself is not subject to discussion. Confusion often arises when a question seeking information is answered with a guess, hunch, theory, or pet belief. Examples of meaningful information-seeking questions illustrate the type:

What factors did the fire chief say contributed to the burning of the Martins' house? (To verify, ask him or someone who heard him.)

How did you do on the English test?

What did you say, Sally, was the number of abortions in University Hospital last year?

By "police" did you mean all law enforcement officers or only uniformed ones?

What does anybody know about the extent of violent crime in our city?

Opinion-Seeking Questions

As we also said in chapter 4, **opinion-seeking questions** ask for others' opinions, interpretations, or judgments about the meaning of a fact. What is sought by a questioner is not a description of events but what those events mean to the answerer. Examples of opinion-seeking questions can be found in any discussion:

How good a president was Harry S. Truman?

How many family-operated farms are there likely to be in the U.S. in 1995?

Is there a need for more interstate highways in the U.S.?

What might be the climactic effects of a nuclear war?

A value-seeking question is a type of opinion-seeking question, of which "How good a president was Harry S. Truman?" is an example. All value-seeking questions ask for an opinion on how good or bad something is.

Policy-Seeking Questions

These are questions which ask what *should* be done to solve a problem, considering all the information found and interpretations of it. When such **policy-seeking questions** are posed, answers acceptable to all members of a group can be found only after answers to relevant questions of information, interpretation, and value have been agreed upon. Examples of policy-seeking questions include:

Should a student be appointed to serve on the Communication Department's curriculum committee?

Should we require all majors to complete a course in rhetoric?

It is usually most productive for a group to consider questions of information-seeking, interpretation, value, and policy in that order. When conflict seems unresolvable among members of a group trying to answer a policy question, it is usually wise to raise questions of value by asking what criteria each member is applying to alternative solutions. It may also be necessary to ask information-seeking and opinion-seeking questions. The group may have jumped to the policy issue before it unearthed adequate information on the problem or before shared values had been expressed as goals and criteria. Backtracking may help solve the problem.

Verbal communication among group members is not all oral; members may address memoranda to each other, provide handouts to accompany oral reports of investigations or readings undertaken for the group, and present charts and other visual aids during meetings. We now examine the most important written messages that coordinate the work of a committee or task force—the official written records of its meetings.

Records of Meetings

Efficient work within a continuing task force or committee depends on accurate, complete written records of meetings. Such records serve many purposes:

Remind members of what was accomplished at a meeting so they do not repeat it at a subsequent gathering.

Provide a reminder to members who have agreed to undertake certain tasks for the group (e.g., investigations, purchases, physical arrangements).

Provide continuity in discussions from meeting to meeting when a group undertakes the solution to a complex problem requiring many deliberative meetings.

Confirm and standardize the recollections members have of what the group decided and what it accomplished.

Provide a legal record of attendance, decisions, and actions (a paper trail).

Bring members who had to miss a meeting up to date.

Keep other interested persons (representative of a parent organization, for example) informed about the group's progress.

Although learning groups rarely keep records of their meetings, problem-solving groups always should. Even a single-meeting *ad hoc* group will benefit from such a record. One of us belonged to a community theatre where the written record of an *ad hoc* personnel review committee provided evidence used in a lawsuit that supported the theatre's assertion that an employee was not fired arbitrarily. Without this written record, which included specific and continuing concerns discussed regarding the employee as well as verification that the board had spoken with the person, the theatre might have lost the case. Most committees of larger groups are required to keep records of their meetings as well as submit reports not only to all members of the committee but also to the parent organization and sometimes other interested groups. For example, at the university where we both work, the committees of the Faculty Senate write reports of each meeting which are distributed to all senate members as well as selected administrators.

Although classroom and other learning groups are typically not required to keep official records of meetings, it is generally a good idea for members of such groups to keep individual journals that can serve as historical records of the group's and the individual member's development. Both of us have required students in our small group communication classes to maintain such journals. After each meeting, students jot down what was discussed, who contributed, what roles members seemed to be enacting, which members appeared to be performing leadership functions, what conflicts occurred and how they were resolved, and so forth. These journals help members keep track of what happened, perceive patterns in the group interaction, and observe their own participation and how it evolved over the group's life. Thus, even unofficial records can serve a useful purpose.

The primary purpose of official written reports or **minutes** is to preserve a record of the important *content* of a discussion, including how decisions were made. In general, the name of the group, the time and place of meeting, the attendance (including absences), all agenda items discussed, major findings, decisions reached bearing on the group's procedures and task, assignments of members, actions to be taken at a later date, and signature of the writer comprise the written record. Committee minutes rarely say much about processes or communication, except to report that a decision had a clear majority or was unanimous. Just as the content of the discussion and decisions reached are the property of the group members, so is the report. It is usually unwise to report *who* suggested what solution or idea, or who presented what information. Sometimes this can be threatening to members and stifle creativity if participants fear the responses of some superior administrator in an organization (e.g., the academic vice-president in the case of a university committee, or the instructor in the case of a class committee). You should record all information, ideas, accepted criteria, decisions, and responsibilities for action—but only in the latter case report names, unless required by some parent organization or authority.

The format and amount of detail included in reports of small group meetings vary considerably, depending on the origins and nature of the group and circulation of the record. Some organizations have a standard format, others do not. Robert's manual on parliamentary procedure says only the following regarding committee minutes: ". . . a brief memorandum in the nature of minutes for the use of the committee."[5] Robert also says that in small committees the chair usually is the secretary, whereas in larger committees a separate secretary *may* be elected or appointed. Regardless, the chair of a formally appointed committee is responsible to see that written records are kept and that the group's reports to its parent organization are written and presented properly.

The written record of a task force or *ad hoc* committee may take the form of a summary report to the members, but a standing committee that considers more than one problem or broad topic per meeting should usually keep more formal minutes like those kept by a parliamentary body. Items should be numbered in the order in which they were taken up during the meeting. Discussion of problems leading to some action or recommendation can be organized around the problem-solving procedure actually followed during the discussion. Here is an example of minutes of a standing committee of a university graduate faculty.

Minutes of April 12, 1985 Meeting of Committee A

Committee A held a special meeting at 1:30 P.M. on Friday, April 12, 1985 in room 14 of the Jones Library.

Attendance: Walter Bradley, Marlynn Jones, George Smith, Barbara Trekheld, Michael Williams.

Absent: Jantha Calamus, Peter Shiuoka

1. The minutes of the April 4 meeting were approved as distributed.
2. Two nominations for membership in the graduate faculty were considered. A subcommittee of Bradley and Trekheld reported that their investigation indicated that Dr. Robert Jordon met all criteria for membership. It was moved that Professor Jordon be recommended to Dean Bryant for membership in the graduate faculty. The vote was unanimously in favor.

   The nomination of Professor Andrea Long was discussed; it was concluded that she met all criteria, and that the nomination had been processed properly. It was moved that Professor Long be recommended for appointment to the graduate faculty. The motion passed unanimously.
3. Encouragement of grant activity. Discussion next centered on the question of how to encourage more faculty members to submit proposals for funding grants. Several ideas were discussed. It was moved that we recommend to President Yardley that
   a. A policy be established to grant reduced teaching loads to all professorial faculty who submit two or more grant proposals in a semester
   b. Ten percent of all grant overhead be returned to the department that obtained the grant for use in any appropriate way.

   This motion was approved unanimously.

Sometimes the written record of meetings of a task force takes the form of a summary report of the discussions. Then, the group prepares a final report for its parent organization. What follows are two meeting reports of a project group from a small group communication class. Group members were preparing to present an instructional program to their classmates on "The Group Polarization Phenomenon." Their examples may help you prepare meeting reports that are concise, yet clear.

Report of Second Meeting of Polarization Instructional Group

Date of Meeting: October 22, 1983
Time and Place: 3:35 P.M. in our regular classroom, CBA 202
Attendance: Beverly Halliday, Bart Bonn, Hal Darling, Judy Hartlieb; Bill Miklas, absent.

Report of Previous Meeting

Judy distributed copies of the last meeting's record to the group members; it was approved.

Phone Numbers

Phone numbers of all members were exchanged.

Test Ideas

Hal read some ideas for test questions from a book he had borrowed from Professor Brilhart. The group discussed criteria for a test question and determined that a question that was "close to home" and applicable to the class members should be sought. The issue was to be considered further when the group next met.

The meeting was adjourned at 3:45 P.M. with plans to meet again on Tuesday, October 29, during class.

Report of Third Meeting of Polarization Instructional Group

Date of Meeting: October 29, 1983
Time and Place: 7:30–9:00 P.M. in Room 151C, Arts and Sciences Hall
Attendance: Beverly Halliday, Bart Bonn, Hal Darling, Bill Miklas, Judy Hartlieb

Report of Second Meeting

Judy distributed copies of the report of the second meeting to all members. It was approved. It was decided that Judy would be responsible for recording and distributing reports of each group meeting.

Goals

A suggested outline for problem solving presented by Bart was followed. This led to a discussion of group polarization and to determining the actions to be taken in solving the group's "problem."

The group goals were identified as (1) understanding group polarization, (2) conducting a presentation on group polarization for the class, and (3) each member being able to write a personal essay about the group experience.

Test Portion of Presentation

After some discussion of the type of test to be used in the presentation, it was decided that Hal would be responsible for trying to locate a book with sample tests that could be considered by the group at the next meeting. Hal will also have primary responsibility for this portion of the presentation and will see that copies of the test are produced and ready for the class. The other group members will individually brainstorm for test ideas, and further discussion of this test will take place during our class meeting of Tuesday, November 5.

Criteria for a test were discussed. It was concluded that the purpose of the test would be to demonstrate the phenomenon of group polarization at work in the small group. The test would be divided in such a way that each individual in the class would first take the test alone and then with a small group.

Leader and Role

The group determined that the leader would be responsible for developing agendas and outlines for future meetings and would serve as an overall controller and fill-in or backup person for other group members. Beverly was selected by unanimous vote to fill this role as primary group leader.

Structure of Presentation

A structure and time schedule for the presentation were decided upon:

5 minutes—Each member of the class will take the test individually

10 minutes—The class is divided into four groups, with four of our small group members serving as observers. Each group of classmates will decide how to answer the test.

5 minutes—One member of our group will present a short report on group polarization research to the class. At the same time, the four observers will be finishing their notes regarding what happened in their respective groups.

5 minutes—The four groups will each discuss what occurred in the group. The observer may start the discussion or serve as a guide/reference person, answering questions and offering insights into what happened relative to polarization within the group.

5 minutes—The class as a whole will have opportunity to share what they observed and experienced within their groups. The observers may again start the discussion and open the floor to any class member's contribution.

Additional Member Roles

Bart agreed to present the five-minute oral report on polarization to the class.

Bill will be responsible for arranging meeting places and will serve as a backup to any other member who might be absent. The meeting adjourned at approximately 9:00 P.M. Further planning will take place on Tuesday, November 5, during class time.

Such records as the previous examples help members recall from meeting to meeting what facts were presented, what assignments were accepted, what progress was made, and so on. Without such a written report, the group "reinvents the wheel" at each meeting, wasting hours from *not* keeping minutes. Moreover, such reports give the group a sense of accomplishment and closure in addition to helping foster cohesiveness.

Summary

Discussion of ideas occurs primarily through the use of verbal communication. Languages consist of codes of symbols, rules for arranging the code units, and assumptions about the world. Symbols have no inherent meaning; to understand each other, people must use the same codes and use symbols to refer to the very same or similar referents. Language can help people understand one another or it can lead to misunderstandings and disruptions of the group's progress. Disruptions include bypassing, where discussants do not realize that they are talking about the same thing using different words, or use the same words to refer to very different things without knowing it. Highly abstract and ambiguous language leads to confusion among members. Clichés frequently circumvent critical thinking and exploration of ideas. Emotive words, particularly those used to stigmatize, evoke defensive reactions and conflicts.

A group's progress is helped if members make concise and unambiguous remarks, relating them to prior remarks and group goals. Asking appropriate questions helps coordinate and clarify group talk. Questions function to seek orientation, seek procedural suggestions, clarify relationships, or seek information, opinion, or policy. Keeping records, such as minutes or summary reports, provides leadership to coordinate members' efforts.

Language is a major medium of effective discussion, but it does not stand alone. The nonverbal communication that accompanies language can clarify, obscure, or reinforce the verbal message. In chapter 7 we consider the nonverbal signals in small group communication.

Exercises

1. Listen to a recorded discussion or to a discussion among several classmates. Each time someone utters a cliché you recognize, write it down. Record your impression of any effect the cliché has on subsequent discussion. What did you discover? Share your findings with fellow observers.

2. Play the Question Dialogue Game. Carry on a dialogue with another student in which you make statements to each other only in the form of questions. Each should reply to the other's previous question with another question. Leading or rhetorical questions are permitted. For example, the dialogue might go as follows:

   A: So, how are you feeling today?
   B: Do you think I have some unusual feeling today?
   A: Don't you?
   B: What makes you ask?
   A: Does it matter why I ask?
   B: How many of your feelings would you like to share with me?

   The first to use the form of a declarative sentence instead of a question loses the round. What did you discover in playing this game?

3. Describe an instance of misunderstanding resulting from one of the following types of verbalization. Be specific in describing what was said and what happened in response.
   a. High level abstraction or ambiguity
   b. Sexist language
   c. Ethnic or racial epithet

4. Watch a videotape or movie of a group deliberation or discussion ("Twelve Angry Men" is excellent for this). As you listen, list each of the types of questions, and count the frequency of each type. Record each actual question, the response it elicited, and whether or not you think it was appropriate and why. Compare your results with others who observe the same discussion.

5. Following a meeting of a committee, task force, or project group of class members, each participant should write a report of the meeting. Circulate reports among members, compare them, and decide as a group the format and content of the most useful report for the group.

Bibliography

Condon, John C. *Semantics and Communication.* 3d ed. New York: Macmillan Company, 1985.

Gulley, Halbert E., and Dale G. Leathers. *Communication and Group Process: Techniques for Improving the Quality of Small Group Communication.* 3d ed. New York: Holt, Rinehart and Winston, Inc., 1977; especially parts 1 and 3.

Hayakawa, S. I. *Language and Thought in Action.* New York: Harcourt, Brace and Company, 1949.

Notes

1. William V. Haney, *Communication and Organizational Behavior,* 3d ed. (Homewood, Ill.: Richard D. Irwin, 1973), 246.
2. Dale G. Leathers, "Process Disruption and Measurement in Small Group Communication," *Quarterly Journal of Speech* 55 (1969): 288–98.
3. Harry L. Weinberg, *Levels of Knowing and Existence* (New York: Harper & Row, Publishers, 1959), 213–16.
4. Randy Y. Hirokawa, "A Comparative Analysis of Communication Patterns within Effective and Ineffective Decision-Making Groups," *Communication Monographs* 47 (1980): 312–21.
5. Henry M. Robert, *Robert's Rules of Order, Newly Revised* (Glenview, Ill.: Scott, Foresman and Company, 1981), 416.

Chapter 7

Nonverbal Signals in Small Group Communication

Study Objectives

As a result of studying chapter 7 you should be able to:

1. Describe three major characteristics of interpersonal nonverbal signals.

2. Explain each of the major functions nonverbal signals perform in the process of small group communication.

3. Name and give an example of eight types of nonverbal cues presented by discussants, and describe at least two types of contributions each makes to communication among group members.

4. Demonstrate increased sensitivity to the nonverbal signals you and your fellow group members send.

Key Terms

Gesture   an expressive motion of the entire body or some part of the body, often symbolic, which represents an idea or emphasizes feelings about an idea.

Kinesics   study of communication via movements.

Nonverbal signals   everything pertaining to communication except the words themselves; not relying on linguistic signals.

Paralanguage   nonverbal characteristics of voice and utterance, such as pitch and pitch changes, rate, tone of voice, fluency, pauses, force, and dialectical variation.

Proxemics   Study of human uses of space and territory when relating to other humans.

Regulators   gestures used to control who has the floor to speak.

Small group communication begins even before any member says a word. You form opinions about other group members as soon as you see them. One member may slink into the room, not looking at anyone, and take a seat in the far corner; you might think, "Better not count on that one to contribute much." Another, dressed in a dark suit, strides confidently to the head of the table and places on it a briefcase which takes up a substantial amount of space. "Arrogant," you think. Their clothes, looks, manner, where they sit, how much space they claim—all these, and other nonverbal signals, contribute to your judgments about fellow group members.

Nonverbal signals, which include everything *except* the words, are *vital* to the process of communication, but they cannot be measured with precision because their impact changes from group to group. Birdwhistell, an early pioneer in the study of body movement signals, believed that only about 35 percent of meaning is communicated verbally when people communicate face to face; the other 65 percent is evoked nonverbally.[1] Mehrabian, a psychologist concentrating on interpersonal communication, put the percentage of meaning derived from nonverbal cues as high as 93 percent.[2] He estimated that, on the average, 55 percent came from facial and 38 percent from vocal cues. The specific percentages are not important; rather, what is important is that you recognize how essential nonverbal cues are to us as we interpret what we think people mean. In chapter 6 we examined the nature and function of language in the communication process. Now, we turn our attention to the nonverbal signals of small group communication. Remember, in an actual communicative setting we do not split the two; they necessarily go hand in hand.

This is especially true when we are talking about human communication in small groups, where almost no communication is entirely verbal or entirely nonverbal. In chapter 5 human communication was defined as a receiver phenomenon, requiring the response of a person (or persons) to perceived signals, including the processes by which signals are created, disseminated, received, and responded to. Conscious human beings invariably interpret signals with words—words in their heads, called *thinking* or *self talk*. For instance, when you see a fellow group member make a face, you might think, "I wonder what's wrong," or "I guess she doesn't like that idea," or even "I wonder what he thought of just then to cause that face." Thus, you have reacted to nonverbal signals with verbal ones. Most interpersonal communication entails both verbal and nonverbal signals. To confirm this principle, try to discover instances where you engage in discussion without words being part of the process of any complete communicative transaction. You are likely to discover that you use words when attributing meaning to almost every signal coming from other group members. Similarly, nonverbal elements accompany the spoken word. When you make a statement, you are necessarily using *some* tone of voice, a nonverbal dimension of communication. You may also accompany the statement with a **gesture** or body movement of some kind. Thus, verbal and nonverbal dimensions are inseparable; we discuss them separately for the sake of convenience and clarity.

Nonverbal cues are the most important medium of exchange in establishing feelings and relationships among group members. Verbal signals are the primary ways by which we exchange information and ideas toward accomplishing our learning objectives or tasks. Nonverbal signals supplement the words we utter, providing clues to listeners about how to interpret the words. They regulate the flow of talk. In the rest of this chapter, we will first consider some basic propositions concerning nonverbal signals and responses to them in the small group setting, then we will discuss how the specific functions previously mentioned are performed by nonverbal signals such as appearance, eyes, movements, voice, space, touch, and uses of time.

Codes of nonverbal signals are culture bound. What follows is about mainstream American culture and *will not necessarily be valid* for persons from countries other than the United States or perhaps some subcultures within the United States. For instance, many members of the Omaha tribe would not look you in the eye during a small group discussion—to do so would show disrespect. A person from China might pause at length before answering a direct question, not out of uncertainty or deviousness but as a sign of respect. What is considered appropriate conversational distance varies widely from culture to culture. Even small groups develop nonverbal norms about things like appropriate distance, seating pattern, showing affection by touching, and so forth that vary according to the group. The moral is clear: be very cautious when interpreting nonverbal signals.

Characteristics of Nonverbal Communication

1. **You cannot stop sending nonverbal signals to other members of a small group.**
   This is often stated as "you cannot *not* communicate," at least in the sense of sending signals that others can potentially receive and interpret. We emit nonverbal signals continuously; we cannot stop them. Signals like body shape, posture, movements, eyes, clothing and accessories, and skin color are all signals to which others may respond, whether or not we so intend. One of us taught a small group seminar where one member, afraid that others would get to know her too well, decided she would not communicate. She refused to look at the other members, made few verbal contributions in the class and even turned her chair slightly aside so that others could not see her face. Of course she communicated—that she did not care about the other members and was "too good" for the rest of the group. This, however, was not the message she intended to send. Thus, while you may not be a verbal participant in the group's discussion, you cannot be physically present without affecting the mood, climate, cohesiveness, and interpersonal relationships of the group. There is no ducking out of the stream of communication when a group meets. Your question, therefore, becomes not "Will I communicate?" but "How?" The only way to stop nonverbal signals is to leave the group.

2. **By themselves, many nonverbal signals are highly ambiguous.**
   To prevent misunderstandings, nonverbal signals should be clarified by verbal explanations. For instance, a smile can signal feelings of friendship, agreement with a proposal, amusement, a private reverie, acknowledgement of another, gloating over someone's misfortune, feelings of superiority, or simple liking. A shake of the head from side to side might be interpreted as disagreement, whereas the head shaker might be feeling disbelief or amazement. Looking at one's watch might be interpreted as boredom, but it could also mean the person has to take medication on a fixed schedule or has another meeting in a few minutes.

3. **When nonverbal and verbal cues seem to contradict each other, a listener-perceiver will usually trust the nonverbal cues.**
   A fellow group member shouts, fists clenched and brows drawn tight, "NO, I'M NOT MAD!" Do you believe him? Marriage counselors are taught to look for these discrepancies, such as the wife who says, "I love my husband," while all the time she shakes her head to indicate "no." There is a good reason for the tendency to believe nonverbal elements when there is an inconsistency. Many nonverbal signals like muscular contractions and physiological conditions are produced automatically by certain emotional states or by a person's habitual outlook on life. These reactions are controlled not by the higher, thinking centers of the brain cortex but by primitive structures of the brain that we share with virtually all other mammals. These structures of the brain—hypothalamus, brain stem, pineal body, limbic system—control bodily processes, hormone output, and feelings. They are subject to little or no conscious control. Few of us can control whether we sweat, whether our blood pressure rises, tension levels in muscles of internal organs, dilation of our pupils, whether we blush, and so forth. Only part of the time in a group meeting are we fully aware of what our feet are doing, our bodily angles, or the set of our head. Few of us exercise conscious control over the tonal quality of the voice, rate of speech, or modulations of pitch. In short, while we largely control the words we utter, we have markedly less control over our nonverbal signals. Thus, the nonverbal is relatively spontaneous and easier to trust than the more easily manipulated stream of words.

When conflict arises, we sense threat through nonverbal signals not in harmony with the words they accompany. Say you love me in flat tones, and I won't believe you. Say to the committee that you want to hear what others think while you proceed to look away and drum the table with a forefinger, and no one will believe you. Tell us how trusting you are while your hand half covers your mouth, and we will be suspicious.

Just as nonverbal cues can be inconsistent with verbal signals, nonverbal signals are sometimes inconsistent with each other. Here, the pattern of nonverbal behavior is more important than any single nonverbal cue. If we catch

"I want it this size."
Nonverbal signals
supplement the verbal
ones.

an incongruity, we become guarded in interpreting nonverbal signals, especially since such mixed sets sometimes result from attempts to conceal or deceive. Think of the group member who looks at you with what appears to be rapt attention, leaning forward, nodding at what you are saying, and stifling a yawn while sneaking a peek at the clock. What are you to make of that? Sincerity, honesty, and total personal integrity as a group member is the best way to prevent sending mixed messages that produce confusion. You may be a consummate manipulator, but as Lincoln said, "You can't fool all of the people all of the time." Our nonverbal behaviors betray us, even as we think we are successfully covering our true thoughts and feelings.

Nonverbal signals may also be mixed as a result of the sender's internal confusion or uncertainty. If you are confused or puzzled as a result of mixed messages you are receiving from another group member, it pays to *say* so, thereby helping the other person clarify his or her intent. In addition, if you as speaker are confused, you will help your fellow group members interpret your remarks by honestly revealing your confusion. Thus, you can avoid being perceived as deceptive or saying one thing but meaning another.

Functions of Nonverbal Signals in Small Group Communication

Your awareness of the functions of nonverbal signals will enable you to respond appropriately to others and make your own signals more clear to them. Nonverbal signals serve six major functions during group interaction:

1. **Supplementing the verbal.**
   Gestures may effectively repeat what is being said, as when a person points to item three on a chart and at the same time says, "Now look at the third item on our list of ideas." Such repetition reinforces the verbal message. Other nonverbal messages complement or elaborate what is said. For instance, a discussant might shake his head from side to side

while saying, "I cannot accept that suggestion. I consider it immoral," in a voice louder and more strained than usual. Or, a member holds up two fingers and says, "There are two things in support of your suggestion."

Some nonverbal signals give emphasis or accent the verbal message. A nod of the head, increased force on a particular word or phrase, and a shake of the finger can all indicate "this is an especially important idea I am now uttering." Thus by repeating, complementing, and emphasizing, nonverbal signals supplement verbal signals.

2. **Substituting for words.**

Many gestures are substitutes for words. Thumb and forefinger forming an "O" with the other three fingers held out stands for "okay;" so does the "thumbs up" signal. If the chair of a small group asks, "Do you want to vote on this?" and observes two people shaking their heads from side to side, no vote will be taken at that time. A finger movement can indicate to another discussant that you want him or her to lean closer to you. An obscene gesture can indicate disagreement or disgust. Because only one person can be speaking at a time in an orderly discussion, most communicating among members is done with nonverbal substitutes for words. Not to be aware of these, or not consciously to look for them, means you will miss potentially important information. One of us, for example, observed a normally reticent group member fold his arms in a closed gesture in response to a question of opinion addressed to the whole group. The chair, recognizing that the gesture could be interpreted in a variety of ways, asked the individual directly to share his opinion with the group. In fact, the member disagreed with an emerging group consensus for several excellent reasons the rest of the group had not considered; thus, his input improved the final proposal. This input would have been missed had the chair not been alert to nonverbal substitutions.

3. **Contradicting verbal messages.**

When something a person says doesn't ring true, often the nonverbal cues contradict the words uttered. Members of therapy and encounter groups are trained to watch for these, but they occur just as readily in learning and problem-solving discussions when someone is lying, conning, or has mixed feelings. For instance, a member might say, "Yes, I'll go along with that," but in such a way that you expect him or her to give no real support to the idea. When you observe nonverbal messages that seem to contradict what someone is saying, it usually pays to point out the contradiction and ask for clarification. For example, "You said you'd go along with the proposal, but something about the way you said it sounded as if you really don't like it very much. You didn't sound very enthusiastic. What do you feel?"

4. **Expressing emotions.**

As the previous example indicated, our feelings are communicated more often by nonverbal cues than by what we say. Try to say "I like you" in a variety of ways, and notice how each seems to indicate a very different feeling. Sitting close to another person can indicate more

Nonverbal signals
regulate interaction.

positive feelings for him or her than any words will convey. A smile or
nod can signal "I like your proposal." Negative feelings are
communicated nonverbally as well. Starkweather, for instance, reported
that some vocal aspects of anxiety were immediately detectable.[3] Davitz
and Davitz were able to associate particular voice characteristics with
both passive and active feelings.[4] Vocal qualities, posture, and facial
expression can all communicate feelings.

5. **Regulating interaction.**
Certain nonverbal messages control or direct the flow of interaction
among group members. A designated discussion leader may use nods of
the head, eye contact, and hand movements to indicate who should
speak next. Favorable nods encourage a speaker to continue, whereas a
lack of overt response or looking away may signal "shut up." People
show they want to speak by leaning forward, raising a hand or finger,
opening the mouth, and possibly uttering a nonword sound like "uh."
Hand signals may be used to speed up a dawdling speaker or slow
someone who is rushing. Many of these regulatory cues are visual. A
group that one of us observed had a blind member who could not see
the visual regulatory cues. Other members began to be upset at the
arrogant and self-centered behavior they perceived when the blind
member seemed to be talking out of turn or cutting other members
short. A discussion about regulatory cues helped the group learn the
extent to which we depend on sight to interpret them. It increased
members' sensitivity to the communicative problems some handicapped
people experience, and enabled the group to work smoothly toward its
goal.

6. **Indicating status relationships.**

We have already discussed how sitting at the end of the table indicates leadership or desire for high influence in the group. A feeling of relative superiority is often indicated by staking out a larger than average amount of territory at a table (briefcase, books, coffee cup, etc.), suddenly getting very close to another, a penetrating stare, loud voice, and a patronizing pat or other touch.[5] Relatively high status persons tend to have more relaxed posture than lower status group members. On the other hand, uncrossing arms and legs, unbuttoning a coat, and a general relaxation of the body often signals openness and a feeling of equality.[6] Body orientation, the angle at which a participant's shoulders and legs are turned in relation to the group as a whole or another person, indicate how much one feels a part of the group and often that one is more committed to a subgroup than to the group as a whole.[7] The example given earlier of the student who turned her back on the rest of the group illustrates the relatively little influence she had on other members.

Types of Nonverbal Signals

Although we usually respond to a pattern of simultaneous nonverbal signals rather than to a single cue, we need to be aware of the types of cues in order to avoid overlooking some of them. Those listed below play an especially important role in communication among members of small groups.

Physical Appearance

Members of a new group react to each other's appearance long before they begin to judge each other's knowledge, reasoning, leadership, commitment, and other verbal skills. Information about one's sex, race, physique, and height cannot be concealed easily. Nonverbal signals can reveal clues to occupation, self-concept, and attitudes toward others. Financial condition, status in the community, educational background, personal tastes, and how friendly one may be are traits typically inferred from what we can see. The judgments may or may not be correct, and may change later, but they are formed initially from nonverbal signals that cannot be concealed.

Cultural factors influence us in our interpretations. For instance, height and physique are major characteristics to which we react, and we have a clear picture of the ideal height and body build. Americans tend to be prejudiced against endomorphs (heavy bodies) who are perceived as lazy, stupid, sloppy, and undependable, but as jolly and easy to get along with. Ectomorphs (tall and skinny) are seen as frail, studious, and intelligent. Mesomorphs (muscular types) are more likely than the others to be perceived as leaders. Height is particularly important; the taller a person is, the more likely he or she is literally to be looked up to as a leader; short people will have to try harder to be seen as potential leaders in a group.[8] We often are not aware we have these prejudices, so it is especially important that we teach ourselves to react to what a person *does* rather than to physical appearances.

Dress influences initial judgments of others, as do hair style and items of adornment. John Malloy has made a systematic study of the influence of dress and reported these findings in his daily newspaper column, "Dress for Success," and his books. Jeans, a T-shirt, and an earring would surely reduce one's chances of being accepted into a task force of managers from a bank. On the other hand, formal dress would be strange at Apple Computer. Inappropriate dress may result in hostility or aggression.[9] A group one of us belonged to included a young woman with a punk hairstyle that was long on one side, nearly shaved on the other, with an orange streak down the middle. "Bimbo," we concluded; we were wrong. The young woman turned out to be one of the most perceptive, hard-working, and reliable members of the group. Looks can deceive; interpret such nonverbal signals cautiously.

Space and Seating

Much has been reported from studies of how we use personal space and territory in communicating, **proxemics.** We signal our need to be included by how we orient our bodies to the group. A person who sits close to other members, directly in the circle in a flexible seating space, close to a circular table, or at a central point on a square or rectangular table, signals a greater sense of belonging or need to belong than a member who sits outside the circumference, pushed back from the table, or at a corner. Sitting within range of touch indicates that we feel intimately or personally involved, whereas sitting from just outside touch distance to several feet away signals a more formal, businesslike relationship.[10] Patterson reported that groups making collective decisions sat closer together than when the same persons were making individual judgments.[11] What is a comfortable distance varies from one individual to another. Females tend to sit closer than males and tolerate crowding better. People of the same age and the same social status sit closer than people of different ages and statuses. One of us has a friend who grew up in Alabama; accustomed to touching others and sitting close, she realized that co-workers and fellow group members in the midwest were giving her signs that they were uncomfortable with her sense of appropriate distance. They discussed these subcultural differences, had a laugh about them, and she made a point of being more sensitive to their feelings.

The better people are acquainted, the closer they tend to sit. Thus, members of a long-standing group characterized by high interpersonal trust would be comfortable sitting close together in a small room, but people just beginning to form into a group would need more space. Even so, humans are highly adaptable, so when a room or other constraints violate our preferred distances from others, we adjust, at least for a short time. If crowded for too long, though, people sweat, grow tense, display more signs of distress, and act defensive. Group leaders should watch for signs of discomfort from either too much or too little space and make adjustments by rearranging the room, taking a short break, or finding a more comfortable room for subsequent meetings.

Once a group has formed, members appear to internalize what seems to be the most comfortable amount of space between them and to develop a space norm. Burgoon et al. found, for instance, that if low-status group members

Figure 7.1
Typical spacing
between designated
leader and other
members of a small
task group.

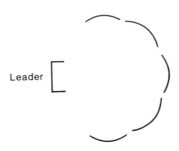

Leader

violate the group's norm regarding space, they suffer from reduced persuasiveness, sociability, and attractiveness in the eyes of other members. In contrast, high-status members enhanced their status by moving either closer or farther away than the group norm, especially if they moved away.[12] Thus, it seems advisable for you to follow group norms rather than violate them. If you have achieved a high level of influence, you may increase this even more by sitting slightly apart from other members.

Leadership emergence in a group is related to space. Dominant people and designated leaders usually choose central positions in the group, such as at the head of a rectangular table or across from as many others as possible. Other members frequently will avoid sitting next to a designated leader (e.g., chair of a committee, program coordinator, work group manager), so the circle looks like the diagram in figure 7.1.[13] This reinforces the leader's position and allows the leader as comprehensive a view of the group as possible. The leader is then able to make appropriate interventions for coordination and control.

People sitting across from each other speak directly to and in response to each other more than people sitting side by side.[14] However, when the group has a dominating leader, "side bar" conversations tend to break out with persons seated beside each other. Thus, we can conclude that conversation normally flows across the circle, and leaders sit where they can maintain eye contact with as many others as possible.

Eye Signals

Eye movements can signal disgust, dislike, superiority, or inferiority as well as liking; they are important nonverbal cues. For most people, establishing eye contact is preliminary to conversing with another. Americans use eye contact to seek feedback, when they want to be spoken to and when they want to participate more actively.[15] Burgoon reported that students given free choice of seating arrangements in small classes chose to sit in a circular or U-shaped arrangement so they could maintain eye contact with as many other persons as possible.[16] Although a stare may indicate competitiveness, in a cooperative group it shows friendship and cohesiveness.[17] As previously mentioned, eye contact is used to regulate the flow of conversation. One of us advised a student organization whose executive committee meetings were characterized by side bar conversations, repetition, and general disorganization. The committee habitually held its meetings using only one side of a long table, with the president in the center of the side. Only members directly next to each other could make eye contact. Members were advised to use a circular or U-shaped pattern for their meetings instead. After just one meeting, members reported a substantial improvement, and the president reported feeling much more organized and in control. This improvement occurred because the group now had eye contact among all members.

Facial Expression

Facial expressions indicate feelings and moods. Without a word being spoken, you can perceive anger, support, agreement, disagreement, and other sentiments. Eckman, Ellsworth, and Friesen found that at least six types of emotion could be detected accurately from facial expressions.[18] Some people change facial expression very little; they are said to have poker faces. They tend to be trusted less than persons whose expressive faces signal their feelings more openly. But even poker-faced people leak their feelings by physiological changes they can't readily control, such as sweating and blushing.[19] If group members show few facial expressions, watch for other revealing physiological signs.

Movements

The science of how we communicate by movement is called **kinesics.** We reveal our feelings by bodily movements and gestures. We show tension by shifting around in a chair, drumming fingers, swinging a foot or twitching an eye. Such behavior may signal frustration, impatience with the group's progress, or annoyance. Alert group members will attempt to track down the source of tension by pointing out the kinesic signs and asking what is producing them.

According to Scheflen, how open to and accepting of others a group member feels is indicated by body orientation.[20] Members turn directly to those they like and away from those they do not like. Leaning toward others indicates inclusiveness, a mutual sense of belonging, whereas leaning away signals a sense of rejection. Members who sit at angles tangential to the rest of the group may not feel included nor want to belong.

When members are "tuned in" to each other they tend to imitate each other's posture and movements. This behavior is called postural echoes, body synchrony, or body congruence. Scheflen observed many instances of parallel arm positions, self-touching behavior, and leg positions indicating congruity.[21] Several studies found that people are more likely to imitate the movements and gestures of people with high status and power than of low status group members.[22] In short, by noting whose behavior seems to be mimicked by others we can infer who has the referent power and what coalitions are being formed.

Some work groups are highly dependent on body movements and gestures to coordinate their efforts: work crews at some distance from each other, athletic teams, troupes of dancers, actors in a play. Carpenters and concrete workers often watch each other to coordinate their moves. Notice how members of a basketball team work together using hand and finger signals to synchronize their plays. In most cases, these nonverbal gestures substitute for words.

In discussion groups, control of the floor for talking is done largely by body movements and eye contact, collectively called **regulators.** Speakers often signal that they are finished speaking by relaxing and stopping hand gestures.[23] Scheflen reported that a speaker who is concluding a point or argument generally changes head and eye position and makes a noticeable postural shift.[24] A listener can bid for the floor by leaning forward, waving a hand and opening the mouth simultaneously. In a small group, regulation of who talks and for how long is done largely with movements.

Vocal Cues

Vocal cues, or **paralanguage,** are any characteristics of voice and utterance other than the words themselves. Included are variables such as pitch, rate, fluency, dialectical variations, force, tonal quality, and pauses. Extensive research since the 1930s indicates that listeners tend to agree on the characteristics they ascribe to speakers based on these vocal cues.[25] Included are attitudes and interests, personality traits, adjustment, ethnic group, education, anxiety, and other emotional states.[26] Tone of voice is an excellent indicator of a person's self-concept and mood. How we react to statements such as "I agree" or "okay" depends much more on the pitch patterns and tone of voice than on the words themselves. Anxiety is indicated by nonfluencies, such as interjections, repetitions, hesitations, sentence correction, and even stuttering.

Misunderstanding of irony and sarcasm occurs if some group members are insensitive to the importance of vocal cues that can indicate that the words should be taken *opposite* to what they seem to mean. Children generally do not understand sarcasm, and even one-third of high school seniors took sarcastic statements literally.[27] Sensitive discussants listen actively for evidence of sarcasm as well as for signals of strong feeling, such as loudness, high pitch, a metallic tone, and fast speech. People who speak quietly in a low key have little persuasive impact. They don't seem to have much personal involvement in what they are saying. However, members whose vocal qualities change too extensively may be seen as irrational, not to be trusted as leaders or sources of ideas. Taylor found, however, that excessive vocal stress was judged more credible than a monotonous vocal pattern.[28]

Nonverbal vocal cues serve as responses, too. Called the backchannel, nonverbal vocalizations, such as "Mm-hmmm," "uh-huh," "mmmmmmm," and other nonverbal sounds indicate signs of interest and active listening. Anderson claims that white Americans do not give such backchannel responses as frequently as blacks, Hispanics, and people of southern European origins.[29] This can lead to friction if members who use the backchannel frequently think those who do not are not really attuned and listening well, while the less active backchannel responders perceive their fellow members as being rude for interrupting so often!

In sum, vocal cues signal how to interpret many ambiguous statements. They reflect positive and negative feelings. They serve as a major channel for feedback when it is not possible to utter discursive sentences by letting the speaker know that the listeners are interested, impatient, seek the floor, agree, or disagree.

Time Cues

Few of us think of time as a nonverbal dimension of communication, but different cultures and subcultures have widely differing conceptions of time that may affect a group's ability to coordinate goal-oriented efforts. Most Americans think of time as a commodity to be spent or saved. People in Western cultures tend to regulate their time by the clock, while people in many other cultures act according to inner biological needs or feelings. For instance, native Americans who live primarily on reservations structure their group activities by events occurring naturally (e.g., sunset, sunrise, the full moon, etc.); in many Third World countries clocks are unknown. In some places work stops when it rains or when the sun is at a certain position in the sky. This makes interaction between these cultures and clock-organized western European and American culture difficult. Even subcultures within the dominant western culture may treat time differently, such as when rural and urban people try to coordinate efforts for cooperative activity. Rural people are more accustomed to a slower pace, more time to chat, and a sense of "we'll get to it when we're ready."

In the fast-paced culture of the American business world, being considerate of fellow group members' time is important; Americans usually will allow a five-minute leeway before they expect an apology.[30] People who come late to meetings (unless due to absolutely unavoidable circumstances) are judged to be inconsiderate, undisciplined, and selfish. Likewise, it is considered improper to leave a meeting before the announced ending time, unless some prior arrangement or explanation has been made. Forcing others to keep to your time schedule is the prerogative of high status individuals.[31] By coming late or leaving early, you are implying that your time is more important than the other group members; this is inappropriate and arrogant in a group of peers. In the long run, you will be perceived as unreliable and will lose influence.

Time also is a commodity within the group's interaction. People can abuse this commodity by talking too much or too little to gain any status. Harper, Weins, and Matarazzo found that persons who talked somewhat above an average percentage of the time for a group were viewed most favorably on leadership characteristics. Those who talked about an average amount were the most liked. Extremely talkative members were regarded as rude and selfish, members the group could do without.[32] Derber refers to this phenomenon of excessive talking as "conversational narcissism."[33]

Pacing a meeting so that all agenda items receive some attention and decisions are made when required is a valuable clock watching service. The leader who is sensitive to this helps curb the narcissistic tendencies of members who shift the topic so they can exploit it for personal attention. A reminder that there are a certain number of minutes left for the meeting and two more items that must be settled will often curb unnecessary reiterating of what others have already said clearly, get a high proportion of relevant remarks, reduce attention-seeking subject changes, and lead to closure on an issue.

Touch

Touch is an important nonverbal dimension in interpersonal communication. It is vital to group maintenance in most primary groups and athletic teams, although it may be nonexistent in many work groups, committees, and activity groups. The kind of touching people expect and enjoy depends on their acculturation and the type of relationship they share with others. For instance, touch between strangers, other than a handshake, is threatening.

Touch among group members can strengthen cohesiveness and teamwork. Families join hands to say grace before a meal; football players pile hands on in a huddle or slap and hug each other. The type of touch, as well as the setting, determines the reaction. Pats are usually perceived as signs of affection and inclusion. Strokes generally are perceived as sensual, inappropriate in a small group meeting. A firm grip on an arm or about the shoulders is usually a control gesture, interpreted as a one-up maneuver; among a group of equals, this will be resented and may provoke conflict. A gentle touch may be a means of getting someone to hold back and not overstate an issue. Many a group member has been restrained from saying some hostile and possibly vicious things by a gentle touch on the arm during a heated argument. We have both experienced this.

As with other nonverbal cues, people vary widely in the extent to which they accept and give touches. It is crucial that you touch others in a group only when you sense they are accepting both of you and of touch. Andersen and Leibowitz found that people range from those who enjoy touch to those who are touch avoiders, reacting *very* negatively to being touched.[34] Have you placed what you thought was a friendly hand on a fellow group member's shoulder at a meeting and been surprised to feel the member flinch, clearly disliking the touch? Although touching can strengthen bonds, you must respect the rights of those who prefer not to be touched, and never touch unless it is comfortable for you. A forced touch is detectable and seems phony or manipulative.

On the other hand, it is appropriate to give a gentle pat as a sign of solidarity to those who like being touched, even in work-related committee and task force meetings. However, jabbing, squeezing, or restraining another will be resented. Inept touches increase tension; our advice is to go easy on this channel of nonverbal communication, especially with work groups and committees. Less diligence is needed with primary groups, where a norm of physical warmth and affection can benefit all.

Summary

In this chapter we have seen how important nonverbal signals are in communicating emotions and establishing relationships among group members. Nonverbal signals supplement and clarify our verbal expressions, substituting for words and regulating the flow of talk and attention. We cannot stop sending nonverbal signals in the presence of others—they are continuous—so one cannot *not* communicate nonverbally with one's fellow group members. Verbal and nonverbal signals are inseparable in a discussion, but when they contradict each other, most perceivers will trust their interpretation of the nonverbal rather than verbal signals.

Many types of nonverbal signals can be perceived and interpreted by group members. Body type, appearance, height, and dress contribute substantially to our initial impressions of personality traits, social status, and relative power. Spatial relations and body angles also indicate relative power, and indicate how much a person feels included in and committed to a group. Seating arrangements influence who talks to and responds to whom. Distances among members reflect norms, position in the group and personal liking. Eye contact signals both inclusion and control. Facial expressions reveal feelings toward specific members and the group as a whole. Body movements, including gestures, are used extensively, along with the eyes, to control turn-taking and to supplement statements. Personality characteristics and moods are interpreted from vocal cues as well as how serious or sarcastic a speaker may be. Nonverbal voice signals, along with facial expressions and gestures, are used extensively in backchanneling to show interest and support. Vocal cues often clarify otherwise ambiguous words.

Americans often regulate their lives by the clock, the time dimension of nonverbal behavior. How we time our behavior in relation to other group members indicates our relative regard for them. Differences in time orientations due to varying cultural practices can lead to severe misunderstandings and mistrust among members with different practices. Pacing work by the clock is often necessary in task groups. Touch, though infrequent among members of most work groups, can be a means of enhancing solidarity or of controlling the actions of those being touched. In primary groups, touch is vital for expressing liking and approval; caution is urged regarding the use of touch in work groups. Touch must always be appropriate and adapted to the preferences and needs of others. At the most basic levels of human grouping, nonverbal signals are integral to the coordinating process of communication.

Now that we have examined the process by which group life goes on—communication—we will turn our attention in chapter 8 to how a small group develops. In some ways, a group's movement toward maturity is analogous to an infant's development through childhood to adulthood.

Exercises

1. In a practice small group discussion session, all members should refrain from giving any bodily or vocal responses to comments of others (i.e., no head nods, leaning forward, hand gestures while another talks, "uh-huh" comments, facial expressions, etc.) for about ten minutes. Each person should make at least one major comment. Then, for the next ten minutes, everyone should react nonverbally (physically and vocally) as fully and completely as possible. Finally, talk about how *you* felt during each nonverbal response pattern and *what this shows* about group communication.

2. Watch a videotape of a small group meeting, but turn off the sound so the words cannot be heard. What do you think the members are talking about? What does each member's individual behavior seem to indicate? Watch the group again, this time with the sound, and see how accurate you were. Discuss what specific nonverbal behaviors contributed to your judgments.

3. Bring a variety of advertisements to class. Have each group member, privately, write down what message(s) the people in the ads seem to convey. Share the results with the group.

4. Secure a play script. Choose a scene at random, and practice changing the meaning of the scene by varying the vocal qualities: pitch, rate, expression, tonal quality, and so forth. Next, practice reading the scene several times, this time keeping the vocal qualities constant but changing the gestures, distances between characters, facial expressions, and so forth. What did you discover?

5. During a fishbowl discussion, any observer may call "freeze" at any time, at which point each discussant should remain motionless, even regarding eye direction. The observer who called "freeze" then asks each other observer to comment on what each discussant's posture, position in the group, eye direction and other nonverbal behavior indicates. Then, both observers and participants should discuss the implications of the observer's interpretations of nonverbal signals.

6. This is a test of sensitivity to nonverbal visual cues in small group discussion. Each of the three photographs on page 153 shows a small group engaged in discussion. Study each photo carefully, then discuss with four or five classmates your perceptions and responses to it. What do you judge each person to be thinking and feeling? What specific cues are you using to form your judgments? What function do the nonverbal cues seem to be serving?

Bibliography

Anderson, Peter A. "Nonverbal Communication in the Small Group." In *Small Group Communication: A Reader.* 4th ed., eds. Robert S. Cathcart and Larry A. Samovar. Dubuque Iowa: Wm. C. Brown Publishers, 1984, 258–75.

Burgoon, Judee K. "Spacial Relationships in Small Groups." In *Small Group Communication: A Reader.* 4th ed., eds. Robert S. Cathcart and Larry A. Samovar. Dubuque Iowa: Wm. C. Brown Publishers, 1984, 276–92.

Burgoon, Judee K., and Tom Saine. *The Unspoken Dialogue: An Introduction to Nonverbal Communication.* Boston: Houghton Mifflin Company, 1978.

Knapp, Mark. *Essentials of Non-verbal Communication.* New York: Holt, Rinehart and Winston, 1980.

Three different
moments of a small
group's life.

Notes

1. Ray L. Birdwhistell, Lecture at Nebraska Psychiatric Institute, Omaha, Nebraska: May 11, 1972.
2. Albert Mehrabian, *Nonverbal Communication* (Chicago: Aldine-Atherton, 1972), 101–8.
3. J. Starkweather, "Vocal Communication of Personality and Human Feelings," *Journal of Communication* 11 (1961): 63–72.
4. Joel R. Davitz and Lois J. Davitz, "Nonverbal Vocal Communication of Feeling," *Journal of Communication* 11 (1961): 81–86.
5. Erving Goffman, *Relations in Public* (New York: Harper & Row, Publishers, 1971), 32–48.
6. Gerald E. Nierenberg and H. H. Calero, *How to Read a Person Like a Book* (New York: Pocket Books, 1973), 46.
7. Stewart L. Tubbs, *A Systems Approach to Small Group Interaction* (Reading, Mass.: Addison-Wesley, 1978), 185.
8. J. Spiegel and P. Machotka, *Messages of the Body* (New York: The Free Press, 1974); J. B. Cortes and F. M. Gatti, "Physique and Propensity," in *With Words Unspoken,* eds. L. B. Rosenfeld and J. M. Civikly (New York: Holt, Rinehart and Winston, 1976), 50–56.
9. L. L. Barker et al., *Groups in Process: An Introduction to Small Group Communication* (Englewood Cliffs, N.J.: Prentice-Hall, 1979), 184.
10. Edward T. Hall, *The Silent Language* (Garden City, N.Y.: Doubleday, 1959).
11. M. L. Patterson, "The Role of Space in Social Interaction," in *Nonverbal Behavior and Communication,* eds. A. W. Siegman and S. Feldstein (Hillsdale, N.J.: Lawrence Erlbaum Associates, 1978), 277.
12. J. K. Burgoon, D. W. Stacks, and S. A. Burch, "The Role of Interpersonal Rewards and Violations of Distancing Expectations in Achieving Influence in Small Groups," *Communication* 11 (1982): 114–28.
13. R. F. Bales and A. P. Hare, "Seating Patterns and Small Group Interaction," *Sociometry* 26 (1963): 480–86; G. Hearn, "Leadership and the Spacial Factor in Small Groups," *Journal of Abnormal and Social Psychology* 54 (1957): 269–72.
14. B. Steinzor, "The Spatial Factor in Face to Face Discussion Groups," *Journal of Abnormal and Social Psychology* 45 (1950): 552–55.
15. J. McCroskey, C. Larson, and M. Knapp, *An Introduction to Interpersonal Communication* (Englewood Cliffs, N.J.: Prentice-Hall, 1971), 110–14.

16. J. K. Burgoon, "Spatial Relationships in Small Groups," in *Small Group Communication: A Reader,* 4th ed., eds. R. S. Cathcart and L. A. Samovar (Dubuque, Iowa: Wm. C. Brown Publishers, 1984), 285.
17. R. V. Exline, "Exploration in the Process of Person Perception: Visual Interaction in Relation to Competition, Sex and the Need for Affiliation," *Journal of Personality* 31 (1963): 1–20.
18. P. Eckman, P. Ellsworth, and W. V. Friesen, *Emotion in the Human Face: Guidelines for Research and an Integration of Findings* (New York: Pergamon Press, 1971).
19. R. W. Buck, R. E. Miller, and W. F. Caul, "Sex, Personality and Physiological Variables in the Communication of Affect via Facial Expression," *Journal of Personality and Social Psychology* 30 (1974): 587–96.
20. A. E. Scheflen, "Quasi-Courtship Behavior in Psychotherapy," *Psychiatry* 28 (1965): 245–56.
21. A. E. Scheflen, *Body Language and the Social Order: Communication as Behavioral Control* (Englewood Cliffs, N.J.: Prentice-Hall, 1972), 54–73.
22. J. K. Burgoon and T. Saine, *The Unknown Dialogue: An Introduction to Nonverbal Communication* (Boston: Houghton Mifflin Company, 1978).
23. S. Duncan, Jr., "Some Signals and Rules for Taking Speaking Turns in Conversations," *Journal of Personality and Social Psychology* 23 (1972): 283–92.
24. A. E. Scheflen, *Body Language and the Social Order: Communication as Behavioral Control* (Englewood Cliffs, N.J.: Prentice-Hall, 1972), 54–73.
25. N. D. Addington, "The Relationship of Selected Vocal Characteristics to Personality and Perception," *Speech Monographs* 35 (1968): 492; Ernest Kramer, "Judgment of Personal Characteristics and Emotions from Nonverbal Properties of Speech," *Psychological Bulletin* 60 (1963): 408–20.
26. Joel D. Davitz and Lois Davitz, "Nonverbal Vocal Communication of Feelings," *Journal of Communication* 11 (1961): 81–86.
27. P. A. Andersen et al., "The Development of Nonverbal Communication Behavior in School Children Grades K–12," (Paper presented at the annual convention of the International Communication Association, Minneapolis, Minn., May, 1981).
28. K. D. Taylor, "Ratings of Source Credibility in Relation to Level of Vocal Variety, Sex of the Source and Sex of the Receiver," (M.A. thesis, University of Nebraska at Omaha, 1984).

29. P. A. Anderson, "Nonverbal Communication in the Small Group," in *Small Group Communication: A Reader,* 4th ed., eds. R. S. Cathcart and L. A. Samovar (Dubuque, Iowa: Wm. C. Brown Publishers, 1984), 265.

30. E. T. Hall, *The Silent Language* (Garden City, N.J.: Doubleday, 1959), 175–76.

31. Martin Remland, "Developing Leadership Skills in Nonverbal Communication: A Situational Perspective," *Journal of Business Communication* 3 (1981): 17–29.

32. R. G. Harper, A. N. Weins, and J. D. Matarazzo, *Nonverbal Communication: The State of the Art* (New York: John Wiley and Sons, 1978).

33. C. Derber, *The Pursuit of Attention* (New York: Oxford University Press, 1979).

34. P. A. Anderson and K. Leibowitz, "The Development and Nature of the Construct 'Touch Avoidance,'" *Environmental Psychology and Nonverbal Behavior* 3 (1978): 89–106.

Part 4

Throughput Processes in the Small Group

Chapter 8

Development of a Group

Study Objectives

As a result of studying chapter 8 you should be able to:

1. Explain the sources, characteristics, and correctives for both primary and secondary interpersonal tensions among group members.

2. List and explain the phases through which most small groups pass, and describe the kinds of statements and processes most prevalent during each.

3. Explain how group rules and norms develop, and be able to recognize, clarify, and adapt to them in small groups to which you belong.

4. Explain group member roles and how they emerge and develop, and the types of behavioral functions that comprise the three broad categories of roles.

5. Describe three communication networks common in small groups and the impact of each on throughput and output.

6. Explain how a status hierarchy forms and the impact of status differences on group process and output.

7. Explain cohesiveness and describe six techniques for enhancing it in a small group.

8. Describe how a fantasy chain contributes to the formation of a small group's culture.

Key Terms

Behavioral function (behavior) how a behavior of a small group member affects the group.

Cohesiveness the degree of attraction members feel for the group; unity.

Communication network the interpersonal channels open for interaction; collectively, who in the group talks to whom. Typical patterns include the wheel, all-channel, and hierarchical arrangement.

Fantasy chain a series of statements by members of a small group in which they dramatize a story about other persons in other places and times in order to create the group's social reality, norms, shared values, and culture.

Group culture the pattern of values, beliefs, and norms shared by group members. It is developed through interaction and incorporates members' shared experiences in the group, the patterns of interaction, and the status relationships.

Idiosyncrasy credit the additional leeway, such as allowing certain rules to be bent, given to a group member for valuable contributions to the group.

Norm an informal rule of conduct or guideline for behavior of members of a group, usually unwritten and unstated, and enforced by peer pressure.

Phase stage in the development of a small group.

Formation phase a collection of individuals form into a group with a structure, set of roles (including a leader), and norms.

Production phase period of time when a mature group is able to concentrate most of its time meeting the task objectives of the group.

Primary tension social unease that occurs when members of a new group first meet or at the beginning of meetings of a long-term group largely resulting from not being able to predict others' responses.

Role a pattern of behavior displayed by and expected of a member of a small group; a composite of a group member's frequently-performed behavioral functions.

Rule a statement prescribing how members of a society, organization, or small group must or should behave; may be stated formally in writing or informally as in the case of norms.

Secondary tension tension and discomfort experienced by members of a group from conflict over values, points of view, or alternative solutions.

Self-centered functions any acts of a small group member, motivated by personal needs, which serve the individual at the expense of the group.

Social or maintenance functions member acts that serve primarily to reduce tensions, increase solidarity, and facilitate teamwork.

Status position of a member in the hierarchy of power, influence, and prestige within a small group; initially attributed by other members on the basis of personal characteristics, then earned on the basis of performance as a group member.

Task functions any act of a member that contributes primarily to accomplishing the goal of the group.

In the previous chapters we have discussed the most important process or throughput variable by which the work of the group is accomplished: the communication itself, including language and nonverbal behavior. In chapter 8 we continue consideration of the process or throughput variables of small groups. In fact, these characteristics can be discussed as both throughput and outcome variables, since the development of functioning processes (throughput) is also one of the accomplishments (outputs) of small group interaction. Our vantage point will be from a system perspective. Small group systems create themselves through their communication behavior, producing outcomes like cohesiveness, a status hierarchy, and decisions. Likewise, they can change themselves, revising these and other outcomes, through their interaction. Rather than focusing on individual behavior per se, we will look at the impact of member behavior on these types of outcomes for the group as a whole. In this chapter, we will examine how a group develops into a functioning system from what is initially a collection of individuals with some common concern. In later chapters, other throughput variables, such as the development of leadership structure, decision making, conflict management, and problem solving will be examined.

Tension among Members

Somehow, what starts as a collection of individuals must become a group that functions smoothly enough to do whatever it is supposed to do. In the process of becoming a unit, the group must solve certain problems for itself and will experience fairly predictable phases in its development. For instance, in order to be able to turn its attention to the task at hand, the group must develop a stable leadership structure for coordinating member behaviors. Only then can it concentrate on its task. This does not happen instantly. As a group works through some of these leadership concerns, it is normal for group members to experience interpersonal tension. We all have experienced moments when we feel irritable, tense, or pressured. Some of this tension actually is functional and helps us perform at peak capacity. Can you imagine taking an exam when you are feeling so totally relaxed that you can hardly motivate yourself to read the questions? If we have too little tension, we are listless and perform poorly. On the other hand, with too much tension, we panic, become uncoordinated, and unable to think or speak clearly.

Just as individuals experience varying levels of tension, so do entire groups. Sometimes a group will become bogged down in apathy; other times it might feel strained and too keyed up to be productive. Ideally, it performs at peak efficiency with just the right amount of energy. These levels of tension are fairly predictable and encompass both primary and secondary tension.

Primary Tension

Bormann first classified the tension a group experiences into the two categories primary and secondary. **Primary tension** is his name for ". . . the social unease and stiffness that accompanies getting acquainted. . . . The earmarks of primary tension are extreme politeness, apparent boredom or tiredness, and considerable sighing and yawning. When members show primary tension, they speak softly and tentatively. Frequently they can think of nothing to say, and many long pauses result."[1] At this early point in the group's development, members do not know each other very well. An individual member wonders, "Will they like me? Will they accept my ideas? Am I going to get along with these people or are we going to fight? Will I be able to work with them smoothly?" People realize they are being judged on how they participate. The apparent boredom and disinterest is only a facade to cover the tension each member feels. If the group is to become a productive one, this primary tension must be reduced. Otherwise, the group will get stuck in a mold of over-politeness, formality, and hesitancy with members believing they are unable to speak frankly and openly. People may feel so uncomfortable they cannot concentrate on their task.

Several things can be done to reduce this primary tension and to hasten the time when group members feel comfortable enough with each other to function effectively. If the group is to be a continuing one, it will pay off in the long run if members deal directly with primary tensions by taking time to get to know each other: to talk about who each person is, ask each other questions, air differences in feelings and backgrounds, chat about hobbies and interests, maybe even have a social hour or party. Joking, laughing together, and finding a common ground of interests help develop a sense of togetherness and trust that will considerably diminish the primary tension. Even members of a one-meeting group, while not experiencing the luxury of time to get to know each other well, can profitably spend a few moments introducing themselves to each other, thus helping the members orient themselves to one another as part of a larger whole, a *group*.

In fact, even members of a continuing group who know each other well can be expected to spend the first few moments of each meeting confirming where they stand with each other and engaging in a certain amount of chitchat before they get down to the business at hand. This, again, is normal and is a vehicle by which primary tension is managed.

Once the high level of primary tension has been reduced so that members can feel comfortable with each other, it is time for a task group to get to work. The designated leader should try to sense when this occurs and help the group focus on its job. It is almost always better to do this early rather than risk having the group lose momentum later.

| Secondary Tension | **Secondary tension** is work-related tension resulting from the differences of opinion among members as they seek to accomplish their task. High levels of secondary tension are inevitable as people differ over their perceptions of a problem, disagree about goals and means for achieving them, and criteria by which to evaluate their ideas. Secondary tensions are a direct result of the need to make decisions *as a group*. Sometimes these tensions become uncomfortably high. Secondary tension looks and sounds different from primary tension. Voices become loud and strained. There may be long pauses followed by two or more members trying to talk at once. Members twist and fidget in their seats, bang fists on the table, wave their arms, interrupt each other, and may even get up and pace around the room. They may try to shout each other down, |

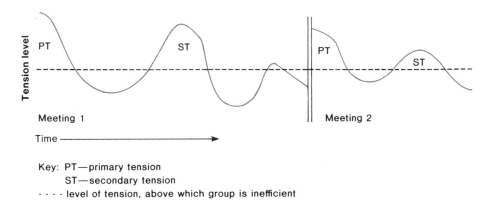

Key: PT—primary tension
     ST—secondary tension
- - - - level of tension, above which group is inefficient

Figure 8.1
The tension cycle in a
hypothetical problem-
solving group.

call each other names, or aggressively question each other's intelligence or motives. While a couple of members attack each other, the rest of the group may sit stiffly and awkwardly, not knowing what to do.

It is normal for a group to cycle between periods of high and low tension among members and high and low productivity. Figure 8.1 represents such cycling in a hypothetical group. Above the dotted line are periods of high tension and low production, while periods of high productivity and lowered tensions are below the line.

While it may seem easier to ignore secondary tensions because dealing with them can be uncomfortable or even painful, the group that deals with these tensions directly will most likely experience several advantages. First, attempts to dodge the tension-producing issue will not cause the issue to go away. As Bormann says, "The problem . . . if ignored or dodged will continue to . . . impede their progress. Facing up to secondary tensions realistically is the best way to reduce them."[2] If this tension is not managed, it will continue to disrupt the group. Second, groups that find integrative ways to manage their secondary tension find they experience greater cohesiveness as a result of having worked through the tension. The members know they can disagree with each other yet still experience a sense of trust and commitment. Finally, the group may find that the tensions have caused the members to look more carefully at task-related issues than they would have if the group members had opted to keep quiet and/or ignore areas of disagreement. The group's final product will usually be better as a result of effective management of secondary tension.

What can group members do to manage secondary tension? Bales found that three categories of behaviors reduced tension among members. He called these "shows agreement," "shows solidarity," and "shows tension release."[3] Showing agreement is socially rewarding to the person agreed with, as if to say to that person, "I value you and your opinion." The more often people agree and are agreed with openly, the more they relax and communicate positively with each other, and the less defensive they become.

A member can show solidarity by indicating commitment to the group. Using *we* to refer to the group, speaking well of other members, offering to help, expressing confidence in the group, and talking about the importance of the group and its task are all ways to show solidarity and encourage other members to move away from self-centeredness and antagonism. The following statements are examples that show solidarity: "Let's all remember that we are in this together." "We're *all* trying to come up with the best possible plan." and "Let's not forget how much we've accomplished so far."

Humor, too, can help release tensions, so long as the disagreement producing the humor is not then ignored. Enjoying a joke together seems to make it easier to listen better and find agreement. Joking can help break uncomfortable tension and move a group past what may seem to be an impasse. In *Pattern for Industrial Peace,* Whyte described how a union staff representative did this repeatedly by using fishing photos whenever discussion among representatives of the steel company and union got overheated with secondary tension.[4] The important principle here is that nobody must seem to win at the expense of the others, or the perceived losers will remain tense. Chapter 10 describes a procedure for managing secondary tension so that cohesiveness can be maintained or increased.

Phases in the Development of Small Groups

We have seen that the occurrence of primary and secondary tensions in a group is predictable and normal. Over the course of time there are other relatively predictable developments within a group. The more group members know about these typical group processes, the more comfortable they will be with them. Members will be able to identify what is usual, what is helpful, and what should be changed in order to help the group function more effectively. A number of researchers have studied how groups develop and change over time and have found that groups progress through relatively identifiable **phases.** Generally this happens gradually, without clear lines of demarcation to separate the phases. The proportion of different kinds of interactions and behaviors can be used to identify the phases as a functioning group develops from an organized collection of people.

Bales was one of the first researchers to investigate a group's progression through predictable phases.[5] Bales said that there are two essential concerns with which a group must deal. First, the group must develop the kinds of interpersonal relationships that provide stability and harmony and allow the group to function smoothly. These are the *socioemotional concerns*. Second, the *task concerns* involve the group's attention to its job, to completion of whatever task it chose or was assigned to accomplish. A group will tend to cycle between these two concerns, focusing first on one, then on the other. Early in the group's **formation phase,** the socioemotional dimension predominates as members attempt to work out the kinds of relationships they will have with each other.

Note the parallel here with what a group must do to overcome primary tension. It is the reduction of primary tension, or working out of interpersonal concerns, that must occur first if a group is eventually to become maximally efficient in completing its task. As the group begins to resolve its early socioemotional issues and becomes increasingly able to take relationships among group members for granted, it begins to concentrate more and more on the task. As socioemotional remarks and behaviors in a group begin to decrease, task-related remarks and behaviors increase and eventually surpass them. In the **production phase** of a group's life cycle, when the group has reached socioemotional maturity, task behaviors will predominate. The group will achieve its peak in task efficiency. This progression can be seen over the life of an effective group as well as over the course of a single group meeting.

More recently, Fisher observed decision-making groups and identified four phases through which groups pass as they work toward making a decision.[6] (Note: these are not the phases of a group's development into a group.) These phases are orientation, conflict, decision emergence, and reinforcement, and they can be identified by the kinds of interactions which occur in each.

Orientation. During the orientation phase, if not already developed as a group, members must get to know each other. They must contend with primary tension as they begin to relate to each other, and concern with maintenance of a harmonious interpersonal atmosphere prevails. They must also figure out what they are supposed to accomplish and how they will accomplish it. They must develop a shared understanding of their task, the facts, and how to interpret them. In this phase, signs of disagreement indicating conflict are minimal; ambiguous and favorable remarks are common. This makes sense, because when group members are uncertain about the facts or worried about how others will perceive them and what relationships will be formed, they will be wary of making strong statements, especially if those statements show disagreement with another member. In the early stages of a group's life, a person is more likely to say, "Well, that idea sounds like it might work, but maybe we should take some time to think about it some more," than to say, "That's not going to work at all. We're going to have to try a lot harder if we are to come up with a decent solution." The first remark is ambiguous and tentative, the second is unambiguous and definite.

Conflict. After group members have resolved primary tension issues and have developed a sense of trust, then they feel freer to offer initiatives, take stands, disagree, offer compromises, argue for and against proposals, and discuss ideas in a more open, less hesitant manner. Ambiguous remarks fall to a low level in this phase, but disagreeing and agreeing remarks are common. One member might say, "I think we should get more information about the impact this might have before we proceed much further." A second member might say, "Naw, we have all the information we need right now to decide." Yet a third member might support the first: "I disagree. We need to know a lot more or we might really mess things up." Members argue for and against proposals, with most people taking sides. Wishy-washy behavior disappears and opinions are expressed clearly and forcefully.

Decision Emergence. A group cannot stay in the conflict phase forever. It must move, somehow, from the position where each member argues a particular point of view to the position where members are willing to relinquish their earlier strong stands and accept reciprocal mutual influence. This movement coincides with the reappearance of ambiguity in the group. Whereas earlier the ambiguity served as a way of managing primary tension, now it allows the members to back off staunchly held positions and save face at the same time. It would be hard on a member's self-image to switch suddenly from "I think we should accept the first proposal" to "I think we should reject the first proposal." A transition is needed, and the ambiguity provides this transition. The member now can move from "I think we should accept the first proposal" to "*Maybe* you are right. There might be some problems with the first proposal that I hadn't considered. Let's look at it more closely before we decide." Members move gradually toward a common group position. Near the end of this phase a consensus decision, with all members in general agreement, will emerge, sometimes suddenly. The members will know when this point is reached, and they will all coalesce around the decision.

Reinforcement. After a group has accomplished its primary objective, it doesn't just immediately move on to a different problem or disband. Members will reinforce each other and themselves for a job well done. They will say such things as, "Wow, it took a long time but we really got some important things done," or "I really like the proposal. It's going to work beautifully," or "I'm really proud of us for coming up with this. You guys are super and this has been a rewarding experience." Members pat each other on the back and reinforce the positive feelings they have toward the decision and toward each other. This good feeling then will be carried over and will positively affect the group at its next meeting.

Fisher believed that unless some outside factor (like severe time pressure) interferes with the group's natural process, these phases will follow each other in a predictable way, although time spent in each phase may vary. It is important to note, however, that he studied interaction in previously developed groups that had already passed through their formation stage. Poole, a current researcher of small group processes, noted that a number of factors influence what phases a group will experience as well as in what order these phases occur.[7] For example, some groups experience long, drawn-out conflict phases with little socioemotional integration after the conflict. Others experience lengthy periods of idea development with no overt conflict. Poole identified two factors in particular that affect a group's phasic progression, task structure, and history. A structured task is well defined, such as how to assemble a swing set. An unstructured task is vague and may have many possible solutions, such as how to solve a campus parking problem. If a task is very unstructured, then it makes sense that a group would need to spend more time orienting itself to the task, and perhaps more time arguing the merits of various ways of solving the problem. With respect to a group's history, such factors as how long members have known each other, how well they have worked together in the past, whether or not they have developed integrative conflict management techniques, how successful the group's solutions have been previously, and how much they like each other are bound to affect the process of that group's discussion of a particular task.

It is essential to keep in mind the distinction between the phases that occur during a decision-making cycle and those that occur in the development of a group. We believe these two processes operate in conjunction with each other and can readily be synthesized. Throughout its entire life, a group must deal simultaneously with process and production concerns. As soon as it meets, it must begin the process of forming into a functioning unit, establishing the interpersonal relationships, leadership structures, and status hierarchies that enable it to work efficiently. This is the formation function that must occur. However, from the very beginning of its formation, the group also is dealing with its task: what its charge is, how the task should be approached, who is to do what, and so forth. Thus, consistent with Bales, the group must contend with both kinds of functions throughout its life span. At first, the interpersonal concerns will predominate, but task concerns are still present. If everything proceeds smoothly for the group, gradually more and more of its time can be spent directly on task concerns and less on interpersonal concerns as it moves to its production stage. However, at no point can group members disregard socioemotional concerns. Thus, we envision a group following essentially two broad developmental stages, a formation phase where process norms unfold and a production phase where group members focus on the task. These phases are not distinct. Instead, a group's attention shifts gradually, but never completely, from process to production concerns.

Within each of these broad phases, a typical group makes a variety of decisions. For instance, early in the formation phase the group may need to decide who will take notes, whether its decisions will require consensus or whether majority vote will suffice, how much information it must gather, how members will address each other, and so on. In the production phase it must decide which of several alternatives is best, how the final report will be written and by whom, to what extent members are satisfied with the group's work and what can be done if they are not, and so forth. (Note that both process and production decisions are represented, no matter what stage in the group's development.) Fisher's work, based on observation of task decision making in a group, provides the information to link the group's developmental stages with its decision-making stages. For each decision a group faces, members must orient themselves to each other and in relation to the group's new task, must argue for and against the various options available, must *decide* something,

Figure 8.2
Decision making within
the development of a
group.

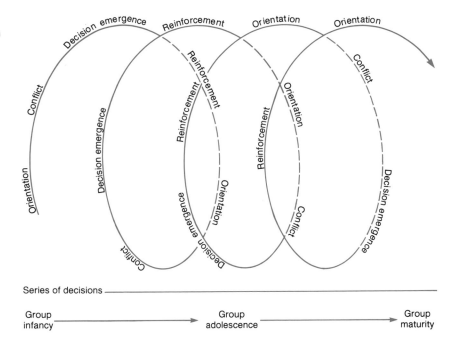

Series of decisions

Group
infancy

Group
adolescence

Group
maturity

and must achieve some sort of closure through reinforcement of the decision. Thus, from our review of the important previous work on phasic progression and from our own experience, we envision a group cycling repeatedly through phases like those Fisher described while moving gradually forward from early formation to full and efficient production. This movement is captured in the spirals of figure 8.2.

Although some writers have confused the two, it is important to be aware that these phases in the group's development, from a collection of individuals into a functioning group system, are not the same as the stages or steps a group goes through in decision making. The latter are a subset of the former, readily incorporated into the developmental stages. Once a group has developed into an operating system, it may repeatedly go through the decision-making or problem-solving steps it needs to complete when working toward a solution to each new problem it tackles. Moreover, it is typical for a group to move back and forth through the various stages, especially if it is a continuing group. As new problems occur, new members are added and old members leave, and former goals are met. This cyclical movement is typical of living organisms. Scheidel and Crowell observed the spiral-like progression of a group's decision-making process and noted that a group does not move in a clear, unbroken line toward a goal.[8] The process is typically messy, going back and forth in a choppy, but ultimately progressive, movement. It is important to know that this type of movement is normal, for that will remove the frustration some members feel if they believe that groups should progress toward their goals in unwavering, unhesitating steps. After all, only when they are *not* engaged do troops march in steady, straight lines!

Development of Group Norms

When individuals begin to interact as members of a group, the full range of human behaviors is potentially available to them. Perhaps they will listen to each other politely, or maybe they will interrupt and insult one another. Somehow, the group must develop a set of rules and operating procedures to coordinate individual behaviors into a system. Some rules are formalized and may even be written down. For example, *Robert's Rules of Order, Newly Revised* is used by many organizations as a code of rules for governing face-to-face interaction based on common law parliamentary procedure.[9] Robert has an entire section of rules that apply to any committee of an organization that adopts his parliamentary manual. These are summarized in chapter 13. Another example of a formal rule might be a rule stating that an individual must be designated at each meeting to take notes and distribute them to members prior to the next meeting.

However, most of the normal operating procedures for a group are developed gradually with the tacit rather than explicit consent of the group members. For instance, if a group member is late to a meeting and the other members make a point of chastising that member, who subsequently arrives on time, a rule proscribing late arrival has been agreed upon by the group members. Such an informal rule, or **norm,** is seldom written down, but rather, as Homans stated, is ". . . an idea in the minds of the members of a group, an idea that can be put in the form of a statement specifying what the members or other *people* should do, ought to do, are expected to do, under given circumstances."[10] This section focuses on these informal rules, or norms.

Norms are not determined by an authority outside the group but are imposed by members on themselves and each other. They are enforced by various types of peer pressure ranging from slight frowns to ostracism. It is important for group members, particularly new members, to be aware of these norms, since to violate them may mean punishment, loss of influence, and perhaps exclusion from the group. Norms reflect cultural beliefs about what is appropriate or inappropriate behavior. While the norms of an individual group may be specific to that group, chances are that they will mirror general cultural norms. For instance, if physical violence is prohibited by the general culture and disagreements are to be handled through discussion, then it is unlikely that a group established in the context of this larger culture will adopt a rule permitting physical violence to settle disputes. Shimanoff stated:

> When group members come together for the first time, they bring with them past experiences and expectations regarding cultural and social rules and rules for specific groups they assume may be similar to this new group. It is out of these experiences and expectations as well as its unique interaction . . . that a particular group formulates its rules.[11]

Rules guide and regulate the behavior of group members. They govern how and to whom members speak, how they dress, what they talk about and when, what language may be used, and so on. The whole process of communication among group members is rule-governed.[12] Rarely do norms specify absolutes, rather they indicate ranges of acceptable and unacceptable behavior. For instance, a particular group may endorse a prompt starting time for its meetings. However, being four minutes late to a meeting may be tolerated without comment, whereas coming half an hour late would not be tolerated.

During the developmental stage of a new small group norms are developed rapidly, often without members realizing what is occurring. The group's first meeting is particularly critical in the establishment of that group's norms. At that time, behaviors that are typical of the primary tension in the orientation phase—speaking quietly, suppressing disagreement, making tentative and ambiguous statements—can become norms if not challenged. Although members may openly discuss and state rules at their first meeting, usually norms evolve over time and seem to exist below the level of consciousness of most members. Often, a norm is brought to the group's awareness only after a member violates it, a new member questions it, or an observer states the norm openly as an apparent rule of the group. The best evidence of the existence of a norm comes when someone violates it and is then punished in some way by the group. For example, others may frown, fail to respond, comment negatively, or even scold the violator: "Let's stick to the issues and not go blaming one another."

Norms may direct the behavior of the group as a whole or of individual members such as the designated leader. Notice that these norms are stated as **rules,** even though they are not imposed on the group by any external authority or parent organization. Examples of each type of norm follow:

General norms
(applicable to every member of the
   group)
Members should sit in the same
   position at each meeting.
Members should address each other
   only by first names.
Other members should not disagree
   with the chairperson's ideas.
No one may smoke during the
   meetings.
Members may leave the meeting to
   get a cup of coffee or a cold drink
   but should return to their places
   promptly after doing so.
Members should arrive on time for
   the meeting.

Role-specific norms
(applicable to specific members of
   the group)
The leader should prepare and
   distribute an agenda in advance
   of each meeting.
The leader should summarize from
   time to time, but other members
   may do so if the leader does not
   when a summary is needed.
The secretary may interrupt the
   leader to clarify a point for the
   minutes, but no one else is
   permitted to interrupt.
Mary may play critical tester of all
   ideas, asking for evidence.
Mike should tell a joke to relieve
   tension when the climate gets
   stressful from an argument over
   differing points of view.

If rules generally exist below the level of conscious awareness, how can group members discover what the rules are? Rules can be inferred and confirmed by observation. It is especially important for new members to become sensitive to the group's norms so they do not inadvertently violate important rules. Fortunately, new members are not usually expected to become active participants right away, so they have time to observe and learn the rules. There are two types of behaviors to watch for especially:

1. Behaviors that occur repeatedly and with regularity, by one or all members. As Shimanoff pointed out, "Because members usually conform to a group's rules, rule generated behavior reoccurs."[13] Repetitions of a behavior are evidence that a norm exists that regulates it. Thus, group members should look for answers to the following questions: "Who talks to whom?" "How do members speak?" "What kind of language do they use?" "What do they talk about and for how long?" "Where do they sit?" "When do they move about and for what reasons?" and "How is the group brought to order?"

2. Punishment of a member for infraction of a rule, perhaps one that has tentatively been inferred. The strongest evidence of a norm is a negative reaction or punishment directed at a member who violates it. Weaker support for the existence of a norm is provided when the violator corrects the sanctioned behavior, and the other members visibly approve the correction. Observers looking for rules should pay attention to negative reactions to preceding actions, ranging from a bit of head shaking to surreptitious and disapproving glances passing between members to forceful negative comments or even threats of violence. Notice behaviors to which members react with gestures of rejection, such as head shaking, frowns, and tongue clucking. What acts do members studiously ignore, as if the person performing the acts were not present? Listen for negative comments, such as "It's about time you got here" and "Maybe you'll have your report ready for our *next* meeting." Note, particularly, those actions that elicit negative responses from more than one person, a sure bet that a rule important to the group has been infringed.

Changing a Norm   Norms have a tremendous impact upon the processes and the outcomes of the group. Therefore, it is important that group members not only be aware of them but act to change them if they appear to be detrimental. For instance, a norm stating that low-status members may not disagree with high-status members interferes with the critical evaluation of ideas. Groups that permit members to criticize ideas as soon as they have been proposed may find that members are reluctant to make innovative suggestions and creativity is stifled. A group in which it is acceptable to address some members with titles and others by first name may find that it gets little output from the first-name members. Meetings may run far beyond the announced time for dismissal because they are late getting started, for instance. This may make it impossible for some members to stay until the end if previous engagements compete for the same time in a schedule. In such cases, individuals should not "sit back and take it" but should work to change the rules. Making a frontal assault, particularly one that may be perceived as a personal attack, is not likely to be successful and will make the person desiring the change seem like a deviant. However, if a few simple guidelines are followed, rules can be changed without unnecessary trauma. First, the member desiring the change must establish an identity as a loyal member of the group and speak not as an outsider but as a member committed to the group's well-being. Second, the member should observe carefully the offending behavior and keep a record of what the behavior is, how often it occurs, what the consequences are, and what norm is inferred from the behavior. Armed with specific information and obvious concern for the other members, the individual is ready for the next step, constructive confrontation.

The member should pick an appropriate time, indicate his or her concern with something that appears to be causing trouble for the group, and state the specifics calmly and clearly. The member should indicate what group rule is inferred, how it detracts from the smooth functioning of the group, and ask whether other members have questions or feel the same concern. For instance, rather than saying, "We never get started on time and I'm sick and tired of it," the member instead should say, "For the past four meetings, we have started our work anywhere from fifteen minutes to a half an hour late. We seem to have a rule that published meeting times do not need to be observed. Two of us have another committee meeting directly following this one, and for each of these late meetings we have had to miss the conclusion of our business. This means that we need to spend additional time at the next meeting bringing us all up to date. Does anyone else share my concern?" If the norm was subconscious, it now has been brought to the attention of the group, and it becomes part of the surface agenda of the group where it can be discussed openly. If the member is wrong about the norm, the group can correct the perception without disparaging the concern. However, if the individual is right, the group will appreciate the concern and will most likely decide that a change is in order. Even if the new rule becomes a consensus norm, members may still need reminders of it for some time until it has become habituated, part of "our way of doing things."

An example will clarify how this works. A study group meeting in a small-town library held weekly discussions of similarities and differences in modern Protestant, Catholic, and Jewish theology. The intent was for the members to come to an understanding of these three religious traditions of the Western world. However, at times members forgot they were there to learn and attempted to convert one another. Discussion often erupted into an uproar with several people talking or shouting at once. One evening, just after the meeting had formally adjourned, one member said, "You know, I'm really bothered by our tendency to all talk at once sometimes, and not listen to each other." He turned to one of the authors, who had been observing the meeting as a researcher equipped with a tape recorder, and said, "Jack, could some of us hear the recording you just made to see how we must sound to you?" When they heard themselves there were signs of irritation and dismay, groans ("Did we sound like that?"), and other indications that people wanted to change the norm that permitted members to interrupt and try to drown each other out. They left the meeting in clusters of two and three, talking about what they had just heard. At the next meeting the game of "uproar" again exploded. Immediately someone said, "Remember the tape recording!" and order resumed. There was no more interrupting for possibly an hour, and when it did occur it lasted only for a few seconds until every participant sheepishly shut up, with several offering apologies. That group had developed a new norm and no more problems with that sort of counterproductive behavior recurred. Many groups we have belonged to or observed have tried out new, more suitable rules in order to improve the quality of their interactions and their output. Thus, although rules are developed generally below the level of awareness, they are not fixed in stone and can be changed as the group's situation warrants.

Development of Role Structure

Most people, when they hear the term **role,** think of parts in a play or movie. Playscripts contain interlocking roles, each of which is a different character in the cast. Just as an actor plays different roles in different scripts, like Meryl Streep as a divorced wife and mother (*Kramer vs. Kramer*), a companion (*The Deer Hunter*), a storyteller and lover (*Out of Africa*), individuals enact many diverse roles in the numerous groups to which they belong. In one group the role might be "daughter" or "son," in another "lead carpenter," and in yet another "church treasurer." In some cases, a given individual might be a leader and in others he or she might play a supporting role. The role that a person enacts in a particular group is a function of that person's personality and abilities, the talents of the other members, and the needs of the group as a whole.

A particular role embraces a set of behaviors which perform some function in the context of the group. There is a difference between a **behavioral function** and behavior. Each act of a group member can be called a behavior, but the meaning of that action in relation to the other members and the group as a whole is its *function,* or what purpose, positive or negative, it accomplishes for the group. For example, one member tells a joke (action or behavior), which functions not only to entertain but to reduce secondary tension. Another member may ask a question (action or behavior) whose purpose (function) is to reorient the group when members seem to be spinning their wheels and have lost sight of the group's goals. Behavioral function, then, is the impact of member behavior on the social structure (throughput) and task accomplishment (output) of the group. A member's role represents the constellation of all the behavioral functions performed by that member, just as an actor's role consists of all the lines and actions of the character in the play. Some necessary functions may be shared widely among all members of the group (such as providing information), and others may become the exclusive domain of one member (such as joking to release tension or keeping group records).

Role Emergence

Some small groups have certain formal roles, usually appointed or elected positions. A chairperson has the responsibility for calling meetings, planning agendas, and coordinating the work of other members. A secretary is responsible for taking notes and distributing minutes of meetings. In these cases, the duties associated with a particular role are specified in advance, sometimes in writing. However, in most small groups members will develop their own roles, creating them and modifying them as the group progresses.

The part a particular individual will play in a small group is worked out in concert with the other members and is determined largely by the relative performance skills of the rest of the group members. This is accomplished primarily through trial and error. For example, one member may have a clear idea of how the group can accomplish its task and will make attempts to structure the group's work. If no one else competes for that role, and if the members themselves see that kind of structuring behavior as helpful to the group, they will reinforce and reward that member's actions. This reinforcement, in turn, is likely to elicit more of those structuring behaviors from that member. On the other hand, if several members also are able to structure the group's work, the group members will reinforce the actions of that person they perceive to be the most skilled in this performance area. Those persons whose behavior is not reinforced positively or consistently will search for other behaviors to perform that will provide assistance to the group and will be valued by the other members. So, if an individual's structuring behavior is not reinforced, that person might turn to joking to relieve tension or to clarifying the proposals of other members instead. *Every member needs a way to make a meaningful contribution to the group.*

Because an individual's role depends on the particular mix of people in the group, that person's role will vary from group to group. Think for a moment of all the groups to which you have belonged. You probably have noticed that your role changed considerably through time as you changed, as new people were added to or left the group, and as the problems facing the group changed. A major principle of small group theory is this: *the role of each member of a group is worked out by interaction between the member and the rest of the group.* Thus, a well-organized person may end up leading in one group and playing a supporting role in another, depending on who the other members of the group are, what they can do to help the group, and how the talents and skills of all the members compare relative to one another.

Behavioral Functions

Many group researchers have developed a number of classification systems to describe roles, or behavioral functions, performed in small groups. These are all oversimplified. One common classification considers the two main functions, discussed earlier, which must be dealt with in small group discussions, task and socioemotional (or maintenance). But even this oversimplifies the actual situation encountered in most groups. If an outside observer suggests that two members who are talking past each other in an excited argument (a

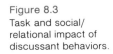

Figure 8.3
Task and social/
relational impact of
discussant behaviors.

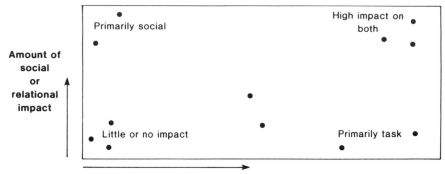

● Specific act or behavior

manifestation of secondary tension) should listen more carefully, that statement, although it focuses on the ways the members are relating to each other, may also have a bearing on the task achievement of the group. Moreover, the statement implies that the observer has the right to intervene with expert information in the group's process and says something about the observer's relationship to the members of the group. Thus, although many researchers consider actions to be *either* task *or* relationship oriented, it is probably more accurate to say that an act can have considerable impact on *both* dimensions. Moreover, recall that the balance of time and attention devoted to these two dimensions shifts as a collection of people develops into a small group system. Thus, we can expect statements made earlier in the group's life to focus more on the relationship dimension than the task, and statements made later to focus more on the task. Figure 8.3 depicts these two major dimensions and illustrates how individual acts can affect each dimension to a greater or lesser degree.

Most researchers agree that both dimensions must be considered for a group to be effective. What follows is a list of behavioral functions needed by most groups to develop from a collection of persons into a coordinated group that can achieve its goals. Several writers have developed lists of roles or functions, but all such lists are arbitrary and have not been subjected to empirical testing. However limited, such a list is useful to help one perceive the dynamics of role emergence and performance. Figure 8.4 illustrates the roles three group members might enact using various combinations of the following behaviors.

Task Functions

Task functions refer to catagories of behavior that have their greatest impact on the task output of the group. Some of the most helpful task functions follow:

Initiating and orienting   proposing goals, plans of action, or activities; prodding the group to greater activity; defining position of group in relation to external structure or goal.

Figure 8.4
Roles of three members
of a small group.

Idea Leader

Opinion
giving

Opinion
seeking

Dramatizing

Supporting

Evaluating

Initiating

Clarifying and elaborating

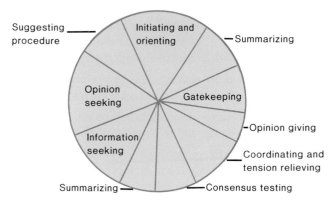

Procedural Leader

Suggesting
procedure

Initiating and
orienting

Summarizing

Opinion
seeking

Gatekeeping

Opinion giving

Information
seeking

Coordinating and
tension relieving

Summarizing

Consensus testing

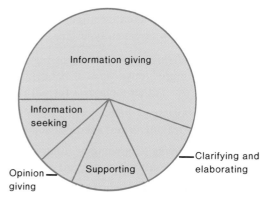

Information Specialist

Information giving

Information
seeking

Clarifying and
elaborating

Opinion
giving

Supporting

Information giving   offering facts and information, evidence, personal experience, and knowledge pertinent to the group task.

Information seeking   asking other members for information; requesting relevant evidence.

Opinion giving   stating beliefs, values, interpretations, judgments; drawing conclusions from evidence.

Opinion seeking   asking other members for their opinions.

Clarifying and elaborating   interpreting issues; clarifying ambiguous statements; developing an idea previously expressed by giving examples, illustrations, and explanations.

Evaluating   expressing judgments about the relative worth of information or ideas; proposing or applying criteria.

Summarizing   reviewing what has been said previously; reminding group of a number of items previously mentioned or discussed.

Coordinating   showing relationships between or among ideas; integrating two or more proposed solutions into one; suggesting how members can work productively together; promoting teamwork and cooperation.

Consensus testing   asking if group has reached a decision acceptable to all; suggesting that agreement may have been reached.

Recording   keeping group records on chalkboard or paper, preparing reports and minutes; serving as group secretary and memory.

Suggesting procedure   suggesting an agenda of issues, outline, problem-solving pattern, or special technique; proposing some procedure or sequence to follow.

Maintenance
(Relationship-
Oriented)
Functions

Maintenance functions focus on interpersonal relationships of members, thus having their greatest affect on the throughput process of the group. We think the following seven types are especially vital to task groups:

Establishing norms   suggesting rules of behavior for members; challenging unproductive ways of behaving as a member; giving negative response when other violates a formal rule or informal norm.

Gatekeeping   helping some member get the floor; suggesting or controlling speaking order; asking if someone has a different opinion.

Supporting   agreeing or otherwise expressing support for other's belief or proposal; following lead of another member.

Harmonizing   reducing secondary tension by reconciling a disagreement; suggesting compromise or new alternative acceptable to all; conciliating or placating angry member.

Tension-relieving   introducing and making strangers feel at ease; reducing external status differences; encouraging informality; joking; stressing common interests and experiences.

Dramatizing   comments that evoke fantasies about persons and places other than the present group and time, including storytelling and fantasizing in a vivid manner; testing a tentative value or norm through fantasy or story.

Showing solidarity   indicating positive feeling toward other group members; reinforcing sense of group unity and cohesiveness.

While the preceding behaviors are considered necessary to the effective functioning of a small group, there is another category of behaviors detrimental to the group. They represent an individual member's hidden agenda.

Self-Centered Functions

Self-centered functions refer to those member actions that serve the performer's unmet needs, usually at the expense of the group. We think the following three types are particularly harmful to groups we have observed:

Withdrawing   avoiding important differences; refusing to cope with conflicts; refusing to take a stand; covering up feelings; giving no response to the comments of others.

Blocking   preventing progress toward group goals by constantly raising objections, repeatedly bringing up the same topic or issue after the group has considered and rejected it. (It is not blocking to keep raising an idea or topic the group has not really listened to or considered.)

Status and recognition seeking   stagehogging, boasting, and calling attention to one's expertise or experience when that is not necessary to establish credibility or relevant to group task; game playing to elicit sympathy; switching subject to area of personal expertise.

This list is by no means exhaustive; it could be expanded considerably with such categories as *special interest pleading, advocating, confessing,* and similar harmful behaviors. It is important to be aware of whether a member is trying to contribute to the interdependent group goal or manipulating and using other members for selfish goals that compete with what the group needs.

Networks of Communication

Concomitant with the development of somewhat specialized roles in a group is the development of a **communication network,** which refers to the pattern of message flow or the linkages, who actually speaks to whom, in discussions. A member who opens a meeting may find the others expecting that initiating behavior at subsequent meetings. A person who speaks frequently will find others looking (literally) to him or her for some comment on each new issue. Infrequent interactants will find themselves increasingly ignored. Networks of who speaks to whom emerge as a function of member expertise, degree of commitment to the group, and level of assertiveness. These networks may

Figure 8.5
Communication
networks.

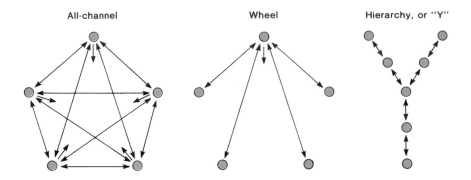

change as new problems or dimensions of problems arise that require specific knowledge or skills or as socioemotional concerns develop in the group. However, every small group is generally typified by one of the major network types described later.

Many types of networks have been identified. In order to understand fully a group's structure, it is important to look at the message links that are possible as well as the ones used. Usually a group of peers has an all-channel network in which all participants are free to comment on a one-to-one basis with all others and to the group as a whole (see figure 8.5). A wheel network, where all comments are directed toward one central person (usually the designated leader) who alone may speak to the group as a whole or to specific individuals, is to be avoided. A Y, or hierarchical network, occurs when an autocratic leader speaks to lieutenants who in turn talk to subordinates. People at the ends of the Y rarely talk to the leader directly. In both the Y and the wheel networks, the central person is generally satisfied with the communication and participation in the group, but the peripheral members are not. Another danger in this type of network is that the central member may suffer from information overload and become frustrated and ultimately dissatisfied. In addition, communication in restricted networks may break down into two or more private conversations during a group meeting. The all-channel network permits rapid communication among all members without having to get clearance from a central gatekeeping authority. Members are free to say what they want while ideas are still fresh in mind and pertinent. Communication flows freely; at least half the remarks are made to group members as a whole so they all feel equal freedom to reply, and all members can hear and attend to one-to-one or one-to-few comments. The all-channel network pays off in several ways. Morale is highest, and such groups tend to perform better on complex tasks when compared with groups with restricted networks. Even in all-channel network groups, the flow of verbal messages may at times resemble a wheel or a hierarchy.

Status Hierarchy

Status refers to the relative importance, prestige, and power of a member in a small group. As group roles emerge, each person is placed in a sort of pecking order or status ladder. Several advantages accrue to members of high status. High status is socially rewarding, and such members feel important and worthwhile. Other group members defer to them, grant them a disproportionate share of the group's attention, agree with their proposals, and seek their advice and opinions. Persons occupying formal, high-status roles, such as that of designated leader, may be given such tangible signs of status as special chairs, large offices, and powers not granted to other members. Moreover, designated leaders are often given deference, support, and more eye contact.

Effects of status differences are numerous. High-status members talk more often than low-status members and address each other more often than do members with low status. Low-status members address their remarks more often to high-status members than to each other.[14] Low-status members also send more positive messages to high-status members than to other low-status members, indicating another reward of high status.[15] Low-status members are interrupted more and their comments are ignored more often than the comments of those with higher status. High-status members tend to talk more to the group as a whole, whereas low-status members express most of their comments to individuals (the classic Y network).

In addition to being granted a number of psychological or material rewards, high-status members are expected to meet certain responsibilities within the group. They are expected to work especially hard to accomplish the group's goals, and they are expected to uphold the group's norms. They may lose status by failing to fulfill the group's expectations although, particularly with regard to norms, they may be given additional leeway, or **idiosyncrasy credit,** that other members do not receive.[16] This means that, for members who have made an exceptionally valuable contribution to the group, certain rules can be bent.

Status within a small group may be *ascribed* or it may be *earned*. At first, before members know each other well and are sure what their respective contributions will be to the group, status is ascribed on the basis of each member's position in the society external to the small group. It is based on such things as wealth, education, work, personal fame, or position in the parent organization of a committee. For example, a committee composed of a college dean, a biology professor, an English instructor, two seniors, and two sophomores will initially have that order of ascribed status. However, status can also be earned or achieved based on a member's individual contributions to the group. The sophomore who conducts considerable research on behalf of the group and is a key contributor will have higher earned status than the biology professor who rarely comes to meetings and completes no assignments.

In some instances, the importance of variables that contribute to higher ascribed status, such as gender, appears to be shifting. For example, in 1978 Bormann, Pratt, and Putnam reported that men tended to resist the efforts of a competent woman to structure and coordinate the group's work regardless of how well she performed.[17] More recently, Bormann and Bormann reported that they found some women resisting efforts of a man to lead groups, largely as a matter of principle.[18] Pratt found that some men were willing to have a woman lead groups of which they were members.[19] The willingness to support and follow members of the opposite sex in groups is changing rapidly and varies from group to group. In some organizations, there is considerable resistance on the part of men to have women group leaders, but almost no resistance in others. Most male university students in our classes are comfortable having a competent woman lead class project groups. However, not many years ago even the most capable women took supporter rather than leader roles. Now that more women are taking visible positions of leadership in society, maleness may cease to be a criterion for high status in American small groups.

The most ideal group climate exists when relationships and relative status differences are somewhat flexible so that different persons can become more dominant as their particular knowledge and skills become pertinent to the issues or problems facing the group at any point in time. It is important to note that lower status does not mean *of little value*. Lower status members are not necessarily unhappy in the group, and cohesive groups value the contributions of each member and every member knows it. Only when members say things like "We could have done just as well without Morgan and Jolene on this committee" can we infer that lower status definitely means inferior. More typically, everyone in the group might follow the lead of a normally recessive, supportive low-status person who seems to have just the information or ability the group most needs at any given moment. That person might later slip back into a more usual low-profile position, but the contribution will have been noted and appreciated.

Cohesiveness

Cohesiveness refers to the common bonds and sentiments that hold a group together. To say that a group is high in cohesiveness is to say that the relationship among members is, on the whole, attractive to them; they have a high degree of "stick togetherness" and unity. Measuring cohesiveness is difficult and involves observing certain selected behaviors. For instance, a researcher might use members' individual assessments of how closely knit they are as a group, how strongly members feel a sense of belonging to the group as expressed on a scale, attendance at meetings, favorable remarks made about the group to outsiders, degree of conformity to group norms that call for behaviors different from the ones members manifest in other social situations, or achievement of consensus (or lack thereof) in expressions of value.

Highly cohesive groups behave differently from less cohesive groups. They have greater rates of interaction, and members express more positive feelings for each other and report more satisfaction with the group and its products. In addition, cohesive groups exert greater control over member behaviors.[20] High cohesiveness is associated with increased ability to cope effectively with unusual problems and to work as a team in meeting emergencies. Production groups, if highly cohesive, *can* produce more than low cohesive groups, but may not do so if the members are being influenced by intragroup norms for less production. Highly successful and cohesive groups tend first to get acquainted and interested in each other as persons and they consistently reinforce the value members place on the group and on each member. Members can be heard saying, "I'm proud of our group, we really thrash out ideas until we arrive at the best, then we team up." High cohesiveness is associated with the group's ability to get members to conform to the majority or to high-status members' desires, which can result in a less-than-thorough critical evaluation of ideas. This phenomenon has been termed *groupthink* by Janis and is discussed in detail in the chapter on conflict.[21]

Although there are pitfalls associated with high cohesiveness, like groupthink, there are benefits as well. A group that accomplishes its objectives, provides members with satisfaction in their participation, offers prestige in belonging, and is successful in competing with other groups is highly attractive to its members. This knowledge can be used to offset the strains produced by uncertainty, risk, and the necessity to defer judgement in order to produce high-quality work. Cohesiveness is fostered to the extent that members know and like each other as individuals, by their frequency of interaction, and by the amount of influence exerted by each on the group. In addition, some evidence suggests that cohesive groups cooperate in creating a dominant sensory metaphor as a group and that cohesiveness can be monitored through metaphor.[22] For example, when a group first is established, members may indicate their understanding by saying, "I see," "I hear you," or "That feels right to me." Each of these metaphors for "I understand" concentrates on a different sense—sight, sound, or touch. In cohesive groups, members will tend to converge on a particular sensory metaphor. If the visual metaphor is chosen, for example, members will all start saying, "I see," "I've got the picture," and "I've spotted a flaw." This is an indication that members have influenced each other in subtle but significant ways.

Interestingly, open disagreement is more frequent in highly cohesive groups, because a climate of trust provides each member with the security needed to permit expressions of disagreement on issues, facts, and ideas—provided that the disagreement is aimed at finding a high-quality solution. On the other hand, if high-status members indicate that they perceive disagreement to be a personal affront, then cohesiveness—willingly following the high-status persons—will be maintained at the expense of high quality in decision making.

Cohesiveness, then, is generally desirable. In order to enhance cohesiveness, Bormann and Bormann suggest that a group should deliberately do the following:

1. **Develop a strong identity as a group and a group tradition or history.**
   This can be done by developing nicknames for the group, insignia indicating membership, referring to past events with pride and pleasure, ceremonies and rituals, and emphasizing the high quality of past accomplishments.

2. **Stress teamwork and give credit to the group.**
   Members, especially the designated leaders, should avoid talking about what they did personally for the group. Members should volunteer to do things for the group and emphasize how important the group is to them. This will help members feel closer.

3. **Recognize contributions to the group goal by members, thus rewarding individual members from within the group.**
   Low-status members especially need reward and praise from other group members and *not* criticism if they are to develop the loyalty that will make them more productive and dependable.

4. **Show human concern for persons who make up the group.**
   Provide warmth, affection, and direct attention to personal tensions and problems that members indicate. As soon as personal needs are dealt with, return the group to its task.

5. **Support both disagreement and agreement, which basically means working for a norm of freedom of expression and openness.**
   Highly cohesive groups show more disagreement, with open conflict encouraged, not repressed. When conflicts are settled, signs of solidarity such as joking, laughing together, compliments to persons who supported rejected ideas that helped build a better group solution, and comments like "Let's get behind this" are needed.

6. **Help the group set clear and attainable goals, which also provide enough of a challenge to yield a sense of pride in group achievement.**
   Continuing groups that fail to reach their objectives tend to display lowered cohesiveness and may even disband. On the other hand, beating a high school team would not enhance the cohesiveness of a college soccer squad.[23]

Development of Group Culture

Group culture is determined by the values the members share and the ways they act toward each other. The roles individuals enact and their interrelationships, the norms and rules which serve to guide the group's interactions, the pattern of interactions, and the status distinctions all are woven together to form the culture of the group. Each group is unique because each group has a mix of members, purposes, rules, and behaviors that cannot be duplicated exactly in other groups. Some groups, for example, will have a freewheeling style of interaction characterized by informality, joking, and a minimum of status distinctions. Other groups are characterized by hostility, aggressive verbal behavior, and personal attacks. Still others can be identified by their adherence to strict rules of interaction and formal, polite, and controlled interaction. How do these differences come about?

Group members seldom discuss the group's values explicitly and do not, as a rule, set out consciously to establish the group's culture. Instead, values are frequently explored and tested for acceptance in what appear to be conversational episodes that are tangential to the group's "real" task. These animated sequences, called **fantasy chains,** were first described by Bales.[24] It is important to note that the use of the term *fantasy* in this context does not mean fictitious or unreal. It means, simply, that during certain periods of a group's interaction, the members will not be discussing events happening in the here-and-now of the group but instead are talking about past events, relating anecdotes or telling stories which have, at the unconscious level, a bearing on the group's process. Bales claimed that fantasy chaining relates to unconscious meanings or needs of one or more participants. Hence, such fantasies have great power to motivate members. This storytelling activity plays a crucial role in determining and passing along the group's culture.[25] Several group members, although not necessarily all, participate in a fantasy chain. Typically, the speed of the interaction picks up, voices become louder, and a sense of excitement can be detected. Members seem interested in participating in the conversation and contributing to the flow. A common psychological theme connects the separate elements, and the fantasy period may last from as little as a half-minute to as much as several minutes.

Morocco demonstrated how the group members interact through fantasy chains to create metaphors that are meaningful to the group and that will ultimately serve to solidify the culture of the group.[26] The process goes as follows. The group experiences a formless feeling and a sense of uncertainty exists. One member begins the fantasy by introducing a core image that relates directly to the uncertainty. Other members diffuse that core image throughout the group by contributing to the fantasy, enabling it to become a group, rather than merely an individual, metaphor. Finally, the fantasy functions to represent some important concept to the group and provides a solution of sorts to the initial uncertainty. For example, Morocco related the story of the first meeting of a research group whose student members believed their leaders were not providing them with enough direction and help (the formless feeling). One member recalled seeing a movie about an experiment in which baby monkeys were deprived of maternal nurturing (introduction of core image) and the other members, who also had seen the movie in school, began to contribute by adding details and developing a plot and dramatic image associated with the movie (diffusion of the core image). The social and sexual development of the monkeys in the movie had been impaired by the lack of parental care, and this image served to portray the reality that the group members currently were experiencing (representation of the conception of the group). This group was saying, in essence, "The lack of attention and help on the part of the leaders will ultimately harm us as individuals and as a group."

In another example, some members of a newly formed project group were interested in creating a panel program on legalizing prostitution in Omaha but knew that other group members were devout members of churches which had a history of fighting such things. One person began a fantasy chain to determine if the members could all work on how to legalize prostitution:

Joan: When I was in Amsterdam I saw these prostitutes sitting in windows inviting passersby to come in, and no one seemed to object. That was a hot section of town!

Jim: (very excitedly, quickly) Yeah, Boston has a place like that, called the Combat Zone; everyone knew where to go for action, and it kept pressure off people in the rest of the city.

Sally: (eagerly leaning forward, excited tones) That could work great near our Old City area! Hookers could work there and liven it up a bit, and maybe end the silly game of cops and working gals that goes on so much!

Jan: (one of the church activists) Prostitutes even advertise in the papers in London. Wouldn't that pep up the staid *World-Herald*?!

Edward: Yeah—and then the guys and gals who wanted to could get together safely.

Jan: I see one good thing—I'd know where *not* to go in town!

The tempo dropped abruptly, and the group returned to discussing what they might do for a panel. Almost at once Jim suggested they take legalization of prostitution in Omaha as their topic, and everyone agreed this was a worthy subject to consider.

Fantasy chains can easily be detected by an observer watching for a sudden change of pace, an electric tension in the air. To interpret the fantasy, Bales suggested that the observer look for a sudden insight into what is going on in the group that has not been openly discussed. Systematic analysis will not work. For example, one of the authors observed the final meeting of a semester-long, intensive group discussion course during which the student members had become attached to the professor. At this meeting, the students began to discuss their parents' divorces, deaths of persons who had been important to them, and endings of relationships. It suddenly became apparent that what the students were *really* discussing, at the psychological level, was their distress at the "abandonment" by the professor, which was about to happen because the semester was coming to a close. Thus, the fantasy theme allows the group to discuss matters which, for whatever reasons, cannot be brought up explicitly. It gives members a way to talk indirectly about what they are unable to discuss directly, to explore values and norms without danger of loss of face, and is linked to the psychological process operating in the group. It is a powerful determinant of the group's culture. Fantasy chaining is a tool for creating shared images of the group and its environment.

Summary

In this chapter we have examined eight major process variables that need to be considered when studying the development of a small group from a loose collection of individual persons: interpersonal tensions, progression of the group through identifiable phases, rules and norms, development of a role structure, communication networks, status hierarchies, cohesiveness, and development of a group culture. All groups experience primary and secondary tensions and must find ways to deal effectively with these tensions. Groups develop in stages typically moving through the stages of development and performance with repeated cyclic phases of orientation, conflict, decision emergence, and reinforcement as they take up major issues on which decisions must be made. While formal rules may exist to govern some of the group's interaction, informal rules, or norms, are developed with the tacit approval of the members themselves to guide their behaviors. From their personal behaviors and skills, group members carve out their individual roles in cooperation with other group members. All groups need both task and maintenance functions to be performed, but self-oriented roles detract from the group's purpose. The ideal communication network for a small group is the all-channel network rather than the Y or the wheel. The combination of roles and placement in the communication network influences each member's status within the group. These factors affect the group's cohesiveness, which is both a product of the group's interaction as well as a process variable that affects the group's outcomes. Finally, all the preceding variables contribute to the group's culture, whose uniqueness is determined in part by the fantasy chaining that serves to help the group define itself.

In the next chapter we will consider one of the most important group processes—leadership.

Exercises

1. Observe a small group during at least one discussion; take notes on what you observe and what norms these behaviors imply. Then, using the format that follows, record all the norms you infer from your observations, stating each as a rule of conduct about what members (or a specific member) of the group must, should or should not, or may do in the group. Try to identify at least fifteen or twenty norms. Briefly describe the observed behaviors on which each norm is based. Finally, indicate whether you think the norm helped the group increase its output ($+$), had no effect on output (0), or reduced the group's output ($-$) in relation to its stated goals.

Norm	Specific Behavior which Provides Evidence of the Norm	Impact

2. Select a small group to which you have belonged since the beginning, and which has met for at least several meetings. Describe the phases in that group's development as best you recall them. What phases did you see? How did you know when the group left one phase and entered the other? Did the phases overlap? Do your fellow group members recall the phases as you do or differently? Also observe the phases of the group's decision making. To what degree do these seem to conform to the four phases described by Fisher?

3. Using the list of behavioral functions as a guide, several observers should classify each remark made by each of several members of a group according to the functions. This gives you a tally of how often each person performs each function. How would you describe each member's role?

4. Rank the members you observed in the previous question according to the status of each in the group. How much relative power and influence do you think each exhibits? Why?

5. Think of at least ten groups to which you have belonged in the past year. What is your role in each? Do you have a different role depending on the group or do you keep the same general role? What have you discovered?

6. Diagram the flow of communication in a discussion group you observe using the form shown on page 340. Be sure to record how many times each person speaks and to whom. What is the proportion of the total statements made by each member? What sort of communication network exists in this group?

7. Think of the most and least cohesive groups to which you have belonged. List as many significant differences as you can that you believe contributed to the cohesiveness or lack of it. What do you conclude?

8. Tape record a group's interaction, and listen to the tape later for the purpose of identifying any fantasy themes. (Listen especially for periods when the group seems excited and the energy level appears to pick up.) What function do you think the fantasy theme is serving? What does it say about the group's social reality?

Bibliography

Bormann, Ernest G. *Discussion and Group Methods: Theory and Practice,* 2d ed. New York: Harper & Row, Publishers, 1975, chapters 8 and 9.

Fisher, B. Aubrey. *Small Group Decision Making: Communication and the Group Process.* New York: McGraw-Hill Book Company, 1980, chapters 5 and 6.

Nixon, Howard L. II. *The Small Group.* Englewood Cliffs, N.J.: Prentice-Hall, 1979, chapters 4 and 5.

Shimanoff, Susan B. "Coordinating Group Interaction Via Communication Rules." In *Small Group Communication: A Reader.* 4th ed., eds. Robert S. Cathcart and Larry A. Samovar. Dubuque, Iowa: Wm. C. Brown Publishers, 1984, 31–44.

Notes

1. Ernest G. Bormann, *Discussion and Group Methods: Theory and Practice,* 2d ed. (New York: Harper & Row, Publishers, 1975), 181–82.
2. Ibid., 190.
3. Robert F. Bales, *Interaction Process Analysis* (Reading, Mass.: Addison-Wesley, 1950).
4. William F. Whyte, *Pattern for Industrial Peace* (New York: Harper, 1951).
5. Robert F. Bales, *Interaction Process Analysis* (Reading, Mass.: Addison-Wesley, 1950).
6. B. Aubrey Fisher, *Small Group Decision Making: Communication and the Group Process,* 2d ed. (New York: McGraw-Hill Book Company, 1980), 144–57.
7. Marshall S. Poole, "Decision Development in Small Groups II: A Study of Multiple Sequences in Decision Making," *Communication Monographs* 50 (1983): 206–32; "Decision Development in Small

Groups III: A Multiple Sequence Model of Group Decision Development," *Communication Monographs* 50 (1983): 321–41.

8. Thomas M. Scheidel and Laura Crowell, "Idea Development in Small Discussion Groups," *Quarterly Journal of Speech* 50: 140–45.

9. Henry M. Robert, *Robert's Rules of Order, Newly Revised* (Glenview, Ill.: Scott, Foresman and Company, 1981), 399–453.

10. George C. Homans, *The Human Group* (New York: Harcourt Brace Jovanovich, 1950), 123.

11. Susan B. Shimanoff, "Coordinating Group Interaction Via Communication Rules," in *Small Group Communication: A Reader,* 4th ed., eds. Robert S. Cathcart and Larry A. Samovar (Dubuque, Iowa: Wm. C. Brown Publishers, 1984), 36.

12. Susan B. Shimanoff, *Communication Rules: Theory and Research* (Beverly Hills: Sage, 1980).

13. Shimanoff, "Coordinating Group Interaction," 42.

14. J. I. Hurwitz, A. F. Zander, and B. Hymovitch, "Some Effects of Power on the Relations among Group Members," in *Group Dynamics: Research and Theory,* 3d ed., eds. D. Cartwright and A. Zander (New York: Harper & Row, Publishers, 1968), 291–97.

15. Dean C. Barnlund and C. Harland, "Propinquity and Prestige as Determinants of Communication Networks," *Sociometry* 26 (1963): 467–79.

16. E. Hollander, "Conformity, Status and Idiosyncrasy Credit," *Psychological Review* 65 (1958): 117–27.

17. Ernest G. Bormann, Jeri M. Pratt, and Linda L. Putnam, "Power, Authority, and Male Responses to Female Dominance," *Communication Monographs* 45 (1978): 119–55.

18. Ernest G. Bormann and Nancy C. Bormann, *Effective Small Group Communication,* 3d ed., (Minneapolis: Burgess Publishing Company, 1980), 80.

19. Ibid., 81.

20. Howard L. Nixon II, *The Small Group* (Englewood Cliffs, N.J.: Prentice-Hall, 1979), 74–76.

21. Irving L. Janis, *Victims of Groupthink* (Boston: Houghton Mifflin Company, 1973).

22. William F. Owen, "Metaphor Analysis of Cohesiveness in Small Discussion Groups," *Small Group Behavior* 16 (1985): 415–26.

23. Ernest G. Bormann and Nancy C. Bormann, *Effective Small Group Communication,* 2d ed., (Minneapolis: Burgess Publishing Company, 1976), 70–76.

24. Robert F. Bales, *Personality and Interpersonal Behavior* (New York: Holt Rinehart and Winston, Inc., 1970), 105–8, 136–55.

25. Eric E. Peterson, "The Stories of Pregnancy: On Interpretation of Small-Group Cultures," *Communication Quarterly* 35 (1987): 39–47.

26. Catherine Cobb Morocco, "Development and Function of Group Metaphor," *Journal for the Theory of Social Behavior,* 9, no. 1 (1979).

Chapter 9

Leadership in Small Groups

Study Objectives

As a result of your study of chapter 9 you should be able to:

1. Define the concepts of leadership, leader, emergent leader, and designated leader.

2. Explain the five types of power on which leadership is based and the four major approaches to the study of leadership, and give appropriate examples of each as it pertains to leadership in small groups.

3. Describe how leadership emerges in an initially leaderless small group.

4. Describe characteristics and behaviors typical of effective discussion leaders.

5. Develop a personal philosophy of group-centered democratic small group leadership.

6. List three major classes of responsibility expected of small group discussion leaders, and explain the general approaches and specific techniques for providing these services.

Key Terms

Autocratic leader a person who for personal goals tries to dominate and control a group, using coercion, rewards, and positional power to influence.

Completer, leader as leader who determines what functions or behaviors are most needed for a group to perform optimally, then attempts to encourage or supply those behaviors.

Contingent behaviors approach study of how outcomes of different leader behaviors vary with differences in input or context variables; adapting leadership services to such variables.

Contingent traits approach study of how outcomes of designated leaders with different traits and styles vary in relation to differences in context variables.

Democratic leader a person who coordinates and facilitates discussion in a small group by consent of the group, thus helping achieve group-determined goals.

Designated leader a person appointed or elected to position as leader of a small group.

Discussion leader leader of a group's verbal interaction; coordinator of discussion process and procedures.

Emergent leader member of an initially leaderless group who in time is named leader by all or nearly all members.

Functional approach study of functions (behaviors) performed by actual small group leaders.

Laissez-faire leader a do-nothing designated leader who provides minimal services to the group.

Leader a person who exercises goal-oriented influence in a group; any person identified by members of a group as leader or a person designated as leader by appointment or election.

Leadership influence exerted through communication that helps a group clarify and achieve goals; performance of a leadership function.

Power potential to influence behavior of others, derived from such bases as ability to reward, coerce, or supply needed expertise, or from personal attraction and charisma.

Pseudodiscussion going through the motions of discussion when the important outcomes have been predetermined by an autocratic leader.

Structuring leadership behaviors that function to organize and coordinate group interaction and work.

Universal behaviors approach belief that there is some set of behaviors appropriate for leaders of all small groups.

Universal traits approach study of personal and behavioral characteristics of both designated and emergent leaders.

The study of leadership is not only interesting, it is critical to understanding the throughput processes and outcome variables of a small group. Leadership has been a focus of study since ancient times, with small group leadership occupying considerable attention of both scholars and group members since the 1930s. While most people agree that leaders are important to the success of discussion groups, there is less agreement on the specific behaviors that provide effective leader services to such groups. (Note: we use the term *discussion group* generically to include decision-making and problem-solving groups that do much of their work via discussion. In addition, we confine our discussion to promotive leadership, that is, behavior which helps a group achieve its goals rather than hindering it.) This chapter has two main purposes. First, we present theoretical information that capsulizes the important information known about small group leadership so that you will have a foundation for understanding the role of the leader in a small group. We will concentrate on those groups that have a **designated** (appointed or elected) **leader** because they are most prevalent, but we also consider the special case of the emergent leader in an initially leaderless group. Second, we offer guidelines for you to use when you find yourself in the leader's position, whether elected, appointed, or through natural emergence. Even when you are appointed or elected as a group's leader, you will still have to earn the respect of the members in order to hold the position and to be effective by emerging in the perception of the members as the leader.

Because small groups are ever-present in our lives, there is virtually no doubt that at some point you will have your turn at group leadership. To serve others as a leader can be a source of self-esteem, recognition, and appreciation, helping you meet your normal human needs for accomplishment, mastery, and meeting challenges. However, for every potential reward of the leadership role there is a concomitant potential for failure and disappointment. We each have experienced both. We offer this information to you so when you operate as a leader, you will do so with awareness, knowledge, and an articulated philosophy of appropriate small group leadership. The leadership role entails high levels of responsibility and visibility from which some members shrink. The sheer amount of work dissuades some members; others avoid leader positions if they think it requires manipulating others. We think that good leaders do not manipulate but facilitate the work of the group, involving other members in the group's task as fully as possible.

Before reading further in this chapter, complete the following scale to find out what *you* think discussion leaders should do and how they should do it. *After* you have completed the scale, use page 220 to score your answers and locate your position on the autocratic-democratic continuum of discussion leader philosophy. Do you think your score accurately reflects your expectations and behaviors in a group? You may want to discuss your findings with classmates. As a result of completing and discussing the Sargent and Miller Leadership scale you should be able to understand this chapter in a more personal way.

A Learning Activity

We are interested in the things that are important to you when you are leading a group discussion. Listed below are several pairs of statements. Read each pair of statements and place a mark in the one you believe to be of greater importance. On reacting to the statements, observe the following ground rules:[1]

1. Place your check marks clearly and carefully.
2. Do not omit any of the items.
3. Never check both of the items.
4. Do not look back and forth through the items; make each item a separate and independent judgment.
5. Your first impression, the immediate feelings about the statements, is what we want.

_____ 1. a. To give everyone a chance to express his opinion.
_____   b. To know what the group and its members are doing.
_____ 2. a. To assign members to tasks so more can be accomplished.
_____   b. To let the members reach a decision all by themselves.
_____ 3. a. To know what the group and its members are doing.
_____   b. To help the members see how the discussion is related to the purposes of the group.
_____ 4. a. To assist the group in getting along well together.
_____   b. To help the group to what you think is their best answer.
_____ 5. a. To get the job done.
_____   b. To let the members reach a decision all by themselves.
_____ 6. a. To know what the group and its members are doing.
_____   b. To let the members reach a decision all by themselves.
_____ 7. a. To get the job done.
_____   b. To assist the group in getting along well together.
_____ 8. a. To help the members see how the discussion is related to the purposes of the group.
_____   b. To assign members to tasks so more can be accomplished.
_____ 9. a. To ask questions that will cause members to do more thinking.
_____   b. To get the job done.
_____ 10. a. To let the members reach a decision all by themselves.
_____   b. To give new information when you feel the members are ready for it.

No discussion group can be effective without appropriate leadership. But what does it take to lead discussions well? This entire book represents an attempt to answer that question. Before we begin to form conclusions regarding appropriate leader behavior, we will consider the general concepts of leader and leadership.

Leadership and Leaders

The terms _leader_ and **leadership** have overlapping, but separate, meanings. For instance, it is possible, though uncommon, for a discussion group to have no designated leader and yet to have excellent leadership. It is also possible for such a group to have a formal leader and yet be woefully lacking in leadership.

Leadership

Social scientists almost unanimously define leadership as interpersonal influence. Probably the most widely used definition is that by Tannenbaum, Wechsler, and Massarik:

> We define leadership as *interpersonal influence, exercised in situation and directed through the communication process, toward the attainment of a specified goal or goals.* Leadership always involves attempts on the part of a *leader* (influencer) to affect (influence) the behavior of a follower (influencee) or followers in *situation.*[2]

This general definition is not limited to small groups. Only attempts to influence behavior with respect to a *group* goal will be considered leadership in the context of small group discussion, thereby excluding behavior through which one member influences another to accomplish something apart from or contrary to the goal of the group. Thus, we exclude such behavior as one member attempting to influence another to sabotage a group goal or to join the first member in a drink after the meeting (unless that is done to achieve greater harmony in the group).

Influence refers to the exercise of *power,* which in groups of relative equals depends on the consent of other members to be influenced. Leaders can influence others only if they have a power base, a source of power which is perceived and acknowledged as such by the other members. French and Raven identified five types of power that give leaders their ability to influence: reward, coercive, legitimate, referent, and expert.[3]

Leaders can reward members by giving them special attention, favors or acknowledgement, or they can coerce members with threats, by removing opportunities for them to speak or ignoring them until they comply. A boss or authority figure may use such power virtually to force acquiescence, but such behavior is not leadership.

Legitimate power stems from acknowledged position or title. Leaders have legitimate power simply because they have the title. Just as a private will accept orders from a sergeant but ignore identical orders from another private, committee members typically attend meetings at the call of an appointed chairperson, accept the agenda prepared by the chair, and willingly comply with reasonable assignments given by the chair. Most discussants also expect the designated leader to exercise some control over the flow of verbal participation and problem-solving procedures.

Referent power is based on attraction of one person to another, or identification. Referent leaders have a type of charisma that causes others to want to associate with them and imitate their behavior. For example, one of us (we won't tell you which one) skipped class in high school because the referent leader of our small group of friends suggested it. Ideally, however, discussion leaders model positive behaviors for the other members to admire and emulate, such as listening, considering all sides of an issue, and keeping remarks orderly and clear. To the degree a leader is admired or liked, his or her behavior is copied and power to influence other members is increased.

Expert power is attributed by members to someone for what that member knows or can do. For instance, if your group is responsible for producing a panel discussion for the rest of your class, and you happen to be the only member who has ever participated in or observed a panel discussion, you have expertise that gives you power within that particular group. Thus, the person with expert power is influential because he or she is perceived as having knowledge and skills vital to the group.

It is possible for a leader's power to rest on more than one base. The more these five power bases are concentrated in one person, the more that person can dominate a small group. On the other hand, the greater the degree to which the bases of power and influence are distributed among members of a small group, the more likely is verbal participation to be shared, decision making to be collaborative, and satisfaction to be high. Even so, numerous studies have indicated that groups that evolve a stable leadership structure are more effective. A group undergoing a struggle for leadership produces poor products, dissatisfaction, and low levels of cohesiveness.[4] In contrast, groups with single designated leaders work more efficiently, have fewer interpersonal problems, and produce better outputs than groups without a designated leader.[5] The conclusion is clear: someone in a group where the bases of power are shared must emerge as *the* recognized leader, not for the purposes of usurping the shared decision-making functions, but to keep the flow of communication orderly and to structure the members' work.

Even when a group leader is appointed or elected chair of a small group, that person must still earn respect from within the group. The designated leader will be challenged and tested in his or her attempts to coordinate activities. If that person's power rests solely on the legitimacy of the title *leader,* problems will occur and someone else with more broadly based power will emerge as the natural leader.

Leaders

Even though all members in a group are theoretically responsible for that group's success or failure, the parent organization of the group will hold a designated leader responsible for the productivity of the group. Designated leaders of small groups in other settings are not free from such responsibility either: ". . . group members and outsiders tend to hold the leader accountable for group beliefs, proposals, actions, and products."[6] Thus, the role or position of leader must be clarified. In this book we use the term **leader** in three different ways: (1) to refer to any person who is perceived by group members as their leader; (2) to refer to any person who has been appointed or elected to a position of leadership, such as chair or coordinator; and (3) to refer to any person who is exerting influence within a group toward achievement of interdependent group goals.

Two important ideas are embedded in this definition. First, it is clear that a designated leader is accountable for the effective functioning of the group. The leader must maintain perspective and see that all needed leadership services are being performed. This sense of leadership was captured by Schutz' concept of **leader as completer**: ". . . the best a leader can do is to observe what functions are not being performed by a segment of the group and enable this part to accomplish them."[7] This makes the designated leader responsible for knowing what are needed group functions, observing and monitoring to see what functions are and are not being performed, supplying or arranging for other members to supply the needed functions and being willing to take necessary action even if that action is not what the leader would prefer to do. This concept of leader as completer is a powerful guide for anyone who wants to be an effective group leader.

Second, somewhat paradoxically, the definition implies that the members as well as the designated leader are accountable for seeing that necessary leadership functions are being performed. The function and duties of the role *leader* depend in part on the skills of the person occupying the role, the abilities, beliefs and expectations of the other members, the group's goals, and the degree of development of the group as a functioning system. Ideally, leadership functions are shared so that each member supplies those services he or she does best, with the designated leader providing what others cannot. For example, someone who is a particularly skilled listener, observing a need to clarify another member's proposal, may attempt to paraphrase it. Someone else may be especially good at organizing complex activities and offer to coordinate member's efforts toward accomplishment of an important group goal. The leader's role depends on the availability of talent within the group, the other members' expectations of leadership behavior, and constraints of the external situation in which the group operates. Thus, group leadership is seen as a set of requisite functions that must be supplied, but not necessarily by the designated leader.

Theoretical Approaches to the Study of Leadership	There have been several approaches to the study of leadership, each one focusing on different dimensions. Jago, reviewing these approaches, organized them into a typology derived from the major assumptions of each approach.[8] One assumption concerns universality versus contingency: is there a set of leadership behaviors or traits that is universal, or does leadership depend on the situation? The other assumption concerns traits versus behaviors: do leaders have certain stable characteristics they carry from situation to situation, or does leadership consist of a set of behaviors that can be learned? Studies of small group leadership can easily be classified into Jago's framework. We see these dimensions not as mutually exclusive, but as poles of a continuum. Thus, we categorize the approaches to leadership study by asking two questions: "To what degree does leadership depend on universality of traits or behaviors, and to what degree is it contingent on the situation?" and "To what degree is leadership a result of persons having stable traits, and to what degree of behaviors which can be learned." Figure 9.1 illustrates our modification of Jago's framework.

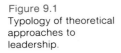

Figure 9.1
Typology of theoretical
approaches to
leadership.

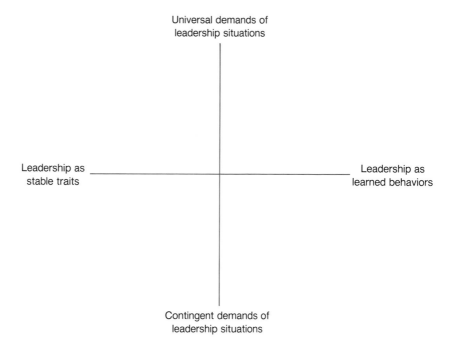

Universal demands of
leadership situations

Leadership as
stable traits

Leadership as
learned behaviors

Contingent demands of
leadership situations

*The Universal
Traits Approach
to the Study of
Leadership*

The earliest leadership studies assumed that leadership consists of a universal set of traits. According to the **universal traits approach,** leaders are a special class of people, distinguishable from followers on the basis of personal, stable characteristics (traits). But is this a valid theory? Some studies have found that leaders tend to have higher IQs, more knowledge, greater verbal facility, behavioral flexibility, and are more attractive as well as physically larger than other group members. They tend to be more sociable than average and are above average in initiative and persistence.[9] However, Stogdill's conclusion from his 1948 review of leadership studies still holds:

> A person does not become a leader by virtue of the possession of some combination of traits, but the pattern of personal characteristics of the leader must bear some relevant relationship to the characteristics, activities, and goals of the followers. . . . The evidence suggests that leadership is a relation that exists between persons in a social situation, and that persons who are leaders in one situation may not necessarily be leaders in other situations.[10]

A leader does not operate in isolation from other members of the group. Leadership behavior will be shaped by the needs of the particular group, so an individual's traits are not as important as other features of the group in combination. What may be appropriate traits for leadership of a committee of university faculty may be inappropriate for leadership of a group of shipwreck survivors. Also, if traits equal leadership, could we have a group where everyone was leader? Of course not. Leadership is *not* a trait!

People who accept the **universal behaviors approach** assume that there is a set of behaviors which is universally appropriate for small group leadership. Focusing on what leaders *do* rather than what they *are,* this approach encourages a search for the best leadership style. Two general style designations have a direct bearing on leadership in small groups. The first, which distinguishes among democratic, autocratic, and laissez-faire behavior, has been the object of considerable study. Research has shown that there are observable differences in the behavior of leaders representing each of the styles. White and Lippett studied adult leaders of boys' craft-making groups and found that democratic leaders allowed the boys to make policy decisions with the leaders' encouragement and assistance. Laissez-faire leaders took almost no initiative but did respond to inquiries, while autocratic leaders made assignments, gave orders, and rigidly controlled all verbal interaction, shutting off boys who did not agree with them.[11] Sargent and Miller, who developed the scale at the beginning of this chapter, discovered that democratic leaders encouraged much more participation in the problem-solving discussion process than did autocratic leaders.[12] Rosenfeld and Plax found that autocratic discussion leaders asked fewer questions but answered more than democratic leaders, expressed more negative reactions (coercion attempts?) and made fewer attempts to get others to participate actively.[13]

Whether a group has a democratic or autocratic leader affects the group's output. For example, in White and Lippett's study democratically led groups were more satisfied. Autocratically led groups worked harder in the presence of the leader but showed the highest frequencies of incidents of aggressiveness and apathy. Most members preferred democratic groups. Jurma studied groups led by individuals who provided structure and coordination (democratic leadership) and those who were nonstructuring (laissez-faire) and concluded that groups with structuring designated leaders are more effective in problem solving as well as more satisfying to participants.[14] Independent judges rated discussions led by structuring leaders to be of higher quality than discussions led by nonstructuring leaders.[15] It appears that a leadership style with some degree of structure produces better outcomes and higher member satisfaction.

The universal behaviors approach also supports the assumptions underlying the **functional approach** to small group leadership. This approach to leadership encourages a search for the kinds of behavioral functions performed by leaders and supports the concept that leadership consists of certain functions that must be performed by *someone* if the group is to be effective, but not necessarily or automatically by the designated leader. The two categories of functions usually described as needed for a group to be maximally effective are those which focus on interpersonal relationships (various writers call this maintenance, socioemotional, or process leadership, or initiating consideration) and those concerned with the group's task (also called initiating structure). There do appear to be some functions common to leaders of several types of groups. Schultz was able to predict, for eight of nine groups, who would become the leader by the communicative functions they performed.

Leaders were more goal directed, direction-giving, summarizing, and self-assured as well as somewhat quarrelsome and sensible.[16] Dobbins and Zaccaro found that members of groups with leaders high in both initiating structure and consideration were more cohesive and satisfied than members of groups with leaders low in these types of behaviors.[17]

Several people have attempted to describe the specific task and maintenance functions needed for effective group leadership. Examples of some of these designations were presented in chapter 8. One of the earliest category systems was the Interaction Process Analysis developed by Bales.[18] Benne and Sheats identified a variety of task and maintenance roles which they claim are productive for the group, along with a set of individual roles that are counterproductive.[19] More recently, Fisher indentified four functions performed by leaders, whom he saw as providing a mediating function between group events and activities and the final outcome:

1. Leaders are well informed and provide a sufficient variety of information as well as the ability to process and handle considerable information.
2. Leaders enact a variety of functions needed within the group.
3. Leaders help group members make sense of decisions made and actions performed within the group by doing such things as supplying good reasons for those actions.
4. Leaders focus on the here-and-now, stopping the group from jumping to unwarranted conclusions or finding formula answers too quickly.[20]

Obviously these process functions are important to the outcomes of a problem-solving or discussion group. Each major function requires many specific types of behaviors. These are described in detail later in this chapter. The important thing to remember about the universal behavior approach to leadership is that it assumes, no matter what the group, certain functions must be performed and some leader styles are more effective than others in supplying these necessary functions. There is considerable support for this approach to the study of leadership.

The Contingent Traits Approach

The **contingent traits approach** assumes that the type of leadership required in any particular situation depends on certain contingencies within the situation itself, such as group purpose, task complexity, organizational context, member characteristics, and other factors. In other words, there is neither a universal set of traits nor a universal set of behaviors that is always appropriate; leadership depends at least in part on the situation. Furthermore, the contingent traits approach assumes that individuals have fairly stable traits, so matching the leader to the situation is more likely to be effective than trying to teach the leader to adapt to the situation.

Fiedler's contingency model of group leadership reflects this approach. He concluded that there are three factors upon which appropriate leader behaviors are contingent: leader-member relations, task structure, and leader position power.[21] The central thesis of Fiedler's work is that individuals' personal needs and characteristics make them suited for leadership only in certain types of contingencies, so it is more productive to match prospective leaders to situations than to try to change the individual's style. This theory also implies that as a group's situation changes through time different types of persons would be needed in the designated leader position. According to Fiedler, problem-solving discussion groups would generally be served best by a democratic structuring leader with concern for persons rather than by autocratic or nonstructuring leadership. However, in other types of situations, such as supervising police or production workers or leading primary groups, a much more autocratic or a socioemotional style of leadership would be more productive.

Members of groups seem to agree that the appropriate leadership functions and style are contingent upon situational variables.[22] Wood asked members of continuing small groups with task, social, and dual task-social objectives what they expected of designated leaders. Three factors emerged: task guidance, interpersonal attractiveness, and team spirit. Members of both task and dual-purpose groups rated task-oriented leadership (analogous to structuring) important, whereas members of social groups rated interpersonal attractiveness high and task orientation low. A moderate degree of team spirit was expected of leaders in all types of groups.[23] Griffin found that the amount of structuring and directive behavior expected from supervisors depended on the level of growth needs of subordinates. Persons with high growth needs (enjoy challenging jobs) most preferred participative, considerate supervisors, whereas employees with lower growth needs accepted more autocratic leadership.[24] Downs and Pickett examined contingencies of leader style and member needs. Groups of participants with high social needs were most productive with task-oriented procedural leaders and least productive with no designated leader. Groups of persons low on interpersonal needs did equally well with designated leaders who provided task-structuring only, leaders who provided both task structuring and socioemotional leadership, and no designated leader. Groups with some members high and some low in interpersonal needs performed somewhat better without a designated leader. A complex relationship was found among member needs, leadership style, and member satisfaction, giving support to the general contingency hypothesis of leadership in small discussion groups.[25] This is supported by Skaret and Bruning, who noted that satisfaction involves a complex interaction between leader behavior and work group attitudes.[26] Differences in follower traits have been known to influence reactions to different leader behavior patterns: degree of authoritarianism and dogmatism, need for achievement and locus of control (whether one feels in control of one's own life or governed by fate).[27] From the research and theory we can safely conclude that a discussion leader needs to be flexible, adapting to situational contingencies, but that in almost all situations a democratic structuring approach will be productive.

Figure 9.2
Task and relationship
needs of maturing
groups.

P. Hersey/K. Blanchard,
MANAGEMENT OF
ORGANIZATIONAL
BEHAVIOR: Utilizing
Human Resources, 4/E, ©
1982, p. 152. Reprinted by
permission of Prentice-Hall,
Inc., Englewood Cliffs, New
Jersey.

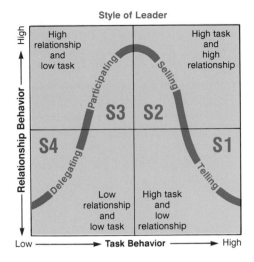

*The Contingent
Behaviors
Approach*

The **contingent behaviors approach** is similar to the previous one in that it focuses on situational contingencies, but it assumes that leaders are capable of more behavioral flexibility than the traits approach. Representative of this approach is the model of leadership adaptability and style developed by Hersey and Blanchard. These authors postulated that leadership behaviors can be located along two dimensions, relationship orientation or task orientation. A given leader can be high on one or the other, on both, or on neither. Figure 9.2 illustrates these dimensions. However, whether or not a leader is effective depends upon his or her ability to adapt to the needs of the members and the life cycle, or maturity, of the group. For instance, a new group probably needs higher task but lower relationship orientation until it understands its charge and objectives. As members become familiar with the task, the leader should begin to increase relationship behavior. Eventually task behavior (coordination efforts, instructions, advice, and so forth) can be reduced, and finally socioemotional support can be withdrawn, since at maturity the group's dependence on the leader is minimal. The group can function well with leadership being widely shared among members based on norms and procedures of a developed system. It is important that the leader be able to analyze the situation and the maturity level of the group members so either task instructions or socioemotional support is not withdrawn prematurely, but also so the leader does not continue to supply either when it is not necessary. The important point, though, is that Hersey and Blanchard assume the behavioral adaptability of the leader.[28]

Wood demonstrated that at least some effective discussion leaders do demonstrate behavioral flexibility. She examined the oral remarks of designated leaders and found that the leaders' comments varied depending on the stated purpose of the discussion and the previous success or failure of the committee. For example, leaders tended to compensate depending on what had occurred at previous meetings, providing more or less structure as needed. Wood noted that "The most important and obvious conclusion is that leaders of purposive discussions do engage in adaptive behavior."[29]

Also consistent with this approach is Chemers's Integrative Systems/Process Model of small group leadership. Chemers's model attempts to integrate the variables studied in all the major approaches to understanding leadership: "The model does assume that leadership process is a multivariate system in which each set of variables is influenced by and in turn influences numerous other sets of variables."[30] Chemers sees the small group as an open system emphasizing leadership. Inputs include the leader's personal characteristics, cultural and situational characteristics, expectations and intentions, and follower characteristics. Process variables include leader and follower behaviors. Output variables include satisfaction, group performance, and feedback. Only by viewing all leader-follower behaviors as parts of a complex process are we likely to develop increasingly valid theories of leadership. We believe that Chemers has developed the first theory reflective of the complexity of leadership in small groups. Other theories have been partial in their explanatory power, oversimplifying what goes on in real small groups.

Leadership Emergence in a Leaderless Group

Most of the groups to which we belong will have either an appointed or elected leader. Occasionally, we find ourselves in an initially leaderless group. College students often are placed in such groups for the purposes of completing various class projects. Others find themselves in casual or activity groups which, though not having a designated leader, nevertheless need leadership functions to be performed. In such situations an **emergent leader** can be expected to evolve naturally.

Leadership studies conducted by Bormann at the University of Minnesota over a period of years revealed a predictable pattern to the emergence of a leader. Study of initially leaderless discussion groups indicated a two-phase pattern. First, all members were in potential contention for the leadership position. The first members to be eliminated were those who were infrequent participants, seemed uninformed about the problem facing the group, or were rigid and dogmatic in the way they spoke. In the second phase, with about 40 percent of the members remaining in contention for leadership, contenders who were authoritarian and manipulative were eliminated in favor of more democratic members. This phase, which usually lasted longer than the first, typically entailed a leadership struggle between two remaining contenders. The final characteristic by which members were eliminated was called *offensive verbalization,* which included constant talking and stilted language. On the other hand, the person who emerged as leader seemed to have an unusual aptitude with words, a knack for saying the right thing at the right time. Often, when one of two remaining contenders for the position emerged as leader, the other served as a kind of lieutenant or supporter of the leader.[31]

Bormann noted that a group tended to select as leader the member who seemed to have the best blend of task and personal concerns for the particular group. Members who are more concerned with relationships are uncomfortable with a strong task leader, and task oriented individuals feel uneasy with a relationship oriented leader. Thus, consistent with Chemers's model, theories regarding leadership emergence must take into account all relevant variables, including the members' expectations and abilities. The leader who emerges will be the one other members trust and perceive to be of most value to the group.

Group-Centered Democratic Discussion Leadership

Up to this point we have examined theory and research concerning small group leaders and leadership without prescribing any specific role functions or techniques. Now, we present suggestions that can be used to guide your behavior the next time you find yourself leader of a small discussion group. These suggestions stem from our personal philosophy about appropriate group leadership; both of us believe that, *all other things being equal,* democratic leadership of learning, discussion, problem-solving and decision-making groups is most appropriate. While it is true that certain situations call for other leadership styles, the kinds of discussion groups you are likely to encounter will generally profit from democratic leadership. Thus, the guidelines lean toward that approach. We think they will be helpful to you. Try them out. Adapt them to your specific personality and the situations you face. Use what you can. In time you will develop your own philosophy, along with a variety of skills in providing leader services. Success comes with practice; now is the time to begin.

We believe that in most situations a designated **discussion leader** helps the group by adopting a democratic group-centered role, with primary attention to task and procedural matters and secondary attention to interpersonal relations. Effective leaders share the multitude of leadership functions and responsibilities. They monitor the group's processes, act as completers to supply needed functions, and accept a large share of the personal responsibility for the success of the group. In most peer groups or work groups of educated employees, an autocrat who pushes personal goals, procedures, beliefs, and solutions will produce apathy, poor quality of outputs, low levels of commitment, interpersonal conflicts, and general dissatisfaction.

Autocratic leaders keep a tight control over the group's interaction, procedures, and outcomes. The result is a **pseudodiscussion** during which the group goes through the motions of discussion but the end result has been predetermined by the leader. An autocrat decides on the agenda alone and the procedure by which a problem will be discussed. He or she decides who will speak when. He or she may listen to advice, but once the autocrat's mind is made up, the decision has been made. Both of us have observed many such groups. In one typical case, the group was the administrative staff of a university campus. The leader, the administrative manager of the staff, presented the agenda, called upon the members one by one to report, made comments to each member, shut off comments by other members, and decided alone when one agenda item had been discussed sufficiently, moving the group immediately to the next item. Members were apathetic and distressed about these meetings. No creativity or enthusiasm was exhibited.

Autocratic leaders who lack the power of an absolute head may use manipulative techniques to secure agreement. They may interrupt, ignore, or argue with anything contrary to their point of view, often without attempting to understand the opposing point. They may use a "divide and conquer" approach by setting up a one-on-one communication network with individuals, using sweet talk and back room politicking to gain support. They distort summaries to fit their views and state ideas with highly emotive language. They manipulate the use of time, coercing agreement by preventing the group from making a decision until time has almost run out, then pressuring others to accept a solution. In the group previously described, the administrative manager frequently said, in a self-assured tone of voice, "Well, no one disagrees with my suggestion, do they?" Few were courageous enough to say "I do."

An autocratic style rests on the belief that a few select people (of which the autocrat is one) are specially endowed, that the majority of people are incapable or irresponsible, and that the way to get people to act is to reward or punish them. On the other hand, democratic leadership style is based on the belief that collective wisdom is greater than that of any single member and all people affected by a decision *should* have a voice in making it. In a democratic climate, attempts to coerce are immoral because they destroy the human capacity to reason and decide for oneself. Attempts to manipulate are impractical because when they are discovered they lead to apathy, resistance, and counterforce. While a democratic leader participates in the group's procedural and substantive decisions, he or she *serves* the group rather than forcing it to satisfy self-serving ends.

The **democratic leader** seeks to discover the group's will and facilitate its achievement. He or she does not predetermine the outcome, which results from the interaction of all members. Discussants speak when they want to within the procedural norms adopted by the group. All ideas are treated as group property; evaluating them is the responsibility of the entire group. Influence comes primarily from information, ideas and skills in doing what is needed to achieve mutually acceptable goals. Establishing the agenda and the procedure for discussing a topic or problem is the prerogative of the group, not of one single member. The leader will suggest and encourage but will not compel, coerce, or manipulate. Leaders may suggest procedures, plans, or solutions but will follow any procedure or accept any solution that the group, by consensus, prefers.

We believe that a democratic leader is superior to an autocratic one, but both are better than a laissez-faire leader for most discussion groups. Laissez-faire leaders do almost nothing; they create a void into which other group members must step. They may open discussions by saying, "It's about time we started our discussion," and then sit back. Skilled group members may proceed successfully, but too often they waste time or an autocrat takes over. Even an autocrat beats chaos!

Another type of leadership appropriate for some situations is bureaucratic leadership. The following are examples of this leadership style: a foreman is charged by his superiors to see that certain tasks are accomplished by the work group; a study-discussion leader is partly responsible to the organization sponsoring the discussion program (often a library or university); a department head is bounded by regulations that cannot be ignored. In a sense, each of these designated leaders has been given a charge that must be met. They must make clear to the group the area of freedom and limits under which they operate. For instance, the leader must tell the group when the decision will be made by the group and when the group is being asked to supply information or advice on which the leader will base the decision. Not to do so will create dashed expectations and unnecessary conflict.

Sometimes members expect the designated task leader, (supervisor, head of department, even committee chair) to provide an analysis of the problem and a tentative solution, which the group will accept or reject apart from its merits in fact and logic. To prevent this, designated leaders are advised to refrain from suggesting solutions, at least until other members have supplied a number of them. One remedy for this may be for the leader to adopt a nondirective style of leading that makes the group accountable for directing its own activities. This is *not* the same as being a laissez-faire or do-nothing leader. In fact, this places great responsibility on the leader to pay careful attention to the group's process, to listen intently, and to reflect observations back to the group, clarifying a problem, supplying information, summarizing, and always asking the group members whether they agree. The leader must exercise great self-control, withholding directions at critical junctures, letting the group flounder, so that members will develop their own skills and motives. The nondirective leader will call attention to problems facing the group but will not solve them. He or she might suggest or invite alternatives but will leave the decision to the group. The leader adopts the role of teacher, developer of individuals, and coach. Although this is difficult at first, consuming more time early in the group's life than appears necessary, it will save time, effort, and group energy in the long run. Once members are accustomed to accepting responsibility for making decisions that affect them, they will not want it any other way.

Personal Characteristics and Behaviors of Effective Discussion Leaders

Knowing what characteristics distinguish effective from ineffective leaders will help you become a better leader as well as select wisely whom to support as group leader. Member input variables like positive attitudes toward self, others, information, and ideas are important, but from leadership studies we list the following specific characteristics of effective discussion leaders.

1. **Effective discussion leaders have a good grasp of the task facing the group, whether the task is learning or problem solving.**
   They are informed, good at analysis, and have promising ideas for solving problems.

2. **Effective discussion leaders are skilled in coordinating group members' thinking and encoding toward a goal.**
   They are above average in ability to think systematically and solve problems. They have to be both goal directed and flexible, providing an agenda of issues and themes, but encouraging contributions of relevant issues and themes from all members. They must be able to detect conversational tangents and bring the group back on track. Effective leaders help others focus on activities relevant to the task.[32]

3. **Effective discussion leaders are active in participation.**
   They are above average for group members in frequency of verbal participation, yet they are not incessant talkers. They are never reticent in a small group, which implies they have a favorable self-concept, nor are they overly sensitive or defensive when criticized or disagreed with. Morris and Hackman found emergent leaders to be frequent, but not necessarily the *most* frequent, participants.[33] Reynolds, too, found leaders to be frequent participants, maintaining "positions of influence through continuous involvement in group discussions and decision-making activities."[34] Remember, quiet members are the first to be eliminated from leadership consideration, but overly talkative ones also are rejected eventually.

4. **Effective discussion leaders encode clearly and concisely.**
   The ability to speak well is important for success in all social contexts. Effective discussion leaders make remarks that are concise, organized, and pertinent. Such leaders, designated or not, are rhetorically sensitive rather than tactless and especially skilled in encoding consensus decisions. For instance, Russell found that problem-solving group leaders had higher degrees of communicative skills than other members.[35] Lashbrook also found that leaders were perceived as speaking more clearly and fluently than other members.[36] Facility in verbalizing the goals, values, ideas, and ideals of the group is important in a discussion leader.

5. **Effective discussion leaders are open-minded.**
   We have found that discussion leaders chosen by participants as future leaders were much more conditional in the way they expressed judgments than those not chosen. Potential leaders might say, "We could try brainstorming to come up with solutions," rather than, "I've decided that brainstorming is the best way for us to solve this." Maier and Solem demonstrated that a leader who suspends judgment and encourages full consideration of minority viewpoints is more effective than one who does not.[37] One of us has repeatedly given dogmatism and authoritarianism scales to students and found that classmates usually chose open-minded leaders. Haiman reported similar findings with his open-mindedness scale.[38] Open-minded leaders manifest the spirit of skeptical inquiry we discussed earlier by considering all information and ideas, even ones contradictory to personal beliefs.

6. **Effective discussion leaders are democratic and group centered.**
   This was developed fully in the preceding section. As Rosenfeld says, ". . . people are equals with whom they work, the rewards and punishments are to be shared."[39]

7. **Effective discussion leaders have respect for and sensitivity to others.**
   To adjust to the changing needs and moods of members of a group, one must be tuned in to the revealing nonverbal cues. Democratic actions rest on trust in the collective wisdom of the group and respect for rights of all members. Building a team spirit and sense of cooperation often depends on finding and emphasizing common interests and values, which takes a high degree of sensitivity and awareness of others. Kenny and Zaccaro found that leadership depends heavily on one's ability to perceive and adjust one's own behaviors to the needs and goals of members.[40] Wood found that leaders are skilled in adapting and tailoring their behavior.[41] The best discussion leaders are excellent listeners, empathic, patient, and able to summarize accurately. Husband found that effective leaders avoid extremes of behavior likely to alienate others.[42]

8. **Effective discussion leaders are flexible in taking their distinctive roles.**
   Many studies have shown that effective discussion leaders take roles distinctly different from those of other group members.[43] We have found that the most effective discussion leaders are those who asked more questions, gave more procedural guidance, and expressed fewer personal opinions than other members. The concept of leader as completer indicates the need for role flexibility, as do all the contingency theories of leadership. Wood observed that committee leaders actually did show such flexibility from meeting to meeting as conditions changed.[44] You are well advised to practice and develop skills in as many of the task, procedural, and maintenance functions of group interaction as possible.

9. **Effective discussion leaders share rewards and give credit to the group.**
They readily praise the group for successes, not taking credit or glory
to themselves. They stress teamwork and look for ways to make
members feel important to the group.

Other terms could be used to characterize the behavioral style of
effective democratic discussion leaders in groups of peers, but these
nine are supported consistently in the research findings. The ideal small
group discussion leader is informed, egalitarian, organized,
knowledgeable, a skilled problem solver, active, outgoing, democratic,
respectful, accepting of other people, nonmanipulative, articulate,
flexible, and group-centered.

Responsibilities and Techniques of Discussion Leaders and Chairpersons

Designated discussion leaders are responsible for seeing that the time and
energy of the group members is spent wisely. Most adults are members of
many groups and have numerous demands upon their time. We often come
rushing into a meeting at the last minute, our minds still occupied with other
matters. We become irritated if our leaders greet us with "Well, what shall
we do today?" In contrast, leaders who are organized and well prepared for
meetings foster group cohesiveness, acceptance of solutions, and member acceptance of responsibility for the work of the group. This does *not* mean the
leader controls. The group still retains power to decide within its area of
freedom, but its time and activities are coordinated by the designated leader.

While being leader of a group can be time consuming, the designated
leader's duties in a continuing group need not require much more effort and
time than are expected of all group members; in fact, in groups of peers they
should *not* require more time. This will be the case, however, only if the other
members view the job of organizing and carrying out the group's work as a
task appropriately shared by all members. For example, a group one of us
belonged to discussed openly how leadership functions were to be distributed;
one person was responsible for calling meetings, a second for taking notes and
having them distributed, and a third for soliciting items for the agenda from
other members. During the discussion periods, the position of discussion leader
rotated among members, as did the position of social chairperson. Another
way of distributing the work is for co-procedural leaders to agree to take on
the primary responsibility of monitoring the group's process, ensuring that all
members have equal opportunity to participate and watching for signs of tension that need to be dealt with. Ideally, every member can assume responsibility to supply whatever leadership services appear to be needed at any given
time. This is the essence of the effective discussion group, even though one
person has emerged as *the* leader.

If the role of primary discussion leader rotates from meeting to meeting,
members should all be relatively equal in ability to perform that role. In addition, if the group decides that it will use co-leaders to alleviate the problem
of overwork, the co-leaders must function as a team, planning who will do
what and how best to serve the group. Periodic review of the procedures is in
order as well.

We presented information earlier about contingencies that may affect the degree of control appropriately assumed by a designated leader. In general, leaders of developing peer groups tend to err on the side of too little control, with a few trying to control too much. As a group begins to mature and its members become more skilled, the designated leader must be flexible enough to release some control needed initially in the group's development. This means that the leader must be perceptive in gauging what the group needs at any given time. Fortunately, leaders can rely on group members to help them by periodic, explicit review of the group's procedures. Considering situational variables can help you optimize your leadership style and functioning:

1. **Group purpose and goals.**
   Learning, personal growth, and value-sharing groups need far less structure and control than groups facing complex problems.

2. **Member expectations.**
   A designated leader will at first need to conform to what members expect of the role, but this can later be changed through explicit discussion of the leader's job.

3. **Specific procedures and group methods often require rather strict procedural control.**
   Brainstorming, buzz group procedures, problem census, or nominal group techniques require that specific procedures be followed and monitored, but discussion not using special procedures requires less control.

4. **Member skills and maturity must be taken into account.**
   As Hersey and Blanchard reported, members who are used to working together may need less leader control.

5. **The leader's skill and confidence should determine how he or she acts.**
   It is harder to share tasks of procedural leadership than to monopolize them. Democratic leadership calls for skills in listening, organizing, summarizing, and timing that may take a long time to develop.

6. **Time urgency may be a factor.**
   Occasionally a decision must be made in a hurry, in which case a group will welcome strict control on its procedures. When time is not limited and members are vitally affected by what they decide, they need less control.

7. **Highly involved groups require less control.**
   When members perceive that the task is important to them personally, they will often resist close procedural control by a leader. Thus, the designated leader should try to help members realize the importance of their task and become involved and concerned.

Now that we have discussed the broad issues regarding degree of control, we turn to the specific duties that small group leaders typically are expected to perform. These fall into three categories: administrative duties, functions performed during group discussions, and responsibilities for helping the group develop. We also include information on how to perform them, basing the suggestions on the research findings and philosophical stances presented earlier. One helpful suggestion is for a group to develop a manual of duties and responsibilities for the group as a whole, the chair, and the members. Once all members have a copy, they will be better able to orient their expectations and behaviors toward each other and the designated leader. We urge all organizations with committees to create such a manual.

Administrative Duties

Administrative duties are those that must be performed for the group to run smoothly and to maintain an appropriate relationship to its parent organization if it has one. Especially important among these administrative services are planning for meetings, following up on members' assignments, making needed reports, and serving as liaison with other groups and the parent organization.

Planning for Meetings

Adequate planning is necessary if members' time is to be used efficiently. The following is a checklist you can follow to facilitate productive meetings:

_____ 1. **Define the purpose of the meeting.**
A meeting should not be held if there is no purpose for it. Furthermore, the meeting's purpose should be defined clearly. "To talk over our coming year as a committee" is *not* adequately defined as an objective; "To establish an agenda of problems for committee actions during the coming six months" gives clear purpose to the meeting.

_____ 2. **List the specific outcomes which should or must be produced from this meeting.**
Has the parent organization demanded a report within a week? Must the board of trustees be given a recommendation within two days or the committee will lose its opportunity to supply input into trustees' actions? The group should know what is to be accomplished, by when, and what form it is to take.

_____ 3. **Establish starting and ending times for the meeting.**
Frequently, committees and study groups meet with strict time limits imposed by other concurrent meetings, class, and work schedules and other factors over which the group has no control. When the group has no such external time limits placed on its meetings, an ending time should be established anyway. Don't run meetings overtime! That will kill member involvement and attendance quickly. Setting an ending time encourages the group to use its time well. If the work cannot be finished, plan extra meetings.

_____ 4. **Notify members of the purpose or agenda, necessary preparation, and time and place of the meeting.**

The chair is responsible for seeing that members are notified and given ample opportunity to prepare for a meeting. In large organizations this duty may be delegated to a staff person, such as a professional secretary, but it still is the *responsibility* of the leader.

_____ 5. **If special resource persons will be needed at the meeting, advise and prepare them for the meeting.**

Small groups frequently need to question specialists with unique knowledge and skills or experience. A student group may want to discuss its dissatisfaction with cafeteria services with the food service manager before making a policy decision, or a collective bargaining committee may want the advice of a financial expert before recommending a negotiating platform. Such members need to be told what information to prepare and what to expect.

_____ 6. **Make all necessary physical arrangements.**

Has the meeting room been reserved? Are handouts, notepads, chalk, charts, ashtrays (if smoking is permitted), and possibly beverages ready? Is the room arranged as a circle or oval to facilitate discussion?

_____ 7. **If needed, prepare a procedure by which the group can evaluate its process.**

If the group needs to evaluate its throughput processes (recommended periodically for continuing groups), an outline of questions should be developed to assure that important variables will not be overlooked. Appropriate postmeeting reaction forms should be prepared also.

Following Up on Meetings

Two kinds of follow-up are needed: reminding group members of assignments to be sure they are completed and getting out necessary reports from the group to other groups or individuals. If adequate reports or minutes are kept, members will be reminded of routine assignments through these written records. Sometimes members agree to undertake special assignments. Someone may agree to find bibliographic items, someone else to conduct a personal interview, and a third to procure copies of a relevant statute—all before the next meeting. The leader can make a brief phone call before the next meeting, tactfully asking whether the member encountered any trouble in completing the assignment will serve as a gentle reminder. This helps keep the group on track.

It is often necessary for a chair to prepare and send letters, memoranda, formal reports, notices of group decisions, advice prepared by the committee, and so forth to appropriate people. This includes getting copies of minutes prepared and distributed, but more especially involves writing formal resolutions, sending advisory policy statements to administrative officers, calling and conducting a press conference, or carrying out whatever decisions for action the group has made. While the group should decide *what* to do and *who* is to do it, the *who* is often the group's designated leader.

Liaison

Someone often has to serve as spokesperson for a committee or task group. Usually this is one of the service duties of the chair. Members expect leaders to represent them to other groups and individuals and will often refer inquiries from outsiders to the chair. In many organizations, the chairs of standing committees maintain contact among the working groups that comprise the organization; many companies, for instance, hold regular meetings of division managers specifically for this purpose. Whenever you act as a liaison person, remember that you represent the *group* and are not speaking from a personal perspective or position.

Several specific occasions call for liaison representation. For instance, when a committee makes a report at an organizational membership meeting or presents a resolution for parliamentary action, the chair invariably speaks for the committee. While the thrust of the remarks may have been approved in advance by the committee, the specific comments are often prepared by the chair alone. Occasionally committee chairs will be interviewed by public media. If you anticipate this happening, you can be prepared to answer reporters' questions. The chair's statements should accurately reflect the group's work, findings, and beliefs. Any statement that seems to lean to one side of a controversy within the committee will cause further friction and division within the group, and the leader will lose the trust of those members who feel misrepresented.

Leading Group Discussions

Administrative responsibilities of designated leaders precede and follow actual meetings of a small group. Now we turn our attention to what designated leaders are expected to do during actual meetings.

Initiating Discussions: Opening Remarks

Opening remarks are designed to set the stage for the meeting by creating a positive atmosphere, initiating the structure for the meeting, explaining the leader's role (especially for new groups), and getting the discussion underway. They should be kept brief. Here are some guidelines for planning your opening remarks:

1. **It may be necessary, especially with a new group, to reduce primary tensions.**
   Members may need to be introduced to each other. An icebreaker activity or brief social activity might be planned. Name tags or tents should be provided if members are not acquainted.
2. **The purpose and importance of the meeting must be described and possibly discussed and the area of freedom (and limitations) made clear.**
   Sometimes this will take little more than to review the meeting notice with the group.
3. **Some effort to create a climate of trust and informality may be needed.**
   This might include suggesting norms, such as confidentiality, respectful active listening, and the need for cooperation. When a new group first meets, the discussion leader should briefly describe his or her role and what is expected of other members during discussion. For example, both of us have explained, in first meetings of departmental

committees, that the leader role would be one of facilitator, coordinator, and process monitor, but not decision maker for the group, arguer for specific proposals, or persuasive speaker for particular policies.

Sometimes an unstructured period where members get acquainted with each other's beliefs, values, backgrounds, and attitudes regarding the problem facing the group can help. This serves primarily a socioemotional function. The designated leader who senses such a need for ventilation and encourages it may later find the job of keeping talk organized, relevant, and objective much easier than if no unstructured ventilation had occurred. The leader must balance the need for ventilation with the need for organization and should not let it go on too long. Look for signs that the group wants order.

4. **Informational and structural handouts may be presented.**
These may include informational sheets, an agenda, outlines to guide discussions, case problems, copies of things to be discussed, etc.

5. **Supply suggested structure and procedures.**
You may want the group to set these up, but be prepared to suggest them. You will find it advisable to provide members with an outline for organizing discussion, then ask members to modify or accept it.

6. **See that any special roles needed are established, such as recorder.**
The group may want to discuss whether such roles will be rotated or whether one person will maintain them for the life of the group.

7. **Ask a clear question to focus initial discussion on the first substantive issue on the agenda.**
This will help launch the group into the substantive portion of the meeting.

Structuring Discussions

Once the group members are oriented to each other and toward the task, the leader can help the group function efficiently by helping to structure the group's deliberations. The following are some suggestions to help you accomplish this:

1. **Keep the group goal oriented.**
Be sure the goal is clearly understood and accepted by all members. At times you may want to ask such questions as "How will this help us achieve our goal?" or to comment "We seem to be losing sight of our objective."

2. **A procedure for problem solving or an outline for learning discussions can be put on a handout, a chalkboard, or chart.**
For instance, you may want to explain a procedure with which the group is not familiar, such as the nominal group technique. This will often do a great deal to keep comments organized and goal oriented.

3. **Summarize or see that a summary is made of each major step in a problem-solving discussion and of each decision reached.**
Ask if the summary is accepted by all members as accurate and complete. In some cases, a secretary can help summarize.

4. **Make a clear transition to each new step or agenda item.**
   A transition can be combined with a summary. For example: "We have heard that time pressure, grade pressure, and inadequate preparation lead to plagiarism on term papers. Are we ready to consider possible solutions? What might we recommend to reduce plagiarism?" When members keep restating the same idea, you can suggest that agreement appears to have been reached (decision emergence) and move on to the next issue.

5. **Be sure that all needed steps in the problem-solving procedure, items on the agenda, or issues for a learning discussion are dealt with adequately.**
   Keep track of the time so you can point out to the group what still needs to be done and how much time is available. Point out any issue of importance that is being overlooked.

6. **Watch for extended digressions and frequent changes of theme.**
   Some digressions will occur in every discussion. The leader needs to be on guard so the group can be brought back on track before the digression becomes extended. When you notice a digression, point it out and perhaps ask the group what to do about it. When a change of issue or irrelevant topic crops up, you may suggest returning to the previous issue. If a member suggests a solution prematurely, you might ask if he or she would bring it up when the group has finished its analysis of the problem.

7. **Bring the discussion to a definite close.**
   This should be done no later than the scheduled ending time for the meeting, unless all members consent to extending the time. The conclusion can include a summary of all progress the group has made, a statement of how the reports of the meeting will be distributed to members and other interested persons, comments about preparations for the next meeting, assignments for follow-up and implementation, commendations for a job well done, or an evaluation of the meeting to improve the group's future interactions.

Equalizing Opportunity to Participate and Influence

While you are keeping the verbal interaction organized and goal directed, you also need to see that everyone has equal opportunity to speak and that some members neither stage-hog nor withdraw. There are several things you can do to produce such equality:

1. **Address your comments and questions to the group rather than individuals.**
   Unless you want to elicit a specific item of information or respond directly to what a member has said, speak to the group as a whole. Be sure that you are making regular eye contact with everyone when you ask questions, especially with less talkative members.

2. **See that all members have an equal chance to participate verbally.**
   No one should be forced to speak, but neither should any member be prevented from speaking by the aggressiveness of others.
   a. Point out in your opening remarks that part of your role will be to see that everyone has an equal opportunity to talk and that you will be primarily a coordinator.
   b. You should make a visual survey of all members every minute or two, looking for nonverbal indications that a member wants to speak. If you see such a reaction, be a "gatekeeper" with a comment such as "Joe, did you want to comment on Mary's idea?" Encourage, but do not embarrass the participant by putting him or her in the spotlight. If you misinterpret the nonverbal signals, then say something like "Joe, what do you think of that idea?" Joe will be put in an embarrassing position. Joe might not have been listening. Always leave room for a member to remain silent without losing face.
   c. Sometimes a quiet member can be assigned to investigate and report on needed information.
   d. You might invite a quiet person to speak if you are sure he or she has special knowledge or interest in an issue: "Belinda, I think you made a special study of that, didn't you?"
3. **Listen with real interest to what an infrequent participant says and encourage others to do so as well.**
   Infrequent speakers may get ignored if the leader does not intervene to elicit some response to their remarks.
4. **Try to control compulsive, dominating, or long-winded speakers.**
   Occasionally a member so monopolizes the conversation that others either have to fight for the right to speak or give up. A few will repeatedly interrupt and drown out voices of others who are speaking. Verbal monopolizing must be controlled for the sake of the group, but often highly verbal people can be valuable assets to the group. You want to control, not stifle, the behavior. These techniques are listed in the approximate order in which they would be used, from most subtle to most blunt:
   a. When feasible, seat talkative members where you can seem to overlook them naturally when asking questions of the group, and try to avoid looking at them when you ask a question.
   b. Establish eye contact with infrequent speakers; avoid eye contact with the talkers.
   c. When a long-winded person has made a point, cut in as tactfully as possible with "How do the *rest* of you feel about that point?" or some similar request for others to participate.
   d. Suggest a group rule that each person make one point, then allow others the floor and that persons not interrupt or drown out others.
   e. In private ask the frequent talker to encourage quiet members to speak.

    f. Have one person keep a count or stop watch on each participant's remarks, then report findings to the group and discuss them during an evaluation period.

    g. Describe the problem openly and ask the group to deal with it as a group.

    h. Even more drastic measures may be needed on occasion, to the point of asking the person to leave the group, but only after discussion of the troublesome behavior has failed.

5. **Avoid commenting after each member remark.**

Some designated discussion leaders do this, perhaps unaware, producing a wheel network of verbal interaction. Often such leader behavior seems to come from a desire to dominate and control the ideas and decisions of the group. Procedural leaders cannot get deeply involved in the substance of the discussion without losing perspective. Listen, speak when you are really needed, but avoid becoming the interpreter or repeater of what others say.

6. **Bounce questions of opinion back to the group.**

There is a tendency in some groups either to accept or reject designated leader opinions, so unless the group is quite mature, you are wise to hold your opinions until after others have expressed theirs. Then, offer your opinions only as another point of view to be considered before making a decision. So if a member asks "What do you think we should do?" you can reply, "Let's see what other members think first. What do the rest of you. . . ."

7. **Generally remain neutral during the argument over the merits of alternatives.**

If you get heavily involved you will have a harder time being objective, seeing that all have equal opportunity to participate, the discussion remains orderly and relevant, other leader services are supplied, and seeking constructive compromises as a basis for consensus. If evaluation seems needed, try to get the other members to provide it. Of course, you should feel free to accept and support emergent decisions.

Stimulating Creative Thinking

All too often problem-solving groups create run-of-the-mill solutions. A thorough analysis of the problem is often a rich source of inventive alternatives. A few special techniques may help:

1. **Apply the principle of deferred judgment.**

Ask "How *might* we . . . ?" rather than "How *should* we . . . ? Suggest waiting to evaluate proposals until no one has any more possible solutions to suggest.

2. **When the flow of thinking seems to have dried up, encourage the group to search for a few more alternatives.**

You might use this idea-spurring question: "What *else* can we think of to. . . ." or "I wonder if we can think of any more possible ways to. . . ."

3. **It sometimes pays to take up various components of a problem one at a time.**
    For instance: "Is there any way to improve the appearance of . . ." or "the durability of. . . ."

4. **Watch for suggestions that could be used to open up whole new areas of thinking, then pose a general question about the area.**
    For example, if someone suggests putting up signs in the library that show the cost of losses to the users, you might ask, "How else could we publicize the cost of losses to the library?"

Stimulating Critical Thinking

A group must subject possible alternatives to rigorous evaluation before it reaches a final position. Sometimes an atmosphere develops where members do not feel free to criticize or assess the potential faults of each other's ideas, whether through defensiveness, the tendency to conform to high-status members, or the need to decide quickly. All information and opinions should be subject to critical judgment. Here are some things you might do to encourage this without evoking unmanageable levels of secondary tension:

1. **If the group gets solution-minded quickly, suggest more analysis of the problem.**
    This is a common problem. Chapter 11 presents a systematic method for helping a group focus on problem analysis.

2. **Encourage group members to evaluate information.**
    For example:
    a. To check relevance of evidence you might ask: "How does this apply to our problem?" or "How is that like the situation we are discussing?"
    b. To evaluate the source of evidence you might ask: "What is the source of that information?" "How well is _____ recognized in the field?" or "Is this consistent with other pronouncements on the subject?"
    c. To check on the credibility of information you might ask: "Do we have any information that is contradictory?"
    d. To test a statistic you might ask how it was derived, who conducted the study, or how an average was computed.
    e. Bring in outside experts to challenge the views of the group and its central members.

3. **See that all group members understand and accept all standards, criteria, or assumptions used in making judgments.**
    For example, you might ask: "Is that criterion clear to us all?" "Is this something we want to insist on?" or "Do we all accept that as an assumption?"

4. **See that all proposed solutions are given a thorough testing before they are accepted as final group decisions.**
   Encourage the group to apply the available facts and all criteria. You may want to remind members of the danger of groupthink explained in chapter 10.
   a. The following are some questions you might as leader ask:

   Do we have any evidence to indicate that this solution would be satisfactory? Unsatisfactory?

   Are there any facts to support this proposal?

   How well would this idea meet our criteria?

   Would that proposal get at the basic problem?

   Is there any way we can test this idea before we decide whether or not to adopt it?

   b. Ask members to discuss tentative solutions or policies with persons outside the group.
   c. One or more members can be asked to take the role of critical evaluator or devil's advocate so that all ideas are challenged and everyone has a chance to air all doubts.
   d. Subdivide the larger group into two subgroups under different leaders to evaluate all alternatives, then rejoin to iron out differences.
   e. Before reaching a binding decision on a policy of far-reaching consequence, hold a "second chance" meeting at which all doubts, moral concerns, or untested assumptions can be explored.

Promoting Teamwork and Cooperation

Group maintenance functions require time that might otherwise be devoted to productive problem solving. However, while too much time spent on interpersonal relationships will lead to frustration and impatience, neglecting these concerns will lead to low morale and perhaps disintegration of the group. The leader's task is to find the right blend of the two for the group in question. You want to strive for a group that produces efficiently and successfully in a climate of mutual respect, cooperation, and team spirit. Here are a few suggestions that may help:

1. **Develop a name or other symbol of group identification.**
   (T-shirts, logos, "in" jokes, slogans, etc.)
2. **Speak of "us" and "we," not so much of "I" and "you."**
   You might ask what it means if another member speaks of the group as "you."
3. **Watch for evidence of hidden agendas at variance with group goals.**
   Bring them to the attention of the group as problems to be solved by the group. Avoiding these problems makes them worse.

4. **If there are competing subgroups, a sense of common fate in a larger conflict often will help members pull together.**
   Try to find a superordinate goal, more important to the members' fate than subgroup goals, behind which all subgroups can rally.

5. **Keep arguments focused on facts and issues.**
   Step in at once if any member starts an attack on another's personality or character.

6. **Don't let the discussion get so serious that persons cannot enjoy themselves.**
   Humor may help reduce the tensions that are generated when persons work hard together at the job of hammering out ideas. Good task leaders may have trouble with humor. Lee observed, for instance, that many of the most efficient leaders were lacking in human warmth: "When men are driven, they lose spontaneity and the zestful interest in what goes on. . . . We need efficiency *and* satisfyingness."[45]
   Lee suggested, essentially, that task masters relax and allow humorous digressions, which can relieve secondary tension. Group discussion shifts between the serious and the playful, kidding and criticism. You as leader *want* to let the group chain out fantasies that enrich its life and contribute to establishing necessary shared beliefs and values. The result of such tension-relieving activity is more concerted effort by group members in the long run. If you are not skilled at tension release, enlist the help of members who are. Bring the group back to the task once the joke is over or the fantasy has chained out.

7. **When a group seems to be deadlocked, look for a basis on which to compromise.**
   Perhaps you can synthesize parts of several ideas into a consensus solution. As Tropman says, "Leadership also involves political and intellectual synthesis. The chair participates a bit less than other members because the chair's contribution is more to provide mortar to join different decisional blocks than to provide the blocks themselves."[46] If you have been doing your job well as designated leader, you have remained somewhat detached from the fray, listening and observing. You are able to maintain a perspective of the forest, and so should be able to help members see where the individual trees fit in. As you combine ideas, suggest that part of one proposal be merged with part of another or find a broader solution that incorporates important notions from several smaller ones. You serve the role of mediator, looking for a common ground, a compromise solution that all parties can accept as the *best achievable solution*. If each party gains something as well as yields something, there is no overwhelming loser whose disappointment will have to be dealt with at a later point.

While the ideal is for all needs of all group members to be met fully in the development of a group solution, this is not always possible and compromises are often necessary. Compromise is not a dirty word; it is the basis of the political process. As Edmund Burke said, "All government,—indeed every human benefit and enjoyment, every virtue and every prudent act,—is founded on compromise and barter."[47] First, point out that compromise is not a sellout. Second, insist that the interests and needs of each participant are clearly understood by all other participants. Next, find the minimum conditions that are acceptable to each conferee and suggest a solution to meet these minimums. Be prepared for this to take considerable discussion.

8. **Share rewards with the group.**
   Leaders often receive praise from the parent organization or power figures. Wise leaders give credit to the group. Your comments about what a fine job *the group* has done, your pride in membership, and acknowledgement of the outstanding service provided by members fosters cohesiveness and team spirit.

Developing the Group

The need for development varies widely from group to group. A one-meeting discussion group may not need to evaluate its process, but a continuing group— a classroom project group, standing committee, administrative staff, quality circle, or autonomous work group—is advised to allow time for feedback and assessment of its meetings. This should be done periodically and generally falls within the domain of the designated leader.

Sometimes the impetus for growth can be given by asking the group at the conclusion of a meeting to examine its discussion: "How well did we do in our discussion?" or "What might we do to make our next meeting more profitable than this one?" If a group is having trouble, the leader might interrupt the discussion with a comment like: "We seem to be making little headway. What's wrong? How might we get more accomplished (or, relieve this tension, make the discussion more interesting, etc.)?" Tailor the question to the specific problem you sense.

It is often helpful for someone to be designated the process observer for the group. A class studying discussion techniques should have at least one such observer, who may break into the conversation to point out what seems to be hampering the group, make a brief report after the discussion, fill out rating forms the group can discuss, or raise questions pertinent to the group's procedures. A continuing group can select someone to serve in this capacity, either one member for one entire discussion or several members for shorter segments. After the discussion, the process observers give the group feedback to help clear up any negative or positive feelings. Advice on how to do this is provided in chapter 14. However process observation is handled, it is an invaluable leadership service.

If you are the designated leader, you can serve the group not only by seeing that such activities as process observation are made a regular part of the group's routine, but especially by serving as a model for the kind of group-centered, open-minded, thoughtful, rhetorically sensitive, and responsible behavior needed from all members. Examine your own attitudes when a committee you chair is doing poorly. Our attitudes and values leak nonverbally despite what we say. Communicate your group-centeredness by dependable service to the group.

Summary

Chapter 9 has explored leadership of discussion, problem-solving, and decision-making groups. The first half of the chapter summarized pertinent research and theory; the second half provided prescriptive advice for designated leaders.

Leadership, leader, and *designated leader* are related concepts. Leadership was defined as group goal-oriented influence; leader as anyone exerting such influence; and designated leader as anyone who is appointed, elected, or who has emerged to fill the leader position in a group. Influence rests on power bases of reward, coercion, legitimacy, reference, and expertise. Leadership implies that power is granted freely to a person from one or more of these power sources and can be shared or distributed among all group members. Small groups are more productive when a stable leadership structure exists.

Early approaches to leadership assumed that certain universal traits were present in all leaders in all situations. Later, the belief that leaders should adopt a universally appropriate set of behaviors led to the search for the best style of leadership. Typically, researchers studied democratic, autocratic, and laissez-faire styles or those that stressed task orientation versus relationship orientation. This belief in universally needed behaviors also provided support for the functions approach to the study of leadership. The functional approach stated that there is a set of task-related and maintenance-related functions that must be performed if a group is to be effective, and any member of the group can and should provide whatever function (behavior) is needed at any time. The contingent traits approach assumed that the type of leadership likely to be most productive depends on certain situational contingencies; effective leadership consists of matching a leader with specific traits to a situation that calls for these traits. Fiedler is the major proponent of this approach. The contingent behaviors approach is similar, but gives the leader credit for more behavioral flexibility than the contingent traits approach. According to the contingent behaviors approach, effective leadership depends on the leader's ability to adapt behavior to the needs of the group and the individual members. Hersey and Blanchard represent this view by saying that a group first needs a strong task orientation. However, as the group matures, the leader should alter his or her behavior, supplying less task and eventually less relationship behavior. Lastly, Chemers has provided us with a systems approach to leadership theory that integrates some aspects of all prior theories into one theory matching the complexity of a small group system.

Designated leaders are responsible for a variety of administrative duties, for leading discussions, and for helping the group develop. Among the major administrative tasks of a group leader are planning and preparing for meetings; following up on group decisions; and liaison with executives, other groups, and sometimes the news media. Developing the group into a more efficient system may entail modeling the kinds of behavior needed from members, running training sessions, compiling brief statements of expectations and norms, and conducting periodic evaluation sessions. Leading discussions during meetings requires planning for and initiating the actual discussion, providing both purpose and structure (including agenda-drafting and outlining), encouraging a cooperative and supportive climate, promoting creative thinking, stimulating thorough evaluation of information and ideas, pointing out common ground and bases for compromise to reach consensus decisions, promoting teamwork, and seeing that all phases of the problem-solving procedure or issues of interest to members are explored.

Exercises

1. Score and interpret the Sargent and Miller Leadership Scale you completed at the beginning of this chapter. Give yourself one point for each of your answers that agree with those in the following key:

   Key:
1. a	6. b
2. b	7. b
3. b	8. a
4. a	9. a
5. b	10. a

   A maximum score of 10 means you are very democratic in your responses; a minimum score of 0 means you are very autocratic. Discuss your choices with your classmates.

2. Based on your most recent experiences in group discussions, make three lists. List your most important strengths as a discussion leader, your most important weaknesses, and the steps you plan to take to remove or reduce your weaknesses.

3. Split the class in half. One half will serve as observers and the other as discussants; later, they will switch roles. The discussants should form groups of four or five, with approximately equal numbers of observers per group. Each group should select a case problem or question of interest (for instance, how to improve the quality of undergraduate education at your college, how to reduce cheating, etc.) and a designated leader to guide discussion. The observers should be prepared to observe the leader's behavior and answer the following questions:

   a. What functions did the leader perform? How effective was each? How appropriate?

   b. At what points during the discussion did the leader fail to supply some needed leadership service? Did someone else step in to provide it? Was the group hurt?

   c. Over all, how effective was the leader?

4. Think of leaders of small groups to which you have belonged and discuss the following with class members.
   a. Who was the *worst* leader? List the specific characteristics and behaviors that contribute to your judgement.
   b. Who was the *best* leader? What specific characteristics and behaviors led to that evaluation?
   c. Which of the above behaviors were most important in distinguishing between the two?

5. You and your classmates should form into several groups of four or five, with two or three assigned nonparticipant observers per group, and discuss case problems that you select or that your instructor provides. Half the groups should select a designated leader; the other half should remain leaderless.
   a. The observers should note carefully what they see. What leadership functions were performed? Were there any differences between the two types of groups? What are the implications?
   b. Each group member and observer should write a set of minutes for the discussion. Compare notes with each other. Which set of minutes would you as a group member prefer to receive? Why?

6. Role play problem-solving discussions in groups (preferably using case problems presented by your instructor). Two or three problem members should be planted in each group to do such things as plead personal interests, sidetrack by introducing irrelevant issues, make cutting personal criticisms, talk incessantly, remain silent, and so forth. Experiment with various leader techniques for handling these problem members and evaluate the results.

7. Interview several group leaders (committee chairs, staff managers, etc.). Ask them to describe their concepts of small group leadership and the specific techniques they use. What common beliefs do they share? What differences?

8. Discuss the notion that different types of groups need different types of leaders. What contingencies can you identify that may have a bearing? Can you give examples, from your experience, where a leader should have modified his or her behavior to fit the group's needs? Do you think there is a *best* style of leadership to fit all situations?

9. Have different group members role-play each of the following situations in a small group discussion: incessant talking, interpersonal conflict over issues, and argumentativeness. Have the designated leader practice handling each of these problems. What seemed to work best? What other things could the leader have tried to solve the problems presented?

10. Select a problem. Then, ask each class member to prepare and deliver a leader's opening remarks for initiating a discussion of the problem. Have the class evaluate each introduction.

Bibliography

Bormann, Ernest G. *Discussion and Group Methods: Theory and Practice.* 2d ed. New York: Harper & Row, Publishers, 1975, chapter 11.

Cathcart, Robert S., and Larry A. Samovar, eds. *Small Group Communication: A Reader.* 4th ed. Dubuque, Iowa: Wm. C. Brown Publishers, 1984, 367–446.

Hollander, Edwin P. *Leadership Dynamics.* New York: The Free Press, 1978.

Maier, Norman R. F. *Problem-Solving Discussions and Conferences.* New York: McGraw-Hill, 1963.

Paulus, Paul B. *Basic Group Processes.* New York: Springer-Verlag, 1983, chapter 2.

Tropman, John E. *Effective Meetings: Improving Group Decision-Making.* Beverly Hills: Sage Publications, 1980.

Notes

1. F. Sargent and G. Miller, "Some Differences in Certain Communication Behaviors of Autocratic and Democratic Group Leaders," *Journal of Communication* 21 (1971), 233–52.

2. Robert Tannenbaum, Irving R. Wechsler, and Fred Massarik, *Leadership and Organizations: A Behavioral Science Approach* (New York: McGraw-Hill, 1961), 24.

3. John R. P. French and Bertram Raven, "The Bases of Social Power," in *Group Dynamics: Research and Theory,* 3d ed., eds. Dorwin Cartwright and Alvin Zander (New York: Harper & Row, Publishers, 1968), 259–69.

4. Ernest G. Bormann, *Discussion and Group Methods,* 2d ed. (New York: Harper & Row, Publishers, 1975), 253–69; Nancy L. Harper and Lawrence R. Askling, "Group Communication and Quality of Task Solution in a Media Production Organization," *Communication Monographs* 47 (1980): 77–100.

5. E. P. Hollander, *Leadership Dynamics* (New York: The Free Press, 1978), 13–16.

6. Ernest Stech and Sharon A. Ratliffe, *Working in Groups* (Skokie, Ill.: National Textbook Company, 1976), 201.

7. William C. Schutz, "The Leader as Completer," in *Small Group Communication: A Reader,* 3d ed., eds. Robert S. Cathcart and Larry A. Samovar (Dubuque, Iowa: Wm. C. Brown Publishers, 1979), 400.

8. Arthur G. Jago, "Leadership: Perspectives in Theory and Research," *Management Science* 28 (1982): 315–36.

9. Ralph M. Stogdill, *Handbook of Leadership: A Survey of Theory and Research* (New York: The Free Press, 1974), 63–82; Marvin E. Shaw, *Group Dynamics,* 2d ed. (New York: McGraw-Hill Book Company, 1976), 274–75 and chapter 6.

10. Ralph M. Stogdill, "Personal Factors Associated with Leadership: A Survey of the Literature," *Journal of Psychology* 25 (1948): 64.

11. Ralph K. White and Ronald Lippett, "Leader Behavior and Member Reaction in Three 'Social Climates'" in *Group Dynamics: Research and Theory,* 2d ed., eds. Dorwin Cartwright and Alvin Zander, (Evanston, Ill.: Row, Peterson and Company, 1960), 527–53.

12. F. Sargent and G. Miller, "Some Differences in Certain Communication Behaviors of Autocratic and Democratic Group Leaders," *Journal of Communication* 21 (1971): 233–52.

13. Lawrence B. Rosenfeld and Timothy B. Plax, "Personality Determinants of Autocratic and Democratic Leadership," *Speech Monographs* 42 (1975): 203–8.

14. William E. Jurma, "Effects of Leader Structuring Style and Task-Orientation Characteristics of Group Members," *Communication Monographs* 46 (1979): 282.

15. Malcolm G. Preston and Roy K. Heintz, "Effectiveness of Participatory versus Supervisory Leadership in Group Judgment," *Journal of Abnormal and Social Psychology* 44 (1949): 344–45; George Graen, Fred Dansfereau, and Takau Minami, "Dysfunctional Leadership Styles," *Organizational Behavior and Human Performance* 7 (1972): 216–36; Norman R. F. Maier and Ronald A. Maier, "An Experimental Test of the Effects of 'Developmental' vs. 'Free' Discussions on the Quality of Group Decisions," *Journal of Applied Psychology* 41 (1957): 320–23; William E. Jurma, "Leadership Structuring Style, Task Ambiguity and Group Members' Satisfaction," *Small Group Behavior* 9 (1978): 124–34.

16. Beatrice Schultz, "Communicative Correlates of Perceived Leaders in the Small Group," *Small Group Behavior* 17 (1986): 51–65.

17. Gregory H. Dobbins and Stephen J. Zaccaro, "The Effects of Group Cohesion and Leader Behavior on Subordinate Satisfaction," *Group and Organization Studies* 11 (1986): 203–19.

18. Robert F. Bales, *Interaction Process Analysis* (Cambridge, Mass.: Addison-Wesley, 1950).

19. Kenneth D. Benne and Paul Sheats, "Functional Roles of Group Members," *Journal of Social Issues* 4 (1948): 41–49.

20. B. Aubrey Fisher, "Leadership as Medium: Treating Complexity in Group Communication Research," *Small Group Behavior* 16 (1985): 167–96.

21. Fred E. Fiedler, *A Theory of Leadership Effectiveness* (New York: McGraw-Hill, 1967).

22. James A. Hunt, "Leadership Style Effects at Two Management Levels in a Simulated Organization," *Administrative Science Quarterly* 16 (1971): 476–85.

23. Julia T. Wood, "Alternate Portraits of Leaders: A Contingency Approach to Perceptions of Leadership," *Western Journal of Speech Communication* 43 (1979): 260–70.

24. R. N. Griffin, "Relationships among Individual, Task Design and Leader Behavior Variables," *Academy of Management Journal* 23 (1980): 665–83.

25. Cal W. Downs and Terry Pickett, "An Analysis of the Effects of Nine Leadership-Group Compatibility Contingencies upon Productivity and Member Satisfaction," *Communication Monographs* 44 (1977): 220–30.

26. David J. Skaret and Nealia S. Bruning, "Attitudes about the Work Group: An Added Moderator of the Relationship between Leader Behavior and Job Satisfaction," *Group and Organization Studies* 11 (1986): 254–79.

27. M. L. Chemers, "Leadership Theory and Research: A Systems-Process Integration," in *Basic Group Processes,* ed. P. B. Paulus (New York: Springer-Verlag, 1983), 9–39.

28. Paul Hersey and Kenneth H. Blanchard, *Management of Organizational Behavior: Utilizing Human Resources,* 2d ed. (New York: Prentice-Hall, 1972); Hersey and Blanchard, "So You Want to Know Your Leadership Style?" in *Readings in Organizational Communication,* eds. Phillip V. Lewis and John Williams (Columbus, Ohio: Grid Publishers, Inc., 1980), 219–34.

29. Julia T. Wood, "Leading in Purposive Discussions: A Study of Adaptive Behavior," *Communication Monographs* 44 (1977): 152–65.

30. Chemers, "Leadership Theory and Research," 28.

31. Bormann, *Discussion and Group Methods,* 253–69; John C. Geier, "A Trait Approach to the Study of Leadership in Small Groups," *Journal of Communication* 17 (1967): 316–23.

32. Robert L. Husband, "Toward a Grounded Typology of Organizational Leadership Behavior," *Quarterly Journal of Speech* (1985): 103–18.

33. Charles G. Morris and J. R. Hackman, "Behavioral Correlates of Perceived Leadership," *Journal of Personality and Social Psychology* 13 (1969): 350–61.

34. Paul D. Reynolds, "Leaders Never Quit: Talking, Silence and Influence in Interpersonal Groups," *Small Group Behavior* 15 (1984): 411.

35. Hugh C. Russell, "Dimensions of Communicative Behavior of Discussion Leaders," (Paper presented to Central States Speech Convention, April, 1970).

36. Velma J. Lashbrook, "Gibb's Interaction Theory: The Use of Perceptions in the Discrimination of Leaders from Nonleaders," (Paper presented to Speech Communication Convention, December, 1975).

37. Norman R. G. Maier and A. R. Solem, "The Contributions of a Discussion Leader to the Quality of Group Thinking: The Effective Use of Minority Opinions," *Human Relations* 5 (1952): 277–88.

38. Franklyn S. Haiman, (From a paper given at the Annual Convention of the Speech Association of America, December, 1964).

39. Lawrence B. Rosenfeld, *Now That We're All Here . . . Relations in Small Groups* (Columbus, Ohio: Charles E. Merrill Publishing Company, 1976), 76.

40. D. A. Kenny and S. J. Zaccaro, "An Estimate of Variance Due to Traits in Leadership," *Journal of Applied Psychology* 68 (1983): 678–85.

41. Wood, "Leading Purposive Discussions," 152–65.

42. Husband, "Toward a Grounded Typology."

43. A. Paul Hare, *Handbook of Small Group Research* (New York: The Free Press, 1962), 103–18.

44. Wood, "Leading Purposive Discussions," 152–65.

45. Irving J. Lee, *How to Talk with People* (New York: Harper & Row, Publishers, 1952), 158–60.

46. John E. Tropman, *Effective Meetings* (Beverly Hills: Sage Publications, 1980), 39–40.

47. Lee, *How to Talk with People,* 90–91.

Chapter 10

Conflict in the Small Group

Study Objectives

As a result of studying chapter 10 you should be able to:

1. Define conflict and explain both the positive and negative effects it can have on a group.

2. Explain how the perceptual, emotional, behavioral, and interaction dimensions operate as a system in small group conflict.

3. Describe the four types of conflict that typically occur in small group interactions.

4. Define groupthink, explain the symptoms, and describe the steps that can be taken to counteract groupthink.

5. Describe the two main behavioral orientations underlying conflict management behavior and the specific conflict management styles which result.

6. Describe the principled negotiation procedure for helping the group resolve conflict.

Key Terms

Accommodation the conflict management style where one person appeases or gives in to the other.

Avoidance the passive conflict management style that ignores the conflict situation.

Collaboration the conflict management style that assumes a problem-solving stance, attempting to find a solution that meets fully the needs of all parties to the conflict.

Competition the conflict management style where one person attempts to dominate the outcome.

Compromise the conflict management style that assumes each party must give up something in order to get something; a shared solution to a conflict situation.

Conflict the process that occurs when one person perceives that another has or is about to frustrate a concern; ranges from intellectual disagreements to physical violence.

> *Affective conflict* conflict resulting from personality clashes, likes, and dislikes.
>
> *Inequity* perceived unequal workloads or contributions of one or more members that produces conflict in a group.
>
> *Procedural conflict* conflict resulting from disagreement about *how* to do something.
>
> *Substantive conflict* conflict resulting from disagreements over ideas, information, reasoning, or evidence.

Distributive orientation the behavioral orientation that assumes there must be a winner and a loser in a conflict situation; assumes the needs of all parties cannot be fully met, that someone must lose.

Groupthink the tendency of high-status cohesive groups to fail to subject information, ideas, proposals, and reasoning to thorough critical analysis; leads to faulty decisions.

Integrative orientation the behavioral orientation that assumes a conflict situation can be resolved so the needs of all parties to the conflict are fully met; win-win orientation.

Principled negotiation a general strategy that enables parties in a conflict to express their own needs, search for alternatives that permit the needs of all parties to be met, and remain decent human beings throughout the process.

If you pick up any popular general interest magazine, you are likely to see an article about how to maintain harmonious relationships at work, with friends, or within the family. American cultural norms emphasize getting along well with others, implying that interpersonal conflict is somehow unusual, undesirable, and unpleasant. If you believe everything you read in these magazines, you might get the impression that conflict is to be avoided at all costs. The truth is that whenever individuals come together in any sort of social context, conflict in one form or another is inevitable and does not automatically have to be harmful. This is especially true of conflict among members of small groups.

Conflict is an integral part of small group discussion and decision making. In fact, combating secondary tension successfully is largely a matter of developing productive ways of settling or managing conflict. When a group of individuals must come to some agreement about an issue or problem, conflict is a natural by-product. Each person will see the situation in a slightly different way from the others, will have different values and priorities, and will perhaps have a preferred outcome unlike the outcomes favored by the others. These variations in perception, values, beliefs, and preferences will be brought out into the open in thorough discussion. In a group that does not need to come to agreement, such as a learning group whose goal is to understand varying points of view, the divergent opinions will not matter much. However, if the goal of the group is to achieve concurrence on a particular alternative or course of action, then these differences *will* matter and must somehow be reconciled.

Americans are typically ambivalent about conflict. Along with our values that stress agreement and "getting along," we espouse values that encourage us to stick to our principles without backing down in the face of opposition. We seem to have trouble reconciling the benefits of *both* harmony and conflict. Other cultures do not experience this tension to the same degree. For example, the same Chinese word means both "crisis" and "opportunity." Eastern cultures in particular see apparently opposing concepts like harmony and conflict as sides of the same coin, parts that constitute the whole. It is important for group members to see the benefits of each without feeling it necessary to function entirely one way or the other. Both processes, managed in an appropriately balanced way, can contribute positively to a group's interaction, to members' feelings for each other, and to the soundness of the eventual decision.

Conflict is at the heart of effective decision making and problem solving. The chief advantage of asking a group rather than an individual to make a decision is the premise that several heads are better than one. Group members collectively have more information available to them than an individual has. Group members also have a variety of approaches to use in solving problems, and they have potentially an accumulated wisdom that should enable them to spot serious mistakes in logic and reasoning, omissions in information, and problems of implementation that an individual might miss. This almost guarantees that conflict will occur. If a group is to receive the full benefit of the collective judgment of its members, the members must be willing to disagree, to point out errors, and to argue. If members meekly concur with everything or suppress their disagreement, the group's solutions will suffer.

Of course, too much conflict can be harmful. Members' feelings may be hurt, they may withdraw, and eventually the group may disintegrate. However, it has been our experience that groups of students err in the direction of too little rather than too much conflict. Most of our students have taken to heart popular prescriptions that stress harmony, preferring to interact with little or no conflict.[1] As a result, student groups typically produce less-than-optimum outcomes. For this reason, we stress in this chapter the benefits of conflict. We will discuss what conflict is, how to distinguish beneficial from detrimental conflict, how to recognize symptoms of groupthink, and how to manage the conflict that occurs. Remember, some conflict is necessary if a group is to produce the best possible decision or solution.

| A Definition of Conflict | A variety of definitions exists for conflict, ranging from something that occurs when individuals have reached an impasse [2] to a state of genuine difference.[3] We have adopted Thomas's definition: |

. . . conflict is the process which begins when one party perceives that the other has frustrated, or is about to frustrate, some concern of his. [It includes] a wide variety of phenomena . . . ranging from intellectual disagreement to physical violence.[4]

This intentionally broad definition encompasses a number of different behaviors and activities that may occur in a small group and implies that conflict can stem from a variety of sources.

First, conflict can occur because individuals have *competing values*. For example, a classroom group, which one of us observed, had two members with incompatible values regarding the use of laboratory animals for research purposes. One member, valuing human harmony with all of nature, believed that the lives of animals were of no less importance than those of people. The other member thought that humans were superior to other forms of life, making it proper for laboratory animals to be used to find cures for diseases and other services to humans. This fundamental difference in values made it impossible for the group to which they belonged to reach consensus on a university policy regarding the use of laboratory animals.

Second, conflict can also occur when members disagree on *goals* to be achieved. We have observed this on numerous occasions within many types of small groups, including student groups. One group member's goal for a group classroom project may be to achieve an A for that project. A second member, perhaps pressed for time or taking the course as an elective, may simply want to complete the project adequately enough to receive a C. These two differing goals will probably create conflict.

Third, group members may agree on values and goals but disagree on *ways to achieve the goals*. This is a situation Deutsch calls conflict from "incompatible activities."[5] For instance, you and another member may each want to earn an A for a group presentation. You would rather involve the class in an exercise followed by discussion, and your fellow member would prefer to show and discuss a movie. While you agree on your ultimate objective of getting an A, you disagree on the best course of action to reach the goal. You are probably beginning to see that the latter conflict will be easier to manage than the former two. In a group, the more members are homophilous with respect to basic values and beliefs, the easier it will be for the group to achieve consensus.

Thomas's definition of conflict contains certain implications important to understanding conflict in the small group, including the fact that conflict involves people's perceptions, feelings, and behaviors, and interaction among individuals. The first dimension is the perceptual one. There is nothing automatic that labels a situation as **conflict;** instead, it depends upon how people describe the situation to themselves. For instance, if you see someone slipping in to the place where you normally park, you can say to yourself, "He took MY place," or "I got here too late, he saw it before I could park." In the first instance, by defining the situation as a conflict, (the other driver frustrated a concern of yours) you are more likely to feel angry and frustrated. Assume one member of your group disagrees with something you propose. You can choose to define that as a conflict (He is knocking my idea) or you can define it as an intriguing difference (Her idea is different from mine; I wonder how she thought of it). Thus, perception is the first step to defining a situation as conflict.

Your emotions, the second dimension, are closely associated with your perceptions. Your feelings can range from mild distress to out-of-control rage, depending on how you see the conflict situation. If a stranger parks in your customary spot, your emotional involvement will probably be slight, and you'll feel no more than annoyed. However, if "your" spot is taken by someone you know and dislike, someone you think of as an enemy who derives great pleasure from frustrating you, then you are likely to be angry. Furthermore, if this "enemy" makes a rude gesture at you while slipping into the parking place, your anger may turn to fury. Each element that escalates the intensity of the conflict in your perception creates a parallel increase in the intensity of your feelings. Thus, your perceptions and feelings are clearly linked. The fact that emotions are involved has important implications for the management of conflict. For instance, conflict cannot be handled satisfactorily if you deal only at the rational level with so-called objective issues. The subjective realities—the feelings of the participants—must be allowed to surface, acknowledged as legitimate, and dealt with directly. Hostile feelings make the management of conflict trickier, and sometimes they linger even after the substantive issues have been resolved.

Your perceptions of the situation and your emotions influence your behavior toward that other person. The third dimension of conflict involves a behavioral component as you act upon these perceptions and feelings. For example, a stranger parking in your usual place may provoke only a shrug of your shoulders, but an enemy taking YOUR place and thumbing his or her nose at you will probably elicit intense anger where you clench your fists, blow

Figure 10.1
Perception, behavior,
and interaction in
conflict.

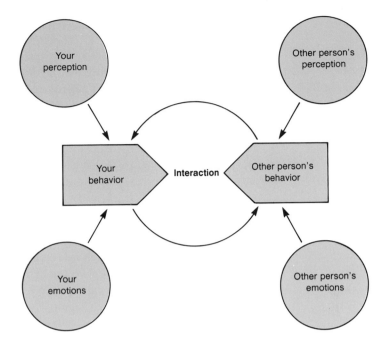

your horn, and make a face or a rude gesture in return. In a group, if you think someone's disagreement is personally directed toward you, you are likely to become defensive and fight back. On the other hand, if you perceive someone's disagreement as a different way of getting to the same goal, you are more likely to listen objectively to what is said. Thus, what you *think* and *feel* about the conflict situation governs what you *do* about it.

Finally, the fourth dimension involves communicative interaction with the other person. As the previous parking example illustrates, your behavior is not performed in isolation. It affects other people. If you honk your horn at the person who took YOUR parking place, that person is likely to honk back. At minimum, he or she will walk away thinking you are inconsiderate. If you become defensive because you perceive you are being verbally attacked, you are likely to elicit defensive behavior in return. That could start a conflict cycle that escalates in intensity, with one person's behavior fueling the other person's anger, and each individual becoming increasingly upset. On the other hand, if you listen to the other person with genuine interest in the spirit of trying to come up with the best possible solution for the group, then the example you set is likely to bring about the same kind of behavior from the other person.

Thus, the four elements present in a conflict situation—perception, emotion, behavior, and interaction—function like a system of interdependent parts, as shown in figure 10.1. Perceptions govern behavior, which in turn influences both the perceptions of the other person and the actual behavioral interaction with that person. Each dimension affects and is affected by the others, so altering any one of the dimensions will change the others.

Positive and
Negative
Outcomes
of Conflict

It has become almost a truism among communication scholars that conflict has both beneficial and negative outcomes.[6] We noted earlier that without the conflict that comes from critical examination of an issue a group will not make as good a decision. We know, also, that conflict can be harmful. We will now examine some of the positive and negative effects of conflict.

Positive Effects
of Conflict

In general, conflict positively affects the group when it produces a better decision, increases cohesiveness and unity, leads to satisfaction with both the process and the product, and enhances member understanding. For instance, Smith, Johnson, and Johnson say positive outcomes of conflict include "high achievement, intrinsic and continuing motivation, perspective-taking ability and positive interpersonal relations."[7] These and other benefits of conflict follow:

1. **Conflict can produce better understanding, of both issues and of people.** We have the tendency to assume that most people see things as we do and feel as we do and are surprised to discover otherwise. We can choose to be upset by this, or we can choose to learn something. For example, Smith, Johnson, and Johnson found that when students discovered others held differing positions on an issue, they became uncertain of their own position, sought actively to get more information about the issue, were able to take the perspective of the other students, and were better able to retain information, both about their own and the other person's position. They demonstrated increased understanding of both the information and the individuals.[8]

2. **Conflict stimulates involvement and increases member motivation.** When group members are participating in a conflict episode, they are actively involved in the issue under consideration. They are interested, excited, and paying close attention. People who do not care will not expend any energy disagreeing about an issue. This stimulation increases motivation to learn more about an issue. A student in one of our classes could not accept a statement by a fellow group member that nonverbal communication contributed more than verbal communication in determining meaning. Unable to resolve the issue to his satisfaction, the student undertook an investigation of his own, using library and personal resources, and discovered the validity of the statement. His search provided some excellent examples the other group members were able to use in their class presentation—all because he got into an intellectual argument.

3. **Conflict can produce better decisions.** This is a very important outcome and is the heart of good group problem solving. Through conflict, you discover first that others disagree, then *why* they disagree. You find flaws in reasoning, holes in arguments, factors that the group failed to consider, or implications that were ignored. This helps the group prevent mistakes. For example, a staff meeting one of us attended was charged with approving a plan for cutting costs at a commuter campus. The developer of the plan

recommended closing down the snack bar at 5:00 P.M. Another member of the staff pointed out that would leave evening students, many of whom had to leave directly from work to attend classes, without food service and might eventually lead to a drop in enrollment. After considerable debate, the committee decided to provide vending machine service, which would accomplish the job of cutting personnel and utility costs, but not leave evening students without food.

4. **Conflict can produce greater cohesiveness among group members.**
When a group experiences a conflict episode and resolves it successfully, it learns that the ties holding the group together are strong enough to sustain disagreement. Most of us who have had serious arguments with spouses or significant others can recall the closeness we feel after we have "made up." Instead of automatically driving us apart, the conflict has served as a catalyst to strengthen the bonds between us. So it is with groups, too. The conflict frequently produces a better outcome than there would have been without the conflict. Thus, the twin outcomes of task success and interpersonal tolerance can increase group cohesiveness. In the food service example, members felt so good about the final outcome and so positive about each other's willingness to listen to opposing arguments that they adjourned for lunch after the meeting in a spirit of camaraderie.

Negative Effects of Conflict

Although conflict can be beneficial, we all have seen how harmful it can be as well. If you have ever said to yourself after a group meeting, "I'll be glad when this project is completed, I hope I never have to work with these people again," you probably have experienced the harmful effects of conflict. These include hurt feelings, lowered cohesiveness, and even group dissolution.

1. **Conflict can cause bad feelings among group members.**
Most of us do not like to have others disagree with us. This is particularly true when others not only disagree with an idea or proposal we give, but in the process appear to devalue us as a person. Their remarks appear caustic, even hostile. This type of perceived personal attack will cause hard feelings; such a response represents the opposite of the attitude of skeptical inquiry we discussed in chapter 3. Moreover, even a conflict over issues and ideas can be carried on too long, increasing tension and wearing group members down.

2. **Conflict, especially if it involves personal attacks or is carried on too long, can lower group cohesiveness.**
If you believe that others in a group do not value your contributions, you will not be eager to spend time with that group. We would rather spend time with people who confirm, not deny, our existence. If you have a choice, you will elect to spend your time with groups that seem to value you. Prolonged conflict and attacks on one's self-concept loosen those bonds of attraction and cohesiveness.

3. **Conflict can split a group apart.**

Ultimately, a member who believes the group dislikes his or her ideas, and then has the opportunity to find support in other groups, will leave the group. Conflict which goes on too long and too intensely will tear members apart. One of us once observed a friendship group split apart over a political issue. One side believed that busing was an appropriate way to achieve racial equality; the other side disagreed. Moreover, the two sides did not simply have an intellectual disagreement; they began to impugn each other's intelligence, loyalty, and ability to reason. Unkind things were said, a rift occurred, and the group never regained its former cohesiveness.

Types of Conflict

From some of the examples given thus far, you probably begin to see that the mere presence of conflict among members in and of itself is neither helpful nor harmful to a group. What the conflict is about, how it is initiated, and how it is managed all have a bearing on what happens to the group. Before we examine various types of conflict that can occur within a group and discuss the potential effects of each, we present a description of a conflict situation that occurred in one of our student project groups.

The students were charged with making an hour-long presentation on listening to the class. Most of the six students were at least average in performance as students, but one woman, Faith, was exceptionally hard-working with a high grade point average. In contrast, one man, Jon, was rather nonchalant about academic matters. Faith, and eventually the others, wanted a high grade. Thus, earning a high grade had become a group goal. Jon would have liked a high grade but not if it meant working hard. Note that the situation is ripe for overt conflict because the members had some divergence of values and goals. At first, members assigned themselves research tasks, which they completed. Although it is typical for student groups to reward each other for whatever work is done, even if that work is sloppy, this group, under Faith's leadership, developed a norm of critical inquiry. Jon's work, in particular, was not acceptable to the rest of the group, especially Faith. At first, assuming that Jon was simply inexperienced at library research work, the group gently suggested other things he could do to bring his contribution up to the standards of the other members. Jon pretended to comply, but his work never improved. He seemed always to be taking the easy way out, finding all kinds of excuses for his lack of quality. At first, Faith was willing to work with him, but later she took an exceptionally hard line with Jon. She had the backing of the other members, who were forming into a highly cohesive unit with high performance standards. What started out as a mild conflict over how to do the work of the group escalated into a serious interpersonal conflict between Jon and the other group members. There are several sources of conflict in this example, which illustrate the following four types of conflict.

*Substantive
Conflict*

Substantive conflict, also called *intrinsic* conflict, is conflict or disagreement over ideas, meanings, issues, and other matters pertinent (intrinsic) to the task of the group.[9] It involves *what* the group should do. In the previous example, Faith refused to accept as appropriate the information originally supplied by Jon; her challenge represents substantive conflict. The example given earlier, with one group member wanting to conduct a class exercise and another wanting to show a movie, is another instance of substantive conflict. When the university where one of us worked was ordered by the governing board to reduce programs costing about $2 million, a committee charged with recommending what programs to cut had severe substantive conflicts among the members. For example, some wanted to eliminate intercollegiate athletics, others thought various service programs could be cut, and still others wanted to do away with religious studies and masters programs in the performing arts. Substantive conflict is the basis of effective decision making and problem solving in a discussion group. This is the vehicle by which ideas, proposals, evidence, and reasoning are challenged and critically examined, doubts are brought into the open, and the group works together to find the solution most likely to be effective.

Affective Conflict

Affective conflict, also called *extrinsic,* is that conflict which originates from interpersonal power clashes, likes, and dislikes extrinsic to the group's task.[10] It represents the "who" of small group conflict. It is generally detrimental to the smooth operation of a group. You probably have observed this sort of conflict many times in groups. Two members do not like each other, and they miss no opportunity to disagree or to belittle each other. Such conflict is both difficult to resolve and exceedingly harmful to the group. In our extended example of small group conflict Jon and Martha, group members, took an instant dislike to each other that went far deeper than any disagreement over work procedures could explain. They rarely failed to make sarcastic comments back and forth during a meeting. Although the origin of this type of conflict is difficult to pin down, our observations of numerous groups suggest that much of it is rooted in one person's acting as if he or she is superior, and another member's refusal to accept this difference in status or power. Most of this "I am superior, more important, more knowledgeable" signaling is nonverbal, projected by a subtle pattern of facial expressions, glances, head angles, vocal tones and pitch patterns, and postures. We each believe that much of what is described as interpersonal conflict emerges from this sort of struggle for position and power.

Procedural Conflict

Procedural conflict is a type of substantive conflict over the procedures a group should follow in working toward its goals. It represents disagreement about the "how" of group interaction. However, it may be used to mask conflict rooted in interpersonal relationships or disagreement regarding the substance of a solution.[11] For instance, members of a group may disagree about whether they should make decisions by consensus or whether majority rule will suffice. It can occur, as Putnam notes, because members genuinely disagree over the set of procedures a group should follow, but it also can be used to withdraw from another substantive conflict by forcing a vote or otherwise regulating the group's work. While procedural conflict may seem a straightforward difference over how the group should accomplish something, it may in fact be rooted in member needs for structure versus freedom, indicating an origin in differing personality traits.

Conflict from Inequity

One of the most prevalent sources of conflict in the groups we have observed is conflict over **inequity** in the group: group members do not seem to have equal work loads, and do not make equal contributions to the group. Inequity reduces satisfaction with the group and is associated with higher levels of conflict.[12] In our extended example, Jon's work was seen initially as inadequate but members believed he was trying his best. As the students got to know each other better, Jon began to be seen not only as ineffectual but as lazy, trying to get away with as little work as possible. This perceived inequity of effort within the group created serious conflict between him and the other members, whose model was the conscientious Faith. The fact that both substantive inadequacies as well as perceptions of inequity were involved caused the group to take a harder stance with Jon, giving him no leeway and evaluating his contributions with perhaps more rigor than those of the other members. He was being required to measure up perfectly to the group's performance norms.

It should be apparent that although we describe these four types of conflict as though they are distinct, they are not mutually exclusive. One type of conflict can easily lead to another type. Frequently, two or more types blend together. Using our extended example again, Faith's initial disappointment in Jon's work and his continued failure to attain the high standards of the rest of the group both contributed to her eventual personal dislike. Martha's initial personal dislike contributed to her disapproval of his task-related work. Martha *looked* for things to disagree with just because she disliked Jon. The inequity the others perceived with respect both to the quantity and quality of Jon's work escalated into a general attack on Jon's person. In case you are curious about what eventually happened to this group, the members gave an outstanding presentation. This was due to the norm of critical evaluation that *all* the members (except Jon) adopted and to the fact that they were willing to confront Jon and force him to redo his work. He did perform, albeit grudgingly, for the group. Except for Jon, the rest of the group was cohesive, unified, and successful. It doesn't always turn out so well, as other stories we could tell would show. Some groups with interpersonal conflicts fail.

Groupthink

We spoke earlier about conflict and harmony being elements of the same phenomenon, sides of the same coin, and noted that a balance must be struck between the two for a group to perform optimally. For the most effective possible decision making or problem solving, neither element should be allowed to overshadow the other. Rather than an either/or approach to conflict versus cohesiveness, the successful group must adopt a both/and stance. Nowhere is the imbalance between conflict and harmony seen more clearly than in the presence of groupthink, where a group allows the desire for harmony, cohesiveness, and solidarity to suppress confrontation and other forms of conflict.

Groupthink refers to the tendency of highly cohesive groups to adopt solutions members have failed to subject to full critical examination and analysis. Consequently, the decisions made or solutions adopted by these groups are seriously flawed. The term was coined by Irving Janis, who has conducted extensive analysis of a variety of group decisions by policy makers.[13] Janis became intrigued by the decision of President John F. Kennedy and his advisers to mount the invasion of the Bay of Pigs in Cuba shortly after Fidel Castro had established a communist government there. That decision is widely believed to have been mistaken, but just because a decision turns out badly does not automatically mean that the processes used to formulate the decision were poor. In the case of the Bay of Pigs, however, rational and systematic examination of the evidence *available at the time of the decision* should have alerted the advisers that the invasion would fail. Janis began his search to discover how, in the face of all evidence to the contrary, this group of educated and intelligent people could have allowed such a defective policy decision to be implemented. He compared the decision-making process in the Bay of Pigs incident with that used two years later for the blockade of Cuba during the Cuban missile crisis. Many of the same advisers were involved in both decisions, but while the first is regarded as a disaster the second is considered a model of effective group decision making. A clear distinction was found between effective and ineffective procedures. Groups making effective decisions and proposing high quality alternatives are willing to engage in open conflict over the ideas, evidence, and reasoning presented in the group. We will now examine the symptoms of groupthink and the steps group members can take to combat this normal tendency.

Symptoms of Groupthink

Groupthink is more likely to occur in highly cohesive groups under pressure to achieve consensus. The eight symptoms identified by Janis fall into three main categories:

1. **The group overestimates its power and morality.**
   A group may be so optimistic that it overestimates the chances for its programs to succeed. Student groups in classes taught by both of us have become so excited about creative activities they had developed for a classroom presentation that they have ignored the rest of the presentation by saying, "The instructor will love it—it's more imaginative than anything else other people have done." Often that was the only part of their presentation we instructors did love! In addition, the group may have such an unquestioned belief in the inherent morality of the group that the group ignores potential moral questions that could be raised. For example, the individuals behind the burglary of the Democratic National Headquarters, which led eventually to the Watergate hearings, believed they had a morally determined duty to protect the American public by gathering intelligence they thought

Figure 10.2
Groupthink in action.

would help the president. Likewise, the National Security Council
under President Reagan thought the cause of the Nicaraguan contras
so right that defying the intent of Congress was appropriate. President
Johnson's cabinet evidently believed that fighting a war in Vietnam
would be to the long-term benefit of the United States and the world,
but the way this war was waged nearly destroyed our national pride
and purpose.

2. **The group becomes closed-minded.**

The group closes itself off to any information contrary to its preferred
course of action, and it stereotypes any outside figures involved so that
it does not have to pay attention to what they might have to say or do.
Some Kennedy advisers who participated in the Bay of Pigs decision
were committed to the invasion before other options had been surveyed,
and they ignored contrary information. Moreover, they underestimated
the resistance of the majority of Cuban people to the invasion,
stereotyping them as weak and ineffectual. Some student groups are so
relieved when they arrive at *any* solution to a problem that they fail to
test their solution to ensure it is the best one, thereby producing an
inferior product.

3. **Group members experience pressures to conform.**

This manifests itself in a variety of ways. First, members censor their
own remarks. This is exemplified in figure 10.2. If you think everyone
in the group is in favor of a proposal, you will naturally tend to
suppress your own doubts and fears. Second, the group members have a
shared illusion of unanimity. They believe because individuals are not
open in expressing their doubts that all members agree. Third, if a
member does venture a contradictory opinion, that member is likely to
experience direct pressure from the rest of the group to conform: "Why
are you being so negative, Jim? The rest of us think it's a good idea."
This makes it obvious to the dissenting member that disagreement is

perceived as disloyalty. Finally, the group may have a number of self-appointed *mindguards* who protect the group from mental threats, just as bodyguards do from physical threats. For example, the member who deliberately prevents dissonant information from reaching the group—by stopping outsiders from addressing the group, by failing to mention contrasting points of view contained in research materials, and so forth—acts as a mindguard, withholding *all* available relevant and contradictory material from the group's consideration.

These symptoms cause the group to make an incomplete survey of the information and options at its disposal as well as a less-than-thorough assessment of the information and ideas. The group becomes biased in its search and assessment procedures, frequently adopting simplistic solutions to complex problems. It is especially important to be alert to groupthink whenever a group *must* achieve consensus. The need for consensus can lead to an "agreement norm" which curtails disagreement, ultimately causing the group to suffer.[14] Agreement reached under duress of such a norm is only a surface consensus, not a decision deeply supported by all members as the best the entire group can support.

Preventing Groupthink

The designated leader of a group often has a dual responsibility for building team spirit as well as doing everything possible to insure full evaluation of all material brought before the group. The following suggestions for combating the tendency toward groupthink are designed to help the leader perform this balancing act.

1. **Assign the role of critical evaluator to each member.**
   Each member must feel responsible for helping the group achieve the best possible solution. However, just *saying* this to the members will not make it happen. Group leaders must make sure by their actions that critical evaluation is more important than apparent harmony or deference to the leaders' position. Leaders should especially welcome criticism of their own ideas and proposals, demonstrating that they are willing to be influenced by reason and evidence. The president of a university where one of us worked had an advisory council established in part for this purpose. Council members were elected or appointed, and they represented each area of the university. At one point, the president proposed a major reorganization of the university and invited the council to review his plan critically, to find all the flaws, and recommend changes. The council tore the plan to shreds. The plan was eventually implemented with substantial changes, which improved it immeasurably. Had the president attempted to put the proposal into effect without first asking for and obtaining criticisms of it, the plan would have failed.
   Likewise, members should feel free to question and challenge information presented by other members. It may be helpful to assign one or two people the specific role of devil's advocate. For example, if other members know that Mary has been assigned this role for a

particular meeting, they are more likely to view her criticisms as being part of her job and less likely to take them personally. That way the group gets the benefit of Mary's critical thinking skills but avoids the potential harm of destructive affective conflict.

2. **Leaders should refrain from stating their preferences at the outset of a decision-making or problem-solving session.**
Janis found that one of the major problems with President Kennedy's Bay of Pigs decision was his own referent power. His advisers admired and respected him so much that they were reluctant to disagree or criticize his ideas. Even leaders who do not have Kennedy's charisma have power that stems from one or more of the sources we discussed in chapter 9. This power enhances their influence in group contexts, making it natural for others to give more credence to their arguments and ideas and agree with what they say. This shortcircuits the decision-making process, which at its most effective is based on an exhaustive search for options and vigilant appraisal of them.

3. **Leaders can establish two or more independent subgroups to work on the same problem.**
This establishes somewhat competing subgroups. The competition alone may spur each of the groups to greater effort on behalf of the larger group. Moreover, each subgroup is likely to think of ideas, solutions, and possible consequences that the other subgroup failed to consider. Therefore, the clash between the subgroups can spark creative and novel solutions as well as highlighting potential flaws.

4. **Leaders should take whatever steps are needed to prevent insulation of the group.**
Sometimes a group can be so cohesive that it fails to consider that others may see situations differently. A committee to which one of us belonged developed a sweeping proposal to alter the undergraduate curriculum. Group members had worked together for an entire year, carrying each other along on their enthusiasm and commitment. However, because they were so caught up in their own shared vision, they failed to consider some implications of their proposal for other faculty, who greeted the recommendations with dismay rather than enthusiasm. The group had become insulated from external opinion.

Leaders can take several specific steps to offset insularity. They can encourage members to get feedback on tentative proposals from trusted associates outside the group, then report back to the group. Had the faculty committee mentioned earlier done this, they would not have been surprised at their proposal's reception. Leaders can also arrange for outside experts to discuss their views with the group, thereby helping to insure a broadly based foundation for making the decision. Hence, consultants have some power!

Managing Conflict

We hope we have convinced you of the value of substantive conflict to the decision-making and problem-solving processes in a small group. Conflict is inevitable when humans meet in a group situation. It should not be avoided, for *to do so circumvents the very reason for engaging in group discussion—* the thinking of several people is likely to be more accurate and more thorough than the thinking of one person acting alone. However, your experience and common sense should alert you that there are effective and ineffective ways of managing conflict when it does occur. We now present information about the behavioral orientations underlying several different conflict management styles and give you suggestions to help you produce satisfactory resolution of conflicts in group situations.

Behavioral Orientations toward Conflict Management

Recall that conflict has a perceptual component. How you perceive the conflict situation will affect how you behave. The same is true regarding the management of conflict. How you see the other people, the context, the relationship among group members, the feasibility of combining alternatives, and the desirability of satisfying all members contribute to the way you attempt to resolve or manage conflict. Your approach may be distributive or integrative.[15]

Distributive Orientation

The **distributive orientation,** also called win-lose, assumes that what one person gains is at someone else's expense. For instance, if two people in a department are competing for the same fixed amount of bonus money, the result will be either that one will receive all the money and the other nothing, or that they will somehow find a way to distribute the money between them. In either case, the amount of money one receives determines directly how much the other receives. One's win is the other's loss. In a group situation, two people may present competing solutions to a problem. If they have a distributive orientation toward managing the conflict, each will assume that one of the solutions will be adopted and the other will not.

A distributive orientation to a conflict situation has direct implications for behavior in that situation. For example, if both people believe that only one of them can win, they are each more likely to fight as hard as possible. If you define the situation as distributive, or win-lose, then you are likely to pursue your own goals at the expense of the group; you will be more closed or secretive in your communication; you will deliberately censor information so that you present only that which favors your own point of view; and you may become more hostile and competitive.

Integrative Orientation

An **integrative orientation** assumes that there is some way to manage the conflict so that the parties involved all receive what is important to them in the situation. The underlying belief is that the concerns of all can be integrated fully into whatever the final solution may be. In a group situation, two members presenting competing solutions but having an integrative orientation toward resolving their differences will explore ways that each of them can get essentially what they want, perhaps by coming up with a new, creative solution combining the proposals of each. Thus, this approach has also been termed *win-win.*

It, too, has a direct effect on behavior. Participants with an integrative orientation to a conflict situation will engage in an honest exploration for alternative solutions which meet all important needs of the members. The group's and other members' needs are considered as important as one's own needs, and communication is open. There is a desire to understand fully the other's point of view. Information is not censored but is made available in full to the group, and the search for alternatives is conducted from the position that all group members are working together against the problem rather than competing with each other.

It may transpire, of course, that integrating the concerns of all group members into the group's final solution or decision is impossible. Perhaps the members' underlying values are so divergent that they cannot be merged, or maybe resources are scarce and needs cannot be met fully. In such cases, perhaps partial integration, or compromise, is the best that can be achieved. The important point to note, however, is that even if your group does not develop a fully integrative solution, it *certainly* will not develop one if members begin with the premise that integration is impossible. Without this initial orientation, the group will expend its energy not in developing creative solutions but in arguing the merits of one proposal over another in an attempt to *win* rather than find the best solution possible.

Conflict Management Styles

The behavioral orientation you have toward a conflict situation determines in part the action you take in dealing with that conflict. An additional element is introduced, which works with the behavioral orientation to produce a specific conflict management style, and that is the degree to which you want to see both your own and the other person's needs satisfied in the conflict situation. Figure 10.3 presents the five styles based on the underlying dimensions of concern for meeting one's own needs and concern for meeting the other's needs. (The model assumes dyadic conflict for simplicity's sake.) It is important to note that each conflict management style is appropriate under certain circumstances; none is *always* best. A contingency view is recommended in which the most productive way for settling a conflict is dependent on time pressures, distribution of information and skills, group member values and needs, and other input variables. In problem-solving discussions, the main focus of this book, the integrative approach is always appropriate.[16]

Avoidance

If you have little concern about whether your own needs or the other person's are met, such as when the issue is not important, you will not want to expend much energy exploring a variety of options satisfactory to the both of you. Another member may make a statement you disagree with, but if it is not important to you, and it will not hurt the group's solution, you may let it pass. This is **avoidance** behavior and is appropriate in some circumstances, such as when the risks are slight. For example, a committee to which one of us belonged was asked to develop a decorating plan for a student lounge/study area.

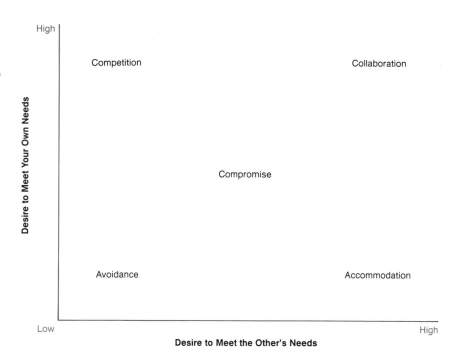

Figure 10.3
Your conflict
management style
depends in part on how
important it is for you to
meet your own and the
other person's needs.

The art instructor on the committee recommended a color scheme not particularly appealing to the chemistry professor on the committee. Since students liked the colors, the chemistry professor kept his objections to himself, reasoning that it was more important to satisfy the students than his own preferences.

Accommodation

Accommodation, also called appeasement, occurs when you give in to someone else. It is more likely to occur when the issue is not important to you and your desire to satisfy your own needs is low, but you see that the issue is important to someone else and your desire is high that the other's needs be met. For example, one of us was a member of a group charged with rewriting some promotional materials for a university. Although other members of the group were not particularly bothered by the use of the word *he* throughout, this was an important issue to one of the coauthors. The rest of the members accommodated, approving the changes to eliminate sexist language.

Competition

If you want very much to achieve a certain outcome in a group situation, and you do not really care whether the other person's needs are met or not, you will probably act in a highly **competitive** way toward resolution of such a conflict. Your orientation is distributive or win-lose. With this stance, sometimes called dominating or forcing, you are not likely to care what the other person thinks of you or what is good for the other person. In some ways, the situation described earlier between Faith, Jon, and the rest of the group exhibited domination by the group, with Faith as its spokesperson. The group members became so disgruntled with what they perceived to be Jon's laziness that they cared less for Jon's feelings and his desires to avoid work than they did for their own desires to meet high standards and earn a top grade.

Collaboration

Collaboration, also called negotiating or problem solving, occurs when you are motivated to meet your own needs in a situation and motivated to help others meet their needs as well. For example, in the committee charged with reviewing the undergraduate curriculum that one of us chaired, one member believed strongly that the students would be served best if the curriculum emphasized theoretical principles. Another member felt equally strongly that practical application was the heart of undergraduate education and insisted on numerous opportunities for students to apply communication techniques. Fortunately, both members had congruent values (each wanted to come up with the best possible curriculum), and each valued the other's continued well being, thereby eliminating avoidance, competition, or accommodation as appropriate behavior. The resulting collaborative (integrative) solution produced a curriculum with strong dual emphases on theory and practice. Each member was completely satisfied that his or her "must have" point was adopted and nothing important was given up. This represents the ideal group problem-solving situation where each party believes she or he has won without the other having lost, and the collaborative solution is superior to what it would have been without the conflict that precipitated the search for a fully integrative outcome. Hare and Naveh gave examples of this creative search for solutions during the Camp David summit meetings. These discussions almost disintegrated, but persistence in seeking integration eventually succeeded.[17]

Compromise

A **compromise**, also called a shared outcome, is attempted when you and another member have intermediate concerns for self and others in the conflict situation. Here, each of you believes you will have to give up something in order to gain something more important. In the previous example, if either party had not been vitally concerned about the merits of theory and practice, each would probably have horse-traded desires: I'll give up the notion that some theoretical underpinning must be included in the public relations courses if you give up the idea that the communication theory courses must include practical course projects. Compromise solutions are often appropriate, but there is an element of loss involved for each party. For this reason, with a decision where all group members are going to be affected, where each member is responsible for implementing the outcome, and where the group is not pressed for time, attempting to reach a collaborative, fully integrative solution is more desirable.

However, we think compromise should *not* be considered a dirty word, nor a poor way to manage or resolve many conflicts. When collaborative resolution is impossible or takes more time than is available, a compromise is a desirable outcome, especially if each group member feels that a standard of fairness has been met.

Expressing Disagreement and Negotiating Agreement

We have stressed the value of sharing your disagreements within the group, but we all have witnessed the harm that can be done by people who disagree in a hostile way. We have seen how hard it is to come to a satisfactory agreement when group conflict has been bitter. We now will discuss how to share your disagreement in ways that are productive for the group, and how to come to a negotiated agreement when conflict has occurred.

Expressing Disagreement in Productive Ways

All group members have the responsibility for expressing their disagreements in constructive ways. A member may spot a serious flaw in the group's deliberations, but if he or she expresses the criticism or disagreement inappropriately, the resulting defensiveness will hurt rather than help the group. The following are suggestions to convey disagreement so that defensive reactions are unlikely:

1. **Do express your disagreement.**
   As we have already noted, failure to express an honest disagreement circumvents the decision-making and problem-solving process in a group. Don't think that by ignoring disagreement it will go away. Instead, premature flight from a conflict is likely to result in stockpiling conflict issues (sometimes called "gunnysacking" or "brown stamp collecting") or piggybacking one issue onto another.[18] This makes conflicts harder to resolve in the long run. Conflict avoiders are less involved and should be encouraged to express their disagreement.[19]

2. **Use rhetorical sensitivity in expressing your disagreement.**
   Recall the definition of rhetorical sensitivity from chapter 3. This implies that you must be perceptive enough, and aware enough of your fellow members, to select words that will not connote negative images. Do not argue for the sake of arguing. You do not want to appear rebellious or to withdraw. Instead, you want to be an "innovative deviant," someone who is strongly committed to the group and its goals but who disagrees with a proposed action or decision of the group. Valentine and Fisher found that innovative deviance accounted for one-fourth of group interaction, serving a critical thinking function.[20] Innovative deviance, which took the form of contradiction, rejection of statements by other members, continuing a disagreement started by others, or agreeing with an assertion someone else has attacked, was particularly helpful in the group's conflict and decision-emergence phases. Furthermore, most innovative deviance occurred immediately prior to consensus, which supports the notion that conflict can contribute to consensus. Social skill is important. Covey found a high correlation between social skill and the use of verbal reasoning in conflict resolution as well as a negative correlation of social skill with verbal aggression and physical violence.[21]

3. **Disagree with the idea but do not criticize the person.**
   Disagreements must be expressed so they do not devalue the person with whom you are disagreeing. Remember that individuals generally would rather have someone disagree honestly with them than disconfirm

them or ignore them. Members of groups who express conflict cooperatively and integratively are more satisfied with the group's process and outcome than members of groups who express conflict competitively and distributively.[22] Thus, "One flaw in your proposal to shut down the snack bar is that it does not consider the food service needs of the evening students" is far superior to "You inconsiderate bozo! What are the evening students supposed to do?" Keep the expression of disagreement issue-oriented rather than person-oriented.

4. **React to disagreement with a spirit of inquiry, not defensiveness**. Alderton and Frey believe that group members' reactions to argument are more important than the arguments themselves in creating group polarization.[23] If someone disagrees with you, do not react defensively as though you have been attacked personally. Listen actively to your fellow member's remarks, be certain that he or she has understood your position correctly, clarify any misunderstandings which have occurred, and work together to search for the best decision and the most effective solutions. In this way, you can make conflict and disagreement work for rather than against the group.

Negotiating Principled Agreement following Conflict

The designated leader should encourage the group to manage conflict productively. The leader must allow all relevant views to be aired, but also should help the group move toward resolution of any particular conflict episode. Clearly, a group cannot remain stuck in conflict. This is not only the responsibility of the designated leader. All members should learn appropriate approaches to the resolution of conflict and use them effectively.

One extremely effective procedure that can help the group negotiate consensus from initially divergent points of view is that of principled negotiation described in detail by Fisher and Ury in their book *Getting to Yes: Negotiating Agreement Without Giving In*.[24] **Principled negotiation** is an all-purpose strategy that encourages all participants in a conflict situation to express their needs and to search for alternatives that meet those needs. Issues are decided on their merits. Where interests compete, issues are decided on the basis of some fair standards independent of the will of either side. Principled negotiation allows participants to adopt the integrative orientation we discussed earlier and put it into practice.

Principled negotiation helps group members get what they want and still remain decent individuals. It is an efficient procedure that encourages the development of a solution that meets the legitimate needs of all parties fairly and therefore is likely to be lasting. This type of negotiation will not harm the relationship among the participants and frequently will improve it. We particularly like the procedure because it recognizes all the elements that enter into conflict—perceptions, emotions, behaviors, and interaction among individuals—and acknowledges that each must be considered. The following description of the procedure shows how a group can incorporate the communication principles we have presented throughout the book, including such concepts as rhetorical sensitivity, assertiveness, active listening, and integrative bargaining, into a practical, effective technique for managing conflict.

1. **Separate the people from the problem**.

   In a conflict situation, two elements operate simultaneously and tend to become tangled: the content of the disagreement and the relationship among the parties. Each should be dealt with directly and separately. For example, parties should share perceptions as they try to put themselves in each other's shoes. If emotions run high, allow them to be vented. Do not react to emotional outbursts, but listen actively and try to show *by your actions and not only your words* that you care about the needs of the other members of the group with whom your interests conflict.

2. **Focus on interests, not positions**.

   When group members stake out certain positions ("I insist that the creation of additional parking lots for students be the main element in our proposal to improve the parking situation on campus."), they become attached to those *positions* rather than the original needs the positions were designed to meet. In their book, Fisher and Ury describe the negotiations between Israel and Egypt which led eventually to the Camp David accords. Initially, Israel's position was that it should keep some of the Sinai, which it had obtained in the 1967 war with Egypt, and Egypt's position was that the entire Sinai should be returned. No agreement was possible so long as each held to its position. However, when negotiators began to discuss the *needs and interests* of each, they discovered that Israel wanted the security of knowing Egyptian tanks were not poised on its border ready to attack, and Egypt was interested in its sovereignty because the Sinai had belonged to Egypt since the days of the Pharaohs. The solution, which met the interests of each, was to create a demilitarized Sinai that would belong to Egypt. Before this solution could be developed, negotiators had to assume that *some* compatible interests existed on each side and had to treat the needs and interests, if not the positions, of each as legitimate.

3. **Invent options for mutual gain**.

   Group members should develop their skill at inventing options, as the previous Israel-Egypt example illustrates. It is suggested that groups separate the invention process from the decision process, and that creative techniques like brainstorming be employed. An integrative approach is recommended, where negotiators assume that the interests of all the parties can be integrated into the group's final solution. For example, one of us was on a committee whose charge was to oversee services to students and help ensure that the important needs of all students were met. One committee member, the academic adviser for evening students, noted that the campus bookstore was open in the evenings only during the first week of the quarter. Evening students, many of whom were driving to the campus directly from work and could not arrive early enough to make the bookstore's regular hours, were unable to exchange books, purchase supplies, or even browse. This committee member's recommendation was to extend bookstore hours to

8:00 P.M. every evening. The budget officer for the campus objected strongly, noting that the proposal would result in cost increases for personnel salaries unlikely to be recovered by purchases made by the evening students. Thus, the positions adopted by each represented attempts to meet the needs of two important groups: evening students and budget watchdogs. However, a solution was invented, through open and honest discussion, that incorporated both sets of needs. The bookstore would remain open two evenings per week throughout the quarter, and would start business later in the morning the rest of the week. The total number of hours of bookstore operation was the same, thus not increasing campus costs, but the distribution of those hours changed to meet the needs of more students.

4. **Insist on using objective criteria**.

Negotiations will be fairer if objective criteria, agreed upon by all parties, are established as a standard. This makes the negotiation less likely to become a contest of wills and more likely to reach a settlement based upon principle instead of pressure. In that way, much of the battle for dominance is removed from the negotiation process. For example, many people use the *Bluebook* to determine what is a fair price range for used cars. When two people agree that the *Bluebook* is an appropriate standard, then arriving at a fair price for a car is easier. One of us chaired a committee responsible for redesigning the undergraduate communication curriculum in the university. Public relations was one of the largest majors in the department of communication, and it needed a drastic overhaul. Before the deliberations began, this committee agreed that the standards for undergraduate public relations majors established by the Public Relations Society of America were appropriate ones to use to guide the committee in developing its final proposal. This agreement to adhere to objective standards saved the committee much fruitless discussion, posturing by individual members, and attempts to protect academic turf. In another example, the United Way organization of a major midwestern city nearly disintegrated as a result of arguments over which agencies should receive money. Finally, the *ad hoc* committee with which the other of us was familiar established a set of cost accounting procedures enabling each agency to determine how many people could be served for what amount. These procedures then served as relatively objective criteria for United Way to use to determine which agencies to fund. Group members will profit from establishing criteria at the beginning of any problem-solving session, but they should *insist* on it in conflict situations.

Sometimes, despite a group's best intentions, attempts at using principled negotiation to arrive at consensus will fail, or the group is operating under a deadline that forces members to use other methods because time is short. We will now describe such fall-back procedures.

When Negotiation Fails: Alternative Procedures

Settlements derived through negotiation by the group itself are preferable because they tend to be more acceptable to all members than solutions imposed by someone. Sometimes, even with best of intentions, a group will not be able to break a deadlock. In that case, when a decision *must* be announced or a proposal submitted, the designated leader has several options.

Mediation by the Designated Leader   If a seemingly irreconcilable conflict emerges over goals or alternatives, the leader might suggest the following procedure, which is an abbreviated form of that used by those who mediate apparently deadlocked negotiations. The procedure represents a last-chance group attempt to arrive at an acceptable decision without resorting to third party arbitration. If this procedure fails, other alternative procedures can be taken to resolve the conflict issue without producing consensus.

1. Presentation of Alternatives
    a. A proponent of each position, solution, goal, or possible decision presents exactly what the subgroup wants or believes and why. Other members supporting the position may add clarifying statements, arguments, evidence, and claims. While this is being done, members who disagree can say *nothing*.
    b. Those in disagreement can now *ask* for clarification, restatements, explanations, or supporting evidence, but may *not* disagree, argue, or propose any other alternative.
    c. A spokesperson for those who disagree is now required to explain the position just presented and clarified to the complete satisfaction of all other group members, both those who agree and disagree with the position originally advanced. (Note the similarity to active listening presented in chapter 5.) Only when this person has restated the first proposal and supporting arguments to everyone's satisfaction is the group ready to advance to the next step.
    d. The *second* alternative is now presented by a spokesperson selected by members of the group supporting it. Exactly the same procedural rules are followed as during presentation and clarification of the first alternative.
    e. In the event that there are more than two alternatives being supported by subgroups, all are presented, clarified, paraphrased, and confirmed in exactly the same way.
2. Charting of Alternatives
    a. The designated group leader now writes both (or all) positions on a chalkboard or large poster and underneath each lists pros (benefits, advantages) claimed by its proponents and evidence advanced in its support. Under the heading cons the leader should list any *disadvantages*, or possible harmful effects or evidence advanced against the alternative. An example of such a chart is shown in figure 10.4.

How to Reduce Damage from Lead Inhalation?

Make regular gas illegal in city.   Eliminate all private cars from central
                                                     city area.

Pros

1. Inexpensive   1. Easy to enforce
2. Chicago precedent   2. Effective in area of greatest
3. Could become federal regulation in   problem
   future

Cons

1. Difficult to enforce   1. Politically unpopular
2. Owners of older cars will fight it   2. No help to suburbs
                                                      3. Disrupt small companies

    b. When all positions have been charted, the group may want to see if there is unanimity about any of the statements on the chart. What, if anything, do all members agree upon?

  3. Search for Creative Alternatives

    a. The designated leader reviews all elements of common ground shared by all group members, such as shared interest in solving the problem, components shared in the competing alternatives, shared history of the group, etc., and then urges group members to seek a win-win resolution, an alternative all could accept. The leader may propose such a solution if she or he has one in mind or

    b. Ask the group members to compromise and create an alternative that meets the minimum requirements of both (all) sides of the conflict.

  4. Resolution occurs when and if a consensus alternative is adopted.

If the procedure is successful, some time should be spent by the group discussing the procedure followed, how they feel about the group and each of the members in it, and how the group can prevent or manage any future conflicts. Generally, when the previously described procedure is followed out of a sincere desire to resolve the conflict, the group will find at least a compromise and will develop increased cohesiveness and team spirit. Lacking a consensus or compromise, other procedures resulting in a decision will be needed.

Voting is one such alternative. Naturally, some members are bound not to like the outcome, but it may be a necessary step in overcoming an impasse. You may recall the example presented earlier where a faculty subcommittee presented a sweeping proposal to the full faculty committee, only to be met with dismay instead of enthusiasm. After repeated attempts to collaborate and develop an integrative solution failed, the committee took a vote to decide the issue. One danger with voting is that the group arrives at premature closure on an issue. Be especially careful, if this is the option you elect, that the group really is deadlocked and unable to achieve consensus.

Forcing   Another option is forcing. Here, the leader breaks the deadlock and decides on behalf of the group. Again, several members are likely to be disappointed, but in instances where an outside group, parent organization, or authority figure demands a report or where the group faces a deadline, the leader may have little choice.

Third Party Arbitration   Third party arbitration occurs when the group brings in an outside negotiator to resolve its differences. This typically happens with joint labor-management disputes and some court-related cases. Arbitrators often have power to resolve issues any way they please, from deciding entirely in favor of one party to splitting the difference between them. Sometimes, just the threat of bringing in a third party arbitrator is enough to force conflict participants to begin negotiating with each other in good faith. Usually, all parties to the conflict end up feeling dissatisfied. Thus, third party arbitration should be proposed only when the leader believes the group has reached an impasse. Of course, the group members must agree to such a resolution procedure.

Summary

An effective group will experience conflict as members discuss a variety of alternatives and evaluate these alternatives on the basis of differing perceptions, goals, values, and preferences. Conflict occurs when one person believes that another has frustrated a goal. It includes perceptual, emotional, behavioral, and interaction dimensions. Conflict is harmful when is causes bad feelings, lowers cohesiveness, or causes a group to disintegrate, but it can also produce a better group decision, increased member understanding of the issues and each other, and a heightened sense of cohesiveness. Types of conflict include substantive (task-oriented), affective (over personality and power differences), procedural (over how the group operates) and inequity (over unequal workloads or contributions by members). Although these are discussed as distinct types, they combine and overlap. One type usually leads to another in an actual conflict situation.

Groupthink is the tendency of cohesive groups not to conduct a thorough search for and evaluation of options and potential solutions. Its symptoms include a group's overestimation of its power and morality, closed-mindedness, and covert and overt pressures to conform. To combat the tendency to groupthink, leaders are advised to assign the role of critical evaluator to each member, to refrain from stating their own preferences at the outset of a group's deliberations, to establish two or more subgroups to work on a problem simultaneously, and to take all steps necessary to prevent the isolation of the group from all relevant outside opinions.

One's behavioral orientation toward a conflict situation can be distributive (win-lose) or integrative (win-win). The orientation one has will determine in part the specific conflict management strategy one selects. Also helping to determine management style is the degree to which one party wants to satisfy his or her own desires as well as the desires of the other in the conflict situation.

Avoidance occurs when desires to satisfy self and others are low. Accommodation occurs when desire to satisfy others is high. The opposite of accommodation is competition, the desire to satisfy oneself. Compromise is sought when desire to satisfy self and others are intermediate, and collaboration, or problem solving, occurs when concern for self and others are both high. Each style is appropriate under certain circumstances.

Ideally, a group arrives at a consensus agreement on its own. Members should follow certain guidelines in expressing disagreement: they should express rather than ignore the disagreement, express disagreement with rhetorical sensitivity, disagree with the idea without criticizing the person, and react nondefensively when someone disagrees with them. Principled negotiation is a procedure a group can use to arrive at consensus. Steps include separating the people from the problem, focusing on interests rather than positions, inventing options for mutual gain, and using objective criteria. If a group cannot achieve consensus, the leader can move the group through a three-step procedure, which includes presentation of alternatives by all sides to the conflict, charting of alternatives in writing, and searching for creative alternatives. If this process fails, the leader may resort to voting, forcing, or third-party arbitration to resolve a stubborn conflict.

Up to this point in part 4, we have been discussing the throughput factors that are the heart of small group discussion. We now turn our attention to procedures for decision making and problem solving, the heart of accomplishing the objective of most task groups.

Exercises

1. Select a group to which you now belong. Try to remember all the recent conflicts or disagreements experienced by the group. On paper, briefly describe each conflict and indicate what type it was and how it was settled. Use the following format:

Description of conflict	Type of conflict	How conflict was resolved

2. Think of an extended conflict in which you were involved or which you observed. Analyze it according to the perception-emotions-behavior interaction model.
   a. How did each element of the system affect each other element?
   b. What was the relationship of the conflicting parties to each other at the beginning of the conflict episode and again at the end?
   c. What do you conclude about conflict from this?
   d. Would you do anything differently if you were faced with the same situation again?
3. Select a contoversial issue for your class about which there are two or more contrasting opinions. Form into discussion groups of four or five so that at least two persons initially are on each side of the issue. Two classmates should serve as observers for each group of discussants.

Discuss the issue and attempt to come to some consensus.

Observers should note and report on the following:

a. What was said?

b. How were the disagreements expressed?

c. Were there any ways that conflict could have been expressed more appropriately? (The observers should pay particular attention to the effect on the *receiver* of the disagreeing remark.)

4. Your class should split into dyads with one nonparticipating observer per dyad. One dyad partner should play the role of quality control manager and the other that of manufacturing manager. Assume that the manufacturing manager wants to get the quality control manager to reject fewer items so that production can be increased. Half the groups should be instructed to negotiate with a distributive behavioral orientation and half with an integrative one. Observers should note and report *exactly* what was said in attempting to settle the conflict and what appeared to be the effect. Discuss how you felt in your particular situation. Were there any consistent differences in the feelings of participants in the two assigned orientations? What did you learn from this activity?

5. In small groups, discuss an issue that has more than one side. Use the fishbowl setup, where first one group is seated around the other to observe the interaction, then the groups trade places. Each member should choose one of the types of conflict (substantive, affective, procedural, or inequity) and enact that type during the discussion. What is the effect of the various kinds of conflict on the group interaction? Do you think any of these types is more harmful to the group than the others? Why or why not?

6. Your instructor should give you a union-management case to discuss. Select seven people from your class to act out the case, three to role play the union team, three to be the management team, and one to be the third-party negotiator. Have this group go through the three-step process under the direction of the negotiator, while the rest of the class observes and takes notes to report on the observations. What worked well? What worked poorly? Do you have any specific advice for the negotiator? What would you have done differently?

Bibliography

Barker, Larry A., Kathy J. Wahlers, Kittie W. Watson, and Robert J. Kibler. *Groups in Process: An Introduction to Small Group Communication.* 3d ed. Englewood Cliffs, N.J.: Prentice-Hall, 1987. See chapter 9, "Conflict Management and Resolution in Small Groups."

Fisher, Roger, and William Ury. *Getting to Yes: Negotiating Agreement Without Giving In.* New York: Penguin Books, 1983.

Janis, Irving L. *Groupthink: Psychological Studies of Policy Decisions and Fiascoes.* 2d ed. Boston: Houghton Mifflin Company, 1983.

Patton, Bobby R., and Kim Giffin. "Conflict and Its Resolution." In *Small Group Communication: A Reader.* 4th ed., eds. Robert S. Cathcart and Larry A. Samovar. Dubuque, Iowa: Wm. C. Brown Publishers, 1984, 326–35.

Putnam, Linda L. "Conflict in Group Decision-Making." In *Communication and Group Decision-Making.* Eds. Randy Y. Hirokawa and Marshall Scott Poole. Beverly Hills: Sage Publications, 1986, 175–197.

Thomas, Kenneth W. "Conflict and Conflict Management." In *Handbook of Industrial and Organizational Psychology.* Ed. Marvin Dunnette. Chicago: Rand McNally, 1976, 890–934.

Notes

1. Victor D. Wall, Jr., Gloria J. Galanes, and Susan B. Love, "Small, Task-oriented Groups: Conflict, Conflict Management, Satisfaction and Decision Quality," *Small Group Behavior* 18 (1987): 31–55.

2. M. R. Shakun, "Formalizing Conflict Resolution in Policy-Making," *International Journal of General Systems* 7 (1981): 207–15.

3. Gordon L. Lippett, "Managing Conflict in Today's Organization," *Training and Development Journal* 36 (1982): 67–75.

4. Kenneth W. Thomas, "Conflict and Conflict Management," in *Handbook of Industrial and Organizational Psychology*, Ed. M. Dunnette (Chicago: Rand McNally, 1976), 891.

5. Morton Deutsch, "Conflicts: Productive and Destructive," *Journal of Social Issues* 25 (1969): 7.

6. Deutsch, "Conflicts," Thomas, "Conflict and Conflict Management," Louis B. Pondy, "Organizational Conflict: Concepts and Models," *Administrative Science Quarterly* 12 (1976): 296–320; Brent D. Ruben, "Communication and Conflict: A System-Theoretic Perspective," *Quarterly Journal of Speech* 64 (1978): 202–12; H. Guetzkow and J. Gyr, "An Analysis of Conflict in Decision-Making Groups," *Human Relations* 7 (1954): 367–82; E. P. Torrance, "Group Decision-Making and Disagreement," *Social Forces* 35 (1957): 314–18.

7. Karl Smith, David W. Johnson, and Roger T. Johnson, "Can Conflict Be Constructive? Controversy versus Concurrence Seeking in Learning Groups," *Journal of Educational Psychology* 73 (1981): 654.

8. Ibid., 654–63.

9. Guetzkow and Gyr, "An Analysis of Conflict," 367–82. Michael R. Cheney and Jane B. Anziano, "An Approach to Conflict and Its Management," in *Small Group Communication: Selected Readings*, ed. Victor D. Wall, Jr. (Columbus, Ohio: Collegiate Publishing, Inc., 1978): 343–53.

10. Guetzkow and Gyr, "An Analysis of Conflict," 367–82. Cheney and Anziano, "An Approach to Conflict," 343–53.
11. Linda L. Putnam, "Conflict in Group Decision-Making," in *Communication and Group Decision-Making*, eds. Randy Y. Hirokawa and Marshall Scott Poole (Beverly Hills: Sage Publications, 1986), 175–96.
12. Victor D. Wall Jr. and Linda L. Nolan, "Small Group Conflict: A Look at Equity, Satisfaction and Styles of Conflict Management," *Small Group Behavior* 18 (1987): 188–211.
13. Irving L. Janis, *Groupthink: Psychological Studies of Policy Decisions and Fiascoes*, 2d ed. (Boston: Houghton Mifflin Company, 1983).
14. Anne Gero, "Conflict Avoidance in Consensual Decision Processes," *Small Group Behavior* 16 (1985): 487–99.
15. Kenneth W. Thomas, "Conflict and Conflict Management," 889–935. Bobby R. Patton and Kim Giffin, "Conflict and Its Resolution," in *Small Group Communication: A Reader*, 4th ed. eds. Robert S. Cathcart and Larry A. Samovar, (Dubuque, Iowa: Wm. C. Brown Publishers, 1984), 326–35.
16. Robert E. Jones and Charles S. White, "Relationships among Personality, Conflict Resolution Styles and Task Effectiveness," *Group and Organization Studies* 10 (1985): 152–67.
17. A. Paul Hare and David Naveh, "Group Development at the Camp David Summit, 1978," *Small Group Behavior* 15 (1984): 299–318.
18. Leslie A. Baxter, "Conflict Management: An Episodic Approach," *Small Group Behavior* 13 (1982): 23–42.
19. Donald D. Morely and Pamela Shockley-Zalabak, "Conflict Avoiders and Compromisers: Toward an Understanding of Their Organizational Communication Style," *Group and Organization Studies* 11 (1986): 387–402.
20. Kristin B. Valentine and B. Aubrey Fisher, "An Interaction Analysis of Verbal Innovative Deviance in Small Groups," *Speech Monographs* 41 (1974): 413–20.
21. Covey, Mark K., "Relationship between Social Skill and Conflict Resolution Tactics," (Paper presented at the annual convention of the Rocky Mountain Psychological Association, Snowbird, Utah, 1983).
22. Gloria J. Galanes, "The Effect of Conflict Expression Styles on Quality of Outcome and Satisfaction in Small, Task-Oriented Groups," (Unpublished doctoral dissertation, Ohio State University, 1985).
23. Steven M. Alderton and Lawrence R. Frey, "Argumentation in Small Group Decision-Making," in *Communication and Group Decision-Making*, eds. Randy Y. Hirokawa and Marshall Scott Poole (Beverly Hills: Sage Publications, 1986), 157–73.
24. Roger Fisher and William Ury, *Getting to Yes: Negotiating Agreement Without Giving In.* (Boston: Houghton Mifflin Company, 1981; Penguin Books, 1983).

Part 5

Small Group Outputs

Chapter 11

Which Shall It Be?
Decision Making
in Small Groups

Study Objectives

As a result of studying chapter 11 you should be able to:

1. Distinguish between the concepts of problem solving and decision making.

2. Describe the relative advantages and disadvantages of group and individual decision making.

3. Understand the differences among decision making by a leader, majority vote, and consensus; and list the advantages and disadvantages of each procedure.

4. Explain five procedural guidelines for making group decisions by consensus and the reasons for these guidelines.

5. Arrive at true consensus decisions in groups.

Key Terms

Assembly effect the decision by a group is qualitatively and/or quantitatively superior to what an adding together of the knowledge, ideas, skills, and wisdom of group members indicates it would be.

Consensus decision a choice among alternatives that all members of the group agree is the best they can make and that is acceptable to all.

Criteria standards for judging among alternatives, often stated as questions.

Decision making choosing among alternatives.

Majority decision decision made by vote, with more than half the members voting for the winning alternative.

Problem solving a several-stage procedure for moving from some unsatisfactory state to a more satisfying one, or developing a plan for doing so.

We have already acknowledged that small groups are permanent fixtures in human society. The need to make decisions in concert with others increases as our society becomes more complex and interdependent. More and more important decisions are made by groups, committees, and boards. As Tropman says, "Only when we begin to recognize the importance and necessity of communal decision-making can we begin to prepare ourselves adequately for these roles."[1]

We are competing with societies—Japanese, Chinese, Korean—that are more skilled than we at collective decision making. We dare not remain complacent. It is a myth, as Anderson notes, that we can work effectively in small groups without understanding their processes and dynamics.[2] One of the most important of these is the decision-making process. Some element of decision making is present in a variety of tasks groups face: solving a complex problem, determining whether or not a defendant is guilty, selecting appropriate punishment, choosing which student receives a scholarship, and so forth. In this chapter we discuss how decisions are made by groups and the implications this has for helping groups make the highest quality decisions possible. First, we differentiate between decision making and problem solving.

Decision Making versus Problem Solving

Some writers have used the terms *decision making* and *problem solving* synonymously, creating considerable confusion. There is a major difference between the two. **Decision making** refers to the act of *choosing* between two or more alternatives. It focuses on evaluating alternatives that already exist so the group can choose the best. **Problem solving** is a more comprehensive, multistage procedure through which an individual or group develops a plan to move from some unsatisfactory present state to a desired goal state. Problem solving usually requires a group to make a multitude of decisions, but it also involves *creating* alternatives as well as deciding among them. Thus, decision making is one subset of problem solving, which will be dealt with in chapter 12. An example illustrates the difference. A screening committee to select the best site for a university performing arts center from among several pre-approved sites is an example of a decision-making group. A task force charged with solving the problem of inadequate facilities for a university's performing arts departments is a problem-solving group. It will make a variety of decisions in the course of developing a proposal to alleviate the situation.

We have chosen to discuss decision making first because it provides a foundation for understanding many kinds of groups with which you will be involved. In addition, knowing something about decision making furnishes you with a more complete understanding of the problem-solving process we will explain later.

Group versus Individual Decision Making

Before reading further, rank the following ways to make decisions in a small group, from 1 (your most preferred) to 7 (your least preferred).

_____ A. Let the leader of the group decide because he or she should have the right to make the decision. After all, the leader has the responsibilities.

_____ B. Find out who is most expert on the topic and let that person decide what is best for the group.

_____ C. Decide by chance, flipping a coin, rolling a die, or drawing straws.

_____ D. Determine the average of what group members think.

_____ E. Wait it out. A decision will finally emerge, or maybe if you wait long enough, a decision will not be necessary.

_____ F. Take a vote and the majority rules. This is the American way to decide after the issues have been discussed.

_____ G. Keep talking until you can arrive at a basic agreement from everyone that the group has arrived at the best possible decision everyone can support.

If possible, compare your rankings with classmates in a small group setting. *Be sure you explain your reasons for your rankings and listen to the reasons of the other people.*

In this book, we have stated that group decision making through discussion is usually superior to individual decision making. In fact, there are times when individual decision making is best. Group decision making takes more time, sometimes one or two members can dominate a discussion, and occasionally the fact that other people are present can push an otherwise well-informed discussant farther in a particular direction than he or she would normally go. Someone who is trying to decide whether to have a group or an individual make a specific decision must balance out these and other factors.

Vroom, for example, says that the decision to ask a group to make a decision should be based on analysis of three dimensions.[3] First, the quality or rationality dimension concerns whether or not one decision is likely to be clearly better than another. There is one best way, for example, to assemble a swingset but many different acceptable ways to plan a party. Second, the leader must determine how important it is that the decision be accepted by group members. Some decisions, particularly those which affect members' jobs or daily lives, may appear perfectly sound but will not work if group members do not accept them. The third dimension is time. The group must have time to engage in discussion, for group decision making is considerably more time consuming than individual decision making. Therefore, a series of trade-offs is involved when someone elects to let a group make a decision.

In general, group decisions tend to be of higher quality than those made by individuals or by averaging individual decisions.[4] In fact, they usually are better even than decisions made by individual high-status members who are considered especially knowledgeable about a problem.[5] Furthermore, it is the verbal interaction itself, not just a summing of individual members' perceptions or opinions, which contributes to the increased quality.[6]

A number of studies support the idea that group involvement in decision making increases the acceptance of the decision.[7] Coch and French demonstrated that when workers have a voice in changing a work procedure, they are more productive and loyal than when the change is imposed on them.[8] As Block and Hoffman wrote, ". . . the effectiveness of gaining members' commitment to change through use of group decision is unquestioned. . . ."[9]

It is important to note, however, that group decision making is not automatically superior. Burleson, Levine, and Samter found that, although eight of ten groups that produced consensus decisions had better decisions than the individual members acting alone, two of the ten produced worse decisions.[10] Miesing and Preble discovered that cohesiveness and performance norms influenced quality. Groups that were very cohesive and had high performance expectations performed better.[11] Hirokawa discovered that groups that approached decision making systematically made better decisions than groups that did not.[12] (This is explained more fully in chapter 12.) On the other hand, Gouran found that group interaction sometimes promotes collective inferential error if members accept unusual cases as representative or allow specialization of knowledge to occur.[13]

We can sum up the meaning of all this research comparing the quality of individual versus group decision making this way: groups are usually superior in making decisions about how to solve discussion-type problems, depending on how high their norms are for quality (performance), whether they have sufficient cohesiveness to enforce such norms, how systematic and organized their problem-solving procedures are, and how skilled and determined the group members are at arriving at valid conclusions based on sound evidence.

As we noted earlier, group members influence each other positively as well as negatively. This contributes to the group polarization tendency, also known as the risky or the cautious shift. Sometimes groups make decisions that are more risky than those the individuals would make alone, and sometimes they are more cautious.[14] It appears that the determining factor is the prevailing cultural norm. If the cultural norm is in the direction of risk (for example, Americans value risk taking when it comes to money or business decisions), a group shifts toward risk. In contrast, when the norm favors caution (for example, when decisions are potentially life threatening), a group shifts toward a safer decision.[15] Either way, decision making can be impaired.

Groups frequently achieve an **assembly effect** in which the decision is qualitatively and quantitatively superior either to the individual decision of the group's most expert member or to the adding or averaging of the wisdom of the members. This is a kind of synergy which occurs in the operation of the small group as a system—the whole becomes greater than the sum of its parts. Burleson et al. found evidence of the assembly effect operating in their recent study.[16] However, the procedures a group follows in making a decision is probably more important than the sharing of responsibility, individual persuasiveness, or societal norms.

Recent research by Hirokawa supports this notion. In one study, the groups who had the highest quality decisions used a vigilant decision making procedure and engaged in second guessing, or retrospective questioning of previous choices.[17] In another study, Hirokawa found that it is not so much the system groups use that determines the quality, but whether or not certain important functions are performed.[18] That is, to make good decisions among possible solutions, groups must thoroughly and accurately understand the problem, must have a variety of acceptable alternatives, and must evaluate each alternative carefully, including assessment of the negative consequences associated with each alternative. Groups that do this, regardless of the decision-making technique used, perform better than otherwise. Hirokawa found that differences in decision quality are linked directly to how well groups satisfy these decisional functions.[19] The two most important factors seemed to be the first and last: superior groups have a better understanding of the choice-making situation and were more thorough and accurate in assessing negative consequences. He also found that assessment of positive and negative qualities are important at different stages of a group's deliberation. For instance, effective groups first seem to spot the serious defects when they initially screen alternatives. Once they find an alternative that appears to be free of fatal flaws, they switch strategies and begin to detail the positive aspects of the alternative. Hirokawa says, ". . . instruction needs to move away from discussion procedures and formats (e.g., 'standard agendas') and more toward the effects or consequences of those procedures and formats."[20]

Methods of Decision Making in Small Groups

The three most common ways small groups make decisions are by consensus, majority vote, or designated leader or head. The following activities are designed to give you experience with the differences among these methods.

The class is first divided into small groups of five or six. One person in each group is appointed leader by the instructor or elected by the group members. Then, each group member should choose from the following list one social activity for your class as a means for getting better acquainted, increasing class cohesiveness, and relaxing.

1. Hold a potluck dinner or picnic at an appropriate location on campus.
2. Attend an intercollegiate sports event together, followed by a dance in the student union.
3. Arrange a class social hour in a private party room at a nearby bar or lounge.
4. Attend a movie together (selected by the leader), followed by an informal discussion of the film over soft drinks and coffee in a private room on campus.
5. As a class, plan and carry out a fund-raising activity to benefit a charitable organization (selected by the leader).

As soon as each person has made a choice, hold a five-minute discussion of the pros and cons of these activities. The leader will then announce to the rest of the group which of the activities your group will recommend to the rest of the class and why it is the best choice. As soon as the leader has made this announcement, complete the postdecision reaction sheet and tabulate the response.

Postdecision Reaction Sheet

Record your answers to the following questions. Then, give the answers to your group's coordinator who will tabulate them, compute averages, and report them to your instructor to record on the board for discussion.

1. How much chance do you feel you had to influence the group decision?

1	2	3	4	5	6	7	8	9
(none)							(a great deal)	

2. How well do you think other members of the group listened to and understood you?

1	2	3	4	5	6	7	8	9
(not at all)							(completely)	

3. How satisfied or confident are you with the result of your group's decision making?

1	2	3	4	5	6	7	8	9
(very dissatisfied)							(very satisfied)	

4. What adjective best describes the atmosphere in your group during the discussion?
   (Note: you will complete this form after each of the next two exercises.)

Sometimes a designated or emergent leader will think the problem through alone and state a decision without discussion or will consult with the group before announcing the decision. Group members then are given instructions for executing the decision. The resulting solution may or may not be a high quality one, but other outcomes will often be resentment, lowered cohesiveness, halfhearted support for the decision, and loss of effective influence on later decisions. Members may even sabotage the decision.

Decision Making by a Majority Vote

Divide the class into different groups of five or six. Look over the following four alternatives for grading students in a small group communication course: should participation in the class be evaluated in computing final course grades? In your groups, discuss your opinions about these alternatives for ten minutes, then vote for your choice by a show of hands. If no alternative gets a majority, vote again between the two top options. If necessary, discuss these briefly before voting.

1. The instructor should grade each student on participation during classroom discussions and make this a major factor in determining each person's final grade.
2. Students should grade each other on class participation, with each receiving the average of all grades received from classmates. This should be a major component of the final grades.
3. Participation should be a major factor in determining final course grades, but both students and instructor should participate in determining this part of the grade. Combine activities 1 and 2.
4. Grading participation would make competitive relationships among students inevitable. This should not be done. Grades should be based entirely on items other than classroom discussion participation.

Now complete the postdecision reaction sheet again.

Making a **majority decision** through voting by a show of hands, saying aye, or with written paper ballot, is probably the procedure used most often to settle a difference of opinion (conflict). This is done when a group has two or more possible alternative solutions to adopt or recommend. Everyone has an equal opportunity to influence the decision by speaking, each vote counts equally, and the decision is reached more quickly than if the group's norms require a consensus decision. (Of course if the vote is unanimous, an integrative consensus has been achieved.) Often the decision is a split vote, a distributive resolution of conflict by the power of the majority, with minority members (losers) doubting that their ideas have been understood fully and treated fairly. People in a minority may even keep silent for fear of being ridiculed for opinions that deviate from those of the majority. Not only does the quality of the decision sometimes suffer, the group experiences lowered cohesiveness and commitment to the decision. Sometimes a group's bylaws require that a vote be taken. In that case, the group may want to discuss an issue until consensus has been reached, then vote to confirm it "legally."

Decision Making by Consensus

A **consensus decision** is one that all members agree is the best that everyone can support. It may be, but is not necessarily, the alternative most preferred by all members. When a true consensus has been reached, the output is usually a superior quality decision, a high level of member satisfaction, and acceptance of the result. However, unless virtual unanimity happens to exist at the beginning of a discussion of alternatives, reaching consensus may take much more time than other procedures. Sometimes a true consensus cannot be achieved, no matter how much time is spent in discussion. Unanimity—the state of perfect consensus in which every group member believes that the decision achieved is the best that could be made—is not at all common. However, if all members accept that a consensus may require compromise and collaboration, all will usually support it even though it may not be the option each would have preferred.

The process of reaching consensus gives all members an opportunity to express how they feel and think about the alternatives and an equitable chance to influence the outcome. Consensus depends on active listening so that all important information and points of view are understood similarly by all discussants. A consensual decision is often a synergistic outcome in which the group produces something superior to a summation of individual ideas and thinking, or the assembly effect discussed earlier. Conflicts, as discussed in chapter 10, must be viewed as means for clarifying and testing alternatives in the process of working toward consensus, not as interpersonal competition for power. Here are some discussion guidelines outlined by Hall for making consensus decisions:

1. Don't argue stubbornly for your own position. Present it clearly and logically, being sure you listen to all reactions and consider them carefully.
2. Avoid looking at a stalemate as distributive conflict (i.e., a win-lose situation). Rather, see whether you can find a next best alternative acceptable to all, a consensus compromise.
3. When agreement is reached too easily and too quickly, be on guard against groupthink. Don't change your position just to avoid conflict. Through discussion, be sure that everyone accepts the decision for similar or complementary reasons and really agrees that it is the best that can be reached.
4. Don't use conflict-suppressing techniques, such as majority vote, averaging, coin tossing, and so forth. While they prevent destructive interpersonal conflicts, they also suppress constructive substantive conflicts.
5. Seek out differences of opinion; they are helpful in testing alternatives and evaluating reasoning. Get every member involved in the decision-making process. The group has a better chance of selecting the best alternative if it has a wider range of information and ideas.

For the following exercise you will be asked to come to a consensus decision but before you form into groups, read the "Subarctic Survival Situation" case and rank the items yourself.

The Subarctic Survival Situation

It is approximately 2:30 P.M., October 5 and you have just crash-landed in a float plane on the east shore of Laura Lake in the subarctic region of the Northern Quebec-Newfoundland border. The pilot was killed in the crash, but the rest of you are uninjured. Each of you is wet up to the waist and has perspired heavily. Shortly after the crash, the plane drifted into deep water and sank with the pilot's body pinned inside.

The pilot was unable to contact anyone before the crash. However, ground sightings indicated that you are thirty miles south of your intended course and approximately twenty-two air miles east of Schefferville, your original destination, and the nearest known habitation. Schefferville (population 5,000) is an iron ore mining town reachable only by air or rail; all roads end a few miles from town. Your party was expected to return from northwestern Labrador to Schefferville no later than October 19th and filed a Flight Notification form with the Department of Transportation via Schefferville radio to that effect.

The immediate area is covered with small evergreen trees (one and one-half to four inches in diameter). Scattered in the area are a number of hills with rocky and barren tops. Tundra (arctic swamps) make up the valleys between the hills. The area is covered by long narrow lakes connected by innumerable streams and rivers. Temperatures during October vary between twenty-five and thirty-six degrees Fahrenheit, but will occasionally go as high as fifty and as low as zero. Heavy clouds cover the sky three-quarters of the time, with only one day in ten being fairly clear. Five to seven inches of snow are on the ground; however, the actual depth varies enormously from clear areas to drifts of three to five feet. Wind speed averages thirteen to fifteen miles per hour.

You are all dressed in insulated underwear, sox, heavy wool shirts, pants, knit gloves, sheepskin jackets, knitted wool caps, and heavy leather hunting boots. You may assume that the number of survivors is the same as the number in your group, that you have all agreed to stick together, and that all the items are dry and in good condition.

Before the plane drifted and sank, you were able to salvage the fifteen items listed below. Your task is to rank these items according to their importance to your survival, starting with 1 for the most important to 15 for the least important.

First, without discussing the situation or consulting anyone, rank the fifteen items individually.

_____ A magnetic compass
_____ A gallon can of maple syrup
_____ A sleeping bag per person (arctic type down-filled with liner)
_____ A bottle of water purification tablets
_____ A twenty by twenty foot piece of heavy duty canvas
_____ Thirteen wood matches in a metal screwtop, waterproof container
_____ 250 feet of one-quarter inch braided nylon rope, fifty pound test
_____ An operating four battery flashlight
_____ Three pairs of snowshoes
_____ A fifth of Bacardi rum (151 proof)
_____ Safety razor shaving kit with mirror
_____ A wind-up alarm clock
_____ A hand axe
_____ One aircraft inner tube for a fourteen inch wheel (punctured)
_____ A book entitled *Northern Star Navigation*

As soon as everyone has ranked all fifteen items without consulting anyone else, the class should form into groups of five or six. Following the rules for decision making by consensus, arrive at a ranking for your group. As soon as your group has completed its consensus ranking, each member should complete a postdecision reaction sheet.

Score both your own answers and your group's answers by comparing them to the right answers arrived at by the Para Rescue Specialists, 413 Transport and Rescue Squadron, Canadian Forces Base on Prince Edward Island. Your instructor has a copy of the correct rankings. Error points for each item are the difference between your rank and that of the experts. Add up your and your group's error points. The smaller the error point total, the closer the answers were to the experts. How did you do? How did your group do? Groups do a better job than individuals on this exercise about 90 percent of the time.

Consensus may be superficial when some members accommodate to other higher-status members, such as "experts" who express their opinions with exceptional force, a designated leader, or a large majority. The first time one of us completed "Lost on the Moon," a similar exercise, it was in a group of mechanical and electrical engineers who appeared to have a great deal of expertise in technical matters. The coauthor in question readily conceded to these experts. Interestingly, the individual ranking in that case was *better* than the group's ranking, but the group had been deprived of the individual's reasoning ability out of compliance to perceived expertise. Do not submerge your doubts!

You will be likely to experience conflict in the course of arriving at consensual decisions. This is to be expected and even welcomed. Follow the suggestions presented in the previous chapter, employ active listening techniques, and use common sense, and your decision-making process should be more effective.

Effective Group Decision Making

There are certain activities a group can perform to help insure that it has made the best possible decision. We have synthesized some of the key elements directly related to decision-making effectiveness in the following guidelines:

1. **Define the problem clearly.**
   Failure to do so will lead a group to choose a decision that attacks symptoms instead of causes or will not work as well as another option. Groups that clearly understand the choice-making situation select more wisely.
2. **Establish criteria carefully.**
   Criteria are those standards that must be met when choosing any option. We introduce the idea here and include details about criteria in chapter 12. For example, if the parent organization for your group has said that you must stay within a prescribed budget or given you other constraints you must consider, these are criteria against which you can evaluate the list of options to choose the one that best meets *all* criteria.

3. **Evaluate all the options, using your established criteria, on the basis of positive and especially negative consequences.**
The most effective groups are able to anticipate all negative consequences and thereby eliminate the worst options. Think of all the things that can go wrong with each option, assessing how serious each consequence will be, then choose appropriately.

4. **Select one option, tentatively, and "second guess" your choice.**
The most effective groups do not simply choose to get things over with. They continue to cycle back over ground previously covered as they encounter new information or think of other things that are pertinent. Once you have made a tentative choice, go back over your choice as a group, reevaluating your information, reasoning, and assessment.

Summary

Decision making involves choosing among specified alternatives; problem solving is an extended process that involves searching for and creating alternatives. Many decisions are made in the process of problem solving. There are numerous ways decisions are made in small groups. When there is an absolute standard of correctness or a formula for decision making, then an individual skilled in the procedure should usually make the decision and explain it to the group. For example, in many groups a skilled mathematician can work out statistics for the group more quickly and just as accurately as the group. However, groups far excel individuals, even experts, in matters of judgment where no alternative can be confirmed as the best when the decision is made. Substantive or task decisions faced by groups are often of this sort. Criteria to use in determining whether a group or an individual should make a decision include: Is there a quality component? Is acceptance of the decision important? and Does the group have time to deliberate? "Yes" answers to all three questions indicate that a group decision is warranted. The quality of the decision can be estimated from these process and output criteria: to what degree was the information and thinking of *all* group members used; how satisfied are members with the decision, and how committed are they to working for it; and to what degree has the decision-making procedure improved the cooperativeness and cohesiveness among members.

Group decisions take longer to make than individual ones, but extensive research shows them to be superior for a number of reasons. First, complementary knowledge of members is pooled to provide a better understanding of the situation and the merits of various alternatives. Second, persons perform better on many tasks when in the presence of others. Discussants stimulate each other to do a better job, leading to an assembly effect. Third, conscientious, confident, and creative people tend to be more active in decision-making discussions than less well prepared people. Fourth, mistakes in individual thinking are detected and corrected by other members. As a general rule, discussing an issue systematically until consensus emerges will produce both a better decision and a more satisfied group. For the most effective decision making, a group should be sure it understands the problem, has established explicit criteria, has thoroughly evaluated all options (especially negative consequences associated with each one), and has reevaluated its tentative decision to insure that nothing important has been overlooked.

In the next chapter we examine the complex process of problem solving, which incorporates all the information we have presented thus far. At this point, you should be viewing the small group as a complex system, with each component interdependent with all the other components. All the parts should come together when we discuss problem solving.

Exercises

1. Read the following case problem, and then break into groups of five or six and come to a consensus decision. Use the following questions to guide your postdecision evaluation:
   a. What problems in choosing did your group have?
   b. What seemed to cause these problems?
   c. Did you make the best choice? Why or why not?
   d. What guidelines can you write to apply what you learned?
   e. What did you learn from this exercise?

Scholarship Awards Committee

You comprise a special scholarship awards committee at State University. A special trust fund was established by an anonymous donor to award one full-tuition scholarship per year to a person with demonstrated need for financial assistance, a reasonable expectation of success as a student, and who is unlikely to attend college if not granted some form of aid. There are no other conditions attached to the award except that a student committee must select the winner from a list of applicants supplied by the admissions office. Admissions has given you a list of five eligible applicants and said no other information can be given to you. Who will receive the scholarship? You can award only one scholarship recipient.

Duane, age 18, finished high school in three years. He says he rushed through because he could not have tolerated another year of the bull. His mother, a widow with two younger children to support, can only work part-time in her field as a registered nurse. Duane's high school grade average was 3.0. University tests predict a 2.6 college grade point average in a science curriculum and 3.1 in non-science. His mother is determined that Duane should be a physician. Duane says he is not sure of what job or profession he wants. He has some emotional problems; a psychiatrist he has seen recommends college because he thinks Duane needs "an intellectual challenge."

Carla, age 17, has very high recommendations from the small town high school where she earned a 3.8 grade average. In her senior year she became engaged to a driver for a feed mill, who wants her to get married at once and forget college. She is known to have spent a few nights with him on a cross-country trip to haul grain. Your university predicts she will earn a 2.6 in science and 3.3 in a non-science program.

She says she wants to become a social worker "to help the poor in some big city." The minister where she attends church says she has a fine mind, but he predicts she will marry and drop out even if she starts college. Her parents are uneducated (less than high school), hard working, law abiding, and very poor.

Melissa, age 26, is a divorcee with a seven-year-old son. She made a 2.8 grade average in high school "because I goofed around," but tests predict a 2.9 in science and a 3.6 in non-science at your university. She says she wants to become an English instructor, "in college if I get lucky, or at least in high school." She was a beauty contest winner at 18, but says she is bitter toward men and will never remarry. She gets no child support or other family assistance. Her present boss, a dress shop owner, gives her a good character reference but predicts she will marry rather than finish college.

Sam, age 19, was offered several football scholarships, but they were withdrawn when an auto accident injured his legs. He can get around well but cannot compete in athletics. His high school grade average was barely passing, but entrance test scores predict a 2.5 average in science and 3.0 in a non-science curriculum. His father, a day laborer, says he can contribute nothing toward a college education for Sam. Sam says he is determined to become a football coach, though he has been advised that may be difficult without a college playing record.

Ray, age 27, earned a medal for bravery and lost his right hand in an Army war game. He earned a high school diploma while in the Army. The university predicts a 2.0 average in science and a 2.8 in a non-science program. He is eligible for some veteran's assistance, but his family needs his help to support a large brood of younger children. Ray says he wants to major in business and "make enough money so I don't have to live like an animal as my parents do."

Bibliography

Hirokawa, Randy Y. "Discussion Procedures and Decision Making Performance: A Test of a Functional Perspective." *Human Communication Research* 12 (1985): 203–24.

Hirokawa, Randy Y. "Group Communication and Decision-Making Performance: A Continued Test of the Functional Perspective." Paper presented at the annual convention of the Speech Communication Association, Boston, 1987.

Janis, Irving L. *Groupthink: Psychological Studies of Foreign Policy Decisions and Fiascoes.* 2d ed. Boston: Houghton Mifflin Company, 1983.

Kline, John A. "Consensus in Small Groups: Deriving Suggestions from Research." *Communication* 10 (1981): 73–78.

Shaw, Marvin E. *Group Dynamics: The Psychology of Small Group Behavior.* 3d ed. New York: McGraw-Hill, 1981. See chapter 3.

Notes

1. John E. Tropman, *Effective Meetings: Improving Group Decision-Making* (Beverly Hills: Sage Publications, 1980), 11.

2. Joseph D. Anderson, "Working with Groups: Little-Known Facts that Challenge Well-Known Myths," *Small Group Behavior* 16 (1985): 267–83.

3. Victor H. Vroom, "A New Look at Managerial Decision-Making," *Organizational Dynamics* (AMACOM: American Management Association, 1973), 66–80.

4. Jay Hall, "Decisions, Decisions, Decisions," *Psychology Today* 5 (November 1971): 51–54, 86–87; Jay Hall and W. H. Watson, "The Effects of a Normative Intervention on Group Decision-Making Performance," *Human Relations* 23 (1970): 299–317.

5. Irving L. Janis, *Groupthink: Psychological Studies of Policy Decisions and Fiascoes* (Boston: Houghton Mifflin Company, 1982).

6. Brant R. Burleson, Barbara J. Levine, and Wendy Samter, "Decision-Making Procedure and Decision Quality," *Human Communication Research* 10 (1984): 557–74.

7. M. L. Chemers, "Leadership Theory and Research: A Systems-Process Integration," in *Basic Group Processes*, ed. P. B. Paulus (New York: Springer-Verlag, 1983), 19–20; Randy Y. Hirokawa, "Consensus Group Decision-Making, Quality of Decision and Group Satisfaction: An Attempt to Sort Fact from Fiction," *Central States Speech Journal* 33 (1982): 407–15.

8. Lester Coch and John R. P. French, Jr., "Overcoming Resistance to Change," *Human Relations* 1 (1948): 512–32.

9. Myron W. Block and L. R. Hoffman, "The Effects of Valence of Solutions and Group Cohesiveness on Members' Commitment to Group Decisions," in *The Group Problem Solving Process*, ed. L. Richard Hoffman (New York: Prager, 1979), 121.

10. Burleson et al., "Decision-Making Procedure," 557–74.

11. Paul Miesing and John F. Preble, "Group Processes and Performance in Complex Business Simulation," *Small Group Behavior* 16 (1985): 325–38.

12. Hirokawa, "Consensus Group Decision-Making," 407–15; Randy Y. Hirokawa, "Why Informed Groups Make Faulty Decisions: An Investigation of Possible Interaction-Based Explanations," *Small Group Behavior* 18 (1987): 3–29.

13. Dennis S. Gouran, "Theoretical Foundation for the Study of Inferential Error in Decision-Making Groups" (Paper presented at the conference on Small Group Research, University Park, Pa., April, 1982).
14. Marvin E. Shaw, *Group Dynamics*, 2d ed. (New York: McGraw-Hill, 1976), 70–77.
15. Robert A. Baron, *Behavior in Organizations: Understanding and Managing the Human Side of Work,* 2d ed. (Boston: Allyn and Bacon, Inc., 1986).
16. Burleson et al., "Decision-Making Procedure," 370–73.
17. Hirokawa, "Why Informed Groups," 557–74.
18. Randy Y. Hirokawa, "Discussion Procedures and Decision-Making Performance," *Human Communication Research* 12 (1985): 203–224.
19. Randy Y. Hirokawa, "Group Communication and Decision-Making Performance: A Continued Test of the Functional Perspective," (Paper presented at the annual convention of the Speech Communication Association, Boston, 1987).
20. Randy Y. Hirokawa, "Discussion Procedures," 221.

Chapter 12

Group Problem Solving

Study Objectives

As a result of studying chapter 12 you should be able to:

1. Analyze any problem from the standpoint of its undesirable present situation, obstacles, and goal.

2. List and explain the importance of seven dimensions of a problem when developing a sequence of steps for problem solving.

3. Present a rationale for following a step-by-step procedure during a problem-solving discussion, or at least of determining that no important step in problem solving has been overlooked.

4. List and explain six principles that serve as guidelines for planning specific problem-solving procedures.

5. List the five steps of the General Procedural Model for Problem Solving in correct order, and be able to adapt this model in outlines for structuring problem-solving discussions of any sort of problem.

Key Terms

Acceptance-technical dimension characteristic of a problem concerned with the degree to which a solution must be acceptable to affected persons in order to work well, be technically excellent, or both.

Brainstorming a procedure for releasing the creative potential of a group of discussants in which all criticism is ruled out for a period of time. The group works for a large number of ideas, and building on others' ideas is encouraged.

Cooperative requirements member's efforts need to be coordinated for a group to complete its task successfully.

Developmental questions specific issues that guide the group's analysis of the problem; answers are thoroughly discussed in order to understand the problem in detail before considering how to solve it.

General Procedural Model for Problem Solving a general procedure involving five steps for structuring problem-solving discussions; the GPMPS can be adapted to suit the characteristics of any problem.

Intrinsic interest extent to which the task itself is attractive and interesting to the participants.

Intuitive problem solving that is nonsystematic, impulsive, or not characterized by any step-by-step procedure.

Program Evaluation and Review Technique (PERT) a procedure for planning the details for solving a complex problem that involves many people and resources.

Population familiarity degree to which members of a group (or society) are familiar with the nature of a problem and experienced in solving similar problems or performing similar tasks.

Problem an existing but undesired state of affairs, a desired state (goal), and obstacles to achieving the goal; difference between what actually happens and what *should* be happening.

Problem question a question calling the attention of a group to a problem without suggesting any particular type of solution.

Problem solving procedure followed by an individual or group to find a way to move from an unsatisfactory condition to a more satisfactory one (goal).

Reflective thinking a generic term for systematic thinking when trying to solve a problem; also, a systematic procedure for organizing group problem-solving discussion that emphasizes criteria and quality as opposed to quantity and innovation in creating alternatives and in which solutions are frequently evaluated as soon as proposed.

Solution question formulation of a problem as a question in which a solution to the problem is suggested or implied.

Solution multiplicity characteristic of a problem such that high multiplicity means many alternatives are possible as solutions.

Structure organization; arrangement among parts of a system, steps in a procedure.

Systematic following a definite series of steps; organized problem solving following a definite sequence.

Task difficulty degree of problem complexity (high-difficulty tasks require extensive effort, knowledge, and skills for solution).

In chapter 11 problem solving was defined as a multi-step procedure beginning with dissatisfaction over an existing situation and ending with a plan of action to produce a more satisfactory state of affairs. Many decisions are made in the process of solving any problem.

If you ask most people what they do when they have a problem to solve, they probably will say, "get the facts, weigh the alternatives, and make a decision." That's not a bad procedure, but extensive observation of individual and group decision making and problem solving reveals that the process is usually more haphazard than that.[1] Have you ever been faced with a troublesome problem you must solve yourself and felt you have ended up chasing your thoughts around in circles without getting anywhere? Most of us have experienced that sensation. If that is typical of individual problem solving, imagine what can happen when a group of individuals try to think together toward a common aim. For instance, Berg found that groups in actual discussions changed themes every fifty-eight seconds, often without completing the topics.[2]

In the typical problem-solving discussion, someone outlines a problem, someone else suggests what to do to solve it, the group briefly discusses the idea, and then it is dropped and something else is discussed. Eventually the group may return to the idea at some point. When time begins to run out, a decision is made quickly. As you might imagine, this haphazard procedure will not produce an adequate decision or solution to the problem. Key elements are likely to have been left out of consideration, and evaluation has surely been less than exhaustive. Some type of systematic procedure is needed for group problem solving to be most effective.

In order to provide a basis for improving problem solving, chapter 12 defines the concept *problem,* analyzes the major dimensions and types of problems, provides evidence that problem-solving procedures for individuals as well as groups can be improved, reviews research that suggests directions for improvement, and provides specific guidelines and sequences for improving the efficiency and effectiveness of group problem-solving discussions.

Problem

The best way for a group to proceed depends on the nature of the problem with which it is concerned. We need to understand the concept **problem** in order to devise effective procedures. All problems consist of the following three major components:

1. **Undesirable present situation.**
   Someone must perceive or something must occur to elicit the feeling that the current state of affairs, the status quo, is undesirable. For example, a club to which you belong has been losing members. Attendance has been dropping gradually to the point where the continued existence of the organization is threatened. At your last meeting, only five of your twenty members showed up and ten were needed to conduct official business.

Figure 12.1
Components of a
problem.

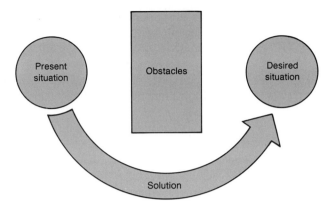

2. **Goal.**

    The recognition of a problem usually is closely associated with the goal. When you call something problematic, you usually have some idea what the desired state of affairs might be. Your organization, for instance, must increase its membership and attendance at meetings in order to survive. You could state the following as a goal: "increase membership by 50 percent and double attendance at meetings."

3. **Obstacles.**

    Certain factors impede smooth progress toward the goal. Obstacles can be such things as contributing causes, lack of resources, lack of information, or anything that must be changed, removed, or gotten around in order to reach the goal. Your dwindling organization may suffer from lack of information regarding why members are not attending meetings, ineffective rewards of membership so that members would rather do something else than participate fully, or perhaps ineffective communication systems that fail to inform members of meetings.

Problem solving is the procedure undertaken to arrive at the solution, which represents the plan by which the obstacles are overcome so that the goal can be reached.[3] Figure 12.1 illustrates this model.

Thus, effective problem solving represents recognition of the discrepancy between what is and what should be, analysis of the reasons for the discrepancy, and delineation of the steps needed to correct the current situation.[4] It is implied that the group or individual engaging in problem solving be able to undertake the steps identified as necessary. A group must learn to recognize what it can and cannot change. *Unless a group has power to overcome obstacles it cannot solve the problem.* Ability to differentiate and discern its limitations is part of the group's problem-solving procedure.

Problem Characteristics

Shaw identified six major dimensions of tasks used in studies of small group process, five of which are characteristics of all problems discussed by problem-solving groups: *difficulty, solution multiplicity, intrinsic interest, cooperative requirements and population familiarity.*[5] We will examine these as well as two additional characteristics, which will help you participate in problem-solving discussions: the acceptance-technical dimension and the area of freedom of the group.

Task difficulty refers to the amount of complexity, effort, knowledge, and skill needed to achieve the goal. For example, establishing what went wrong when the space shuttle Challenger exploded and making recommendations for improvements in launch procedures is much more difficult and requires considerably more expert knowledge than recommending a theme and publicity program for the junior-senior prom. Only the general components of the problem-solving procedure will be the same. For instance, group performance on difficult problems was enhanced more when members expressed their feelings and opinions freely than when they were restricted.[6] Full participation increases group satisfaction as well.[7]

Solution multiplicity refers to the number of conceivable or feasible alternatives for solving the problem. To illustrate, there usually are only a few ways to obtain drinking water for a farmhouse, but there are innumerable ways to decorate a living room. Shaw and Blum found that directive leadership was more effective with a smaller number of alternatives, nondirective leadership better where many solutions were possible.[8] Several studies have shown that highly structured procedures like brainstorming produce more possible *good* solutions than little or no structure.[9]

Intrinsic interest was defined by Shaw as ". . . the degree to which the task in and of itself is interesting, motivating and attractive to the group members."[10] Discussants' interest is related to how important they perceive a problem to be and the degree to which the solution will directly affect them. Berkowitz found that when members were extremely involved with the task they preferred sharing in procedural control, whereas strong procedural control by the designated leader was preferred for less interesting problems.[11] Our personal experience verifies this. If interest is high, members at first want to express their opinions and will resist strong control. Later, after they have vented their feelings, procedural control will be acceptable.

Ideally, groups would discuss only intrinsically interesting problems. In actuality, people are assigned to committees that deal with a variety of problems, some of little interest to them. If this is the case, it should be brought up openly in the discussion, perhaps leading either to a change of attitude or to a request that the problem be reassigned to another group.

Cooperative requirements refers to the degree to which coordinated efforts are essential to satisfactory completion of a group task. Obviously, arriving at a consensus solution for a complex problem requires a high level of cooperation when members initially have different perceptions of the problem and different ideas about how to solve it. Complexity and the need to cooperate are intertwined. Unless some systematic procedures are followed for complex decisions requiring considerable cooperation, the group's discussion will be desultory and ultimately unproductive.

Population familiarity refers to the degree to which members have previous experience with the task and possess information essential to its successful completion. Groups with experienced members tend to perform better than groups with inexperienced ones.[12] A tendency of experienced members to become complacent and closed-minded can be offset by using such procedures as brainstorming.[13] Shared knowledge facilitates the problem-solving process, so spending time orienting members to the problem will pay off in the long run if they are not fairly conversant with the problem.

The **acceptance-technical dimension,** stressed by Maier, refers to the degree to which the decision must be acceptable to those whom it will affect, rather than simply being feasible technically. For instance, it might be technically feasible to replace retiring workers with robots on an automobile assembly line, but if remaining workers do not accept this type of automation, the solution will fail. The amount of human acceptance needed is always a characteristic of the problem; sometimes acceptance is critical, sometimes not.

The *area of freedom of the group* was defined in chapter 4 as the amount of authority given the group. As mentioned earlier, problem-solving groups may seek answers to questions of interpretation, value, or policy. Problems of interpretation require the group to assemble a body of information and interpret it with some generalization. Such is the work of the so-called fact finding or investigative committee. Some examples of this type of group are a jury or legislative committee. The solution for such a group is to decide what meanings to assign to a given body of relevant data. The problem-solving procedures of such a group entail fewer steps than those of a group charged with answering a question of value, which requires not only interpretation of facts but also determination of relative worth. A question of policy implies one additional step, making a decision about what should be done. For example, the blue-ribbon committee charged with investigating the shuttle disaster was also instructed to recommend procedures to prevent future disasters. All these types of questions are more similar than different. Interpreting information often requires making value judgments (for instance, which are credible sources and which are not), and deciding policy involves making a value determination. With all three, the basics of problem solving exist: current unacceptable situation, desired goal, and obstacles.

A complete problem-solving procedure includes still another step—a definite *action taken* to remove barriers or overcome obstacles in reaching the desired goal. Only advisory or purely study groups terminate their work with a body of interpreted knowledge, value judgments, or statements of policy.

With that in mind, groups should formulate their goals in terms of what we *will* do or *what action will be taken* rather than *what we should do,* including an action plan as a final step. For instance, our club members worried about declining attendance will develop a plan that includes assessing current members to determine their attitudes toward the club and reasons for lack of attendance, will formulate a communication campaign to remind members of meetings and recruit new members, and so on.

In summary, it is vital to consider all the dimensions of a problem before attempting to solve it. This enables members and the designated leader to determine the appropriate degree of structure and control needed from the designated leader for the group to perform effectively.

Organizing Problem-Solving Discussions

A group faced with a problem to solve does not itself think; it is the individuals in the group who think. Examination of how individuals solve problems provides a background to the study of problem solving by groups.

The Need for Structure

Some people are **intuitive** problem solvers who size up a situation, then arrive at a solution without consciously following any perceptible procedure. The steps between identification of the problem and finding the solution for it cannot be observed—suddenly the solution is *there*. This is the so-called "Ah-ha!" or "Eureka!" experience.

Systematic thinkers, on the other hand, go through a set of logical steps or **structure** in solving a problem. American philosopher John Dewey, in his famous book *How We Think,* described the **reflective thinking** process by which many of us systematize our decision-making and problem-solving activities. First, we are aware of a felt difficulty, then we define the difficulty, think of possible solutions for it, evaluate those potential alternatives, and finally make a decision, including, if possible, testing the solution we have chosen.[14] Although Dewey was describing the individual thought process, small group writers and researchers have adopted and modified the steps so that groups can take advantage of systematic problem-solving procedures. In fact, Dewey's model provides the foundation for one commonly taught system for structuring group discussions, the Reflective Thinking model.

The advantages for structuring group problem-solving procedures are well documented. Without some preplanned structure, discussions are usually disorganized, jumping back and forth among issues. Scheidel and Crowell, for instance, noted that groups tend to spiral considerably from discussing problem issues to problem solutions.[15] Observers rate the quality of such nonstructured discussions lower than organized discussions.[16] This was confirmed by Jurma, who examined discussions where some leaders provided structure in the form of procedural guidance, goal setting, and reminders about the passage of time, while other leaders did not. Not only did observers rate structured discussions higher in quality, but even the more intuitive, low task-oriented participants rated the structured discussions higher.[17] Hirokawa instructed some groups to use a systematic strategy in making a consensus decision; other groups were simply told to come to consensus. The systematic groups made higher quality decisions.[18]

In a study by one of the authors, participants following a structured rather than unstructured discussion made a larger majority of statements relevant to the phase of problem solving announced by the leader and only a small number of irrelevant statements.[19] Poole concluded that following a structured procedure reminded discussants of the norm or ideal pattern, often reminding group members of something they forgot to do (such as analyze the problem thoroughly) in an earlier step.[20] Later, Poole argued that logical time sequences do not guide the discussion so much as they function to specify the logical priorities that shape the discussions (for example, problem definition and analysis comes before solution generation).[21]

While it appears that some systematic procedure is superior to none, no system appears consistently to surpass the others. In a study by Brilhart and Jochem, three discussion strategies each produced high quality decisions with no significant differences among the three.[22] This finding was supported by Bayless, who also found no significant differences in solution quality among three different formats[23] and by Larson, who discovered that using no pattern was definitely inferior, but one specific discussion pattern was not better than another.[24] Recent verification comes from Hirokawa again, who noted that as long as all major aspects of problem solving are dealt with in the course of the discussion, the particular discussion format does not appear to matter.[25]

Finally, if systematic procedures appear to be associated with higher quality decisions, can systematic procedures be taught? It appears that they can be. None of us is a purely intuitive or purely systematic thinker or problem solver. We operate largely on the basis of what we were taught by our parents, our teachers, and significant others. Nisbett and Ross taught subjects to replace simplistic intuitive strategies, which lead to many errors in problem solving, with the formal systematic and statistical procedures of scientists.[26] Sternberg, convinced that people who are most successful on mental problems like IQ tests approach problem solving systematically, showed that impulsive problem solvers can be taught by showing them how erroneous procedures lead to erroneous solutions and how they can proceed more systematically and effectively.[27]

Why do systematic procedures work? Hirokawa believes that it is not the procedures themselves that lead to effective problem solving.[28] Rather, he says that certain functions must be performed if a group is to be successful. The two most requisite functions are careful analysis and understanding of the problem and thorough, vigilant appraisal of the solutions. In a recent investigation of this functional perspective, Hirokawa asked observers to rate the quality of interaction regarding several important group functions and found that three functions—analysis of the problem, assessment of the positive aspects of the alternatives, and the negative aspects of the alternatives—accounted for most of the variation in decision quality.[29] Thus, merely using a system will not guarantee good results. However, an appropriate system used well should insure that the problem is carefully assessed and the potential solutions diligently evaluated. It is *this* which improves the problem-solving procedure. We turn now to just such a set of guidelines, the **General Procedural Model for Problem-Solving** Discussions. The following are basic steps of the model:

   I. Problem description and analysis. (What is the nature of the problem facing the group?)

  II. Generation and elaboration of possible solutions. (What might be done to solve the problem?)

 III. Evaluation of possible solutions. (What are the relative merits and demerits of the possible solutions?)

 IV. Emergence of a consensus decision. (What seems to be the best possible solution we all can support?)

  V. Planning for implementation of the solution decided upon. (How will we put our solutions into effect?)

A General Procedural Model for Problem-Solving Discussions

As we noted earlier, the effectiveness of specific problem-solving procedures is determined by the contingencies affecting the group: problem characteristics, member experience and values, involvement in the problem, and so forth. The need to insure that certain key functions are present in group discussion has led to the development of the following General Procedural Model, which is flexible enough to adjust to various contingencies.

The model assumes that the leader, perhaps with the help of members, has formulated a written outline containing questions about issues the group must consider if no important contingency is to be overlooked. The following is an explanation of what is done at each procedural step in problem solving and will help you as either designated leader or group member to organize the process. Feel free to adapt the model to your specific circumstances.

I. What is the nature of the problem facing us?

Here the group must focus most of its talk on determining the details of what is unsatisfactory, what led to this undesirable situation, what is ultimately desired, and what the obstacles are. Important discussion principles included under this step are

A. Focusing on the problem before thinking about how to solve it. What would you think if you drove your car into a garage and the mechanic, without so much as looking under the hood, said, "You need a new carburetor and a set of spark plugs." Most of us would drive away. A competent mechanic, after questioning you about how the car was acting, might put it on a computerized engine analyzer and gather whatever information possible before making a tentative diagnosis. Group problem analysis is no different. This example illustrates one of the most common failings in group (and individual) problem solving—getting solution-centered too early.

Several people have noted this tendency and the potential harm it can cause.[30] Time spent with this step will save you headaches as well as time later on. Shortcutting this problem analysis step leads to both process and outcome deficiencies:

1. **Partisanship is encouraged.**

   Participants spend a lot of time arguing for their favorite proposals. Different perceptions and approaches are presented because there is no common understanding of the problem. Distributive resolution is likely.

2. **Time is wasted.**

   The back-and-forth process of this type of discussion moves the group very slowly forward; the cycle is repeated, with the group rarely achieving closure on any one topic.

3. **Ineffectual solutions tend to be adopted.**

   This, of course, is the most serious outcome. If the problem is not thoroughly analyzed and all obstacles identified, the group's solution will only partially overcome the obstacles. Key information will be ignored because the group was too hasty. For example, a university where one of us worked implemented a hefty (ten dollar) fee for dropping and adding classes after the preregistration period. The assumption registration officials made was that students arbitrarily and capriciously changed their minds. In fact, the vast majority of students had good reasons for changing schedules: work changes, courses cancelled or rescheduled, or instructor names not posted accurately. Registration officials had to process so many exceptions to the rule that the fee penalty was eventually dropped. This illustrates what can happen when the solution is determined before the problem is fully understood.

B. Begin with a single, unambiguous problem question. How a problem is formulated into a question makes a great deal of difference in the problem-solving process a group adopts. It is usually better to begin with a **problem question** than a **solution question.** Differences between the implications of these two types of questions are

Problem Questions	**Solution Questions**
Many alternative solutions are implied, none suggested.	One type of solution is suggested.
Focus is on what's wrong?	Focus is on what to do?

If the problem has previously been analyzed by someone else and your charge is only to implement the solution, then a solution question is appropriate. However, if your group is to engage in the full problem-solving procedure, from problem analysis through solution selection and implementation, a problem question is appropriate. Now consider each of the following questions and apply the General Procedural Model for Problem-Solving Discussions to them.

How can I transfer a man who is popular in his work group but slows down the work of other employees in the group? (a solution question, implies that the solution is transferring the man)

versus

How can I increase the work output of the group to the desired level? (a problem question, implies a variety of acceptable solutions)

How can we increase our publicity regarding our club's activities so that attendance will be increased? (a solution question, implying that lack of publicity is causing the problem)

versus

What can we do to increase attendance at our club's activities? (a problem question, implying there may be a variety of factors contributing to lack of attendance)

C. Map the problem thoroughly. Think of the problem as an uncharted area with only vague boundaries. To chart the map, the group must discover the who, what, why, when, where, how, how long, and how serious of the problem. Participants should share all they know about the situation: facts, complaints, conditions, circumstances, factors, details, happenings, relationships, disturbances, effects, etc. In short, what have you heard, read, and observed that bears in any way on the problem? What have other members heard, read, and observed? What does this all add up to?

Such mapping should be as precise and detailed as possible. Kepner and Tregoe pointed out that one of the greatest dangers is that a group will too quickly accept an apparent cause without adequate gathering of facts, analysis, and interpretation of them— "jumping to conclusions without cause." Instead of being very critical when comparing possible causative forces, discussants may collect arguments in support of a pet theory, resist other possible explanations, and pridefully fight to protect their intellectual turf. Instead, Kepner and Tregoe advise that each member should "closely examine each hypothesis, looking for loopholes, for inconsistencies, for exceptions, for partial explanations," even with regard to one's own brainchildren.[31] This is integrative conflict at work.

Figure 12.2 illustrates this mapping process where information is gathered and shared. The large circle represents the whole problem. Each of the members A, B, C, and D come to the initial

Figure 12.2
Maps of a problem
before and after
discussion.

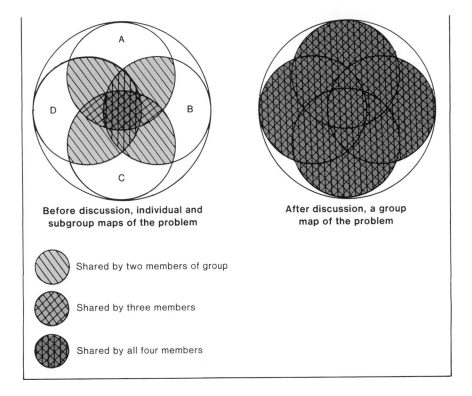

Before discussion, individual and
subgroup maps of the problem

After discussion, a group
map of the problem

Shared by two members of group

Shared by three members

Shared by all four members

meeting with some information and opinions about it, a unique personal map represented by one of the four inner circles. Some information is shared by two members, some by three, and a smaller amount by all four. Once the members have discussed the problem freely and openly, sharing all information at their disposal, the group map of the problem looks like the second large circle in the figure.

One of the greatest obstacles to problem-centered thinking is the leader or member who comes to the group with the problem already solved in his or her own mind. The presenter of the problem must set preconceived solutions aside. Mutual influence is a hallmark of group discussion; be willing to explore any and all solutions without favoring one at the start.

D. Be sure the group members agree on criteria. Unless agreement is reached on criteria that the solution must meet, agreement is unlikely. For instance, a group may decide that one important criterion that must be met is that their solution for improving attendance at meetings must not cost any more money. Or, a group of managers trying to find ways of cutting costs may decide that it will be unacceptable to fire or lay off workers as part of the solution.

Criteria are expressions of values shared by members of a group. Recall the illustration supplied by Rubenstein mentioned in chapter 4, where both Arabs and Americans were asked to indicate who should be saved from a boat wreck: a man's mother, wife, or child. All the Arabs chose the mother but none of the Americans did. The criteria, based on different values, are different for Arabs and Americans. Hence, said Rubenstein: This is the problem of problems, the subjective element of problem solving and decision making. A person's values and priorities guide behavior. Thus, two people, each using rational tools of decision making, can arrive at different solutions because they operate from different frames of values.[32]

The more group members are alike, the less they will have to discuss criteria explicitly. Individuals whose values are similar, like the groups of Americans and Arabs mentioned previously, will tacitly agree on priorities. If, however, a group to which you belong gets involved in a protracted conflict and criteria have *not* been discussed, you will render a valuable service by pointing out the possible lack of agreement regarding the standards, or criteria, for judging solutions.

It is important to rank criteria, giving priority to those that *must* be met. Ideas proposed can then be rated yes or no on whether they meet all the absolute criteria, and from excellent to poor on how well they measure up to the less important criteria. Moreover, criteria should be measurable. Words like *efficient* are too vague to be measurable by themselves, but they can be used as guidelines to specify other criteria. For instance, the following criteria may be applied to plans for a club's annual picnic:

Absolute criteria	**Important criteria**
Must not cost over $400 for entertainment.	Location should be convenient (i.e., within thirty minutes driving time for all members).
Must be enjoyable to both members and their families. (*Enjoyable* means: provide a variety of activities designed to appeal to people ranging in age from three years old to eighty.)	Facilities should be comfortable (e.g., shelter available in case of rain, electrical outlets provided, hot and cold running water, and bathroom facilities provided, etc.)

E. Be sure members understand the group's area of freedom. From the outset, the group must be aware of the limitations on its freedom to act. The group that exceeds its area of freedom, or its charge, will end up confused and frustrated. For example, the area of freedom for a group of university students includes recommending changes in teaching methods, but students have no authority to make or enforce policy governing such matters. Remember the example, in an earlier chapter, of the student services committee charged to make recommendations regarding the types of activities that ended up creating a sweeping proposal that included firing some individuals? Any policy solution must be evaluated from the standpoint of the group's charge.

In this first step of the General Procedural Model, it is helpful to focus on specific **developmental questions** which can guide the group's description and analysis of the problem. The following examples of developmental questions are presented in logical order, but not all will fit every situation:

What does this problem question mean to us?

What is our area of freedom (charge)?

What is unsatisfactory at present?

    Who (or what) is affected?

    When, where, and how?

    How serious do we judge the problem to be?

    How long has the problem existed?

    Do we need to gather any additional information to assess the nature and extent of the problem adequately?

What conditions have contributed to the problem?

    What appear to be causative conditions?

    What precipitated the crisis leading to our discussion?

What exactly do we hope to accomplish (the goal, desired situation)?

    What obstacles to achieving the desired goal exist?

What information do we need before we can find a satisfactory solution?

    What additional subquestions must we answer?

    How might we find answers to these subquestions?

    What are the answers to these subquestions?

How can we summarize our understanding of the problem to include the present and desired situation and causal conditions?

II. **What might be done to solve the problem?**

The ultimate solution will only be as good as the alternatives from among which the group must choose. It is crucial in this step that members generate a variety of creative solutions. A couple of suggestions should be followed:

Defer judgment when seeking solutions. Following this suggestion is both more efficient and potentially more creative. Idea gathering should be separate from idea evaluation because judgment stifles unusual and novel ideas. Sometimes the possible problem-solving options are few, or thorough exploration of the problem leads to a sudden insight into a solution. In those cases, the group should still try to think of other ideas with which the first solution can be compared by asking, "What else *might* we do?" If nothing is discovered, the solution should nevertheless be evaluated thoroughly; it may undergo considerable revision and improvement.

One structured way to generate ideas is by using the technique of **brainstorming.** Developed initially by Alex Osborn for use in advertising, brainstorming relies on the deferring of judgment. It can be used in any phase of problem solving to increase the number of alternatives before a group but typically is used in the solution generation phase.

Often during this phase of problem solving one member will think of some detail of the problem that ought to be explored more fully. The group will then need to cycle back to further exploration of the problem; it can pick up later where it left off. Hirokawa found that this type of second-guessing was characteristic of effective groups.[33] You can see *how vital it is that each proposed solution be recorded in writing,* preferably on a chart or board where everyone can see.

III. **What are the relative merits and demerits of the possible solutions?**

At this point, once the problem has been analyzed, criteria have been agreed upon, and as many alternatives as possible have been identified, the group is ready to evaluate the alternatives. If group problem solving is to work optimally, the pros and cons of each solution must be explored fully. Each member must feel free to express opinions openly and honestly as the group compares the potential solutions against the criteria. Here is a suggestion to help you in this phase; it will recall information we have provided earlier in the book:

A. Use constructive argument and other techniques to avoid groupthink. We have already discussed groupthink, which is the tendency of cohesive groups to foster compliance and forego critical thinking when making decisions or solving problems. It occurs when respected leaders promote their own solutions, when members fail to express their doubts, and when members consider disagreement tantamount to disloyalty. Norms stressing critical examination of issues counteract this tendency:

1. The group should strive to search for creative solutions where everyone participates in the process and no one is seen as losing an argument.

2. Each member must participate openly; that is the only way to attain the advantage of group problem solving. Feelings, ideas, opinions, and even intuition and hunches should be shared freely and evaluated thoroughly.

3. Members should insist on exploring the assumptions and implications of every idea, especially potentially negative consequences. The person proposing the solution should first ask for such a critical evaluation.

4. Every response to one's ideas should be valued, taken seriously, and given a full hearing.

5. Members should be critical of *all* ideas, but not of the people proposing them. Use all the information you have learned and the sensitivity you have developed to avoid placing people on the defensive.

6. Members should frequently state *what they think* are the positions, feelings, and values of others with whom they disagree. Such active listening, explained previously in chapter 5, prevents bypassing and unnecessary tension.

7. All ideas should be evaluated on their own merits, not on the basis of who suggests them. Status and power should be equalized in the evaluation process to avoid interpersonal conflicts from erupting. As noted in chapter 10, disagreements should be focused on issues rather than personalities, and the leader should set the tone by asking for critical evaluation of his or her ideas.

8. The importance of teamwork in striving for consensus should be stressed.

9. Controversy should be introduced when there is enough time to discuss the point at issue thoroughly, not just before adjournment time.

10. Trickery, bargaining, manipulation, and deception must be avoided, pointed out, and rebuked when detected.[34]

Here are some questions you may want to use during this step to guide and simplify the process:

Are there any ideas we can screen out quickly as being unsupported by uncontested fact?

Is there any way to combine and simplify our list of possible solutions?

What are the advantages and disadvantages of each idea?

What groups or individuals must accept and support the solution?

From the point of view of each affected group, what would be the ideal solution?

All things considered, what solution seems most likely to be accepted and supported by all persons involved?

IV. **What is the best possible solution we can all support?**
Sometimes no such question is needed if a decision has emerged from the previous discussion. If several alternatives still remain under consideration, the leader (or members) can ask such follow-up questions as the following:

Which solution seems most likely to be accepted and supported by all persons affected by it?

Is there a compromise solution we can all accept as being likely to solve our problem?

Could we combine these ideas, or parts of them, into a solution?

Once the group has agreed on a policy, findings, recommendation, or other outcome it set out to achieve, the final stage of problem solving—implementation—should be discussed.

V. **How will we put our solution into effect?**
Unfortunately, groups sometimes arrive at policy decisions or solutions with no plans for putting the decision into effect. For example, a committee making recommendations to a parent body should decide who will make the report, whether seconding or supporting speeches must be prepared and who will prepare them, and who will organize a campaign to prepare the general membership to accept the suggestions. Good leaders see that the group has worked out the details of implementation. At this point, the group should ask the following questions:

Who will do what, when, and in what way?

Do we need any follow-up to determine how well our solution is working?

Using the **Program Evaluation and Review Technique (PERT)** is a concrete suggestion to help a group keep track of who will do what. Siebold summarized the main points of PERT as follows:

1. Determine the final step (ie., how the solution should appear when fully operational).
2. Enumerate any events that must occur before the final goal state is realized.
3. Order these steps chronologically.
4. If necessary, develop a flow diagram of the process and all the steps in it.
5. Generate a list of all the activities, resources, and materials needed to accomplish each step.
6. Estimate the time needed to accomplish each step, then add all the estimates to get a total time for implementation of the plan.
7. Compare the total time estimate with deadlines or expectations and correct as necessary (by assigning more persons or less time to a given step).
8. Determine which members will be responsible for each step.[35]

While groups often have problems sticking exactly to a step-by-step sequence for problem solving, attempting to follow such a procedure will help insure that no important function has been overlooked. The General Procedural Model for Problem Solving is flexible by design; you can tailor it to suit the needs of your particular group. The following is a list of problem characteristics we presented at the beginning of the chapter matched to the steps in the problem-solving sequence:

Problem Characteristic	**Emphasize in Problem Solving**
1. Intrinsic interest is high.	A period of ventilation before systematic problem solving.
2. Task difficulty is high.	Detailed problem mapping; many subquestions.
3. Solution multiplicity.	Brainstorming.
4. Cooperative requirements high.	A criteria step, creating and ranking explicit standards.
5. High level of acceptance required for solution.	When evaluating solutions, focus on concerns of persons affected.
6. High level of technical quality is required.	Focus on evaluating ideas, critical thinking; perhaps invite outside experts to group to testify.
7. One or a few stages of the problem-solving process.	Shorten procedure to only steps required.

Two Application Examples

The following two examples of a leader's outline are designed to show you specifically how the General Procedural Model can be used to suggest questions to guide the group's discussion and be modified for specific problems. In the first, provided by Maggie Merken, the group needed to focus on the acceptability dimension of potential solutions to university registration procedures, which had been the subject of complaints by students, faculty, and staff members:

I. What is the nature of the problem with registration?
  A. What exactly is the scope of our concern with registration?
    1. Do we need to clarify any terms?
    2. Do we need to determine the duties of departments involved in registration?
    3. What is our group's area of freedom?
  B. What is unsatisfactory about the present registration procedure?
    1. How do we know that an unsatisfactory registration process exists?
      a. Have any studies been done concerning the problem? If so, what were the conclusions?
      b. Are there any written complaints from faculty, staff, or students?
      c. Is there any other type of feedback about the registration procedure? If so, what?
  C. What are our goals to be achieved by changes that might be made in registration?
  D. What factors (causes) seem to have contributed to the registration problem?
  E. What obstacles stand in the way of solving the problem?
    1. Do we have enough information?
    2. Is enough interest expressed from parties involved?
    3. What resources are needed to solve the problem (money, time, personnel)?
    4. Are there any obstacles to improving registration?
  F. How can the problem best be summarized?
    1. Do we all perceive the problem the same?
    2. In what order should each subdivision of the problem be tackled?
II. What would be an ideal solution to registration problems from the standpoint of each of the interested groups or persons?
  A. Students?
  B. Faculty?
  C. Staff?
  D. Others we ought to consider?
III. What solutions are possible in the present situation at our university?
IV. What solution(s) best fits the problem and desires of the parties who must accept it?

V. How will we make our recommendations concerning the registration problem?
   A. Who will do what, when, how?
      1. To whom will our recommendations be given?
      2. What format will we use to make them?
         a. Writing?
         b. Telephone?
         c. In person?
         d. As a group, or representative?
   B. Do we need to plan any follow-up?

The following is a simple leader's outline for a problem on which the possible options were limited and for which discussion was brief:

I. What sort of written final exam should we have for our class?
   A. How much authority (area of freedom) do we have?
   B. What facts and feelings should we take into account as we seek an answer to this question?
II. What are our objectives (criteria) in deciding on the type of exam?
   A. Learning objectives?
   B. Grades?
   C. Type of preparation and study?
   D. Fairness to all?
III. What types of written final exam might we have?
IV. What are the advantages and disadvantages of each?
V. What will we recommend as the form of our written exam?

Summary

In this chapter we have considered the factors that affect group problem solving. The concept *problem* was defined as an unsatisfactory present condition, a goal or desired state, and obstacles to the achievement of that goal. There are seven major characteristics of problems groups must consider as they organize their problem-solving procedures: task difficulty, solution multiplicity, intrinsic interest, cooperative requirements, population familiarity, acceptance vs. technical feasibility, and area of freedom. While a group cannot always follow a specific procedure in discussions, structuring the process helps insure that nothing important is ignored. Using the General Procedural Model for Problem Solving, tailoring it as needed, can be beneficial. Whatever procedure a group elects to use, it is more productive to analyze and map the problem thoroughly so all members have a high degree of common understanding. In addition, it is usually better to establish the criteria the solution must meet and to generate a variety of solutions before discussing their merits. If acceptance is a major factor, a specific stage of discussion should be devoted to it. The leader of a group engaged in problem solving should help the group organize its problem solving by providing an outline, which members can freely modify, to guide the discussion.

Exercises

1. Select a problem you are faced with, and analyze it according to the problem components model presented in this chapter. Use the following format:

   Problem question—
   What is unsatisfactory about current situation—
   Goal (desired state)—
   Obstacles and barriers—

2. As a class, select a problem affecting all members of the class, such as the type of final exam for the course or some campus or community issue. Analyze the problem according to the problem characteristics presented:

   Task difficulty—
   Solution multiplicity—
   Intrinsic interest—
   Cooperative requirements—
   Population familiarity—
   Acceptance versus technical feasibility—
   Area of freedom—

3. As a class, select two problems, one which presents considerable solution multiplicity and one which does not. Each class member should write a leader's outline for structuring discussion of each of these problems, adapting the General Procedural Model as needed. Compare your outlines in groups of four or five. Then, as a group, write one outline for structuring the discussion for each.

4. After the class has completed exercise 3, each small group should elect two leaders, one to guide each discussion, and conduct the problem-solving session following the discussion outlines developed earlier. After the discussion, determine as a group what worked and what did not, what could have improved the discussion, and what you learned from this exercise.

5. Obtain a videotape of a problem-solving discussion or videotape one yourselves (for instance, one or more of the groups in the previous discussion could be videotaped). Either as a whole class or in small groups, analyze the discussion, pointing out specific instances where the discussion could have been improved and places where the leader or one of the members demonstrated either exceptionally good or poor discussion skills. Did the solution selected by the group appear to be the best possible under the circumstances? Did you see any specific instances in the discussion that contributed directly to making the solution either a good or a poor one?

Bibliography

Dewey, John. *How We Think*. Boston: D.C. Heath and Company, 1910.

Maier, Norman R. F. *Problem Solving and Creativity in Individuals and Groups*. Belmont, Cal.: Brooks/Cole Publishing Company, 1970.

Osborn, Alex. F. *Applied Imagination*. Rev. ed. New York: Charles Scribner's Sons, 1957.

Shaw, Marvin E. *Group Dynamics*. 3d ed. New York: McGraw-Hill, 1981, chapter 10.

Notes

1. Irving L. Janis, *Groupthink: Psychological Studies of Foreign-Policy Decisions and Fiascoes*, 2d ed. (Boston: Houghton Mifflin Co., 1983); Irvin L. Janis and L. Mann, *Decision Making: A Psychological Analysis of Conflict, Choice and Commitment*. (New York: Free Press, 1977).

2. David M. Berg, "A Descriptive Analysis of the Distribution and Duration of Themes Discussed by Task-Oriented Small Groups," *Speech Monographs* 34 (1967): 172–75.

3. Kenneth R. MacCrimmon and Ronald N. Taylor, "Decision Making and Problem Solving," in *Handbook of Industrial and Organizational Psychology*, ed. Marvin D. Dunnette (Chicago: Rand McNally, 1976), 1397–1453.

4. Charles H. Kepner and Benjamin B. Tregoe, *The Rational Manager* (New York: McGraw-Hill, 1965), 20.

5. Marvin E. Shaw, *Group Dynamics*, 3d ed. (New York: McGraw-Hill, 1981), 364.

6. Marvin E. Shaw and J. M. Blum, "Effects of Leadership Style upon Group Performance as a Function of Task Structure," *Journal of Personality and Social Psychology* 3 (1966): 238–42.

7. Beverly J. Hartung Hagen and Genevieve Burch, "The Relationship of Group Process and Group Task Accomplishment to Group Member Satisfaction," *Small Group Behavior* 16 (1985): 211–33.

8. Shaw and Blum, *"Effects of Leadership,"* 238–42.

9. John K. Brilhart and Lurene M. Jochem, "Effects of Different Patterns on Outcomes of Problem-Solving Discussion," *Journal of Applied Psychology* 48 (1964): 175–79; Ovid L. Bayless, "An Alternative Model for Problem Solving Discussion," *Journal of Communication* 17 (1967): 188–97; Sidney J. Parnes and Arnold Meadow, "Effects of 'Brainstorming' Instruction on Creative Problem-Solving by Trained and Untrained Subjects," *Journal of Educational Psychology* 50 (1959): 171–76.

10. Shaw, *Group Dynamics*, 364.

11. Leonard Berkowitz, "Sharing Leadership in Small Decision-Making Groups," *Journal of Abnormal and Social Psychology* 48 (1953): 231–38.

12. James H. Davis, *Group Performance* (Reading, Mass.: Addison-Wesley, 1969).

13. Alex F. Osborn, *Applied Imagination,* rev. ed. (New York: Charles Scribner's Sons, 1957).
14. John E. Dewey, *How We Think* (Boston: D. C. Heath and Company, 1910).
15. Thomas M. Scheidel and Laura Crowell, "Developmental Sequences in Small Groups," *Quarterly Journal of Speech* 50 (1964): 140–45.
16. Dennis S. Gouran, Candace Brown, and David R. Henry, "Behavioral Correlates of Perceptions of Quality in Decision-Making Discussions," *Communication Monographs* 45 (1978): 62.
17. William E. Jurma, "Effects of Leader Structuring Style and Task Orientation Characteristics of Group Members," *Communication Monographs* 46 (1979): 282–95.
18. Randy Y. Hirokawa, "Consensus Group Decision-Making, Quality of Decision and Group Satisfaction: An Attempt to Sort Fact From Fiction," *Central States Speech Journal* 33 (1982): 407–15.
19. John K. Brilhart, "An Experimental Comparison of Three Techniques for Communicating a Problem-Solving Pattern to Members of a Discussion Group," *Speech Monographs* 33 (1966): 168–77.
20. Marshall S. Poole, "Decision Development in Small Groups II: A Study of Multiple Sequences in Decision Making," *Communication Monographs* 50 (1983): 224–25.
21. Marshal S. Poole, "Decision Development in Small Groups III: A Multiple Sequence Model of Group Decision Development," *Communication Monographs* 50 (1983): 321–41.
22. Brilhart and Jochem, "Effects of Different Patterns," 177–78.
23. Bayless, "An Alternative Model," 188–97.
24. Carl E. Larson, "Forms of Analysis and Small Group Problem Solving," *Speech Monographs* 36 (1969): 452–55.
25. Randy Y. Hirokawa, "Discussion Procedures and Decision Making Performance," *Human Communication Research* 12 (1985): 203–24.
26. Richard Nisbett and Lee Ross, *Human Inference: Strategies and Shortcomings of Social Judgment* (Englewood Cliffs, N.J.: Prentice-Hall, 1980).
27. Robert J. Sternberg, "Stalking the IQ Quark," *Psychology Today* 13 (September 1979): 42–54.
28. Hirokawa, "Discussion Procedures," 203–24.
29. Randy Y. Hirokawa, "Group Communication and Decision-Making Performance: A Continued Test of the Functional Perspective," (Paper presented at the annual convention of the Speech Communication Association, Boston, 1987).

30. Irving J. Lee, *How to Talk with People* (New York: Harper & Row, Publishers, 1952), 62; Norman R. F. Maier and R. A. Maier, "An Experimental Test of the Effects of 'Developmental' vs. 'Free' Discussions on the Quality of Group Decisions," *Journal of Applied Psychology* 41 (1957): 320–23; Randy Y. Hirokawa, "Group Communication and Problem-Solving Effectiveness: An Investigation of Group Phases," *Human Communication Research* 9 (1983): 291–305.

31. Kepner and Tregoe, *The Rational Manager,* 117–18.

32. Moshe F. Rubenstein, *Patterns of Problem Solving* (Englewood Cliffs, N.J.: Prentice-Hall, 1975), 1–2.

33. Randy Y. Hirokawa, "Why Informed Groups Make Faulty Decisions," *Small Group Behavior* 18 (1987): 3–29.

34. David W. Johnson and Frank P. Johnson, *Joining Together: Group Theory and Group Skills,* 2d ed. (Englewood Cliffs, N. J.: Prentice-Hall, Inc., 1982), 240.

35. David R. Siebold, "Making Meetings More Successful: Plans, Formats, and Procedures for Group Problem Solving," in *Small Group Communication: A Reader,* 4th ed., eds. Robert S. Cathcart and Larry A. Samovar (Dubuque, Iowa: Wm. C. Brown Publishers, 1984), 187–201.

Part 6

Group Discussion
and Observation Techniques

Chapter 13

Special Discussion Techniques and Methods for Learning and Organizational Settings

Study Objectives

You may choose to read only selected parts of chapter 13, using it as a reference for some special techniques or procedures. If you study the entire chapter, you should be able to:

1. Explain the benefits of cooperative learning discussions.

2. List seven guidelines for conducting learning discussions.

3. Explain the *encounter* concept, and list eight guidelines for making feedback during encounter sessions productive of personal growth.

4. Plan and moderate either a panel or forum discussion for a large group meeting.

5. Explain how to keep discussions orderly by using *Robert's Rules of Order, Newly Revised* for committees of organizations governed by Robert's Rules of Order.

6. Conduct buzz groups involving all members of a large gathering.

7. Describe the value of and procedures for conducting a problem census.

8. Describe the eight major steps of the Nominal Group Technique in chronological order.

9. Explain the purposes, basic procedures, and organizational climate in which quality circles can enhance work outputs.

10. Explain the value of the RISK technique and describe the procedure.

11. Describe both advantages and disadvantages of teleconferences in comparison to face-to-face meetings and how both types can best supplement each other for participants scattered geographically.

Key Terms

Affective discussion members of a small group express and explore their feelings, especially fears, in relation to some topic or concept.

Buzz group session large group meeting is divided into small groups of approximately six persons each, who discuss a target question for a specified number of minutes, then report their answers to the entire large group.

Case problem discussion learning discussion beginning with consideration of a specific case problem about which group members exchange perceptions, ideas, and possible solutions.

Comparative outline a set of questions asking the discussants to compare two or more things, institutions, or other concepts on certain criteria or characteristics.

Encounter discussion open expression of feelings and reactions of members of a group to each other and the group as a whole.

Feedback information given to a member to indicate how other people perceive his or her behavior in the group.

Fine arts discussion format a sequence for discussing some product of human creativity beginning with an examination of the object, discussion of perceived features, interpretation of the whole, evaluation, and ending with reexamination of the object.

Focus group a special group procedure that encourages freewheeling discussion focusing on a specific topic or issue, often used to analyze people's interests and values for a market-research analysis.

Forum discussion verbal interaction within a large audience, controlled by a moderator, usually following some presentation, such as a lecture, panel discussion, or film.

Learning discussion any of several types of discussions the goal of which is learning or the personal growth of the participants or listeners.

Moderator designated leader of a public discussion, such as a panel, group interview, or forum.

Nominal Group Technique special procedure in which six to nine persons work individually in silence to generate ideas, then interact to pool, clarify, and evaluate these ideas until a plan to solve a major problem has been adopted by voting.

Panel discussion informal discussion among members of a small group, coordinated by a moderator, for benefit of a listening audience.

Problem census technique in which members of a small group are polled for topics and problems that are posted, ranked by voting, and used to create agendas for future meetings.

Quality circle a group of employees meeting on company time to investigate work-related problems and make recommendations to management for solving these problems.

RISK technique a small group procedure for communicating and dealing with all risks, fears, doubts, and worries members have about a new policy or plan before it is implemented in an organization.

Teleconference a conference among participants geographically distant from each other in which signals are carried among them via electronic devices, such as television, telephone, and computers.

Up to now we have concentrated on small group dynamics, including communication processes and procedures. Chapter 13 shifts the focus from more general principles to specific techniques and group formats that can serve a number of purposes. We first discuss learning groups, then a variety of group techniques used in organizations.

Learning Discussions

Learning discussions are held primarily for the enlightenment of either the discussants themselves or a listening audience. No matter whether the learning discussion is private or public, learning is more than the acquisition of facts. It assumes change comes about in a person due to experience, with *education* meaning the structuring of situations to facilitate change. *Cognitive* or intellectual learning ranges from the ability to recognize and recall specific information to the ability to combine and create, *affective* learning involves changes in feelings and values, and *psychomotor* learning pertains to physical skills. The group approach to learning is well documented as frequently superior to lecture, video, or an individualized instruction format.[1] Cooperative group interaction is an effective way to learn for students of all ages.[2] From years of observing learning groups as researchers; leading various kinds of learning groups; conducting training programs for teachers, students, and study-discussion leaders; and serving as consultants, we have attempted to develop some principles and techniques for planning and conducting learning discussions. There are a number of settings in which learning discussions occur. They range from impromptu situations, which arise when members of an informal social gathering discover common interests, to occasions organized for the purpose of engaging in learning discussions, including study groups of all kinds. Much of our learning outside the traditional collegiate structure occurs in discussion groups sponsored by continuing education divisions of universities, churches, libraries, and other civic and educational institutions. Because of the prevalence of such learning activities, we will describe both private and public discussion formats.

Private Learning Discussions

Private learning discussions exist not for the purpose of reaching decisions but for the *personal growth and enlightenment of their members*. There is no need to reach agreement; rather, what is sought is appreciation for and understanding of other points of view. Examples include classroom groups, study groups, library discussion groups, training programs, encounter and other experiential growth groups. Private learning discussions are suitable for such diverse purposes as discussing a book, film or other work of art, debating the merits of one policy over another, analyzing case problems or generating ideas to implement a proposal of some kind.

Organizing Learning Discussions

While not all private learning discussions, such as affective groups or encounter sessions, need to be organized, discussions for classes and study-discussion groups generally benefit from some structure. Many of the same logical patterns used to organize informative public speeches can be applied. Usually, the designated leader will provide the organizing framework:

1. **Organizing learning discussions by topic or major issue.**
   In this common pattern, the group discusses a set of topics or issues, each of which is phrased as a question. These should be basic issues that must be understood for members to gain an overall view of the subject and to share their differing reactions to it. The designated leader should prepare a set of questions and subquestions to guide exploration of these major issues, but the group should ultimately decide what will be discussed, modifying the leader's guide as desired. The following outline is an example of general questions used by a group to discuss the films they saw:

   I. What was the reaction to the theme of the picture?
   II. How good was the acting?
   III. How well was the picture staged and costumed?
   IV. How effective were lighting and photography?
   V. Would we recommend this picture to our friends?

2. **Organizing learning discussions by comparison sequence.**
   A **comparative outline** might be used to compare two or more policies, objectives, or organizations. The group might begin by discussing criteria and goals, or with the first of the topics to be compared. For example, a classroom group comparing the merits of various teaching-learning techniques used the following outline:

   I. What are the advantages and disadvantages of lecturing?
   II. What are the advantages and disadvantages of discussions?
   III. What are the advantages and disadvantages of seminar or tutorial methods?
   IV. What are the advantages and disadvantages of programmed instruction?

3. **Organizing learning discussions by other sequences.**
   Other logical sequences can be employed to structure the discussion. For instance, a chronological sequence fits a discussion of a historical trend, such as the changing role of women in the United States from revolutionary times to the present. A causal sequence is appropriate for discussing possible effects of new technologies. In short, the subject matter should determine the sequence.

*Discussions of
Works of Art*

Many learning groups, both in and out of the classroom, have found enlightenment and pleasure in discussing such works of art as poetry, paintings, short stories, sculpture, or architecture. A **fine arts discussion format** has proven helpful in countless discussions: (1) the group examines the work of art together; (2) group members discuss what they perceive in the work of art and what it means to them; and (3) the group again examines the work of art. This format allows relatively little time to be spent discussing the artist, the artist's motives, or the artist's life. If artistic techniques are considered, they are left until near the end of the discussion.

Literature   The following set of questions can be used to guide discussion of a poem. With appropriate modifications, a similar sequence of questions could be used to organize discussion of any other art form. With any specific work of art, some questions may be fruitless or meaningless, and others may be needed to open up other avenues of perception and interpretation. Beliefs of members about how one *ought* to react to a poem or other work should not be allowed to block discussion.

Introduction: A member of the group reads the poem aloud.

    I. What situation occurs in the poem?
       A. What is actually taking place? What do you see in the poem?
       B. What other actions are described by the persons in the poem?
   II. How does the speaker in the poem feel about the situation he or she is discussing?
       A. At the beginning of the poem?
       B. In the middle?
       C. At the end?
       D. What is the nature and direction of the change of his or her feelings?
  III. What kind of person does the speaker appear to be in the poem?
       A. What kind of person would feel like this?
       B. What kind of person would change in this way (or remain unchanged)?
  IV. What broad generalizations underlie the poem?
       A. What ideas does the poet assume to be true?
       B. Does he or she arrive at any insights, answers, or solutions?
       C. How do we feel about these generalizations?
    Conclusion: A group member reads the poem aloud.

Some of the questions in the previous general outline may not fit a particular poem. You must plan questions for the specific poem, depending on what it is about, how it is written, and the reactions it evokes in you. This adaptation is illustrated in the following poem and outline for a discussion of it by a group of college students.

Invictus
William Ernest Henley

Out of the night that covers me,
    Black as the Pit from pole to pole,
I thank whatever gods may be
    For my unconquerable soul.

In the fell clutch of circumstance
    I have not winced nor cried aloud.
Under the bludgeonings of chance
    My head is bloody, but unbowed.

Beyond this place of wrath and tears
    Looms but the Horror of the shade,
And yet the menace of the years
    Finds, and shall find, me unafraid.

It matters not how strait the gate,
    How charged with punishments the scroll,
I am the master of my fate;
    I am the captain of my soul.

   I. What do you think this poem is about?
      A. What might *night* refer to in the first line?
      B. What might the black pit represent?
  II. What sort of person does the speaker appear to be to you?
      A. What does the second stanza tell you about the speaker?
      B. What do you think is the speaker's attitude toward dying?
      C. What do you understand about the speaker's view of life and afterlife?
      D. How do you interpret the last two lines?
 III. What beliefs or assumptions underlie the poem?
      A. What does the poem assume to be true?
      B. How do we feel about these beliefs?
 IV. Do you like this poem? Why or why not?

A group might follow a similar outline for discussion of almost any literary work such as a short story, essay, or even a novel or play.

Visual Objects   An outline of questions for discussing a visual object, such as a painting, sculpture, clothing, building, or photograph should focus on various characteristics or features of the object, not the whole. The discussants are led to shift the visual focus in this way and to describe what they see from each new perspective such as shape, color, line, texture, and area. As part of her work in one of our classes, a student prepared the following outline to lead discussion of an abstract painting.

Introduction: A painting is hung in front of the group seated in a semicircle, and the group is asked to examine it silently.

I. What different elements do you see?
   A. What do you notice about the texture?
   B. What colors do you notice?
   C. What do you notice about the shapes?
   D. Do you observe anything in the lines?
II. Overall, what do you perceive?
   A. Does it seem to portray any specific object, idea, or event?
   B. Do your personal experiences or ideas affect your perceptions in any way?
III. What feelings do you experience from looking at the picture?
   A. What emotions does it arouse?
   B. Does it move you to want to take any action?
   C. What seems to be evoking your reaction or arousal?
IV. What does the painting seem to say to you?
   A. Does it have any specific message or theme for you?
   B. What might be the purpose of this painting? Is it strictly aesthetic?
V. How do you evaluate the painting?
   A. Do you think the artist said what he wanted to say?
   B. Do you feel it was worth saying?
   C. How did the artist achieve this, or what prevented him from achieving it?
   D. Has the painting or our discussion of it revealed anything new or important to you?
   E. Does it have any universality or significance?

Learning Discussions of Case Problems

A group of persons wanting to explore possible ways to cope with some type of problem they may encounter as individuals could structure a **case problem discussion** around the General Procedural Model for Problem Solving, without needing to come to any decisions or solution as a group. The desired output is for each member to achieve a better understanding of what is involved and to have more options when encountering a problem similar to that discussed. If the members are quite heterogeneous in backgrounds and values, more learning by each is possible than if they all are likely to perceive and handle the problem in the same way.

Often learning discussion is desultory when concerned with a vague, non-specific, general problem such as "What should you do if someone threatens your life?" Rather than begin with such general questions, the leader can usually evoke more interest and involvement by using a real or hypothetical situation as the focus of discussion. First, the case problem is discussed as if the group were actually trying to solve it. Then, members of the group are invited to generalize from the specific case to similar situations they have faced or may encounter in the future. The following cases illustrate the type of problem presentation that can be used to stimulate learning discussion following a problem-solving procedure.

The Grade Inflation Case

In recent years, a pervasive problem has arisen on many American college and university campuses—grade inflation. Cumulative final averages have never been so high. This problem has hit home at Robert Burns University. Recently, employers who interview graduates have complained to the chancellor, voicing strong objections to grading policies. They claim that it is now impossible to use a student applicant's grades as a basis for comparison with other applicants and for predicting what sort of employee a student might make. Corporate representatives say that almost all students have above average grades, and 60 percent have at least a 3.1 average.

A preliminary check of records revealed some eye-opening statistics. In 1962, the average SAT score of freshmen was 1,148 and the average final cumulative grade was 2.3 for those students when they graduated. In 1985, the average SAT score of freshmen was 997, but the average final grade point average was 3.2 when those students graduated. Prior to 1967, the SAT served as a dependable predictor of a student's academic accomplishments, but it no longer does so.

A survey of teaching practices at Robert Burns University revealed that most professors curve grades on at least half of their assignments in order to raise the class average. Professors say they are reluctant to give below a C grade because low grades are damaging to students' self-concepts and to their chances for employment in desirable jobs as well as admission to graduate schools. Many said they are reluctant to grade below a B.

College textbook publishers report that they are editing for a tenth-grade reading level, because the higher levels at which they used to edit are too difficult for the majority of today's beginning college students. Some publishers say they must edit freshman texts at even lower reading-difficulty levels, or the books are not adopted.

The provost of Robert Burns University has charged you, as a committee of concerned students from the student senate, to consider whether grade inflation is a serious problem at the university. If you find that it is, he has asked you to recommend a new grading policy to combat the problem and to suggest how to implement the policy and make it effective in restoring grades to their former usefulness and credibility.

The Teacher's Dilemma

An English teacher in a consolidated, rural high school has had extensive dramatic experience and as a result was chosen by the principal to direct the first play in the new school. Its success may determine whether or not there will be future plays produced at the school and if well done can bring prestige to both the teacher and the school. As a result, the teacher (a friend of mine) is exhausting every means available to her to make the play an artistic success.

She has chosen the cast except for the leading female part. The principal's daughter wants the part, and the principal told the teacher he wants his daughter to have it. But—she is a poor actress and would jeopardize the success of the show. Tentatively, the teacher has chosen someone who should do an excellent job in the role, but the principal has implied that if his daughter is not selected, he will appoint another director in the future.

What should I tell my English teacher friend to do?

Guidelines for Leading Private Learning Discussions

Based on educational research and philosophy, the following specific guidelines can be formulated for setting up cooperative learning discussions:

1. **Always establish a cooperative group goal.**
   Remember the concept of promotive interdependence? The group's outcome should be presented as *sharing* individual knowledge to help all members understand each other, listen, and consider each other partners, not competitors.
2. **Give rewards to the group, not to individual members.**
   Praise for good work is directed to the group. Such comments as "That was a really fine discussion" or "I got a lot from all of you" are group oriented and stress the cooperative relationship.
3. **Keep the focus on common experience.**
   Similar to mapping the problem, participants should be reading the same articles or books, looking at the same painting or movie, or studying the same problem. Meaningful discussions evolve from members sharing differing perceptions of the same phenomena. Members are more satisfied when discussion is kept relevant than when it rambles to peripheral topics.[3]
4. **Limit the number of issues or topics.**
   Greater learning and more satisfaction are found in groups where the average number of distinguishable topics per two-hour session is fewer than eleven than in groups where it is more than fourteen.[4] Plan three or four basic issues per hour, including several subquestions under each broad issue.
5. **Plan a variety of open-ended questions.**
   Open-ended questions encourage a variety of answers from different points of view. For example, "Which political party do you think has done the most to help the poor?" is a relatively closed question, but "What kinds of activities and policies help poor people?" is more open-ended. While closed-ended questions are appropriate, especially for helping establish facts, open-ended questions elicit greater discussion.
6. **Be guided by the nature of the subject.**
   The pattern for a learning discussion, as explained earlier, is usually inherent in the subject. Let the topic and the information guide the logical sequence for discussion.

7. **Focus on how the subject relates to interests of the members as a group.** Recall the information about intrinsic interest from the previous chapter? Groups perform best when members are interested in the discussion. One method of insuring this is to poll the group, orally or in writing, for questions members would like to explore. However the leader elects to do this, the discussion will be more productive if it relates to the personal concerns and experiences of the members. For example, compare the following two sets of questions for guiding a discussion of Arthur Miller's *Death of a Salesman*. Which would *you* rather use?

   1. What method of character introduction is used?
   2. Which point of view does the author use?
   3. What are some figures of speech used by Miller?

   versus

   1. Does anything seem unhealthy about Willy's inability to face reality?
   2. Do we think it was wrong for Biff to quit trying after he surprised Willy in the hotel in Boston? Why or Why not?
   3. What should we do when someone else fails us, like a teacher or parent?

8. **Don't confuse pseudodiscussion with a cooperative learning discussion.** In a pseudodiscussion, as explained in chapter 10, the leader has already arrived at an interpretation, value, or solution. Unfortunately, many so-called learning discussion leaders employ the *form* of discussion to disguise a lecture or a persuasion attempt. The purpose of a learning discussion is not to discover the *correct* interpretation but to explore people's opinions, perceptions, and interpretations. If you want to promote one interpretation or position, say so; do not hide behind a pseudodiscussion.

Special Techniques for Learning Groups Concerned with Feelings and Interpersonal Relations

Many groups exist to provide support and psychological learning for their members. Two techniques are presented here that can apply to a wide range of such situations and types of groups.

Affective discussion, a term coined by Epstein, was originally developed to help school children ventilate their feelings. However, the technique can be adapted for any learning group where fears, suspicions, prejudices, and other negative feelings interfere with productive thinking, communicating, and relating to others.[5] The purpose of an affective discussion is to help persons express and explore strong feelings. The group usually consists of six to ten people seated in a tight circle. In a traditional classroom, a teacher can seat part of the class in front or back of the room, while other students work at their seats, or can divide the class into several smaller groups who have been instructed in the procedure. The technique has been used most successfully by one of us to help groups of graduate students cope with their fear of statistics or thesis writing. It also is excellent for dealing with issues like racial prejudice.

An affective discussion begins with the assumption that all persons have feelings and that any feeling is "okay" to have. We need to express our feelings without apology and have them accepted in a supportive atmosphere, without criticism, in order for adequate intra- and interpersonal communication to occur. In an affective discussion, the designated leader plays little part other than to facilitate expression and empathic listening. Judgment and other defensive responses likely to elicit defensive reactions are to be avoided at all costs; otherwise, the free and honest sharing of feelings is inhibited. Comments to avoid include

That's right.

That's wrong.

Don't you mean. . .?

That's not a nice thing to say.

Gasp.

How can you say something like that?

We shouldn't use such language here.

Helpful comments that facilitate candid expression might be

What do *you* think?

How do you feel about that?

Let him finish his thought.

It's all right to say what you feel.

I don't know.

It's not a matter of right or wrong but what you feel.

The key, again, is nonevaluation. The leader must be totally accepting. Present the opening question, then *listen,* perhaps making an occasional facilitative comment showing understanding and acceptance. Here the leader for once is advised to be laissez-faire.

Encounter discussion can be a means to personal growth and improving interpersonal relations for the participants. Encounter means that members of the learning group explore their reactions to each other, describing openly and honestly what they feel. If done in an accepting and caring way, such descriptions by other members of a group regarding how they are responding to you can be a means for gaining self-insight and self-acceptance. A high degree of interpersonal trust is essential if encounter discussion is to be productive because members can feel threatened when others let them know how their behavior is perceived and responded to.

The value of receiving such information is that the person will have more energy available for constructive work rather than protecting an image. As we express some of our inner feelings, others can better understand us, accept us, and identify with our feelings, fears, and needs. For example, an encounter group to which one of us belonged had a member perceived by others as aloof, withdrawn, and cold. After encounter discussion, this individual revealed her fear of interacting with others and her shyness. Others began to respond to her differently once they understood her better and she began to see how her refusal to talk was misinterpreted by others.

The vehicle by which such growth can be facilitated is interpersonal **feedback,** which is defined as information one person gives to another person about how the first has perceived and been affected by the behavior of the second. A mirror provides an analogy—the member giving the feedback holds a mirror up to the person receiving the feedback, describing and reflecting the behavior but *not judging it*. Since self-images are based on what we *think* others think of us, such feedback can modify our self-concepts by providing a "reality check" with what other members really *do* see in our behavior.

In feedback sessions, comments should be limited to what happens among members of the group while it is in session. Talking about other situations members have been in, topical issues, theorizing, or conducting amateur psychoanalysis sessions should be avoided. Participants should state their remarks as their personal reactions and feelings, describing how they feel and what they were reacting to. Members must avoid namecalling, accusing, or telling each other how they *should* behave.

Feedback sessions should be conducted in the presence of your instructor or some experienced group trainer. If no experienced trainer is available, you can still benefit from limited interpersonal feedback. The important thing is for each member to be free to invite or not to invite the reactions of others. The following guidelines may be helpful:

1. **Describe rather than pass judgment.**
   No one should feel condemned as a person. A description of one's own reactions leaves the receiver of feedback free to react as he or she sees fit. For example,"You were nasty" is evaluative and may elicit defensiveness, but "I felt myself growing angry when you . . ." gives the person valuable information free of judgment.

2. **Be as specific as possible.**
   To be told "You are domineering" may do more harm than good. In contrast, "When we were talking about how to proceed, I thought you refused to consider anyone else's ideas, so I felt forced to accept your suggestions, face an attack from you, or leave the group," gives the receiver concrete, helpful information.

3. **Consider the needs of the receiver.**
   What can the receiver hear, accept, and handle at this time? A lambasting to relieve your own tension will be counterproductive. Strive for balance between negative and positive feedback.

4. **Deal only with behavior the receiver can change.**
   For example, you would not tell a stutterer that such hesitations drive you nuts. However, you might let someone know that withdrawal from conversation looks like sulking and you don't like it.

5. **Don't force feedback on another.**
   Let the recipient invite comments (unless you respond immediately after something is said or done). If someone indicates he or she wants to hear no more, stop. What you say won't be accepted or heard in any case.

6. **Check to see whether your feedback is understood.**
   Did the receiver understand what you mean? Watch for reactions, perhaps asking the person to restate your point.

7. **See whether the other members agree with you.**
   You may find that other participants do not respond as you did to a particular person. Ask, "How do the rest of you feel about that?" often. Lack of agreement can provide you with important feedback about your *own* perceptions, reactions, and behavior.

8. **Expect slow moments.**
   At times there will be a lot of hesitation and fumbling. Group members typically are hesitant to express feelings openly until interpersonal trust has been established and they feel safe. Expect the exchange of frank feedback to take a long time to develop.

All the previously described types of learning discussions were conducted for the benefit of the participants. However, not all learning discussions are private. Some are conducted for the benefit of a listening audience.

Public Learning Discussions

A public discussion is conducted primarily for the learning of an audience, not discussants in a small group. No matter what format the public discussion takes, public speaking is involved. When a small group of people discuss for the benefit of an audience, special planning, organization, and procedures must be established in advance. Moving too quickly loses an audience, but constant recycling over the same points is boring. A balance between spontaneity and planned performance is ideal.

Public discussions require a **moderator** who is responsible for keeping the discussion flowing smoothly. To plan and organize the discussion, the moderator typically contacts individuals to participate in the program and describes the general topic or issue, the purpose of the discussion, the reasons for the person's selection as a participant, who the other participants will be, and who is likely to compose the audience.

Participants in public discussions should be chosen for their expertise, fluency, and diversity. They should be knowledgeable on the topic or representatives of special points of view and able to state their views clearly and concisely. The two most frequently used types of public discussion are the panel and the forum.

Panel Discussions

As you recall, **panel discussion** involves a group of specialists interacting informally in front of and for the benefit of an audience. A variety of viewpoints should be represented. For example, a panel convened to discuss how to reduce

A panel discussion is a form of public speaking.

traffic congestion and air pollution while improving transportation might include a city planner with information about rapid transit systems, an air pollution control expert, a highway engineer, an urban business person, and an automotive designer.

Public discussions call for special physical arrangements. First, all discussants should be in view of each other and the audience at all times to facilitate a sense of direct interaction. Seat discussants in a semicircle in front of the audience, with the moderator either at one end or the center; thus, panelists have eye contact with each other and the audience. Second, panelists should be seated behind a table, preferable with some sort of cover on the front. Two small tables in an open V make an excellent arrangement. Third, a large name card should be placed in front of each panelist. Fourth, microphones, if needed, should be plentiful enough and unobtrusive. In a large assembly, if a floor mike is required for questions from the audience, it should be placed strategically and audience members should be instructed in its use. Fifth, visual displays of the topic or question under consideration help keep the discussion organized. A chalkboard or easel can be used for this purpose.

The outline for a panel discussion could follow a problem-solving pattern or one of the learning discussion formats suggested earlier. The moderator should ask panelists in advance to suggest questions and subquestions for discussion. After these are compiled into a rough outline the moderator intends to use, panelists should receive a copy in advance so they have a chance to investigate and think of possible responses to each question.

During the panel discussion, the moderator uses a special outline he or she has prepared, with an introduction, sequence of questions to be raised, and a planned conclusion format. The moderator acts as a conversational traffic officer directing the flow of the discussion. Moderators ask questions of the group of panelists, see that all panelists have an equal opportunity to speak, clarify ambiguous remarks, or ask panelists to do so. They do not participate directly in the discussion. They summarize each major topic or have the panelists do so and keep the discussion moving along the major points of the outline. A moderator's outline might look like this:

Introduction

"What should be the law in the U.S. governing abortions?"

I. Ladies and gentlemen, the question of what the law should be governing abortions in the U.S. has been a subject of heated argument, physical confrontation, intensive lobbying, court cases, sermons, and pamphlets—and far too little calm, thoughtful discussion.

II. Today we are fortunate to have a panel of thoughtful experts who represent all major points of view on this subject.
   A. Father Jon McClarety has made an intensive study of the Catholic theology and arguments underlying the church's stand against legalizing abortions. He is a member of the Department of Philosophy and Theology of Holy Name Academy.
   B. Robert Byron is an attorney for the Legal Aid Society who has served his society in appeals to the Supreme Court which led to the current legal status of abortions.
   C. Dr. Robert Splando is a specialist in obstetrics and gynecology and has performed hundreds of therapeutic abortions.
   D. Ms. Dorothy Mankewicz, a social worker and volunteer lecturer for "Zero Population Growth," has assisted many women who wanted abortions.
   E. Professor Maha Kazakrim is historian of ethical and social values at Western State University, and author of two books dealing with the abortion law controversy.

III. Our panelists have agreed to discuss four specific issues which are part of the question you see on the poster before you. "What should be the law in the U.S. governing abortions?"
   A. When does a human life begin?
   B. Who has the right to decide whether or not a woman should be allowed to have an abortion?
   C. What would be the effects of greater restrictions on the right of choice to have an abortion?
   D. Under what conditions, if any, should abortions be legal?

IV. Each panelist will give a brief statement of his or her position on each issue and the reasoning behind it, then the panelists will question and debate their positions informally. After fifty minutes the floor will be opened for questions from you, our listening audience. While the discussion is proceeding, you may want to jot down questions as they occur to you so you can remember them for the forum period.

Body of the Discussion

I. "When does a human life begin?"
   A. Dr. Splando: _____.
   B. Father McClarety: _____.
   C. Ms. Mankewicz: _____.
   etc.

(All four issues are discussed, with the moderator summarizing; seeing that each panelist gets an opportunity to present a position on each issue and question, support, or argue with the others; and moving the group to the next major question at a pre-arranged time.)

Conclusion

I. Let's see if we can summarize what we have learned about each other's positions. I'd like each of you to summarize in a minute or less your position and arguments. (Often the moderator does the summing up, with panelists being free to correct or supplement.)

II. I believe all of us in this room are now better prepared to cope with this vital issue. We now understand each other's positions as well as possible, and the values and beliefs supporting them.

III. Now I wonder what questions our listeners have for the panel? Please raise your hand if you want to ask a question, and wait for me to recognize you by pointing. I will give each person a chance to ask one question before allowing anyone to ask a second question. Your questions can be directed to a particular panelist or to the entire group. If you want a particular panel member to answer, state the name of that person. Okay, what's our first question? The lady to my right wearing the maroon blazer—please state your question loudly enough for all present to hear it.

Forum Discussions   A **forum discussion** is often conducted following a speech, panel discussion, educational film, public interview or symposium. Strict procedural control is needed for a successful forum. The moderator or chair should control the forum so that the discussion is both interesting and fair to all persons involved. The following are guidelines to ensure fairness without letting the discussion bog down on one issue:

1. During the introduction to the panel or other program, announce that there will be a forum or question and answer period. This allows listeners to be thinking of questions and remarks.

2. State whether only questions or both questions and comments will be permitted.

3. Just before the audience participation segment, announce definite rules to assure equal opportunity for all to speak:
   a. Raise your hand and wait to be recognized before speaking.
   b. No one may speak a second time until each person who wants the floor has had it once.

    c. Comments or questions should be addressed either to a specific panelist by name or to the entire panel.

    d. Remarks must be limited to not more than _____ seconds.

    e. Speak loudly enough to be heard by everyone (or go to the floor microphone).

4. Tell the audience whether there will be a definite length of time for the forum and stick to the time.

5. If the audience is large, recognize persons from various parts of the room in a systematic pattern.

6. Encourage different points of view by asking for them: "Does anyone want to present a *different* point of view from that which we have just heard?"

7. If a question cannot be heard by all, restate it to the originator's satisfaction.

8. If a question is unclear or lengthy, restate it to the originator's satisfaction.

9. When the alloted time is nearly up, state that there is just enough time for one or two more questions or comments.

10. If no one seeks the floor, wait a few seconds, then thank the panel and audience for their participation and either dismiss the meeting or go on to the next item on the agenda.

Regulating Problem-Solving and Decision-Making Discussions with Discussion Rules

It is important that group discussions of all sorts be structured so that participants have equal opportunity to speak. Moderators help provide that function for panel discussions and forums. Sometimes committees have specific rules to establish fairness and equity, make discussions more predictable, and maintain order. Many large assemblies use formal rules, usually *Robert's Rules of Order, Newly Revised,* to organize their interaction.[6] Robert also has developed a code of rules for committees established by parent organizations using Robert's rules as parliamentary authority. Parliamentary procedure is modified in formality and detail for small groups and committees. The member of such a group who keeps uttering "point of order," "question," or "I move to table the motion" is showing off or is ignorant of the basic purpose of rules of order for small groups. He or she certainly does *not* know what rules exist for committees governed by *Robert's Rules of Order.*

Committees may have formal rules governing them created in the bylaws of a parent organization. Any such rule replaces any of Robert's rules with which it clashes. We summarize Robert's rules specifically for committees here for two reasons. First, they are legally in force when the parent organization has adopted Robert. Second, many chairs of small committees who would like to use some type of structure for organizing actions, like voting, are hesitant to employ formal parliamentary procedure and are not aware that *Robert's Rules of Order* has created less formalized procedures for committees.

1. The chairperson of a committee may be appointed by the parent organization. That organization can ask the committee to appoint its own chair, or else the first person named to the committee is automatically the chair.
2. A committee meets on call of its chair or any two members.
3. A quorum (minimum number of members needed for the committee to take any legal action) is a simple majority of committee members, unless specified otherwise by the parent organization.
4. The chair is responsible for records of the committee and writes minutes or reports unless a separate secretary position is created. If a professional secretary from the parent organization is assigned to keep records, the chair is still responsible for supervising and signing these records.
5. Members do not need to obtain permission from the chair by formal recognition before speaking or making a motion. They may speak whenever they want so long as they do not interrupt others.
6. Motions do not need a second. A motion is a proposal to take some action as a group.
7. There is no limit on how many times a member can speak on an issue, and motions to limit or close discussion are never appropriate.
8. Informal discussion is permitted with no motion pending. Whereas in a parliamentary discussion members cannot discuss an issue without a motion, in a committee meeting no motion is usually made until *after* consensus or at least a majority has been achieved through extended discussion.
9. A majority vote (of those actually voting) is required before any decision can be said to have been made. Usually a vote is taken to confirm a decision already sensed by the group. "Straw" votes can be taken at any time to determine whether majority or consensus exists before a binding vote is taken. The leader might say, "Let's see how we stand on this. Would all who favor it please raise your right hand."
10. When a proposal is clear to all members, a vote can be taken and the outcome recorded as a decision even though no motion has been introduced.
11. The chair can ask if all members consent or agree with an idea or proposal. Then if no one objects, the decision has been made and is reported in the minutes. For example: "It was decided by consent that we should have Jean and Bob draft a resolution to present at the next meeting of the club."
12. Committee chairs can speak up in a discussion, taking a stand on a controversial issue, without leaving the chair. They can also make motions and vote on all questions as do all other members of the committee. (In some large committees it may be decided that the chair will act as if in a large assembly; if so, he or she should do so *at all times,* voting only to break a tie and not participating in the substance of the discussion.)

13. A motion to reconsider a previous vote can be made at any time and there is no limit on how many times a question can be reconsidered. Unlike in a parliamentary body, any person who did not vote with the losing side can move to reconsider. Thus, a person who was absent or did not vote can ask for the reconsideration of a previous decision or vote if the action has not yet been carried out.

14. Motions can be amended in committee, but this is best done informally. Voting on the proposed change in a motion should only occur if a consensus decision cannot be made in the time available for a meeting.

15. Many of the motions required in an assembly are irrelevant. A member can discuss virtually anything informally in committee sessions, so there is no need for points of order, motions to table, or matters of personal privilege. In short, the bulk of what is called parliamentary law is not needed; in fact, it can be obstructive.

16. Formal reports of committees should contain only what was agreed to by a majority vote of those present at a regular and properly called (notice given to each member) meeting at which a quorum was present. Usually the chair makes formal reports from a committee in writing. Reports of less formal actions or work in progress may be given orally to a parent organization. If a committee is unable to reach consensus and a minority of its membership wants to make a report or recommendation different from that of the majority, it usually is permitted to do so as soon as the "majority" committee report has been made. This is not a *right* of a committee minority, but during debate under parliamentary rules the members who did not agree with the majority position can speak their opposition. However, no one has the right to allude to what happened during the committee's private discussions unless the entire committee has agreed that this is to be permitted.

In summary, only a minimum of rules of order and precedence is required in committees of organizations which have adopted *Robert's Rules of Order, Newly Revised*. Voting is done to show that a legal majority supported all reported findings, recommendations, and actions. Voting is not done to shut off discussion or suggest that majority vote is the best way of making decisions by a committee. Any issue within the freedom of the committee can be presented for discussion at any time, and discussion of it can be quite informal and as lengthy as needed.

Techniques for Groups within Organizations

There is a variety of special discussion techniques for encouraging small group involvement within a large meeting, for facilitating communication within small groups that are part of large organizations, and for increasing communication necessary for participatory management or autonomous work groups. Those selected (there are others as well) for inclusion in this chapter are all group centered, are discussional in nature, and can be of value in a number of contexts. If you elect to use any of these techniques, make sure the coordinator explains the procedures carefully before the group tries it. Often a sheet of instructions is handed to participants to explain the purpose and procedures.

The Problem Census

The **problem census** is a "posting" technique used to identify important issues or problems. It is particularly useful for building an agenda for future problem-solving meetings, program planning by an organization, or discovering problems encountered by a group of employees or students. For instance, a university department where one of us worked periodically conducted a problem census that developed into an agenda for a series of future meetings. Different faculty members committed themselves to investigate the various problems and prepare a presentation of information and an outline for each problem as it came up. The following are the steps to take when leading a problem census:

1. Seat the group in a semicircle facing a chart or board.
2. Explain the purpose of the technique, which is to bring out all problems, concerns, questions, or difficulties any member of the group would like to have discussed.
3. The leader then asks each participant to present one problem or question, going around the group clockwise. Anyone not ready to present a new problem may pass to the next person. After one round, anyone who passed may now add a question or problem. This continues until all problems have been presented.
4. The leader posts each problem as it is presented by writing it clearly on the chart or board. Each filled page of a chart is fastened to the wall with tape. The leader must be totally accepting of whatever is presented, never challenging its validity or disagreeing, but asking for clarification or elaboration if necessary. Often, the leader will need to distill a long problem statement to a concise phrase or question but should always ask the speaker whether that is what was intended before posting the rephrased problem.
5. The group now evaluates the list for priority by voting, usually with each member voting for his or her top three or four choices. *All* problems are included on the agenda; voting just prioritizes the list.
6. The group may now find that some of the questions can be answered or solved at once by other members to the satisfaction of the presenter. Such questions or issues are removed from the list; those remaining are in order for future consideration.
7. Each problem is dealt with in turn. Some issues may call for factual presentation by a consultant. Others may be handled by a brief lecture or other informational technique and some by printed materials. However, the core problems should be analyzed and handled by the entire group or a subcommittee, following an appropriate problem-solving procedure.

Figure 13.1
Buzz group seating in
an auditorium.

Buzz Groups

A **buzz group session** is used to organize a large group meeting into many small groups that work concurrently on the same question. Purposes may be to generate questions for a speaker or panel, identify problems or issues, compile a list of ideas or possible solutions, and generally to stimulate personal involvement and thinking by members of a large group. One of us was a participant among 500 educational leaders in Kentucky who met to work out techniques for promoting a "minimum foundation program" for public education in that state. Organizers sought a favorable vote of taxpayers in a special election to support a state tax for local schools based on need. This meant higher taxes and a flow of money from wealthier to poorer districts. Several times the buzz group technique helped identify specific local problems, inexpensive advertising and promotional techniques, arguments for the program, and so forth. This procedure was developed and popularized by J. Donald Phillips, President of Hillsdale College in Michigan, who served as consultant for the Kentucky Conference. The conference was held in 1954 at Eastern Kentucky State College. Although the conference was large, every participant was active in discussion and the sense of enthusiasm and involvement was remarkable. The procedure is as follows:

1. The chair presents a target question—as concise, limited, and specific as possible—to the entire assembly, which may be seated in rows in an auditorium or at small tables. The question should be displayed on a large poster or blackboard where all can see it. The following are examples of such questions:

   What techniques could be used to publicize the Minimum Foundation Program to citizens of each county or city?
   What new projects might local unions undertake to help members with social problems?
   What questions would you like Coach Paterno to answer about his proposals to improve academic achievement by athletes?

2. Divide the large group into work groups of six by seating them at small tables or in a large auditorium by counting off by three in each row. Then have alternate rows turn to face each other as shown in figure 13.1. Each group should be given a copy of the target question on an index card.

3. Appoint a recorder-spokesperson for each group based on seating. For example, the leader might say, "The person sitting in the forward left-hand seat of each group will be its recorder. The recorder should write on the card *all* ideas presented, then have the group rank order them." Assistants should then pass out blank cards.

4. Next, ask each group to record as many answers to the target question as it can think of in five minutes. Spend one minute evaluating the list to decide whether any items should be eliminated and in what order to present them. Thus, discussion occurs in groups of six members for six minutes! This procedure is sometimes called Phillip's 66.

5. When the five minutes are up, warn the groups and allow an extra minute if all seem involved. Then, ask each group to evaluate and rank order their list.

6. At this point you may do any of several things, depending on group size and plan of the overall meeting:

   a. The cards are collected and edited to eliminate duplications. A tally of the number of times each item was mentioned on the cards is kept. The total list is duplicated and distributed to the entire group at a subsequent meeting or is presented to some special group for processing.

   b. The chair asks each recorder to report orally from his or her seat one *new* item from the card without explanation, or a recorder may pass if all the items have been presented. A secretary writes all items on a chart or chalkboard in the front of the room. The list is then processed as above or according to the problem census technique described earlier.

   c. The questions listed are presented in rotation to the speaker or panel.

Many variations in the buzz group technique are possible. It is a useful technique for teachers in such courses as social problems, literature, political science, and psychology. The groups may have more than six minutes and may even follow a brief outline provided by the teacher.

| The Nominal Group Technique | Some research into brainstorming showed that people working individually in the presence of others can generate more ideas for solving problems than the same number of people interacting. Interacting groups sometimes suppress divergence on their way to consensus.[7] Delbecq and Van de Ven developed the **Nominal Group Technique** as an alternative that attempts to derive the major advantages of group discussion without the major disadvantages.[8] A nominal, or "in name only," group alternates between verbal interaction and individual work in the presence of others. It works better for major problems and long-range planning than for routine meetings.[9] The Nominal Group Technique helps reduce secondary tension, controls destructive conflict, and eliminates the chance for some members to make speeches. On the other hand, it is not a complete problem-solving process, may reduce cohesiveness, and produces |

less member satisfaction than fully interactive formats.[10] One of us successfully used a modification of this technique to help a manufacturer identify and generate possible solutions for problems consumers were having with package directions for a product.

Essentially, Nominal Group Technique members (six to nine) work individually in each other's presence by writing their ideas, recording these ideas on a chart as a group and clarifying them, and evaluating them by a ranking procedure until a decision has been reached. The procedure may vary, but it always involves a cycle of individual work followed by discussion. The following are the steps for the designated leader as outlined by Delbecq:

1. State the known problem elements or characteristics of a situation that differ from what is desired. At this point there should be *no* mention of solutions and no interaction. Members are seated at a table facing a chart easel. A large group can be divided into several small working groups, each with a leader.

2. Ask the participants to generate a list of the emotional, personal, and organizational features of the problem. Then give a clear definition of the problem. (Steps 1 and 2 can be combined, with no discussion as in step 2 and the leader presenting the problem and moving the group at once into step 3.)

3. Allow the group five to fifteen minutes to work silently. Each person is asked to write all problem-solving ideas that he or she can think of.

4. In a round robin session the results are compiled on a chart in front of the group where all can see the list.
   a. Ask each person in turn to give *one* item from his or her list. This item is recorded on the chart. No discussion is allowed at this time.
   b. Do not record who suggested the idea or record more than one idea per person at a time.
   c. Keep going around the group until *all* ideas have been posted on the chart. Additional ideas may occur to members while this is going on; be sure they too are stated and listed.
   d. If someone has the same idea as another, put a tally mark by it on the chart. Don't record it twice.
   e. The leader also has generated a list and posts his or her ideas in turn just as for the other members.

5. Clarification interaction—anyone may ask another person for clarification of an idea or proposal on the list. Questions such as "What does item 6 mean?" or "Do you understand item 4?" are now in order for discussion. The leader should take the group through the list item by item, but only to clarify and elaborate, *not* to evaluate. At this point, allow no lobbying, criticism, or argument for an idea.

6. Each person is now given a set of note cards on which to write the five or so items (each should have the same number of cards) he or she most prefers. These cards are now ranked, with 5 the highest and 1 the

lowest, and collected by the leader. Sum the rank for each item and divide by the number of people in the group to derive a weighted value for each item.

7. Now engage in an evaluation discussion of the several items with the highest ranks. This should be a full and free evaluative discussion with critical thinking, disagreement, and analysis encouraged.

8. If a decision is reached, fine. If not, revote and discuss further. This process can be repeated several times if necessary until a clear synthesis of a few ideas or support for one idea has emerged. The result is submitted to the appropriate planners, executive, or parent group for action.

The RISK Technique

Once a group has decided on a solution, that solution has to be evaluated carefully. Recall that earlier we talked about second chance meetings where members can raise last-minute doubts, and we reported Hirokawa's research showing that one crucial function a group should perform is evaluation of possible negative consequences.[11] The **RISK technique** is designed specifically to allow an organization to assess how a proposed change or policy will affect the individuals and groups involved.[12]

Groups employing RISK may use or modify the basic procedures for problem census or the Nominal Group Technique, but the focus is on what possible negative consequences (RISKs) will occur if the solution tentatively selected is implemented. The basic steps of the RISK technique follow:

1. The leader presents the proposed solution or change in detail, and asks members to think of any risks, fears, or problems with the proposal.

2. Members may either brainstorm as a group to generate problems, or may work individually in the presence of others, using the solo brainstorming step of the Nominal Group Technique.

3. The problems are posted in round-robin fashion on a chart or blackboard. Once this has been done, members should study the list and add to it any additional concerns that may occur to them. It is *absolutely imperative* that the leader be nonjudgmental. If members feel threatened, they will not reveal their real concerns. Often the risks felt to be most serious by some members will be voiced after a lull, when considerable time has elapsed.

4. After this initial meeting, all risks are compiled into a master list and circulated to all participants, who are asked to add anything else that occurs to them.

5. At a second meeting, additional risks felt by any member are added to the master list. Then the members discuss each risk one by one. They decide whether each is a serious problem or one that can be readily resolved and removed from the list. Affective interaction should be encouraged as members share fears, doubts, and concerns.

6. The remaining risks are processed into an agenda and handled with the same general procedure as items from the problem census.

Quality Circles

The name **quality circle** has been given to small groups of employees who meet at regular intervals on company time to discuss work related matters. The ultimate purpose of the quality circle is to increase productivity, improve the quality of what is produced, and enhance employee involvement.[13] Quality circle members share their opinions with management in an attempt to solve all sorts of job-related problems. American consultants charged with helping postwar Japan prepare to compete for world markets introduced quality control techniques of participative management to the Japanese, which meshed well with that culture, although they had been rejected by U.S. managers. One tool for enacting participative management was the quality circle, a joint invention of American and Japanese management experts.

In recent years, a variety of American companies have instituted quality circles, sometimes called *work effectiveness teams,* to help U.S. industries compete more successfully. Corporations using quality circles or some variation of them include Ford Motor Company, General Motors, Hewlett-Packard, Burlington Industries, Ethyl Corporation, Anchor Hocking, Control Data, Galion, Sheller-Globe, 3M, Dresser Industries, Firestone, W. R. Grace, Sony, Honda, Weyerhauser, Northrup, SmithKline, American Airlines, and dozens of others.[14] Nonprofit organizations like the Red Cross and Boy Scouts also have quality circles. Workers participating in these groups perceive improvements in their communication with superiors, subordinates, and peers as well as positive effects on their power and influence.[15]

Employees in a quality circle meet with a team leader (in the U.S., usually a supervisor; in Japan, an elected worker) on company time to discuss production problems, or to react to problems presented to them by management. Usually they meet for an hour a week, but time varies from company to company. All ideas agreed upon are submitted to management, which must react to every suggestion, either reporting that it has been adopted, is being investigated, has been adopted with modifications, or is rejected with an explanation why. Many companies combine the quality circle with employee bonus systems, which reward either individuals or groups for profit-making or money-saving ideas. You will note that any of the techniques discussed thus far—standard decision-making and problem-solving methods, the RISK technique, the problem census, and the Nominal Group Technique—can be used as needed by the quality circle to enhance its effectiveness.

While quality circles can be quite effective, merely instituting them in a company will not guarantee a positive outcome. Sometimes unions see them as a ploy to increase production without improving benefits (perhaps a valid criticism in some cases), and occasionally managers implement quality circle programs without giving enough foresight into how the programs will work within that company's culture. Potential problems identified by Lawler and Mohrman include middle managers who are threatened and resist the ideas presented, failure to implement ideas, groups becoming discouraged by management's failure to respond, and management's failure to reward groups financially for their contributions.[16] If quality circle programs are to work, they cannot be used as a cosmetic device to mask deep-seated problems within the company. Management must be strongly committed to the quality circle program, the program must be part of a long-range plan for organizational development, and participants must be adequately trained in small group dynamics and participative problem solving.[17]

For the quality circle form of consultative management to work, employees must have job security. They must feel assured that their ideas for increasing their efficiency will not ultimately cost them jobs or earnings. They must know that their ideas are eagerly sought and will be dealt with seriously and thoroughly. They must have a sense both of commitment to the company and of the company's commitment to them. They must truly share in the growth, profits, and future of the company. When employees are treated like machines that can readily be replaced or if they have no job security other than that provided through a hard-fought union contract, quality circles are not going to work very well.

Focus Groups

Several other techniques exist that can be used to solve specific problems. One of the most common is the focus group. Long used in advertising and marketing, **focus groups** enable a company to identify problems or issues by encouraging nonstructured, freewheeling group interaction. One of us, a former public relations officer for a small campus, used a focus group to discover more effective ways of redesigning and promoting the evening course schedule. A group of evening students was given instructions simply to talk about what it was like to be an evening student. From the discussion, campus officials discovered a way of scheduling evening courses more convenient for most evening students. In addition, the students' comments provided a wealth of ideas for advertising and promoting evening offerings imaginatively to the right audiences.

Electronically Mediated Meetings: Teleconferencing

Another group technique which holds promise for many organizations is the teleconference. Face-to-face meetings are expensive, but representatives of departments in large corporations, administrators and faculty of multicampus universities, and individuals involved in cooperative ventures among different organizations and nations must find ways to share ideas and information. One such solution is the electronically mediated meeting, the **teleconference.** These can take the form of video conferences, where each participant can see each other; computer conferences, where participants send messages printed at computer terminals; and audio conferences where participants can hear but cannot see each other. The first is prohibitively expensive for most companies at present. The second, still a fairly new technique, holds some promise. Recent studies have shown that decisions made by computerized conference groups were just as good as ones made by face-to-face groups, but computer groups were less likely to reach agreement.[18] The *type* of computerized technique appears to make a difference. Murrell found that using the window method, where each participant could see the responses of all other participants at once, produced higher decision quality than a message system where participants had to complete a message before they could interact.[19] The window system mimics face-to-face interaction more closely. The audio conference is both readily available (via telephone lines, satellite, or microwave towers) and reasonably priced.

From the more than 100 studies of teleconferencing, we can develop practical guidelines for making electronic meetings productive.[20] For audioconferencing, speaker phone equipment is readily available, relatively inexpensive, and requires no special studios. It can be set up in any office. However, audio conferences lack "social presence."[21] When linked by sound waves of rather low fidelity, the sense of sharing, belonging, and recognition of each other as individuals can be low. Many key nonverbal cues are absent. Moreover, electronic equipment can fail at the most inopportune times. On the other hand, the potential for *greater* equality of opportunity to participate exists in the control equipment used by conference leaders.

For teleconferencing to work best, Johansen, Vallee, and Spangler recommend that the participants hold an extended face-to-face conference beforehand to form a sense of "groupness."[22] A post-teleconference meeting can be useful as well. It seems that for complex tasks, especially where the level of conflict is likely to be high, face-to-face meetings are still preferable. Teleconferences are well suited to routine meetings.

Several factors will enhance such routine meetings. A trained moderator is essential; all participants should be aware of the rules and guidelines for speaking; and all speakers should abide by specified time limits.[23] These meetings are not qualitatively different from face-to-face ones, but additional coordination efforts are required with less information (e.g., nonverbal cues) provided. They are likely to increase in the future, as travel costs increase and technological limitations decrease.

Summary

A variety of discussion methods and techniques was presented in this chapter. Learning discussions have as their intent the cognitive, affective, and/or behavioral change of participants. In general, the focus of private learning discussions is not consensus but sharing and understanding perceptions. Various formats can be used and should be guided by the subject matter under consideration. Personal feelings and interpersonal relationships can be dealt with through affective discussion or group encounter. Interaction in such groups must be accepting and free of judgment. Discussion of social and political issues can be organized in sequences like those for informative speeches. Discussions of craft or artistic products should focus attention on various characteristics of the item being discussed.

The most common types of public discussion are panel presentations and large group forums. Special procedures for each were described in detail. Each format requires close control by a designated moderator.

Small groups that are part of large organizations hold considerable promise for increasing employee participation. Involvement of every individual in a large group is facilitated through such techniques as the buzz group. A problem census can be taken to develop an agenda based on member concerns. Management groups doing long-range planning can increase their productivity with the Nominal Group Technique. The RISK procedure can be used effectively to evaluate the possible negative consequences of a proposed course of action or change in policy. Most widely used is the quality circle, which increases both the quality and the quantity of work when it is used appropriately.

Modern electronic developments have made possible video, audio, and computer conferences of people in remote locations. Video is expensive and complex, but audio is readily available and inexpensive. It requires careful coordination with a skilled moderator and prepared participants. It can supplement, but not replace, face-to-face meetings.

The techniques described in this chapter are designed to be useful in a variety of contexts. As you have occasion to use these discussion methods and techniques, feel free to modify and adapt them to your circumstances.

Exercises

1. Select a poem, short story, brief essay, painting, sculpture, or other work of art that intrigues you. Your class will be divided into several groups of five to seven members. If you have selected something written, make a copy for each member of your group. Plan an outline for leading discussion on the work of art. The discussion will be limited to fifteen to twenty minutes. Each member of your small group will in turn lead the discussion using the outline prepared. You may want to have one member sit out as a critic-observer, and then lead a brief evaluation discussion.

2. Break into groups of five or six. Using one of the case problems ("The Teacher's Dilemma" or "The Grade Inflation Case") presented in the chapter, each member should develop an outline to organize discussion of the problem. Share your outlines with each other and select the one you like best. Choose a designated leader and conduct the discussion. What did you learn? What did you like best about the outline you chose? How did you feel about the discussion?

3. Conduct a problem census focusing on the question "What topics should our class select for discussion that would be intrinsically interesting and involve the whole class?" You will use the rank ordered topics in future exercises.

4. Select a topic identified by the problem census which is likely to produce strong feelings, and conduct an affective discussion in small groups of five or six. What things were easy for you to discuss and what were difficult? What did you learn?

5. With a trained facilitator, conduct an encounter session with volunteers from the class.

6. Following a series of discussions, have a feedback session. On a chart or chalkboard write a set of terms for guiding the feedback. These should be selected by the group, possibly including some of the following: attitudes, preparation, speaking, supportiveness, acceptance of others, self-acceptance, personal insight, openness, and warmth.

7. Break into groups of six or more, and have each group select a topic identified in your problem census. Each group should prepare a panel discussion for the rest of the class, and conduct a buzz session following the panel discussion.

8. Select a topic from your problem census and use the Nominal Group Technique to discuss the problem. Your instructor will coordinate and time the exercise, but students should lead each of the groups.

9. With the instructor's blessing, form a quality circle of volunteers to meet every two weeks, discuss problems in the class, what might be done to solve them, and other ways the class could be made more interesting. The circle should give consensus recommendations to the instructor. The instructor should make some reaction to each suggestion at the next class meeting, incorporating it if possible or explaining why the suggestion was declined.

Bibliography

Baird, John E. Jr. *Quality Circles: Leader's Manual.* Prospect Heights, Ill.: Waveland Press, 1982.

Barker, Larry L., Kathy J. Wahlers, Kittie W. Watson, and Robert J. Kibler. *Groups in Process: An Introduction to Small Group Communication.* 3d ed. Englewood Cliffs, N.J.: Prentice-Hall Inc., 1987, chapter 10.

Delbecq, Andre L., A. H. Van de Ven, and D. H. Gustafson. *Group Techniques for Program Planning: A Guide to Nominal Group and Delphi Processes.* Glenview, Ill.: Scott, Foresman and Company, 1975.

Deming, W. Edward. "What Top Management Must Do." *Business Week,* 20 July 1981, 20–21.

Elton, Martin C. J., W. A. Lucas, and D. W. Conrath, eds. *Evaluating New Telecommunications Systems.* New York: Plenum, 1978.

Johansen, Robert, J. Vallee, and K. Spangler. *Electronic Meetings: Technical Alternatives and Social Choices.* Reading, Mass.: Addison-Wesley, 1979.

Moore, Carl M. *Group Techniques for Idea Building.* Newbury Park, Cal.: Sage Publications, 1987.

"Quality Circles Pay Off Big," *Industry Week,* 29 October 1979, 17–19.

Robert, Henry M. *Robert's Rules of Order, Newly Revised.* Glenview, Ill.: Scott, Foresman and Company, 1981.

Ruch, William V. *Corporate Communications, A Comparison of Japanese and American Practices.* Westport, Conn.: Quorum Books, 1984.

Siebold, David R. "Making Meetings More Successful: Plans, Formats, and Procedures for Group Problem-Solving." In *Small Group Communication: A Reader.* 4th ed., eds. William S. Cathcart and Larry A. Samovar. Dubuque, Iowa: Wm. C. Brown Publishers, 1984, 187–201.

Notes

1. D. W. Johnson and R. T. Johnson, *Learning Together and Alone* (Englewood Cliffs, N.J.: Prentice-Hall, 1975), 191–92; W. J. McKeachie, "Recitation and Discussion," in *Achieving Learner Objectives,* 3d ed., ed. O.E. Lancaster (University Park, Pa.: The Pennsylvania State University, 1963), section F.

2. John W. Powell, *Research in Adult Group Learning in the Liberal Arts* (White Plains, N.Y.: Fund for Adult Education, 1960), 3; P. H. Witte, "The Effects of Group Reward Structures on Interracial Acceptance, Peer Tutoring and Academic Performance," (Unpublished doctoral dissertation, Washington University, 1972); Johnson and Johnson, *Learning Together and Alone,* 193–96; Elizabeth Hunter, *Encounter in the Classroom* (New York: Holt, Rinehart and Winston, 1972), 1–15.

3. John K. Brilhart, "An Exploratory Study of Relationships between Evaluating Process and Associated Behaviors of Participants in Six Study-Discussion Groups," (Ph.D. dissertation, Pennsylvania State University, 1962), 283–93.

4. Brilhart, "An Exploratory Study," 275–82.

5. Charlotte Epstein, *Affective Subjects in the Classroom: Exploring Race, Sex and Drugs* (Scranton, Pa.: Intext Educational Publishers, 1972), 12–13.

6. Henry M. Robert, *Robert's Rules of Order, Newly Revised* (Glenview, Ill.: Scott, Foresman and Company, 1981).

7. Anne Gero, "Conflict Avoidance in Consensual Decision Processes," *Small Group Behavior* 16 (1985): 487–99.

8. Andre L. Delbecq, Andrew H. Van de Ven, and David H. Gustafson, *Group Techniques for Program Planning: A Guide to Nominal Group and Delphi Processes* (Glenview, Ill.: Scott Foresman and Company, 1975), 7–16.

9. Ibid.,3–4.

10. Andre L. Delbecq, "Techniques for Achieving Innovative Changes in Programming," (Presentation at the Midwest Regional Conference of the Family Service Association of America; Omaha, Neb., 20 April 1971).

11. Randy Y. Hirokawa, "Discussion Procedures and Decision-Making Performance: A Test of a Functional Perspective," *Human Communication Research* 12 (1985): 203–24.

12. Norman R. F. Maier, *Problem-Solving Discussions and Conferences: Leadership Methods and Skills* (New York: McGraw-Hill, 1963), 171–77.

13. Jane P. Elvins, "Communication in Quality Circles: Members' Perceptions of Their Participation and Its Effects on Related Organizational Communication Variables," *Group and Organization Studies* 10 (1985): 479–507.

14. William V. Ruch, *Corporate Communications* (Westport, Conn.: Quorum Books, 1984), 205–19.

15. Elvins, "Communication in Quality Circles," 479–507.

16. E. Lawler, and S. Mohrman, "Quality Circles after the Fad," *Harvard Business Review* (1985): 65–71.

17. Gerald M. Goldhaber, *Organizational Communication,* 4th ed., (Dubuque, Iowa: Wm. C. Brown Publishers, 1986), 283.

18. Starr Roxanne Hiltz, Kenneth Johnson, and Murray Turoff, "Experiments in Group Decision Making: Communication Process and Outcome in Face-to-Face versus Computerized Conferences," *Human Communication Research* 13 (1986): 225–52.

19. Sharon L. Murrell, "The Impact of Communicating through Computers,"(Unpublished doctoral dissertation, State University of New York at Stony Brook, 1983).

20. Robert Johansen, J. Vallee, and K. Spangler, *Electronic Meetings: Technical Alternatives and Social Choices* (Reading, Mass.: Addison-Wesley, 1979), 2.

21. John A. Short, E. Williams, and B. Christie, *The Social Psychology of Telecommunications* (London: John Wiley and Sons, 1976).

22. Johansen, Vallee, and Spangler, *Electronic Meetings,* 113–15.

23. Larry L. Barker et al., *Groups in Process: An Introduction to Small Group Communication,* 3d ed. (Englewood Cliffs, N.J.: Prentice-Hall, 1987), 208.

Chapter 14

Observing and Evaluating Small Group Discussions

Study Objectives

As a result of studying chapter 14, you should be able to:

1. Explain the benefits of having nonparticipating observers for small groups and the roles of reminder, consultant, student, and critic observer.

2. Prepare a set of questions to guide your observations of any small group discussion.

3. Explain ways to make the report of your observations both acceptable and helpful to group members.

4. Devise instruments for obtaining postmeeting reactions from group members to chart the flow and frequency of verbal participation and to rate groups, individual members, and designated leaders.

5. Make, record, and report observations of discussion inputs, processes, and outputs.

Key Terms

Consultant-observer a nonparticipant observer whose primary responsibility is to give assistance and advice based on observations of group input, process, and output to a discussion group or a designated small group discussion leader.

Content analysis an analysis of the content (topics, behaviors, specific words or ideas, fantasy themes, etc.) of a group's discussion.

Critic-observer a nonparticipant observer of a small group discussion who evaluates the functioning of the members and group as a whole.

Postmeeting reaction form (PMR) a form completed by group members following a discussion on which they evaluate the discussion, the group, and the leader; responses are usually tabulated and reported back to the group.

Rating scale a pencil-and-paper instrument, usually completed by a critic-observer, to render a numerical evaluation of some factor involved in the discussion.

Reminder-observer a nonparticipant observer of a small group discussion, selected from the regular membership of the group, who tries to determine what is missing that might be helpful to the group (information, functions, roles, procedures, etc.), then suggests to the group what has been overlooked.

Student-observer a nonparticipating observer whose only purpose is to learn about groups by observing, usually to develop skills in small group communication or as a researcher investigating questions about the nature of small groups.

Verbal interaction analysis an analysis of who talks to whom and how often group members speak in a small group.

Throughout this book we have stressed the importance of observing group inputs and processes as well as participating in them. You cannot both participate and observe in the same instant. Rather, the participant-observer shifts attention back and forth between the two activities. At times you have seen clearly what your group needs and been able to supply the requisite function, but there undoubtedly have been things you have missed. Sometimes the most skillful of us becomes so engrossed in the interaction over an important issue that we lose the perspective of the observer entirely.

Thus, a nonparticipating observer can be of real assistance in helping the group perceive what is going on. The entire group as well as the designated leader can benefit from the feedback observations of a nonparticipating observer. We have two main purposes in this chapter. First, we will explain the various roles observers can take. Second, we will present a variety of instruments, including member and observer rating scales, interaction analysis diagrams, and content analysis schemes, which observers and members alike may use both to gather information and present it to the group. Seeing the group's interaction represented in a diagram or displayed on a chart may produce just the insight members need to improve their own performance.

The Role of the Observer

Every student of discussion and group processes needs the experience of observing discussion groups at work. Many of our students have remarked, "It looks different when you are sitting outside the discussion." We have seen the "Ah ha!" reactions of student-observers as they finally *see* a phenomenon occurring that previously had been only an abstract idea. These observations frequently lead to voluntary behavior change, so we encourage you to do as much observing as you can.

When you observe a group you may become overwhelmed by all the things going on simultaneously. Planning your observation in advance will help you focus on the things which are most important. One additional suggestion for coping with information overload while observing is to tape record the group's discussion (only with the group's prior permission, of course). That way, you will worry less about missing something and can make notes on areas of the discussion to review later.

Here is a list of questions that you can use as a general guide from which to select a more limited list of questions to answer as an observer. For example, if you have been asked either as a member of the group or as an outside consultant to help the group identify areas it can improve, the list can help you screen out those processes that appear to be operating well so that you can focus on those the group members may want to change.

Group Goals

Are there clear and accepted group goals?

Has the committee a clear understanding of its charge?

Do all members know and accept limits on their area of freedom?

Do members know what output is needed?

Setting

Are any environmental factors disrupting the group, such as poor seating arrangements, lack of privacy, or unpleasant surroundings?

Communication Skills and Network

How well do members encode their ideas, verbally and nonverbally?

How well are members listening and trying to understand each other?

How well is the verbal participation spread among all members?

Is the pattern of verbal interaction all-channel or unduly restricted?

Communication Climate and Norms

To what degree does the group climate seem open, trusting, and cooperative?

What attitudes toward themselves, each other, and the substance of the discussion are members manifesting?

Are there any hidden agenda items interfering with group process?

Are any norms interfering with progress and cohesiveness?

Leadership and Member Roles

If there is a designated leader, what style of leadership is being provided?

Does leadership seem appropriate for what the group needs?

Does the role structure provide optimal inputs from all members?

Are any needed behavioral functions missing?

Decision-Making and Problem-Solving Procedures

Do members seem adequately prepared with information?

Are information and ideas being evaluated or accepted at face value?

Do you see any tendency toward groupthink?

When evaluating ideas and opinions, is the group making use of information brought out in earlier discussions?

Are periodic internal summaries needed to help members recall and maintain perspective on the discussion and move the group forward without undue redundancy?

Are the information, interpretations, proposals, and decisions being adequately recorded?

Has some procedure or agenda for discussion been provided or developed by the group? If so, how well is it being followed? Does it serve the group's needs?

How are decisions being made?

Do members share the same values and criteria in making decisions, or do criteria need to be clarified?

In problem solving, has the group defined and clarified the problem before focusing on finding solutions?

How creative is the group in generating potential solutions to its problem and in interpreting information?

Has judgment been deferred until solutions have been listed and understood by all members?

If needed, has the group made adequate plans to implement decisions, including member responsibilities, future meetings, and so on?

Are special procedural techniques (brainstorming, committee procedural rules, problem census, etc.) being used as needed?

Could procedural changes benefit the group?

You cannot look at all of these at once. You should first concentrate on the one or two areas that seem most important or most in need of assistance. After more experience as an observer you will find that you can pay attention to more areas.

The nonparticipating observer can do four things with his or her observations: learn from the example of others, remind the group of techniques or principles of discussion it has overlooked, give advice to improve the group's communication and procedures, or supply critical evaluations of the discussion. We now examine the role of observers who do each of these.

The Student-Observer

The **student-observer's** purpose is to learn from observing and evaluating the functioning of small groups. Such an observer does not normally make a report of observations to the group, although a report might be given when observing a group which is part of a small group communication class. Small group researchers, many of whose studies have been cited in this book, frequently gather data by observing small groups in their natural settings. Such student-observers seek to establish valid generalizations about small groups.

You are free to observe any small group meeting legally declared open to the public, such as most meetings of boards, councils, and committees of governments where a "sunshine" law has been passed. You also can obtain permission to observe many other small groups by describing your purpose as a learner and promising to maintain the confidentiality of details which are the business only of the group. Our students have observed such groups as church study-discussion groups, student activity groups, executive committees of sororities and fraternities, teaching-team meetings, school board meetings, meetings of department managers, quality circles, and so forth.

Here are a few suggestions to make your observation more successful. It usually produces more insight into a group's processes to take a team of observers; you will learn quite a bit from discussing your observations with each other. Your observation team can use a fishbowl arrangement, surrounding the

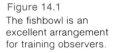

Figure 14.1
The fishbowl is an excellent arrangement for training observers.

group in a circle (see figure 14.1). Observers may each focus on the same aspect of group dynamics, such as leadership, or may each watch for and report on different phenomena (e.g., leadership, member roles, use of information, nonverbal communication, etc.). Or, each observer may be assigned to watch the behavior of a specific participant on a one-on-one basis. In some situations, observers may have the opportunity to share their observations with their assigned *alter egos* as well as with the rest of the observation team.

The Reminder-Observer

Often group members need just to be reminded of principles and techniques they know but have temporarily forgotten in the heat of a lively debate. The **reminder-observer** is a group member who focuses attention on group interaction and procedures while other members are involved with the content. When the observer notices some difficulty with the process, he or she reminds the group of the communication principles or techniques that have momentarily been overlooked. A useful procedure for most classroom discussion groups is to rotate this assigned role among members so each has the chance to develop the skill, but also so that one person is not left out of the discussion for too long. When you have become very skilled as a participant-observer you may be able to act as an unappointed reminder to nonclassroom groups to which you belong. A few guidelines follow:

1. Focus on processes, not issues or content.
2. Remember that the group, not you personally, is responsible for its own changes. Phrase your remarks neutrally in the form of questions and suggestions. For example: "I wonder if the group realizes we have discussed _____ , _____ , and _____ in the space of only five minutes?" "Are we ready to list possible solutions or do we need to explore the problem in more detail?" "I wonder if Jake and Marcia understand

each other's proposals?" or "Some members do not appear to have much chance to be heard. Does the group want to do more gatekeeping?" Comments phrased in such ways remind the group of principles of effective discussion without criticizing specific members.

3. Focus on trends and tendencies; avoid singling out individual members.
4. Give the group a chance to correct itself. Interrupt the discussion only when you believe the group will not become aware of the problem until it has wasted a lot of time and experienced harmful tension and frustration.

The Consultant-Observer

Many designated leaders and groups will benefit from the advice and coaching of a **consultant-observer.** With the advent of autonomous work groups and quality circles, workers who select coordinator-leaders from their own ranks and decide as a group how to manage their work routines must become proficient in group discussion as well as able to serve as discussion leaders. Committees and task forces of all kinds may need someone to help them resolve communication, relational, and procedural difficulties; hence, the need for small group communication consultants. Any organizational communication specialist should be prepared to serve as a consultant-observer to small groups in the organization.

As a small group consultant, you will need a thorough grasp of small group dynamics and techniques. You are likely to need to know and use a variety of observational, feedback, and evaluation techniques and instruments as appropriate. Examples are presented in the next section of this chapter. The following are guidelines for improving your performance as a consultant-observer:

1. Begin your postdiscussion remarks by *stressing the positive* and pointing out what a leader or group is doing well.
2. Emphasize what you think matters most or most needs improvement. Do not overwhelm the group with more advice and suggestions than it can accept and handle.
3. *Avoid arguing.* Present your observations, opinions, and advice, make sure they are understood, then leave group members free to decide whether or how your evaluations and advice will be used.
4. If you advise a leader during the actual meeting, do so *without interrupting the meeting.* If possible, whisper or write suggestions.
5. When group members ask your advice, give it clearly, precisely, and as briefly as possible. If the group asks for a presentation or demonstration of some technique, prepare and present it.
6. Critical comments to a leader should usually be made *in private* where the person will not appear to be under attack before the rest of the group.

The Critic-
Observer

A **critic-observer** may do considerable consulting, but his or her primary function is to evaluate and render judgments. Such an observer belongs primarily in a classroom or training program. The critic-observer may also act as an advisor. For example, your instructor may interrupt a discussion of a student group to point out what he or she thinks is going wrong and suggest a different procedure or technique. After you have become a proficient observer you might take on the role of critic-observer for a small group in a speech class or other course at your school. The critic usually makes a detailed report after observing a discussion, describing and interpreting selected aspects of the discussion, and expressing opinions about the strong and weak points. This must be done with tact! Discussants can be helped to accept criticism by applying two guidelines. All criticism should be constructive. When you point out a problem, you should also suggest what to do to correct it in a spirit of helpfulness. All critiques should include positive comments before pointing out what needs to be changed.

In general, a critic-observer's postmeeting judgments should cover at least four aspects of a discussion: (1) the group product, including how well it has been evaluated by the group, how appropriate it is to the problem described by the group, and how likely members are to support it; (2) the group process, including patterns of interaction, communication, decision making, and problem solving as a whole; (3) contributions and functional roles of members; and (4) leadership, especially the role of the procedural leader. As a critic-observer, you should use criteria appropriate for the type of discussion you observe, whether it is a public or private learning discussion or a problem-solving, advisory, or action group.

Instruments for
Observing and
Evaluating
Discussions

Whether or not your group employs a consultant, it will benefit from periodic self-evaluation. Such regular reviews should be scheduled, perhaps at the conclusion of each meeting. For instance, Hill's *Learning Thru Discussion* procedure includes evaluation of the meeting as the last stage.[1] If such sessions are not scheduled, too often they are never completed. In addition to regular brief evaluations, taking a break for an unplanned evaluation may correct a dangerous pattern of behavior or procedure before a serious breakdown occurs. Thus, both routine and spontaneous evaluations are useful.

The remaining section of chapter 14 is devoted to instruments for observing and evaluating groups and individual members. Many of these were developed especially for classes in small group communication, discussion, and leadership. They can be used as is or adapted to suit particular situations and groups.

Figure 14.2
Verbal interaction
diagram.

Group _____

Time _____

Begin _____

End _____

Place _____

Observer _____

**Frequency and Direction
of Participation**

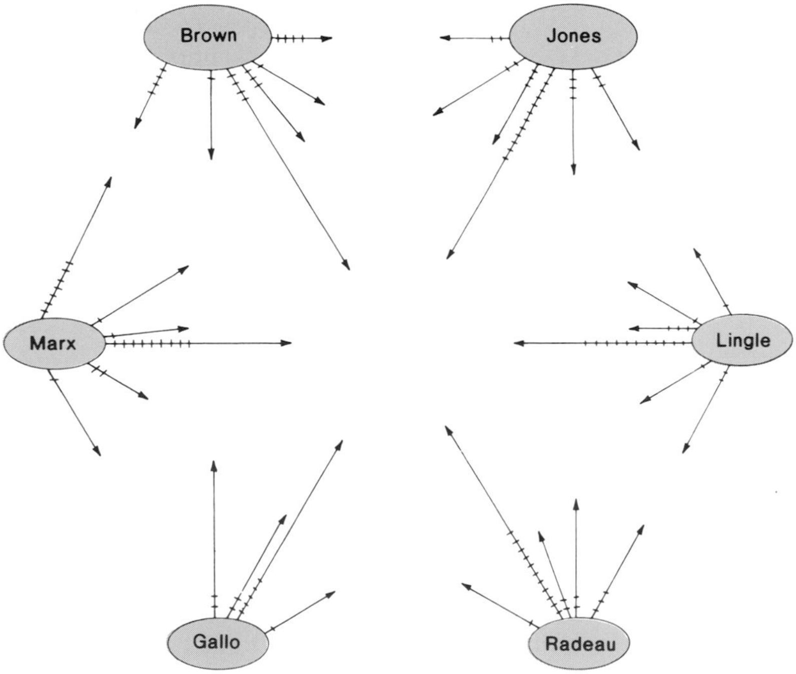

Verbal Interaction Analysis

A diagram of a **verbal interaction analysis** made by an observer reveals a lot about the relationships among members of a group. The diagram shows who talks to whom, how often each member participates orally, and whether the group has any members who dominate. A model interaction diagram is shown in figure 14.2. Notice the data at the top of the sheet; the names of all participants are located around the circle in the same order in which they sat during the discussion. Each time a person speaks, an arrow is drawn from his or her position toward the person to whom the remark was addressed. If a member speaks to the entire group, a longer arrow points toward the center

Figure 14.3
Displaying data from a
verbal interaction
diagram.

Group __CURRICULUM COMMITTEE__   Place __CRAIG HALL__

Observer __SMITH__   Date __8-28-87__

Beginning time __9:00 A.M.__   Ending time __10:30 A.M.__

TO:

FROM:	Brown	Jones	Lingle	Radeau	Gallo	Marx	Group	Total
Brown	—	5	2	4	2	5	5	23 / 16.1
Jones	3	—	3	4	4	3	13	30 / 21
Lingle	2	2	—	3	2	4	12	25 / 17.5
Radeau	3	3	4	—	0	2	12	24 / 16.8
Gallo	3	3	2	0	—	0	6	14 / 9.8
Marx	8	2	2	3	2	—	10	27 / 18.9
Total number / percent	19 / 13.3	15 / 10.5	13 / 9.1	14 / 9.8	10 / 7	14 / 9.8	58 / 40.6	143 / 100

of the circle. Subsequent remarks in the same direction are indicated by short cross marks on the base of the arrow.

Later, for ease of interpretation, the numbers and percentages can be displayed in a chart as in figure 14.3. From the frequency of participation to the group as a whole and to specific members, who might you guess is the leader of this particular group? Are there any other observations you can make about this group from the verbal interaction analysis? Note, too, that you can modify this procedure to capture frequency of nonverbal interaction, such as eye contact, as well as verbal interaction.

Content Analysis Procedures

One type of **content analysis** focuses on who does what and how often. The example in figure 14.4 uses the member roles designations (task, maintenance, and individual) to help the observer identify what functions are being performed and by whom. The specific behaviors are listed along the left margin and the participants' names across the top. Each time a member speaks, the group function performed by his or her remarks is tallied by placing a mark in the appropriate box. Later, the tally marks are converted to numbers and percentages as shown in figure 14.5. Can you tell who is probably the task leader of this group? Who is the maintenance leader? Do any individuals seem to be interfering with the group's progress?

Note that *any* category system can be used as a content analysis scheme. For example, you might want to focus on confirming or disconfirming statements members make to each other, as we discussed in chapter 3. In that case, you would record all the individual confirming and disconfirming categories along the left side.

There are other content analyses that can be performed. For example, you might want to trace the development of any fantasy chains in the group, the progression of an idea from its initial introduction by one member through its

Figure 14.4
Content analysis of
behavioral functions of
discussants.

Group _____ Place _____ Observer _____

Date _____ Beginning time _____ Ending time _____

Behavioral Functions	Participants' Names					
1. Initiating and orienting						
2. Information giving						
3. Information seeking						
4. Opinion giving						
5. Opinion seeking						
6. Clarifying and elaborating						
7. Evaluating						
8. Summarizing						
9. Coordinating						
10. Consensus testing						
11. Recording						
12. Suggesting procedure						
13. Gatekeeping						
14. Supporting						
15. Harmonizing						
16. Tension relieving						
17. Dramatizing						
18. Norming						
19. Withdrawing						
20. Blocking						
21. Status and recognition seeking						

Figure 14.5
Displaying data from
analysis of behavioral
functions of
discussants.

Group ___EXECUTIVE COMMITTEE___   Place ___CU LOBBY___
Observer ___ANDY___   Date ___8-28-87___
Beginning time ___4:30 P.M.___   Ending time ___6:30 P.M.___

Participants' Names

Behavioral Functions	Mary	John	Edna	Dave	Jodi	Total number / percent
1. Initiating and orienting	5	3				8 / 5.7
2. Information giving	6	5		2	3	16 / 11.4
3. Information seeking			3			3 / 2.1
4. Opinion giving	8	8	4	2	1	23 / 16.4
5. Opinion seeking			2			2 / 1.4
6. Clarifying and elaborating			3			3 / 2.1
7. Evaluating	2	4			1	7 / 5
8. Summarizing	2					2 / 1.4
9. Coordinating	8					8 / 5.7
10. Consensus testing				3		3 / 2.1
11. Recording			5			5 / 3.6
12. Suggesting procedure	3	6				9 / 6.4
13. Gatekeeping			1	5		6 / 4.3
14. Supporting	2		2	6		10 / 7.1
15. Harmonizing				3	2	5 / 3.6
16. Tension relieving					6	6 / 4.3
17. Dramatizing		5			3	8 / 5.7
18. Norming				4		4 / 2.9
19. Withdrawing		1				1 / .7
20. Blocking	2	5				7 / 5
21. Status and recognition seeking		4				4 / 2.9
Total number / percent	38 / 27.1	35 / 25	26 / 18.6	25 / 17.9	16 / 11.4	140 / 100

modification by the group to its final form, types of conflicts, or the use of
information to support ideas. If you decide to do this, it will make your job of
observer easier if you tape record the group's interaction (with permission, of
course).

Member and Observer Rating Scales

Many different **rating scales** and instruments have been prepared for a variety
of purposes. You may use any of the following or create your own to meet your
group's unique needs. The scales and forms that follow should give you some
good ideas for creating others.

PMR sheets can help
diagnose problem
groups.

*Postmeeting
Reaction Forms*

Postmeeting reaction forms, or **PMRs,** are used to get objective feedback from group members. Since they are anonymous, participants can be honest. A PMR may be planned by the chair or leader, by an instructor, by the group as a whole, or by organizers of a large conference. The forms are distributed, completed, and collected following a discussion. Results should be tallied and reported back to the group as soon as possible, either on a duplicated summary sheet or posted on a chart. They can then provide the content for further discussion and for planning changes in group procedure.

PMR questions should be tailored to fit the purposes and needs of the person(s) preparing the questionnaire. Sometimes the questions concern substantive items, sometimes interpersonal matters, and sometimes matters of technique and procedure. Two or more types of questions may be mixed on a PMR. Three examples of PMRs are shown in figures 14.6, 14.7, and 14.8.

Figure 14.6
Postmeeting reaction
form.

Instructions: Check the point on each scale that best represents your honest judgment. Add any comments you wish to make that are not covered by the questionnaire. Do *not* sign your name.

1. How clear were the *goals* of the discussion to you?

   _____

   very clear   somewhat vague   muddled

2. The *atmosphere* was

   _____

   cooperative and cohesive   apathetic   competitive

3. How well *organized and systematic* was the discussion?

_____

disorderly   just right   too rigid

4. How effective was the *style of leadership* supplied by the chairperson?

_____

too autocratic   democratic   weak

5. *Preparation for this meeting* was

_____

thorough   adequate   poor

6. Did you find yourself *wanting to speak* when you didn't get a chance?

_____

almost never   occasionally   often

7. How satisfied are you with the *results* of the discussion?

_____

very satisfied   moderately satisfied   very dissatisfied

8. How do you feel about *working again* with this same group?

_____

eager   I will   reluctant

Comments:

Figure 14.7
Postmeeting reaction
form.

1. How do you feel about today's discussion?

   excellent _____ good _____ all right _____ so-so _____ bad _____

2. What were the strong points of the discussion?

3. What were the weaknesses?

4. What changes would you suggest for future meetings?

(You need not sign your name.)

Figure 14.8
Postmeeting reaction
questionnaire.

Instruction: Circle the number that best indicates your reactions to the following questions about the discussion in which you participated:

1. *Adequacy of Communication* To what extent do you feel members were understanding each others' statements and positions?

| 0 | 1 | 2 | 3 | 4 | 5 | 6 | 7 | 8 | 9 | 10 |

Much talking past each   Communicated directly with
other, misunderstanding   each other, understanding well

2. *Opportunity to Speak* To what extent did you feel free to speak?

| 0 | 1 | 2 | 3 | 4 | 5 | 6 | 7 | 8 | 9 | 10 |

Never had a   All the opportunity to
chance to speak   talk I wanted

3. *Climate of Acceptance* How well did members support each other, show acceptance of individuals?

| 0 | 1 | 2 | 3 | 4 | 5 | 6 | 7 | 8 | 9 | 10 |

Highly critical   Supportive and receptive
and punishing

4. *Interpersonal relations* How pleasant and concerned with interpersonal relations?

| 0 | 1 | 2 | 3 | 4 | 5 | 6 | 7 | 8 | 9 | 10 |

Quarrelsome, status   Pleasant, empathic,
differences emphasized   concerned with persons

5. *Leadership* How adequate was the leader (or leadership) of the group?

| 0 | 1 | 2 | 3 | 4 | 5 | 6 | 7 | 8 | 9 | 10 |

Too weak ( ) or   Shared, group-centered,
dominating ( )   and sufficient

6. *Satisfaction with role* How satisfied are you with your personal participation in the discussion?

| 0 | 1 | 2 | 3 | 4 | 5 | 6 | 7 | 8 | 9 | 10 |

Very dissatisfied   Very satisfied

7. *Quality of product* How satisfied are you with the discussions, solutions, or learnings that came out of this discussion?

| 0 | 1 | 2 | 3 | 4 | 5 | 6 | 7 | 8 | 9 | 10 |

Very displeased   Very satisfied

8. *Overall* How do you rate the discussion as a whole apart from any specific aspect of it?

| 0 | 1 | 2 | 3 | 4 | 5 | 6 | 7 | 8 | 9 | 10 |

Awful, waste of time   Superb, time well spent

Leader's Name _____

Instruction: Circle number on each scale that best indicates your reaction.

1. *Preparation* for leading the discussion seemed
thorough and appropriate   very inadequate

| 7 | 6 | 5 | 4 | 3 | 2 | 1 |

2. *Organizing and guiding* the discussion were
clear and orderly   rigid or haphazard

| 7 | 6 | 5 | 4 | 3 | 2 | 1 |

3. *Spreading of participation* was
just right   completely neglected

| 7 | 6 | 5 | 4 | 3 | 2 | 1 |

4. The *style* or philosophy of the leader was
group centered stimulator   autocratic ("expert")

| 7 | 6 | 5 | 4 | 3 | 2 | 1 |

5. *Participating* in the discussion was
satisfying and enjoyable   boring or frustrating

| 7 | 6 | 5 | 4 | 3 | 2 | 1 |

Comments:

1. What did you especially *like* or *dislike* about the discussion?

2. What, if anything, do you believe you learned?

3. What do you most *approve* and *disapprove* of in the leader's behavior?

Specialized PMR forms for learning discussions are presented in figures 14.9, 14.10, and 14.11. The first was developed for a group discussing creative products like stories, movies, poems, paintings, and so forth. The second can be used as feedback for almost any learning group and is easily modified for a specific group. The last is designed to be used after an encounter session.

Figure 14.11
PMR for encounter
sessions.

Instruction: Circle number indicating your reaction on each scale.

1. How well was discussion focused on the "here and now" experience of the group?

| 1 | 2 | 3 | 4 | 5 | 6 | 7 |

little,
mostly
story telling
                 totally on
here-and-now

2. How open were members in describing feelings and reactions?

| 1 | 2 | 3 | 4 | 5 | 6 | 7 |

no self-disclosure   open, much self-disclosure

3. How descriptive and supportive were members?

| 1 | 2 | 3 | 4 | 5 | 6 | 7 |

evaluative and critical,   neutral   entirely descriptive
a "hatchet job"   of reactions and
others' behaviors

4. How specific and clear were comments?

| 1 | 2 | 3 | 4 | 5 | 6 | 7 |

vague, general and   clear, specific
theoretical   and focused

5. How much responsibility did members assume for the session?

| 1 | 2 | 3 | 4 | 5 | 6 | 7 |

leader dominated, much   members assumed responsibility
dependency behavior   for success of session

Comments:

*Scales for Rating
Group Inputs,
Process, and
Outputs*

Rating scales can be used by critic-observers to record judgments about any aspect of the group and its discussion, including group climate, cohesiveness, efficiency, satisfaction, degree of mutual respect, organization of discussion, and adequacy of information. Groups or class members may devise their own scales or modify the ones presented here. The first scale given, in figure 14.12, can be used to evaluate any small group discussion. The scale shown in figure 14.13 is adapted from a similar one developed by Patton and Giffin to identify deficiencies in problem-solving procedures.[2]

Figure 14.12
Discussion rating scale.

Date _____   Group _____

Time _____   Observer _____

Group Characteristic	5 Excellent	4 Good	3 Average	2 Fair	1 Poor
Organization of discussion					
Equality of opportunity to speak					
Cooperative group orientation					
Listening to understand					
Evaluation of ideas					

Comments:

Figure 14.13
Problem-solving
process scale.

Instructions: On each scale indicate the degree to which the group accomplished each identified behavior. Use the following scale for your evaluations:

Poor	Fair	Average	Good	Excellent
1	2	3	4	5

Circle the appropriate number in front of each item.

1 2 3 4 5   1. The concern of each member was identified regarding the problem the group attempted to solve.

1 2 3 4 5   2. This concern was identified *before* the problem was analyzed.

1 2 3 4 5   3. In problem analysis, the present condition was carefully compared with the specific condition desired.

1 2 3 4 5   4. The goal was carefully defined and agreed to by all members.

1 2 3 4 5   5. Valid (and relevant) information was secured when needed.

Figure 14.13
(*continued*)

1   2   3   4   5   6. Possible solutions were listed and clarified before they were evaluated.

1   2   3   4   5   7. Criteria for evaluating proposed solutions were clearly identified and accepted by the group.

1   2   3   4   5   8. Predictions were made regarding the probable effectiveness of each proposed solution, using the available information and criteria.

1   2   3   4   5   9. Consensus was achieved on the most desirable solution.

1   2   3   4   5   10. A detailed plan to implement the solution was developed.

1   2   3   4   5   11. The problem-solving process was systematic and orderly.

Forms for Evaluating Individual Participants

Almost any aspect of individual participation can be evaluated by preparing appropriate forms. Figure 14.14 shows a simple rating form that can be completed and given to each participant or can be completed by a critic-observer. This form was written by a group of students and has been used extensively to rate students engaged in practice discussions. It is brief and simple, yet focuses on some of the most important aspects of participation. A somewhat more detailed form is shown in figure 14.15. As before, feel free to modify it or develop your own forms.

Figure 14.14
Participant rating scale.

Date _____

Observer _____

_____
(Name of participant)

1. Contributions to the *content of the discussion*? (well prepared, supplied information, adequate reasoning, etc.)

5	4	3	2	1
Outstanding in quality and quantity		Fair share		Few or none

2. Contributions to *efficient group procedures*? (agenda planning, relevant comments, summaries, keeping on track)

5	4	3	2	1
Always relevant, aided organization		Relevant, no aid in order		Sidetracked, confused group

3. Degree of *cooperating*. (listening to understand, responsible, agreeable, group centered, open-minded)

5	4	3	2	1
Very responsible and constructive				Self-centered

Figure 14.14
(*continued*)

4. *Speaking.* (clear, to group, one point at a time, concise)

5	4	3	2	1

Brief, clear,   Vague, indirect,
to group   wordy

5. *Value* to the group? (overall rating)

5	4	3	2	1

Most valuable   Least valuable

Suggestions:

Figure 14.15
Discussion participant
evaluation scale.

Participant's name _____

Instruction: Circle the number that best reflects your evaluation of the discussant's participation on each scale.

Superior   Poor

1 2 3 4 5	1. Was prepared and informed.
1 2 3 4 5	2. Contributions were brief and clear.
1 2 3 4 5	3. Comments relevant and well timed.
1 2 3 4 5	4. Spoke distinctly and audibly to all.
1 2 3 4 5	5. Contributions made readily and voluntarily.
1 2 3 4 5	6. Frequency of participation (if poor, too low ( ) or high ( ).
1 2 3 4 5	7. Nonverbal responses were clear and constant.
1 2 3 4 5	8. Listened to understand and follow discussion.
1 2 3 4 5	9. Openminded.
1 2 3 4 5	10. Cooperative and constructive.
1 2 3 4 5	11. Helped keep discussion organized, following outline.
1 2 3 4 5	12. Contributed to evaluation of information and ideas.
1 2 3 4 5	13. Respectful and tactful with others.
1 2 3 4 5	14. Encouraged others to participate.
1 2 3 4 5	15. Overall rating in relation to other discussants.

Comments: Evaluator _____

Figure 14.16 is an observer form for assessing the assertiveness of members of a small group. The observer completes one of these scales for each participant, or participants can complete the scales for themselves and each other. A check at either end indicates that a participant was either more aggressive or passive than desirable.

Figure 14.16
Assertiveness rating
scale.

Discussant _____   Date _____

Observer _____   Time _____

The check mark on each scale indicates my best judgment of your degree of assertiveness as a participant in the discussion.

Behavior	Nonassertive	Assertive	Aggressive
Getting the floor	yielded easily	usually refused to let other take over or dominate	interrupted and cut others off
Expressing opinions	never expressed personal opinion	stated opinions, but open to others' opinions	insisted others should agree with you
Expressing personal desires (for meeting times, procedures, etc.)	never, or did so in a pleading way	stated openly, but willing to compromise	insisted on having own way
Sharing information	none, or only if asked to do so	whenever information was relevant, concisely	whether relevant or not; long-winded, rambling

Personal Manner			
Voice	weak, unduly soft	strong and clear	loud, strident
Posture and movements	withdrawn, restricted	animated, often leaning forward	unduly forceful, "table pounding"
Eye contact	rare, even when speaking	direct but not staring or glaring	stared others down
Overall manner	nonassertive	assertive	aggressive

Forms to Evaluate the Leader and Group Leadership

Previous forms can be used or modified to assess designated discussion leaders, but because group leadership is so important, a number of forms exist for that specific purpose. The one presented in figure 14.17 is one of the most comprehensive. Figure 14.18 is designed specifically for discussion leadership.

Figure 14.17
Comprehensive leader rating scale.

Date _____ Leader _____

Time _____ Observer _____

Instructions: Rate the leader on all items that are applicable; draw a line through all items that do not apply. Use the following scale to indicate how well you evaluate his or her performance:

> 5—superior
> 4—above average
> 3—average
> 2—below average
> 1—poor

Personal Style

To what degree did the leader

_____ Show poise and confidence in speaking?

_____ Show enthusiasm and interest in the problem?

_____ Listen well to understand *all* participants?

_____ Manifest personal warmth and a sense of humor?

_____ Show an open mind toward all new information and ideas?

_____ Create a supportive, cooperative atmosphere?

_____ Share functional leadership with other members?

_____ Behave democratically?

_____ Maintain perspective on problem and group process?

Preparation

To what degree

_____ Were all needed physical arrangements cared for?

_____ Were members notified and given guidance in preparing to meet?

_____ Was the leader prepared on the problem or subject?

_____ Was a procedural sequence of questions prepared to guide discussion?

Procedural and Interpersonal Leadership Techniques

To what degree did the leader

_____ Put members at ease with each other?

_____ Equalize opportunity to speak?

_____ Control aggressive or dominant members, with tact?

_____ Present an agenda and procedure for group problem solving?

_____ Encourage members to modify the procedural outline?

_____ State questions clearly to the group?

_____ Introduce and explain the charge or problem so it was clear to all?

_____ Guide the group through a thorough analysis of problem before discussing solutions?

_____ Stimulate imaginative and creative thinking about solutions?

_____ Encourage the group to evaluate all ideas and proposals thoroughly before accepting or rejecting them?

_____ See that plans were made to implement and follow-up on all decisions?

_____ Keep discussion on one point at a time?

_____ Rebound questions asking for a personal opinion or solution to the group?

_____ Provide summaries needed to clarify, remind, and move group forward to next issue or agenda item?

_____ Test for consensus before moving to a new phase of problem solving?

_____ Keep complete and accurate records, especially of all proposals and decisions?

_____ If needed, suggest compromise or integrative solutions to resolve conflict?

_____ (Other—name the technique or procedure _____)

Instructions: Rate yourself on each item by putting a check mark in the "Yes" or "No" column. Your score is five times the number of items marked "Yes." Rating: *excellent*, 90 or higher; *good*, 80–85; *fair*, 70–75; *inadequate*, 65 or lower.

Figure 14.18
(*continued*)

	Yes	No
1. I prepared all needed facilities.		
2. I started the meeting promptly and ended on time.		
3. I established an atmosphere of permissiveness and informality; I was open and responsive to all ideas.		
4. I clearly oriented the group to its purpose and area of freedom.		
5. I encouraged all members to participate and maintained equal opportunity for all to speak.		
6. I used a plan for leading the group in an organized consideration of all major phases of the problem.		
7. I listened actively, and (if needed) encouraged all members to do so.		
8. I saw to it that the problem was discussed thoroughly before solutions were considered.		
9. I integrated related ideas or suggestions and urged the group to arrive at consensus on a solution.		
10. My questions were clear and brief.		
11. I saw to it that unclear statements were paraphrased or otherwise clarified.		
12. I prompted open discussion of substantive conflicts.		
13. I maintained order and organization, promptly pointing out tangents, making transitions, and keeping track of the passage of time.		
14. I saw to it that the meeting produced definite assignments or plans for action, and that any subsequent meeting was arranged.		
15. All important information, ideas, and decisions were promptly and accurately recorded.		
16. I actively encouraged creative thinking.		
17. I encouraged thorough evaluation of information and all ideas for solutions.		
18. I was able to remain neutral during constructive arguments, and otherwise encourage teamwork.		
19. I suggested or urged establishment of needed norms and standards.		
20. I encouraged members to discuss how they felt about the group process and resolve any blocks to progress.		

Summary

In chapter 14 we have examined the role of the nonparticipant observer as learner, reminder, consultant, or critic. Students who observe small group communication can hasten development of insights and skills by observing numerous small group discussions. They may also be called upon to assist groups in such roles as reminder or consultant. Since no one can keep track of everything at once, it is important that the observer(s) focus on certain variables ahead of time. Preplanned observation forms and rating scales help observers do this.

Numerous forms were provided to help you function as an observer or to get responses from members that can be tabulated and used to improve future meetings of the group. You may use the forms as provided, modify them as needed, or create forms to serve your specific purposes. What is important now is for you to *use* the forms in actual observation projects.

Exercises

1. Divide your class into groups of five or six. Select an area of small group discussion to evaluate and, individually, develop a form to assess that phenomenon. Then share your individual forms and as a group come up with one to evaluate that same phenomenon.
2. Divide your class into project groups of five or six members. Each group should select an existing small group to observe and evaluate. You may want to check your student activities or similar office for lists of on-campus organizations or groups whose meetings you can observe. This project will last for the entire term. Although you may be given time in class to meet, expect that you will have to meet outside class as well.

   You should plan what group you will observe, what aspects of the group you will focus on (e.g., leadership, member roles, decision-making effectiveness, conflict management effectiveness, use of information, etc.), and what observation techniques and/or forms you will use. Then you should carry out your observations and prepare to report your findings to the rest of the class, using charts and audiovisual aids as appropriate.

   In addition, since you will be a *member* of a group that forms this observation team, you should assume the role of participant observer for your project group. Pay particular attention to how your group develops from a collection of individuals to a real group, what norms develop and how, how leadership emerges, how effective it is, and what functions the members perform. Then, write an essay describing the group and evaluating its functioning, using for an outline a set of questions such as those that follow. Remember, these are only suggestions; your group will be unique, so concentrate on those factors that are most important for understanding and assessing your group.

Guidelines for Evaluating Your Project Group

1. What was the *goal* of the group? How did the group develop this as an objective? How adequately did this goal represent the interests and concerns of the members (individual goals)? What hidden agendas existed, and how did these contribute or detract from the surface agenda?

2. What *phases* were there in the emergence of a group structure? How could you tell when the group had progressed from one stage of development into another?

3. What do you perceive to be the *role* of each member? How did members come to have their roles? Were any needed behavioral functions missing? If so, what was the impact on the group? Did a procedural *leader* emerge in your group? Who? *How* did this person become acknowledged as leader? What responsibilities did the leader perform? What leadership functions did others perform? If no leader emerged, how were necessary leadership services provided (or were they)?

4. What *communication network* exists in the group? How well do members listen to each other? Have there been problems in communicating, such as ambiguity, bypassing, or the mood of dismissal? How did the group handle these? Have adequate records been kept and reports made from meeting to meeting?

5. What *norms* governing individual and group behavior emerged? How did these evolve? What effects do they have on group productivity and maintenance? If there were counterproductive norms, were these changed? How? Did you have any problem members? If so, who? How were these persons handled?

6. How were discussions *structured*? What overall procedure did the group follow for its problem solving? How adequate was this procedure? How well were all members' resources of knowledge, creativity, reasoning, and evaluating used? Did each meeting have a clear objective and an agenda to follow?

7. How well were *decisions* made? What decision-making techniques were employed? What sorts of conflicts developed? If prolonged conflicts occurred, how were they resolved?

8. What *climate* or atmosphere existed and now exists among members? How did it develop? Were there serious interpersonal conflicts? How have tensions been handled? Are members committed, task oriented, or accepting and supportive of each other? Are members appropriately flexible?

9. Overall, how do you evaluate your group and your personal contribution to it? What changes would you make if you could? How and why?

Notes

1. W. Fawcett Hill, *Learning Thru Discussion* (Beverly Hills: Sage Publications, 1977), 30–31.

2. Bobby R. Patton and Kim Giffin, *Problem-Solving Group Interaction* (New York: Harper & Row, Publishers, 1973), 213–14.

Author Index

Subject Index